DEDICATION

TO MY MOTHER, WHO COULD USE A DRINK, FOR HAVING
BEEN BLESSED WITH ME.

-STEPHEN

ACKNOWLEDGEMENTS

Special Thanks!

To Mom and Dad, Stuart and Cindy. To Cara, Brittany, Jacquie, and David Howe and the rest of my relatives whom I don't see often enough.

To Cyril Clark, Kelly and Jay Cappelli, Brad Parker, Jeff Irvin, Donny Richards, Bryan Miller, Paul Masiello, Murray (Buddy) Bortman, Will Norris, Mike Shaw, Joe Kaszuba, Mark Stuart, Mike Hamori, Frank Sullivan, Walter Hall, Scott Blanchette, Mark Farrin, Matthew Olga, Kurt Weltler, Russ Hodge.

To Chris Hall and Mind and Body Martial Arts, Boston; Glen and crew at Glen's Galley, Newburyport; Caroline and Joshua and everybody at Curious Liquids, Boston; Frankie at the Hog's Breath Saloon, Key West; The Castle Hill Foundation; The 1640 Hart House; The Choate Bridge Pub; Ipswich Clam Bake Company, Ipswich; CHF Inc., Salem, NH; Everybody at the Marshall House, Boston; Everybody at the 21st Amendment, Boston; Everybody at the Peabody Marriott, Peabody; The friendly staff at the Boston Sports Club (Bullfinch Place), Boston; Everyone I served with at Combat Support Company 3/18th INF, Danvers.

Publisher's Cataloging-in-Publication
(Provided by Quality Books, Inc.)
**Publisher: The Bartender's Black Book Co., Inc.
Brockton, Mass. 02301**

Cunningham, Stephen Kittredge.
    The bartender's black book / Stephen Kittredge
Cunningham. -- 5th ed.
    p. cm.
    Includes index.

    1. Bartending- Handbooks, manuals, etc.
2. Cocktails. I. Title.

TX951.C86 2000   641.8'74
                          QB100-500125

ISBN 1-891267-36-1

THE BARTENDERS BLACK BOOK
TABLE OF CONTENTS:

A MESSAGE TO OUR READERS

What makes THE BARTENDER'S BLACK BOOK unique from all other recipe guides on the market is that the book is updated on a yearly basis. Look for Mr. Parker's "Vintage Guide" and "The World's Greatest Wine Values" to be updated at the same time.

At that time, the latest recipes and new sections will be added to THE BARTENDER'S BLACK BOOK in order to keep the book current. Thank you for purchasing this edition of THE BARTENDER'S BLACK BOOK.

The Publisher

MIXING

Glassware
In recent years the trend of establishments to have specialized glassware has changed. Multi-purpose glassware has taken over. Many busy businesses have made it using only shaker glasses and snifters. The choice is yours.

Flaming
Any alcohol concentration of 87 proof or greater will ignite if exposed to a direct flame. Many liquors and liqueurs of lesser proof will ignite if heated first and then exposed to a direct flame. *CAUTION*, people have been maimed drinking flaming shots.

Floating
To make floating drinks, layered drinks, pousse-café, one must pour the heaviest liqueurs or liquors first, then slowly pour the lighter ones on top over the back of a spoon. If you have time to make drinks ahead of time you can refrigerate, and the individual ingredients will separate themselves in an hour or so.

Frosting and Chilling Glasses
To frost a glass simply run cold water all over glass and place in freezer. Allow 5-10 minutes for ample frosting.
To chill a glass, if time allows just place in a refrigerator for 5 to 10 minutes. If time does not permit, fill glass with ice and let set a minute or two.

Shaking
Most bars have in their arsenal metal or plastic shaker cups which fit over their glasses. If no shaker cups are available you can pour from one glass to another until mixed.

Stirring
Stir with spoon in a home atmosphere. In an establishment it is more appropriate to stick a straw or a stirrer into drinks and let the patron stir their own drink. Be careful not to over stir drinks containing Champagne, sodas or other sparkling ingredients.

Straining
The easiest way to strain a drink is to acquire a metal mixing cup and a drink strainer which fits over the cup. In a bind you can place straws or a knife over cup, and pour very gently.

GARNISHES

Wash fresh fruit and vegetables thoroughly. Many are grown in foreign soil and may have been exposed to harmful insecticides.

Bananas: Ripe yellow cross sections of bananas make a colorful and stylish garnish. Before peeling and adding fresh banana to a blended drink, cut a 1/2-3/4 inch cross section from the middle. Then cut from the center through the peel. This should make it fit nicely onto the rim of a glass.

Celery: Always wash celery thoroughly. Cut off the base as well as the tips of the leaves, so that there is no discoloration, just healthy light green celery. When making a drink calling for celery as a garnish, make sure you leave room to accommodate the stick of celery. Keep celery in ice water, in a refrigerator until needed.

Cherries: Red Maraschino cherries are essential for adult drinks, as well as children's drinks. After opening the jar be sure to refrigerate.

Cinnamon: Ground cinnamon as well as cinnamon sticks are used in many recipes. It is easy to overpower a drink with cinnamon. Use ground cinnamon sparingly. Drinks calling for cinnamon sticks, leave whole unless specified. Long sticks can make excellent stirrers.

Cocktail Shrimp: Shrimp make delicious exotic garnish for drinks such as a Bloody Mary or a Red Snapper. Cook them as if they were for a shrimp cocktail, removing the black vein in the back. If shrimp, after cooking and waiting to be used become slimy, throw them away.

Coffee Beans: Coffee Beans are a traditional garnish for Sambuca drinks. Three beans represent Health, Wealth and Happiness.

Cucumber: Cut either into spears or wheels, cucumbers are a great garnish instead of, or in addition to celery for a Virgin Mary and other drinks of that nature. Wash thoroughly. Peeling is optional.

Lemons: *Wedges*. Cut off the ends of a lemon, then cut down the middle from flat end to flat end making two halves. Make a 1/4 inch incision in the center of the halves against the grain, then cut 3 or 4 equal sized wedges from the half. The tiny incision was made so your wedge will fit snugly on rim of glass.

Twists. Cut off the ends of a lemon, then make 4 long lengthwise cuts into the rind (Be careful not to cut into the meat of the lemon). Soak lemon in hot tap water for 5 minutes. Separate the rind from the meat, and cut the rind into long 1/4 inch strips. When a twist is called for a drink, it should be twisted over the drink, then rubbed around the lip of the glass.

Limes: *Wedges.* Cut off the ends of a lime, then cut down the middle from flat end to flat end making two halves. Make a 1/4 inch incision in the center of the halves against the grain. Cut 3 or 4 equal sized wedges from the half. The tiny incision was made so your wedge will fit snugly on the rim of a glass.

   Wheels. Cut off the ends. Cut 1/6th inch cross sections. Cut the rind to allow a place to sit on the glass.

Olives: Green olives (with or without pimentos) are essential for martinis. Refrigerate after opening a fresh container.

Onions: Cocktail onions are the distinguishing difference between a Martini and a Gibson. They can be found in most grocery stores. Refrigerate after opening.

Oranges: Cut the ends off an orange. Cut down the middle from flat end to flat end. Cut half wheels across the grain approximately 1/6th inch thick. A slight pull on the the ends will allow you to sit it on the rim of the glass.

Pineapples: *Sticks.* Cut off the top, bottom and sides, making a solid block of pineapple meat. Cut this into equal sized sticks.

   Wedges. Cut off the top and bottom, then quarter the pineapple the long way. Cut off pointed part of quarter. Slice straight down flat side about 1/4 inch deep. Cut into 1/2 inch wedges.

Salt (Kosher): Salt is primarily used to rim glasses by moistening the glass with either water or fruit juice from a cut piece of fruit (lemon, lime, orange) and dipping the glass into the salt (which should be laid out in a dish or any contained flat surface).

Shaved Almonds: Commonly found in a cook's arsenal, they make a very appealing decoration for drinks with traces of Almond Liqueurs (Amaretto, Creme De Nouyax). Sprinkle them on whipped cream or float them on a creamy drink's surface.

Shaved Chocolate: A favorite at fancy establishments is freshly shaved dark chocolate. Just buy a block of chocolate and introduce it to your friendly cheese grater, and you're in business.

Sprinkles or Jimmies: Pleasant to the eye as well as the palate, they do justice to hot coffee drinks and many frozen concoctions. They are available at most convenience stores.

Strawberries: Fresh ripe strawberries enhance any drink containing berries or strawberry liqueur. Wash berries thoroughly. Cut large ones in two; leave small ones whole. Simply push a berry onto the rim of a glass until it fits snugly.

Whipped Cream: You can use either fresh or canned. Whipped cream is expected to top many hot drinks. If fresh whipped cream is used, you may want to add 1/2 tsp of sugar to your drink due to the fact that processed whipped cream is sweetened.

RECIPES A-Z

A-BOMB
Fill glass with ice.
1/2 oz Vodka
1/2 oz Coffee Liqueur
1/2 oz Irish Cream
1/2 oz Orange Liqueur
Shake.
Strain into shot glass.

ABBY ROAD
Fill glass with ice.
1 oz Amaretto
1 oz Black Raspberry Liqueur
1 oz Coffee Liqueur
Stir.

ABBY ROAD COFFEE
1 oz Amaretto
1 oz Black Raspberry Liqueur
1 oz Coffee Liqueur
Fill with hot Black Coffee.
Top with Whipped Cream.
Drizzle with Chocolate Syrup.

ABC (floater)
1/2 oz Amaretto (bottom)
1/2 oz Irish Cream
1/2 oz Orange Liqueur or Cognac
(top)

ABSINTHE COCKTAIL
Fill glass with ice.
1 1/2 oz Absinthe
1 1/2 oz Water
Dash of Bitters
Dash of Sugar Syrup
Shake.
Strain into chilled glass.

ABSINTHE DRIP COCKTAIL
1 or 2 oz Absinthe
Place slotted spoon or strainer
Holding sugar cube over glass.
Drip cold water over sugar until
it melts into drink.

ACAPULCO
Fill glass with ice.
1 oz Brandy
1 oz Gin
Dash of Grenadine
Dash of Sour Mix
Dash of Orange Juice
Fill with Ginger Ale.
Garnish with Orange and Cherry.

ACAPULCO GOLD
Fill glass with ice.
1 oz Tequila
1 oz Amber Rum
1 oz Cream of Coconut
1 oz Pineapple Juice
1 oz Grapefruit Juice
Shake.

ADIOS MOTHER aka CODE BLUE
Fill glass with ice.
1/2 oz Vodka
1/2 oz Rum
1/2 oz Tequila
1/2 oz Gin
1/2 oz Blue Curacao
Fill with Sour Mix.
Shake.

ADULT HOT CHOCOLATE aka PEPPERMINT KISS, COCOANAPPS, SNUGGLER
2 oz Peppermint Schnapps
Fill with Hot Chocolate.
Stir.
Top with Whipped Cream.
Sprinkle with Shaved
Chocolate or Sprinkles.

AFTER EIGHT (floater)
1/2 oz Coffee Liqueur (bottom)
1/2 oz White Creme De Menthe
1/2 oz Irish Cream (top)

AFTER FIVE (floater)
1/2 oz Coffee Liqueur (bottom)
1/2 oz Irish Cream
1/2 oz Peppermint Schnapps (top)

AFTER FIVE COFFEE
1/2 oz Coffee Liqueur
1/2 oz Irish Cream
1/2 oz Peppermint Schnapps
Fill with hot Black Coffee.
Top with Whipped Cream.
Sprinkle with Shaved
Chocolate or Sprinkles.

AFTERBURNER
Fill glass with ice.
1 oz Peppered Vodka
1 oz Cinnamon Schnapps
1 oz Coffee Liqueur
Shake.
Strain into shot glass.

AFTERBURNER 2
Fill glass with ice.
1/2 oz 151-Proof Rum
1/2 oz Jaegermeister
1/2 oz Coffee Liqueur
Stir.
Strain into chilled glass.

AGENT 99 (floater)
3/4 oz Orange Liqueur (bottom)
3/4 oz Blue Curacao
3/4 oz Sambuca or Ouzo (top)

AGENT O.
Fill glass with ice.
1/2 oz Vodka
1/2 oz Orange Liqueur
Fill with Orange Juice.
Shake.
Garnish with Orange.

AGGRAVATION aka TEACHER'S PET

Fill glass with ice.
1 oz Scotch
1 oz Coffee Liqueur
Fill with Milk or Cream.
Shake.

AIR GUNNER

Fill glass with ice.
2 oz Vodka
Dash of Blue Curacao
1 oz Sour Mix
Shake.
Strain into chilled glass.

ALABAMA

Fill glass with ice.
1 1/2 oz Brandy
1/2 oz Triple Sec
Fill with Sour Mix.
Shake.

ALABAMA SLAMMER

Fill glass with ice.
3/4 oz Vodka
3/4 oz Southern Comfort
3/4 oz Amaretto
Dash of Sloe Gin or Grenadine
Fill with Orange Juice.
Shake.
Garnish with Orange.

ALABAMA SLAMMER 2

Fill glass with ice.
1 oz Vodka
1 oz Southern Comfort
Dash of Sloe Gin or Grenadine
Fill with Orange Juice.
Shake.
Garnish with Orange.

ALABAMA SLAMMER 3

Fill glass with ice.
1 oz Southern Comfort
1 oz Amaretto
Dash of Sloe Gin or Grenadine
Fill with Orange Juice.
Shake.
Garnish with Orange.

ALABAMA SLAMMER 4

Fill glass with ice.
1/2 oz Southern Comfort
1/2 oz Triple Sec
1/2 oz Galliano
1/2 oz Sloe Gin
Fill with Orange Juice.
Shake.
Garnish with Orange.

ALABAMA SLAMMER 5

Fill glass with ice.
1/2 oz Whiskey
1/2 oz Southern Comfort
1/2 oz Amaretto
1/2 oz Sloe Gin
Fill with Orange Juice.
Shake.
Garnish with Orange.

ALABAMA SLAMMER (frozen)

In Blender:
1/2 cup of Ice
1 oz Vodka
1 oz Southern Comfort
Dash of Sloe Gin or Grenadine
Scoop of Orange Sherbet
Blend until smooth.
If too thick add Orange Juice.
If too thin add ice or sherbet.
Garnish with Orange.

ALASKAN ICED TEA

Fill glass with ice.
1/2 oz Vodka
1/2 oz Gin
1/2 oz Rum
2 oz Blue Curacao
2 oz Sour Mix
Fill with Lemon-Lime Soda.
Garnish with Lemon.

ALBATROSS (frozen)

In Blender:
1 cup of Ice
1 oz Gin
1 oz Melon Liqueur
1 Egg White
1 oz Lime Juice
Blend until smooth.

ALEXANDER

Fill glass with ice.
1 oz Gin
1 oz White or Dark Creme De Cacao
Fill with Milk or Cream.
Shake.

ALEXANDER THE GREAT

Fill glass with ice.
1 1/2 oz Greek Brandy
1/2 oz Dark Creme De Cacao
2 oz Milk or Cream
Shake.
Strain into chilled glass.

ALEXANDER'S SISTER

Fill glass with ice.
1 oz Gin
1 oz Green Creme De Menthe
Fill with Milk or Cream.
Shake.

ALGONQUIN

Fill glass with ice.
1 1/2 oz Whiskey
1 oz Dry Vermouth
1 oz Pineapple Juice
Shake.
Strain into chilled glass.

ALICE IN WONDERLAND aka DALLAS ALICE

Fill glass with ice.
3/4 oz Tequila
3/4 oz Orange Liqueur
3/4 oz Coffee Liqueur
Shake.
Strain into shot glass.

ALIEN ORGASM
Fill glass with ice.
3/4 oz Amaretto
3/4 oz Melon Liqueur
3/4 oz Peach Schnapps
Fill with equal parts Orange
and Pineapple Juice.
Shake.

ALIEN SECRETION
Fill glass with ice.
1 oz Coconut Rum
1 oz Melon Liqueur
Fill with Pineapple Juice.
Shake.
Garnish with Cherry.

ALIEN URINE SAMPLE
Fill glass with ice.
1/2 oz Coconut Rum
1/2 oz Banana Liqueur
1/2 oz Peach Schnapps
1/2 oz Melon Liqueur
Fill with Sour Mix leaving 1/2 inch
from top.
Shake.
Splash Soda Water.
Top with 1/2 oz Blue Curacao

ALMOND ENJOY
Fill glass with ice.
1 oz Amaretto
1 oz Dark Creme De Cacao
1 oz Cream of Coconut
Fill with Cream or Milk.
Shake.

ALMOND JOY
Fill glass with ice.
1 oz Coconut Rum
1/2 oz Dark Creme De Cacao
Fill with Milk or Cream.
Shake.

ALMOND KISS aka COCOETTO
2 oz Amaretto
Fill with Hot Chocolate.
Stir.
Top with Whipped Cream.
Place Chocolate Kiss on top
or Shaved Chocolate.

ALMOND MOCHA COFFEE
1 oz Amaretto
1 oz Creme De Cacao
Fill with hot Black Coffee.
Top with Whipped Cream.
Sprinkle with Shaved Almonds
and/or Shaved Chocolate.

AMARETTO *(type liqueur)*
Bring 2 cups of Water mixed with
1 1/2 cups of Brown Sugar and
1 cup of Granulated Sugar to a boil.
Stir often.
Lower heat and let simmer 5 minutes.
Let cool 2 minutes.
Pour mixture into glass container.
Add 1 qt Vodka, 6 tsp Vanilla, 8 tsp
Almond Extract.
Stir and pour into bottles with screw top.
Place in a dark cool place for 1 week.

AMARETTO SOUR
Fill glass with ice.
2 oz Amaretto
Fill with Sour Mix.
Shake.
Garnish with Orange and Cherry.

AMARIST
1 oz Amaretto
1 oz Orange Liqueur
Microwave for 10-15 seconds.

AMBER CLOUD
1 1/2 oz Cognac
1/2 oz Galliano
Microwave for 10 seconds.

AMBER MARTINI
Fill glass with ice.
1 oz Vodka
1/2 oz Amaretto
1/2 oz Hazelnut Liqueur
Stir.
Strain into chilled glass.

AMBROSIA
Fill glass with ice.
1 oz Brandy
1/4 oz Triple Sec
Fill with Champagne.

AMBUSH COFFEE
1 oz Irish Whiskey
1 oz Amaretto
Fill with hot Black Coffee.
Top with Whipped Cream.
Sprinkle with Shaved Almonds.
Dribble 4-5 drops of Green Creme
De Menthe on top.

AMERICAN GRAFFITI
Fill glass with ice.
1/2 oz Light Rum
1/2 oz Dark Rum
1/2 oz Southern Comfort
1/2 oz Sloe Gin
Dash of Lime Juice
Fill with equal parts Sour Mix and
Pineapple Juice.
Shake.
Garnish with Lime.

AMERICAN SOUR
Fill glass with ice.
2 oz Bourbon
Dash of Orange Curacao
or Triple Sec
Dash of Orange Juice
Fill with Sour Mix.
Shake.

AMIGO aka WHITE BULL
Fill glass with ice.
1 oz Tequila
3/4 oz Coffee Liqueur
Fill with Milk or Cream.
Shake.

AMORE-ADE
Fill glass with ice.
1 1/2 oz Amaretto
1/2 oz Triple Sec
Fill with Soda Water.
Stir.

ANGEL FACE
Fill glass with ice.
1 oz Gin
1/2 oz Apricot Brandy
1/2 oz Apple Brandy
Shake.
Strain into chilled glass.

ANGEL KISS (floater)
1 oz Dark Creme De Cacao (bottom)
1 oz Milk or Cream (top)

ANGEL WING (floater)
1 1/2 oz White Creme De Cacao
(bottom)
1/2 oz Irish Cream (top)

ANGEL WING 2 (floater)
1 oz White Creme De Cacao
(bottom)
1 oz Brandy
1/2 oz Milk or Light Cream (top)

ANGEL'S TIT (floater)
1 oz Dark Creme De Cacao (bottom)
1 oz Milk or Cream (top)
Garnish with Cherry on toothpick
across top of glass.

ANISETTE (type liqueur)
Bring 2 cups of Water and
2 cups of Granulated Sugar to a boil.
Simmer 10 minutes, stirring often.
Add 1 tsp Vanilla, 1 1/2 tsp Anise
Extract, 1 qt Vodka.

ANKLE BREAKER
Fill glass with ice.
1 1/2 oz 151-Proof Rum
1 oz Cherry Brandy
1 oz Lime Juice
1 tsp Sugar Syrup
Shake.

ANNA'S BANANA (frozen)
In Blender:
1/2 cup of Ice
2 oz Vodka
1/2 fresh ripe Banana
1 tsp Honey
Dash of Lime Juice
Blend until smooth.
If too thick add fruit.
If too thin add ice.
Garnish with Banana.

ANTI-FREEZE
Fill glass with ice.
1 oz Vodka
1 oz Green Creme De Menthe or
Melon Liqueur
Shake.
Strain into shot glass.

ANTI-FREEZE 2
Fill glass with ice.
1 oz Mentholated Schnapps
1 oz Blue Curacao
Shake.
Strain into chilled glass.
Top with Lemon-Lime Soda.

ANTIQUAN KISS
Fill glass with ice.
1/2 oz Light Rum
1/2 oz Dark Rum
1/2 oz Apricot Brandy
1/2 oz Peach Schnapps
Dash of Cranberry Juice
Fill with Orange Juice.
Shake.

ANTIQUAN SMILE
Fill glass with ice.
1 1/2 oz Dark Rum
1/2 oz Banana Liqueur
Pinch of Powdered Sugar
Fill with Orange Juice.
Shake.
Garnish with Lime.

APOLLO COOLER
Fill glass with ice.
1 1/2 oz Metaxa
1/2 oz Lemon Juice
Shake.
Fill with Ginger Ale.

APPENDECTOMY aka
APPENDICITIS
Fill glass with ice.
1 oz Gin
1/2 oz Orange Liqueur
1 oz Sour Mix
Shake.
Strain into chilled glass.

APPETIZER
4 oz Red Wine
Fill with Orange Juice.
Dash of Bitters (optional)

APPLE COOLER
Fill glass with ice.
1 oz Light Rum
1 oz Brandy
Fill with Apple Cider or Juice.
Shake.
Strain into chilled glass.
Float 1/2 oz Dark Rum on top.

APPLE MARGARITA (frozen)
In Blender:
1 cup of Ice
1 oz Tequila
1 oz Apple Brandy
2 tbsp Applesauce
1 oz Sour Mix
Blend until smooth.
If too thick add applesauce or Sour Mix.
If too thin add ice.
Rim glass with Cinnamon and Sugar.

APPLE PIE
Fill glass with ice.
1 1/2 oz Vodka
1/2 oz Apple Cider or Juice
Strain into chilled glass.
Sprinkle with Cinnamon.

APPLE PIE (floater)
3/4 oz Apple Brandy (bottom)
3/4 oz Cinnamon Schnapps
3/4 oz Irish Cream (top)

APPLE POLISHER
2 oz Southern Comfort
Fill with hot Apple Cider.
Garnish with Cinnamon Stick.

APRES SKI
Fill glass with ice.
1 oz Peppermint Schnapps
1 oz Coffee Liqueur
1 oz White Creme De Cacao
Shake.

APRES SKI 2
1 oz Brandy
1 oz Apple Brandy
Fill with Apple Cider.
Garnish with Cinnamon Stick.

APRICOT FRAPPE
Fill large stemmed glass (Red Wine glass, Champagne saucer) with crushed ice.
1 oz Brandy
1 oz Apricot Brandy

APRICOT SOUR
Fill glass with ice.
2 oz Apricot Brandy
Fill with Sour Mix.
Shake.
Garnish with Orange and Cherry.

APRIL IN PARIS
1 oz Orange Liqueur
Fill with Champagne.
Garnish with Orange Slice.

ARIZONA LEMONADE
Fill glass with ice.
2 oz Tequila
2 tsp Powdered Sugar
Fill with fresh Lemon Juice.
Shake until sugar dissolves.
Garnish with Lemon.

ARMORED CAR
Fill glass with ice.
2 oz Bourbon
Dash of Simple Syrup
1 oz Fresh Lemon Juice
Stir.
Strain into chilled glass.

AROUND THE WORLD
Fill glass with ice.
1 1/2 oz Gin
1 1/2 oz Green Creme De Menthe
1 1/2 oz Pineapple Juice
Shake.

ARTIFICIAL INTELLIGENCE
Fill glass with ice.
1/2 oz Dark Rum
1/2 oz Light Rum
1/2 oz Coconut Rum
Dash of Lime Juice
3 oz Pineapple Juice
Shake.
Strain into chilled glass.
Float 1/2 oz Melon Liqueur on top.

ASIAN MARTINI
Fill glass with ice.
2 oz Vodka
1/2 oz Ginger Liqueur
Stir.
Strain into chilled glass
or pour contents (with ice)
Into short glass.
Garnish with Lemon Twist.

ASPEN COFFEE
3/4 oz Coffee Liqueur
or Orange Liqueur
3/4 oz Irish Cream
3/4 oz Hazelnut Liqueur
Fill with hot Black Coffee.
Top with Whipped Cream.
Sprinkle with Shaved Chocolate.

ASPEN HUMMER
1 oz 151-Proof Rum
1 oz Coffee Liqueur
Fill with hot Black Coffee.
Top with Whipped Cream.

ASSASSIN (floater)
3/4 oz Banana Liqueur (bottom)
3/4 oz Blue Curacao
3/4 oz Orange Liqueur (top)

ASSISTED SUICIDE
Fill glass with ice.
2 oz Grain Alcohol
1 oz Jaegermeister
Fill with Cola
Stir.

ATOMIC BODYSLAM
Fill glass with ice.
1/2 oz Vodka
1/2 oz Gin
1/2 oz Dark Rum
1/2 oz Blackberry Brandy
Fill with Orange Juice or
Grapefruit Juice.
Shake.

ATOMIC WASTE
Fill glass with ice.
3/4 oz Vodka
3/4 oz Melon Liqueur
1/2 oz Peach Schnapps
1/2 oz Banana Liqueur
Fill with Milk.
Shake.
Strain into chilled glass.

AUGUST MOON
Fill glass with ice.
1 oz Amaretto
1 oz Triple Sec
1 oz Orange Juice
Shake.
Strain into chilled glass.

AUNT JEMIMA (floater)
1/2 oz Brandy (bottom)
1/2 oz White Creme De Cacao
1/2 oz Benedictine (top)

AUNT MARY
Fill glass with ice.
2 oz Rum
1 tsp Horseradish
3 dashes of Tabasco Sauce
3 dashes of Worcestershire Sauce
Dash of Lime Juice
3 dashes of Celery Salt
3 dashes of Pepper
1 oz Clam Juice (optional)
Dash of Sherry (optional)
1 tsp Dijon Mustard (optional)
Fill with Tomato Juice.
Pour from one glass to another
until mixed.
Garnish with Lemon and/or Lime,
Celery and/or Cucumber and/or
Cocktail Shrimp.

AVALANCHE (floater)
1/2 oz Coffee Liqueur (bottom)
1/2 oz White Creme De Cacao
1/2 oz Southern Comfort (top)

B & B
1 oz Brandy
1 oz Benedictine
Stir gently.

B-12 (floater)
1 1/2 oz Irish Cream (bottom)
1/2 oz Orange Liqueur (top)

B-50 (floater)
1 1/2 oz Irish Cream (bottom)
1/2 oz Vodka (top)

B-51 aka CONCORD (floater)
1/2 oz Coffee Liqueur (bottom)
1/2 oz Irish Cream
1/2 oz 151-Proof Rum (top)

B-52 (floater)
1/2 oz Coffee Liqueur (bottom)
1/2 oz Irish Cream
1/2 oz Orange Liqueur (top)

B-52 (frozen)
In Blender:
1/2 cup of Ice
3/4 oz Coffee Liqueur
3/4 oz Irish Cream
3/4 oz Orange Liqueur
Scoop of Vanilla Ice Cream
Blend until smooth.
If too thick add Milk or Cream.
If too thin add ice or Ice Cream.
Garnish with Chocolate
shavings or Sprinkles.

B-52 (rocks)
Fill glass with ice.
1 oz Coffee Liqueur
1 oz Irish Cream
1 oz Orange Liqueur
Shake.

B-52 COFFEE
1/2 oz Coffee Liqueur
1/2 oz Irish Cream
1/2 oz Orange Liqueur
Fill with hot Black Coffee.
Top with Whipped Cream.
Garnish with Orange.

B-52 ON A MISSION (floater)
1/2 oz Coffee Liqueur (bottom)
1/2 oz Irish Cream
1/2 oz Orange Liqueur
1/2 oz 151-Proof Rum (top)

B-52 WITH A MEXICAN
TAILGUNNER
3/4 oz Coffee Liqueur (bottom)
3/4 oz Irish Cream
3/4 oz Orange Liqueur
1/4 oz Tequila (top)

B-52 WITH BOMBAY DOORS
(floater)
1/2 oz Coffee Liqueur (bottom)
1/2 oz Irish Cream
1/2 oz Orange Liqueur
1/2 oz Dry Gin (top)

B-53 (floater)
3/4 oz Coffee Liqueur (bottom)
3/4 oz Sambuca
3/4 oz Orange Liqueur (top)

B-54 aka DC-10 (floater)
1/2 oz Coffee Liqueur (bottom)
1/2 oz Irish Cream
1/2 oz Amaretto (top)

B-57 (floater)
1/2 oz Coffee Liqueur (bottom)
1/2 oz Amaretto
1/2 oz Cognac or Brandy (top)

B. M. P.
Fill glass with ice.
1 3/4 oz Amber Rum
1/2 oz Light Rum
3 oz Pineapple Juice
1 oz Lime Juice
Dash of Bitters
Shake.
Strain into glass.

BABBIE'S SPECIAL
Fill glass with ice.
1 oz Gin
3/4 oz Apricot Brandy
Fill with Milk or Cream.
Shake.

BACARDI COCKTAIL
Fill glass with ice.
2 oz Rum
Dash of Grenadine
Fill with Sour Mix.
Shake.
Garnish with Orange and Cherry.

BAD ATTITUDE
Fill glass with ice.
1 oz Coconut Rum
1 oz Spiced Rum
2 oz Pineapple Juice
Shake.
Strain into chilled glass.
John Couture

BAHAMA MAMA
Fill glass with ice.
1 oz Light Rum
1 oz Dark Rum
1 oz Amber Rum
2 oz Sour Mix
2 oz Orange Juice
2 oz Pineapple Juice
Shake.
Put dash of Grenadine in second glass and fill with mixture.
Garnish with Orange and Cherry.

BAHAMA MAMA 2
Fill glass with ice.
1 oz Light Rum
1 oz Coconut Rum
1 oz Amaretto
Dash of Grenadine
Fill with equal parts Orange and Pineapple Juice.

BAHAMA MAMA 3
Fill glass with ice.
1 oz Light Rum
Fill with Pineapple Juice leaving a 1/2 inch from the top.
Shake.
Top with 1/2 oz 151-Proof Rum and 1/2 oz Dark Rum.

BAILEY'S AND COFFEE
2 oz Irish Cream
Fill with hot Black Coffee.
Top with Whipped Cream.

BAILEY'S COMET
Fill glass with ice.
1 1/2 oz Vodka
1/2 oz Irish Cream

BAILEY'S FIZZ
Fill glass with ice.
2 oz Irish Cream
Fill with Soda Water.

BAJA MARGARITA
Fill glass with ice.
1 1/2 oz Tequila
1/2 oz Banana Liqueur
Dash of Lime Juice
3 oz Sour Mix
Dash of Orange Juice (optional)
Shake.
Rub rim of second glass with Lime and dip into kosher salt.
Pour contents (with ice) or
Strain into salted glass.
Garnish with Lime.

BALALAIKA
Fill glass with ice.
1 1/2 oz Vodka
1/2 oz Triple Sec
2 oz Sour Mix
Shake.
Strain into chilled glass.
Garnish with Lime.

BALI HAI
Fill glass with ice.
1 oz Gin
1 oz Rum
Dash of Amaretto
Fill with Sour Mix leaving 1/2 inch from top.
Shake.
Top with Champagne.

BAMBINI ARUBA
Fill glass with ice.
1 oz Vodka
1 oz Rum
1 oz Bourbon
Dash of Grenadine
Fill with equal parts Sour Mix, Orange and Pineapple Juice.
Shake.
Garnish with Orange and Cherry.

BANANA BOAT
Fill glass with ice.
1 oz Coconut Rum
1 oz Banana Liqueur
2 oz Pineapple Juice
Shake.
Strain into chilled glass.

BANANA COLADA (frozen)
In Blender:
1/2 cup of Ice
2 oz Light Rum
2 tbsp Cream of Coconut
1 whole peeled ripe Banana
1 tbsp Vanilla Ice Cream
Blend until smooth.
If too thick add more fruit.
If too thin add ice or Ice Cream.
Garnish with Banana.

BANANA COW (frozen)
In Blender:
1/2 cup of Ice
1 1/2 oz Dark Rum
1/2 oz Banana Liqueur
1/2 peeled ripe Banana
Scoop of Vanilla Ice Cream
Blend until smooth.
If too thick add Milk.
If too thin add ice or Ice Cream.
Garnish with Banana.

BANANA CREAM PIE (frozen)
In Blender:
1/2 cup of Ice
1 oz Vodka
1/2 oz Irish Cream
1/2 oz Banana Liqueur
1/2 peeled ripe Banana
Scoop of Vanilla Ice Cream
Blend until smooth.

BANANA DAIQUIRI (frozen)
In Blender:
1 cup of Ice
1 1/2 oz Rum
1/2 oz Banana Liqueur
Dash of Lime Juice
1 whole peeled ripe Banana
Blend until smooth.
If too thick add more fruit.
If too thin add ice.
Garnish with Banana.

BANANA FROST (frozen)
In Blender:
1/2 cup of Ice
1 1/2 oz Amaretto
1/2 oz Banana Liqueur
Scoop of Banana
or Vanilla Ice Cream
1/2 peeled ripe Banana
Blend until smooth.
If too thick add Milk.
If too thin add ice or Ice Cream.
Garnish with Banana.

BANANA POPSICLE (frozen)
In Blender:
1/2 cup of Ice
1 oz Vodka
1 oz Banana Liqueur
1/2 scoop Orange Sherbet
1/2 scoop Vanilla Ice Cream
1/2 peeled ripe Banana
Blend until smooth.
If too thick add Orange Juice or Milk.
If too thin add ice or Ice Cream.

BANANA SANDWICH (floater)
1/2 oz Coffee Liqueur (bottom)
1/2 oz Banana Liqueur
1/2 oz Rum Cream (top)

BANANA SOMBRERO
Fill glass with ice.
2 oz Banana Liqueur
Fill with Milk or Cream.
Shake.

BANANA SPLIT
Fill glass with ice.
1 1/2 oz Vodka
1/2 oz Banana Liqueur
1/2 oz Strawberry Liqueur
1/2 oz Dark Creme De Cacao
Fill with Milk.
Shake.

BANANA SPLIT (frozen)
In Blender:
1/2 cup of Ice
1 oz Rum
1 oz Coffee Liqueur
1 tbsp Cream of Coconut
1/2 peeled ripe Banana
Scoop of Vanilla Ice Cream
1 tbsp Chocolate Syrup
1/4 cup fresh or canned Pineapple
2 Maraschino Cherries (no stems)
Blend until smooth.
Top with Whipped Cream.
Garnish with Cherry.

BANANA STRAWBERRY
DAIQUIRI (frozen)
In Blender:
1 cup of Ice
1 oz Rum
1/2 oz Banana Liqueur
1/2 oz Strawberry Liqueur
1/2 cup fresh or frozen
Strawberries
1/2 peeled ripe Banana
Blend until smooth.
If too thick add fruit.
If too thin add ice.
Garnish with Banana and Strawberry.

BANGING THE CAPTAIN 3 WAYS ON THE COMFORTER
Fill glass with ice.
1 oz Spiced Rum
1 oz Southern Comfort
Fill with equal parts Orange,
Pineapple and Cranberry Juice.
Shake.

BANSHEE aka CAPRI
Fill glass with ice.
1 oz Banana Liqueur
1/2 oz White Creme De Cacao
Fill with Milk or Cream.
Shake.

BANSHEE (frozen)
In Blender:
1/2 cup of Ice
1 oz Banana Liqueur
1/2 oz White Creme De Cacao
Scoop of Vanilla Ice Cream
1 whole peeled ripe Banana
Blend until smooth.
If too thick add Milk.
If too thin add ice or Ice Cream.
Garnish with Banana.

BARBADOS PUNCH
Fill glass with ice.
1 1/2 oz Spiced Rum
1/2 oz Triple Sec
Dash of Lime Juice
Fill with Pineapple Juice.
Shake.

BARBARELLA aka BARBELLS
Fill glass with ice.
2 oz Orange Liqueur
1 oz Sambuca
Shake.
Serve or strain into chilled glass.

BARBARY COAST
Fill glass with ice.
1/2 oz Rum
1/2 oz Gin
1/2 oz Scotch
1/2 oz White Creme De Cacao or
White Creme De Menthe
Fill with Cola.
Shake.
Serve or strain into chilled glass.

BARBELLS aka BARBARELLA
Fill glass with ice.
2 oz Orange Liqueur
1 oz Sambuca
Shake.
Serve or strain into chilled glass.

BARRACUDA
Fill glass with ice.
1 oz Amber Rum
1 oz Light Rum
1/2 oz Galliano
Dash of Lime Juice
1/2 tsp Powdered Sugar
2 oz Pineapple Juice
Shake.
Top with Champagne.

BART SIMPSON
Fill glass with ice.
1/2 oz Vodka
1/2 oz Coconut Rum
1/2 oz Melon Liqueur
Shake.
Strain into chilled glass.

BARTMAN
Fill glass with ice.
1 oz Light Rum
1 oz Apple Brandy
Dash of Grenadine
Dash of Sour Mix
Fill with Orange Juice.
Shake.
Garnish with Orange and Cherry.

BAT BITE
Fill glass with ice.
2 oz Rum
Fill with Cranberry Juice.
Garnish with Lime.

BATTERED BRUISED AND BLEEDING (floater)
3/4 oz Grenadine (bottom)
3/4 oz Melon Liqueur
3/4 oz Blue Curacao (top)

BAVARIAN COFFEE
1 oz Peppermint Schnapps
1 oz Coffee Liqueur
Fill with hot Black Coffee
Top with Whipped Cream.

BAY BREEZE aka HAWAIIAN SEA BREEZE, DOWNEASTER
Fill glass with ice.
2 oz Vodka
Fill with equal parts Cranberry and
Pineapple Juice.
Garnish with Lime.

BAY CITY BOMBER
Fill glass with ice.
1/2 oz Vodka
1/2 oz Gin
1/2 oz Tequila
1/2 oz Triple Sec
Fill with equal parts Sour Mix,
Cranberry, Orange, and Pineapple
Juice.
Shake.
Top with 1/2 oz 151-Proof Rum.

BAZOOKA
Fill glass with ice.
1 oz Southern Comfort
1 oz Banana Liqueur
Dash of Grenadine
Shake.
Strain into shot glass.
Top with Whipped Cream.

BAZOOKA JOE
Fill glass with ice.
3/4 oz Irish Cream
3/4 oz Banana Liqueur
3/4 oz Blue Curacao
Shake.
Strain into shot glass.

BBC
1 oz Brandy
1 oz Irish Cream
Fill with hot Black Coffee.
Top with Whipped Cream.

BEACH HUT MADNESS (floater)
1/2 oz Irish Cream (bottom)
1/2 oz Amaretto
1/2 oz Sambuca (top)

BEACHCOMBER
Fill glass with ice.
1 1/2 oz Rum
1/2 oz Triple Sec
Dash of Grenadine
Fill with Sour Mix.
Shake.

BEACON HILL BLIZZARD
Fill glass with ice.
1 oz Dark Rum
1 oz Coconut Rum
Fill with equal parts
Cranberry and Grapefruit Juice.
Garnish with Lime.

BEAM ME UP SCOTTI
Fill glass with ice.
1 oz Vodka
1 oz Irish Cream
1 oz Banana Liqueur
Shake.
Strain into shot glass.

BEAM ME UP SCOTTI (floater)
1/2 oz Coffee Liqueur (bottom)
1/2 oz Banana Liqueur
1/2 oz Irish Cream (top)
Dash of Vodka or Hazelnut Liqueur (optional).

BEARHUG (Floater)
1/2 oz Coffee Liqueur (bottom)
1/2 oz Sambuca
1/2 oz Orange Liqueur (top)

BEAUTIFUL THING
Fill glass with ice.
1 oz Peppermint Schnapps
1 oz Irish Cream
Stir.

BEE STING
Fill glass with ice.
1 oz Jaegermeister
1 oz Bärenjäger

BEE'S KNEES
Fill glass with ice.
1 1/2 oz Rum
1 tsp of Honey
1 oz Sour Mix
Shake.
Strain into chilled glass.

BEEHIVE
Fill glass with ice.
2 oz Bourbon
1 tsp Honey
Fill with Grapefruit Juice.
Shake.

BEER BUSTER
In chilled beer glass:
2 oz chilled 100-Proof Vodka
3 dashes of Tabasco Sauce
Fill with Beer.

BEETLE JUICE
Fill glass with ice.
1 oz Dark Creme De Cacao
1 oz White Creme De Cacao
1/2 oz Peppermint Schnapps
1/2 oz Coffee Liqueur
Fill with Milk or Cream.
Shake.

BELFAST BOMBER (floater)
1 oz Irish Cream (bottom)
1 oz Irish Whiskey (top)

BELLINI
In Blender:
1 fresh Peach (no pit or skin) or
1/2 cup canned Peaches (no juice)
Blend.
Pour pureed peach into glass.
Fill with cold Champagne.

BELLY BUTTON SHOT
Find an attractive desirable belly
button (inny).
Ask permission to use it.
If yes, lay owner of belly button on
their back (totally nude if possible).
Fill belly button with favorite straight
liquor or liqueur (be careful not to
spill any or you'll have to clean it up
with a rag or your tongue).
Place lips over belly button and
slurp out drink as loudly as
possible. Take turns and repeat
process until interests change.

BELMONT
Fill glass with ice.
1 1/2 oz Gin
1/2 oz Black Raspberry Liqueur
Fill with Milk or Cream.
Shake.

BEND ME OVER
Fill glass with ice.
1 oz Vodka
or 1/2 oz Vodka and 1/2 oz
Whiskey
1 oz Amaretto
1 oz Sour Mix
Shake.
Strain into chilled glass.

BENT NAIL
Fill glass with ice.
1 1/2 oz Canadian Whiskey
1/2 oz Drambuie
Stir.

BERLIN WALL
Fill glass with ice.
1 1/2 oz Vodka
1/2 oz Irish Cream
Stir.

BERMUDA TRIANGLE
Fill glass with ice.
1 oz Spiced Rum
1 oz Peach Schnapps
Fill with Orange Juice.
Shake.

BETSY ROSS
Fill glass with ice.
1 oz Brandy
1 oz Port
1/2 oz Triple Sec
Dash of Bitters
Stir.
Strain into chilled glass.

BETWEEN THE SHEETS
Fill glass with ice.
1 oz Rum
1 oz Cognac or Brandy
1 oz Triple Sec
Dash of Sour Mix
Shake.
Strain into chilled glass.

BEVERLY HILL (floater)
1 oz 100-Proof Cinnamon
Schnapps (bottom)
1 oz Jaegermeister (top)

BIBLE BELT
Fill glass with ice.
2 oz Bourbon
or Southern Comfort
1 oz Triple Sec
2 oz Lime Juice
2 oz Sour Mix
Shake.
Rim glass with Powdered Sugar.
Garnish with a Lemon.

BIG BAMBOO
Fill glass with ice.
2 oz 151-Proof Rum
1 oz Dark Rum
1/4 oz Triple Sec
2 oz Orange Juice
2 oz Pineapple Juice
1/2 oz Sugar Syrup
Dash of Bitters
Shake.
Strain into 3 or 4 shot glasses.

BIG DADDY
Fill glass with ice.
1/2 oz Vodka
1/2 oz Rum
1/2 oz Tequila
1/2 oz Whiskey
Fill with Lemon-Lime Soda.
Garnish with Lime.

BIG KAHUNA
Fill glass with ice.
1 1/2 oz Gin
1/2 oz Triple Sec or Blue Curacao
1/2 oz Sweet Vermouth
2 oz Pineapple Juice
Shake.
Strain into chilled glass.

BIG TITTY ORGY
Fill glass with ice.
1 oz Grain Alcohol
1 oz Vodka
1 oz Strawberry Liqueur
Fill glass with Orange Juice.
Shake.

BIKINI
Fill glass with ice.
1 oz Vodka
1 oz Rum
tsp Sugar
1 oz Sour Mix
1 oz Milk or Cream
Shake.
Strain into chilled glass.

BIKINI LINE
Fill glass with ice.
3/4 oz Vodka
3/4 oz Coffee Liqueur
3/4 oz Raspberry Liqueur

BIKINI LINE (floater)
1/2 oz Strawberry Liqueur (bottom)
1/2 oz Orange Liqueur
1/2 oz Vodka (top)

BILLIE HOLIDAY
Fill glass with ice.
2 oz Vodka
Dash of Grenadine
Fill with Ginger Ale
Garnish with Cherry.

BIMINI ICE-T
Fill glass with ice.
1/2 oz Vodka
1/2 oz Gin
1/2 oz Rum
1/2 oz Tequila
1/2 oz Blue Curacao
1 oz Sour Mix
1 oz Orange Juice
1 oz Pineapple Juice
Shake.
Top with Cola.
Garnish with Lemon.

BIRD OF PARADISE
Fill glass 3/4 full with ice.
Fill 3/4 with Champagne.
Fill with Pineapple Juice.
Dash of Grenadine

BISCUIT NECK
Fill glass with ice.
1/2 oz 101-proof Bourbon
1/2 oz Amaretto
1/2 oz Irish Cream
1/2 oz Hazelnut Liqueur
Shake.
Strain into shot glass.

BIT OF HONEY (frozen)
In Blender:
1/2 cup of Ice
1/2 oz Scotch
1 tbsp Honey
Scoop of Vanilla Ice Cream
Blend until smooth.
Float 1/2 oz of B&B on top.

BITCH FIGHT
Fill glass with ice.
1 oz Peach Schnapps
1 oz Orange Liqueur
Dash of Lime Juice
Fill with Cranberry Juice.
Shake.
Garnish with Lime.

BLACK AND BLUE MARTINI
(CAUTION: DRY usually means
less Vermouth than usual.
EXTRA DRY can mean even less
Vermouth than usual or no
Vermouth at all.)
1 oz Top Shelf Gin
1 oz Top Shelf Vodka
1/2 oz Dry Vermouth
Stir.
Strain into chilled glass or pour
contents (with ice) into short glass.
Garnish with Lemon Twist or
Olives or Cocktail Onions.

BLACK AND TAN
Fill glass 1/2 with Amber Ale.
Fill glass 1/2 with Stout.

BLACK BARRACUDA
Fill glass with ice.
1 oz Dark Rum
1/2 oz Banana Liqueur
1/2 oz Blackberry Brandy
Dash of Lime Juice
Dash of Grenadine
Fill with Orange Juice.
Shake.
Garnish with Lime and Orange.

BLACK CAT
Fill glass with ice.
1 oz Vodka
1 oz Cherry Liqueur
Fill glass with equal parts
Cranberry Juice and Cola.

BLACK COW
In glass:
Scoop of Vanilla Ice Cream
Fill with Root Beer.
Serve with straw and spoon.

BLACK COW 2
Fill glass with ice.
1 oz Vodka or Vandermint
1 oz Dark Creme De Cacao
Fill with Cream or Milk.
Shake.

BLACK DEATH
1 oz 12 year old Scotch
Fill with Stout.

BLACK DOG
Fill glass with ice.
2 oz Bourbon
1 oz Blackberry Brandy
Stir.

BLACK EYE
Fill glass with ice.
1 1/2 oz Vodka
1/2 oz Blackberry Brandy
Stir.

**BLACK-EYED SUSAN aka
KENTUCKY SCREWDRIVER,
YELLOW JACKET**
Fill glass with ice.
2 oz Bourbon
Fill with Orange Juice.

BLACK FOREST (floater)
1/2 oz Coffee Liqueur (bottom)
1/2 oz Black Raspberry Liqueur
1/2 oz Irish Cream
1/2 oz Vodka (top)

BLACK FOREST (frozen)
In Blender:
1/2 cup of Ice
3/4 oz Vodka
3/4 oz Coffee Liqueur
3/4 oz Black Raspberry Liqueur
Scoop of Chocolate Ice Cream
Blend until smooth.
If too thick add Milk.
If too thin add ice or Ice Cream.
Garnish with Shaved Chocolate or
Sprinkles.

BLACK HAWK
Fill glass with ice.
1 1/2 oz Whiskey
1 1/2 oz Sloe Gin
Stir.
Strain into chilled glass.
Garnish with Cherry.

BLACK ICED TEA
Fill glass with ice.
3/4 oz Dark Rum
3/4 oz Brandy
3/4 oz Triple Sec
1 oz Orange Juice
Fill with Cola.
Garnish with Orange.

BLACK JAMAICAN
Fill glass with ice.
1 1/2 oz Rum
1/2 oz Coffee Liqueur
Stir.

BLACK LADY
Fill glass with ice.
2 oz Orange Liqueur
1/2 oz Coffee Liqueur
1/2 oz Brandy
Shake.
Strain into chilled glass.

BLACK MAGIC
Fill glass with ice.
1 1/2 oz Vodka
1 oz Coffee Liqueur
Dash of Sour Mix
Stir.
Garnish with Lemon Twist.

BLACK MAGIC 2
3/4 oz Amaretto
3/4 oz Irish Cream
3/4 oz Coffee Liqueur
Fill with Hot Chocolate.
Top with Whipped Cream.
Sprinkle with Shaved Chocolate.

BLACK MARTINI 1
Fill glass with ice.
2 oz Vodka or Gin
1/2 oz Blackberry Brandy or Black
Raspberry Liqueur
Stir.
Strain into chilled glass.

BLACK MARTINI 2
Fill glass with ice.
2 oz Gin or Rum
1/2 oz Blackberry Brandy
or Black Raspberry Liqueur
Stir.
Strain into chilled glass
or pour contents (with ice) into
short glass.
Garnish with Lemon Twist
or Black Olive.

BLACK PRINCE
1 oz Blackberry Brandy
Dash of Lime Juice
Fill with Champagne.

BLACK ROSE
Fill glass with ice.
2 oz Rum
1 tsp Sugar
Fill with cold Black Coffee.
Shake.

BLACK ROSE (frozen)
In Blender:
1 cup of Ice
1/2 oz Gold Tequila
1/2 oz Coffee Liqueur
1/2 oz Black Raspberry Liqueur
1/2 cup fresh or frozen
Strawberries
1/2 oz Cream or Milk
Blend until smooth.
If too thick add cream or milk.
If too thin add ice.

BLACK RUSSIAN
Fill glass with ice.
1 1/2 oz Vodka
1 oz Coffee Liqueur
Stir.

BLACK RUSSIAN (frozen)
In Blender:
1/2 cup of Ice
1 1/2 oz Vodka
1 oz Coffee Liqueur
Scoop of Chocolate Ice Cream
Blend until smooth.
If too thick add Milk or Cream.
If too thin add ice or Ice Cream.
Garnish with Chocolate Shavings
or Sprinkles.

BLACK SABBATH
Fill glass with ice.
3/4 oz Bourbon
3/4 oz Dark Rum
3/4 oz Jaegermeister
Shake.
Strain into chilled glass.

BLACK SHEEP
Fill glass with ice.
1 oz Blackberry Brandy
1 oz Black Raspberry Liqueur
1/2 oz Lime Juice
Stir.
Strain into chilled glass.
Garnish with Lime.

BLACK STRIPE
2 oz Dark Rum
tsp Molasses or Honey
Twist Lemon over glass and drop
in.
Fill with Hot Water.
Garnish with Cinnamon Stick.
Stir.

BLACK TIE (floater)
1/2 oz Amaretto (bottom)
1/2 oz Drambuie
1/2 oz Scotch (top)

BLACK VELVET
Fill glass 1/2 with Champagne.
Fill glass 1/2 with Stout.

BLACK VELVETEEN
Fill glass 3/4 with Hard Cider.
Fill glass with Stout.

BLACK WATCH
Fill glass with ice.
1 1/2 oz Scotch
1/2 oz Coffee Liqueur
Stir.

BLACK WITCH
Fill glass with ice.
1 1/2 oz Amber Rum
1/4 oz Dark Rum
1/4 oz Apricot Brandy
1/2 oz Pineapple Juice
Shake.
Strain into chilled glass.

B

BLACKBERRY SWIZZLE
Fill glass with ice.
1 1/2 oz Gin
1/2 oz Black Raspberry Liqueur
Fill with Blackberry Flavored Spring Water.

BLACKJACK
Fill glass with ice.
1 oz Brandy
1 oz Blackberry Brandy
1 oz Cream
Shake.
Serve or strain into chilled glass.

BLAST
Fill glass with ice.
1 oz Rum
1 oz Brandy
Dash of Sour Mix
Fill with equal parts Orange and
Pineapple Juice.
Shake.

BLEACHER CREATURE
Fill glass with ice.
1/3 oz Vodka
1/3 oz Tequila
1/3 oz Rum
1/3 oz Triple Sec
1/3 oz Melon Liqueur
1/3 oz Green Creme De Menthe
Fill with Sour Mix.
Shake.

BLINKER
Fill glass with ice.
2 oz Whiskey
Dash of Grenadine
Fill with Grapefruit Juice.
Shake.

BLIZZARD
Fill glass with ice.
2 oz Vodka
Fill with Lemon-Lime Soda.
Garnish with Lemon or Lime.

BLIZZARD (frozen)
In Blender:
1/2 cup of Ice
1/2 oz Dark Rum
1/2 oz Brandy
1/2 oz Coffee Liqueur
1/2 oz Irish Cream
Scoop of Vanilla Ice Cream
Blend until smooth.

BLOOD AND SAND
Fill glass with ice.
1 oz Scotch
3/4 oz Cherry Brandy
1/2 oz Sweet Vermouth
1 oz Orange Juice
Stir.
Strain into chilled glass.

BLOOD CLOT
Fill shot glass with:
2 oz Southern Comfort
Drop shot glass into larger glass:
Filled 3/4 with Lemon-Lime Soda
And a dash of Grenadine

BLOOD CLOT (floater)
1 1/2 oz 151-Proof Rum
Dash of Grenadine
Float 1/4 oz Cream on top.

BLOODY BASTARD
Fill glass 1/2 with ale.
1 tsp Horseradish
Fill with Bloody Mary Mix.
Rub rim of second glass with Lime
and dip into Kosher Salt.
Pour drink into second glass.

BLOODY BRAIN
1 oz Strawberry Liqueur
Dash of Grenadine
1/2 oz Irish Cream

BLOODY BREW
1 1/2 oz Vodka
2 oz Tomato Juice
Fill with Beer or Malt Liquor.
Dash of Salt

BLOODY BULL
Fill glass with ice.
2 oz Vodka
1 oz Beef Bouillon
1 tsp Horseradish
3 dashes of Tabasco Sauce
3 dashes of Worcestershire Sauce
Dash of Lime Juice
3 dashes of Celery Salt
3 dashes of Pepper
1 oz Clam Juice (optional)
Dash of Sherry (optional)
Fill with Tomato Juice.
Pour from one glass to another until
mixed. Garnish with Lemon and/or
Lime, Celery and/or Cucumber
and/or Cocktail Shrimp.

BLOODY CAESAR
Fill glass with ice.
2 oz Vodka
1 tsp Horseradish
3 dashes of Tabasco Sauce
3 dashes of Worcestershire Sauce
Dash of Lime Juice
3 dashes of Celery Salt
3 dashes of Pepper
Dash of Sherry (optional)
1 tsp Dijon Mustard (optional)
Fill with equal parts tomato and
Clam Juice.
Pour from one glass to another until
mixed. Garnish with Lemon and/or
Lime, Celery and/or Cucumber
and/or Cocktail Shrimp.

BLOODY HOLLY aka
DANISH MARY
Fill glass with ice.
2 oz Aquavit
1 tsp Horseradish
3 dashes of Tabasco Sauce
3 dashes of Worcestershire Sauce
Dash of Lime Juice
3 dashes of Celery Salt
3 dashes of Pepper
1 oz Clam Juice (optional)
Dash of Sherry (optional)
1 tsp Dijon Mustard (optional)
Fill with Tomato Juice.
Pour from one glass to another until mixed. Garnish with Lemon and/or Lime, Celery and/or Cucumber and/or Cocktail Shrimp.

BLOODY JOSEPHINE
Fill glass with ice.
2 oz Scotch
1 tsp Horseradish
3 dashes of Tabasco Sauce
3 dashes of Worcestershire Sauce
Dash of Lime Juice
3 dashes of Celery Salt
3 dashes of Pepper
1 oz Clam Juice (optional)
Dash of Sherry (optional)
1 tsp Dijon Mustard (optional)
Fill with Tomato Juice.
Pour from one glass to another until mixed. Garnish with Lemon and/or Lime, Celery and/or Cucumber and/or Cocktail Shrimp.

BLOODY MARIA
Fill glass with ice.
2 oz Tequila
1 tsp Horseradish
3 dashes of Tabasco Sauce
3 dashes of Worcestershire Sauce
Dash of Lime Juice
3 dashes of Celery Salt
3 dashes of Pepper
1 oz Clam Juice (optional)
Dash of Sherry (optional)
1 tsp Dijon Mustard (optional)
Fill with Tomato Juice.
Pour from one glass to another until mixed. Garnish with Lemon and/or Lime, Celery and/or Cucumber and/or Cocktail Shrimp.

BLOODY MARISELA
Fill glass with ice.
2 oz Light Rum
1 tsp Horseradish
3 dashes of Tabasco Sauce
3 dashes of Worcestershire Sauce
Dash of Lime Juice
3 dashes of Celery Salt
3 dashes of Pepper
1 oz Clam Juice (optional)
Dash of Sherry (optional)
1 tsp Dijon Mustard (optional)
Fill with Tomato Juice.
Pour from one glass to another until mixed. Garnish with Lemon and/or Lime, Celery and/or Cucumber and/or Cocktail Shrimp.

BLOODY MARY
Fill glass with ice.
2 oz Vodka
1 tsp Horseradish
3 dashes of Tabasco Sauce
3 dashes of Worcestershire Sauce
Dash of Lime Juice
3 dashes of Celery Salt
3 dashes of Pepper
1 oz Clam Juice (optional)
Dash of Sherry (optional)
1 tsp Dijon Mustard (optional)
Fill with Tomato Juice.
Pour from one glass to another until mixed. Garnish with Lemon and/or Lime, Celery and/or Cucumber and/or Cocktail Shrimp.

BLOODY MOLLY
Fill glass with ice.
2 oz Irish Whiskey
1 tsp Horseradish
3 dashes of Tabasco Sauce
3 dashes of Worcestershire Sauce
Dash of Lime Juice
3 dashes of Celery Salt
3 dashes of Pepper
1 oz Clam Juice (optional)
Fill with Tomato Juice.
Pour from one glass to another until mixed.
Garnish with Lemon and/or Lime, Celery and/or Cucumber and/or Cocktail Shrimp.

BLOW JOB aka
PEARL NECKLACE (floater)
1/2 oz Cream (bottom)
1/2 oz White Creme De Cacao
1/2 oz Vodka (top)
Top with Whipped Cream.
Contents should mix slightly.
To drink, place hands behind back and pick up using only mouth.

BLOW JOB 2 (floater)
3/4 oz Coffee Liqueur (bottom)
3/4 oz Orange Liqueur
3/4 oz Banana Liqueur (top)
Top with Whipped Cream.
To drink, place hands behind back and pick up using only mouth.

BLOW JOB 3 (floater)
1 oz Irish Cream (bottom)
1 oz Orange Liqueur (top)
Top with Whipped Cream.

BLUE BAYOU (frozen)
In Blender:
1 cup of Ice
1 1/2 oz Vodka
1/2 oz Blue Curacao
1/2 cup fresh or canned Pineapple
2 oz Grapefruit Juice
Blend until smooth.
If too thick add juice.
If too thin add ice.
Garnish with Pineapple.

BLUE BIJOU (frozen)
In Blender:
1 cup of Ice
1 1/4 oz Rum
1 oz Blue Curacao
3 oz Orange Juice
3 oz Pineapple Juice
3 or 4 drops of Lime Juice
Blend on low speed for 3-5 seconds.

BLUE CANARY
Fill glass with ice.
1 1/2 oz Gin
1/2 oz Blue Curacao
Fill with Grapefruit Juice.
Shake.

BLUE DAIQUIRI (frozen)
In Blender:
1 cup of ice.
1 1/2 oz Rum
1/2 oz Blue Curacao
Dash of Lime Juice
Dash of Sour Mix
1/2 tsp Sugar
Blend until smooth.
If too thick add Sour Mix.
If too thin add ice.

BLUE HAWAIIAN
Fill glass with ice.
1 oz Rum
1 oz Blue Curacao
1 oz Cream of Coconut
Fill with Pineapple Juice.
Shake.
Garnish with Pineapple.

BLUE HAWAIIAN 2
Fill glass with ice.
1 1/2 oz Vodka
1/2 oz Blue Curacao
Fill with equal parts Orange and Pineapple Juice.
Shake.
Garnish with Pineapple.

BLUE KAMIKAZE aka NUCLEAR KAMIKAZE
Fill glass with ice.
2 oz Vodka
1/2 oz Blue Curacao
Dash of Lime Juice
Shake.
Serve or strain into chilled glass.
Garnish with Lime.

BLUE LADY
Fill glass with ice.
1 1/2 oz Gin
1/4 oz Blue Curacao
1 oz Sour Mix
Stir.

BLUE LEMONADE
1 oz Citrus Vodka
1 oz Blue Curacao
Dash of Sour Mix
Dash of Lemon-Lime Soda
Stir.

BLUE MARGARITA
Fill glass with ice.
2 oz Tequila
1 oz Blue Curacao
Dash of Lime Juice
3 oz Sour Mix
Shake.
Rub rim of second glass with Lime and dip rim into Kosher Salt. Either pour contents (with ice) or strain into salted glass.
Garnish with Lime.

BLUE MEANIE
Fill glass with ice.
1 1/2 oz Vodka or Tequila or Gin
1/2 oz Blue Curacao
2 oz Sour Mix
Shake.
Strain into shot glass.

BLUE SHARK
Fill glass with ice.
1 oz Vodka
1 oz Tequila
3/4 oz Blue Curacao
Shake.
Strain into chilled glass.

BLUE TAIL FLY
Fill glass with ice.
1 oz Blue Curacao
1 oz White Creme De Cacao
Fill with Milk or light Cream.
Shake.

BLUE VALIUM
Fill glass with ice.
2/3 oz 151-Proof Rum
3/4 oz Whiskey
3/4 oz Blue Curacao
Dash of Sour Mix
Shake.
Strain into chilled glass.
Dash of Lemon-Lime Soda

BOARDWALK BREEZER
Fill glass with ice.
1 1/2 oz Dark Rum
1/2 oz Banana Liqueur
1/2 oz Lime Juice
Fill with Pineapple Juice.
Shake.
Top with dash of Grenadine.
Garnish with Orange and Cherry.

BOB MARLEY
Fill glass with ice.
1 oz Dark Rum
1 oz Tia Maria
Dash of Cream of Coconut
Dash of Milk or Cream
Dash of Pineapple Juice
Shake.
Strain into chilled glass.

BOCCI BALL
Fill glass with ice.
1 1/2 oz Vodka
1/2 oz Amaretto
Fill with Orange Juice.
Splash with Soda Water.
Garnish with Orange.

BODY SHOT
Pour shot of Tequila.
Lick unclothed area of favorite person.
Sprinkle dampened area with salt.
Place Lime in favorite person's mouth.
Lick salted area. Drink shot.
Suck Lime from friend's mouth.
Take turns.

BOG FOG aka
RUM MADRAS
Fill glass with ice.
2 oz Rum
Fill with equal parts Orange and Cranberry Juice.
Garnish with Lime.

BOILERMAKER
Fill shot glass with Whiskey.
Fill chilled glass 3/4 with Beer.
Either drink shot and chase with beer or drop shot glass into beer and drink.

BOMB
Fill glass with ice.
1/2 oz Scotch
1/2 oz Bourbon
1/2 oz 151-Proof Rum
1/2 oz Dark Rum
Dash of Grenadine
Fill with equal parts Orange and Pineapple Juice.
Shake.

BON BON
Fill glass with ice.
3/4 oz Irish Cream
3/4 oz Black Raspberry Liqueur
3/4 oz Truffles Liqueur
Shake.
Strain into chilled glass.

BONGO
Fill glass with ice.
1 1/2 oz Rum
1/2 oz Blackberry Brandy
Fill with Pineapple Juice.
Shake.

BOOMER
Fill glass with ice.
1 oz Tequila
1 oz Apricot Brandy
Fill glass with equal parts Orange Juice
And Sour Mix.
Shake.

BOOTLEGGER
Fill glass with ice.
3/4 oz Bourbon
3/4 oz Tequila
3/4 oz Southern Comfort
Shake
Strain into chilled glass.

BOP THE PRINCESS
Fill glass with ice.
2 oz Premium Whiskey
Fill with equal parts Cranberry Juice and Lemon-Lime Soda.
Garnish with Cherry and Lemon.

BORDER CROSSING
2 oz Tequila
Dash of Lime Juice
Fill with Cola.

BOS'N MATE
Fill glass with ice.
1 oz Light Rum
1 oz Dark Rum
Dash of Triple Sec
Dash of Grenadine
Fill with equal parts Lime and Pineapple Juice.
Garnish with Lime and Pineapple.

BOSOM CARESSER
1 1/2 oz Brandy
1/2 oz Curacao
Dash of Grenadine
1 Egg Yolk
Shake.

BOSS
Fill glass with ice.
3/4 oz Bourbon
1/2 oz Amaretto
Stir.

BOSSA NOVA
Fill glass with ice.
1 oz Galliano
1 oz Amber Rum
1/4 oz Apricot Brandy
Dash of Sour Mix
1/2 Egg White
Fill with Pineapple Juice.
Shake.
Garnish with Orange and Cherry.

BOSTON ICED TEA

Fill glass with ice.
1/2 oz Vodka
1/2 oz Gin
1/2 oz Rum
1/2 oz Coffee Liqueur
1/2 oz Amaretto or Orange Liqueur
2 oz Sour Mix
Fill with Cola.
Garnish with Lemon.

BOSTON MASSACRE

Fill glass with ice.
Dash of Irish Cream
Dash of Orange Liqueur
Dash of Coffee Liqueur
Dash of Hazelnut Liqueur
Dash of Irish Whiskey
Dash of Amaretto
Dash of Dark Creme De Cacao
Fill with Cream.
Shake.

BOSTON MASSACRE (frozen)

In Blender:
1/2 cup of Ice
Dash of Irish Cream
Dash of Orange Liqueur
Dash of Coffee Liqueur
Dash of Hazelnut Liqueur
Dash of Irish Whiskey
Dash of Amaretto
Dash of Dark Creme De Cacao
Scoop of Vanilla Ice Cream
Blend until smooth.
If too thick add Milk or Cream.
If too thin add ice or Ice Cream.
Pour into glass. Insert straw in glass against side and dribble Grenadine into straw. It should run down inside of glass and look like dripping blood.

BOTTOM LINE

Fill glass with ice.
2 oz Gin
1/2 oz Lime Juice
Fill with Tonic Water.
Stir.
Garnish with Lime.

BOURBON MANHATTAN

Fill glass with ice.
2 oz Bourbon
Dash of Sweet Vermouth
Stir.
Strain into chilled glass or pour contents (with ice) into short glass and serve.
Garnish with Cherry.
CAUTION: SWEET means extra Sweet Vermouth.
DRY can mean either use Dry Vermouth instead of Sweet Vermouth, or less Sweet Vermouth than usual and garnish with a Lemon Twist or Cherry.

BOURBON OLD FASHIONED

Muddle together in short glass:
stemless Maraschino Cherry,
Orange Slice,
1/2 tsp of Sugar, and
3 dashes of Bitters.
Fill glass with ice.
2 oz Bourbon
Dash of Soda Water
Stir.

BOURBON SATIN

Fill glass with ice.
1 1/2 oz Bourbon
1 oz White Creme De Cacao
2 oz Milk or Cream
Shake.
Strain into chilled glass.

BOX CAR

Fill glass with ice.
1 1/2 oz Rum
1/2 oz Triple Sec
Fill with Sour Mix.
Shake.
Garnish with Orange and Cherry.

BRAHMA BULL

Fill glass with ice.
1 1/2 oz Gold Tequila
1/2 oz Coffee Liqueur
Stir.

BRAIN

1 oz Strawberry Liqueur
or Peach Schnapps
1/4 oz Grenadine
1/2 oz Irish Cream.
Put in drop by drop.

BRAIN (floater)

Fill glass with ice.
1 oz Coffee Liqueur (bottom)
1 oz Peach Schnapps
1 oz Irish Cream (top)

BRAIN ERASER

Fill glass with ice.
1 oz Vodka
1/2 oz Coffee Liqueur
1/2 oz Amaretto
Splash with Club Soda.
Supposed to be drunk in one shot through a straw.

BRAIN TUMOR

Fill glass with ice.
2 oz Irish Cream
5 or 6 drops of Strawberry Liqueur

BRAIN WAVE (floater)

1 1/4 oz Irish Cream (bottom)
3/4 oz Vodka (top)
Place a drop of Grenadine into center of drink.

BRANDY ALEXANDER
Fill glass with ice.
1 1/2 oz Brandy
1/2 oz Dark Creme De Cacao
3 oz Cream or Milk
Shake.
Serve or strain into chilled glass.
Sprinkle Nutmeg on top.

BRANDY ALEXANDER (frozen)
In Blender:
1/2 cup of Ice
1 1/2 oz Brandy
1/2 oz Dark Creme De Cacao
Scoop of Vanilla Ice Cream
Blend until smooth.
If too thick add Milk or Cream.
If too thin add ice or Ice Cream.
Sprinkle Nutmeg on top.

BRANDY ALMOND MOCHA
1 oz Brandy
1 oz Amaretto
Fill with equal parts Hot
Chocolate and hot Coffee.
Stir.
Top with Whipped Cream.
Sprinkle with Shaved Almonds.

BRANDY GUMP
Fill glass with ice.
2 oz Brandy
Dash of Grenadine
Fill with Sour Mix.
Shake.
Serve or strain into chilled glass.
Garnish with Orange and Cherry.

BRANDY HUMMER (frozen)
In Blender:
1/2 cup of ice
1 oz Brandy
1 oz Coffee Liqueur
Scoop of Vanilla Ice Cream
Blend until smooth.
If too thick add Milk or Cream.
If too thin add ice or Ice Cream.

BRANDY MILK PUNCH
2 oz Brandy
1 tsp Sugar or Sugar Syrup
Fill with Milk or Cream.
Shake.

BRASS KNUCKLES
Fill glass with ice.
1 1/2 oz Bourbon
1/2 oz Triple Sec
Fill with Sour Mix.
Shake.

BRASS MONKEY
Fill glass with ice.
1 oz Vodka
1 oz Rum
Fill with Orange Juice.
Garnish with Orange.

BRAVE BULL
Fill glass with ice.
1 1/2 oz Tequila
1/2 oz Coffee Liqueur
Stir.
Strain into shot glass.

BRAVE COW
Fill glass with ice.
1 1/2 oz Gin
1/2 oz Coffee Liqueur
Stir.
Serve or strain into chilled glass.

BRAZILIAN COFFEE
3/4 oz Coffee Liqueur
3/4 oz Brandy
3/4 oz Orange Liqueur
Fill with hot Black Coffee.
Top with Whipped Cream.
Sprinkle Brown Sugar on top.

BRIGHTON PUNCH
Fill glass with ice.
3/4 oz Brandy
3/4 oz Benadictine
3/4 oz Bourbon
Fill with equal parts Sour Mix and
Orange Juice.
Shake.
Top with Soda Water.

BROKEN DOWN GOLF CART
Fill glass with ice.
1 oz Vodka or Melon Liqueur
1 oz Amaretto
1 oz Cranberry Juice
Shake.
Strain into shot glass.

BROKEN HEART
Fill glass with ice.
1 oz Vodka
1 oz Black Raspberry Liqueur
Dash of Grenadine
Fill with Orange Juice.
Shake.

BRONCO COCKTAIL
Fill glass with ice.
1 oz Orange Liqueur
2 oz Orange Soda
Fill with Champagne.
Garnish with Orange.

BROWN COW
Fill glass with ice.
2 oz Dark Creme De Cacao
Fill with Milk or Cream.
Shake.

BROWN DERBY
Fill glass with ice.
2 oz Vodka
Fill with Cola.

BROWN SQUIRREL
1 oz Amaretto
1 oz Dark Creme De Cacao
1 oz Cream or Milk
Shake.
Strain into chilled glass.

BROWN SQUIRREL (frozen)
In Blender:
1/2 cup of Ice
1 oz Amaretto
3/4 oz Dark Creme De Cacao
Scoop of Vanilla Ice Cream
Dash of Milk
Blend until smooth.
If too thick add Milk.
If too thin add ice or Ice Cream.

BRUT AND BOGS aka
CHAM CRAN CHAM,
SCARLET LETTER
Fill glass 3/4 with ice.
Fill glass 3/4 with Champagne.
Dash of Black Raspberry Liqueur
Fill with Cranberry Juice.

B-STING
Fill glass with ice.
1 1/2 oz B&B
1/2 oz White Creme De Menthe

BUBBLE GUM
Fill glass with ice.
1 oz Vodka
1 oz Southern Comfort
1 oz Banana Liqueur
Dash of Grenadine
1 oz Cream
Shake.
Strain into chilled glass.
Garnish with Bubble Gum Stick.

BUBBLE GUM 2
Fill glass with ice.
1 oz Melon Liqueur
1 oz Amaretto
or Creme De Nouyax
1 oz Milk or Cream
Dash of Grenadine (optional)
Shake.
Strain into chilled glass.
Garnish with Bubble Gum Stick.

BUCK
Fill glass with ice.
2 oz desired Liquor
Fill with Ginger Ale.
Garnish with Lemon.

BUCKAROO
Fill glass with ice.
2 oz Rum
Fill with Root Beer.

BUCKHEAD ROOT BEER
Fill glass with ice.
2 oz Jaegermeister
Fill with Club Soda.
Garnish with Lime and Orange.

BUCKING BRONCO (floater)
1 oz Southern Comfort (bottom)
1 oz Tequila (top)

BUFFALO PISS
Fill glass with ice.
2 oz Tequila
Fill with equal parts Grapefruit
Juice and Lemon-Lime Soda.

BUFFALO SWEAT
2 oz Bourbon
Dash of Tabasco Sauce
Stir.

BUFFALO SWEAT 2
1 oz Tequila
1 oz 151-Proof Rum
Dash of Tabasco Sauce

BULL SHOT
1 oz Vodka
1 oz Beef Bouillon
Dash of Worcestershire Sauce
Dash of Salt
Dash of Pepper

BULL'S MILK
Fill glass with ice.
1 1/2 oz Brandy
1/2 oz Dark Rum
1/2 tsp Sugar
Fill with Milk.
Shake.
Sprinkle with Cinnamon.

BULLDOG
Fill glass with ice.
1 oz Vodka or Rum
1 oz Coffee Liqueur
Fill with equal parts Cream and
Cola.

BULLFROG aka KAMIKAZE
Fill glass with ice.
2 oz Vodka
1/2 oz Triple Sec
1 oz Lime Juice
Shake.
Serve or strain into chilled glass.
Garnish with a Lime.

BULLFROG 2
Fill glass with ice.
2 oz Vodka
Fill with equal parts Sour Mix and
Grapefruit Juice.

BUMBLE BEE
Fill glass with ice.
2 oz Tia Maria
Fill with Milk.
Shake.
Top with Peach Schnapps.

BUNGEE JUMPER
Fill glass with ice.
2 oz Irish Mist
Dash of Cream
Fill with Orange Juice.
Shake.
Top with Amaretto.

BURNING BUSH aka PRAIRIE FIRE
2 oz Tequila
Add Tabasco Sauce until pink.

BURNT ALMOND aka ROASTED TOASTED ALMOND, ORGASM
Fill glass with ice.
1 oz Vodka
1 oz Coffee Liqueur
1 oz Amaretto
Fill with Milk or Cream.
Shake.

BURNT ALMOND (frozen)
In Blender:
1/2 cup of Ice
1 oz Vodka
1 oz Coffee Liqueur
1 oz Amaretto
Scoop of Vanilla Ice Cream
Blend until smooth.
If too thick add Milk or Cream.
If too thin add ice or Ice Cream.

BURNTOUT BITCH
Fill glass with ice.
1/2 oz Vodka
1/2 oz Rum
1/2 oz Tequila
1/2 oz Triple Sec
Fill with Orange Juice.
Shake.

BUSH DIVER (floater)
3/4 oz Coffee Liqueur (bottom)
3/4 oz Irish Cream
3/4 oz Apple Brandy (top)

BUSHWACKER aka SHILLELAGH
Fill glass with ice.
1 oz Irish Whiskey or Irish Mist
1 oz Irish Cream
Stir.

BUSHWACKER 2
Fill glass with ice.
1 1/2 oz Dark Rum
1/2 oz Coffee Liqueur
1/2 oz Dark Creme De Cacao
1 oz Cream of Coconut
Fill with Cream or Milk.
Shake.

BUSTED CHERRY (floater)
1/2 oz Coffee Liqueur (bottom)
1/2 oz Cream
1/2 oz Cherry Brandy (top)

BUSTED RUBBER (floater)
1/2 oz Raspberry Liqueur (bottom)
1/2 oz Irish Cream
1/2 oz Orange Liqueur (top)

BUTT MUNCH
In Blender:
1/2 cup of ice
1 oz Brandy
1 oz Rum
1 oz Coffee
1 oz Chocolate Syrup
1 oz Milk
tsp Honey
Blend until smooth.
Top with Whipped Cream.
Sprinkle with Cinnamon.

BUTTAFINGER
Fill glass with ice.
1/2 oz Vodka
1 oz Cookies and Cream Liqueur
1 oz Butterscotch Schnapps
Fill with Cream or Milk.
Shake.

BUTTAFINGER 2
1/2 oz Vodka
1/2 oz Irish Cream
1/2 oz Coffee Liqueur
1/2 oz Butterscotch Schnapps
Dash of Milk or Cream
Shake. Strain into shot glass.

BUTTER BALL (floater)
1 1/2 oz Butterscotch Schnapps (bottom)
1/2 oz Irish Cream or Orange Liqueur (top)

BUTTER SHOT aka BUTTERY NIPPLE (floater)
1 oz Butterscotch Schnapps (bottom)
1/2 oz Irish Cream
1/2 oz Vodka (top)

BUTTERNUT COFFEE
1 oz Amaretto or Hazelnut Liqueur
1 oz Butterscotch Schnapps
Fill with hot Black Coffee.
Top with Whipped Cream.
Drizzle with Butterscotch.

C & B
1 oz Cognac
1 oz Benedictine

C-DROP
Fill glass with ice.
1 oz Coffee Liqueur
1 oz Irish Cream
1/2 oz Banana Liqueur
Shake.
Strain into shot glass.

CABLE CAR
Fill glass with ice.
1 1/2 oz Gin
1/2 oz Triple Sec
1/2 oz Lime Juice
Shake.
Strain into chilled glass.

CABLEGRAM
Fill glass with ice.
2 oz Whiskey
1/2 oz Sour Mix
1 tsp Sugar Syrup
Shake.
Fill glass with Ginger Ale.
Garnish with Lemon.

CACTUS BANGER aka FREDDY FUDPUCKER
Fill glass with ice.
1 1/2 oz Tequila
Fill with Orange Juice.
Top with Galliano.
Garnish with Orange.

CACTUS JUICE
Fill glass with ice.
1 1/2 oz Tequila
1/2 oz Amaretto
Fill with Sour Mix.
Shake.

CADIZ
Fill glass with ice.
3/4 oz Blackberry Brandy
3/4 oz Dry Sherry
1/2 oz Triple Sec
1/4 oz Cream
Shake.

CAFÉ AMORE
1 oz Cognac
1 oz Amaretto
Fill with hot Black Coffee.
Top with Whipped Cream.
Sprinkle with Shaved Almonds.

CAFÉ BARBADOS
1 1/2 oz Dark Rum
1/2 oz Coffee Liqueur
Fill with hot Black Coffee.
Top with Whipped Cream.
Sprinkle with Powdered Chocolate.

CAFÉ DIABLO
3/4 oz Cognac or Brandy
3/4 oz Sambuca
3/4 oz Orange Liqueur
Fill with hot Black Coffee.
Sprinkle with grated Orange Rind,
Allspice and Brown Sugar.
Garnish with Orange.

CAFÉ FOSTER
1 oz Dark Rum
3/4 oz Banana Liqueur
Fill with hot Black Coffee.
Top with Whipped Cream.
Garnish with Banana.

CAFÉ GATES
3/4 oz Tia Maria
3/4 oz Orange Liqueur
3/4 oz Dark Creme De Cacao
Fill with hot Black Coffee.
Top with Whipped Cream.
Sprinkle with Shaved Chocolate or
Sprinkles.

CAFÉ GRANDE
3/4 oz Orange Liqueur
3/4 oz Dark Creme De Cacao
3/4 oz Coffee Liqueur
Fill with hot Black Coffee.
Top with Whipped Cream.
Garnish with Orange.

CAFÉ ITALIA
1 1/2 oz Tuaca
1 tsp Sugar or Sugar Syrup
Fill with hot Black Coffee.
Top with Whipped Cream.
Sprinkle with Cinnamon.

CAFÉ MAGIC
3/4 oz Amaretto
3/4 oz Irish Cream
3/4 oz Coffee Liqueur
Fill with hot Black Coffee.
Top with Whipped Cream.
Sprinkle with Shaved Chocolate.

CAFÉ MARSEILLES
3/4 oz Hazelnut Liqueur
3/4 oz Black Raspberry Liqueur
3/4 oz Coffee Liqueur
Fill with hot Black Coffee.
Top with Whipped Cream.

CAFÉ ORLEANS
1 oz Coffee Liqueur
1 oz Praline Liqueur
Fill with hot Black Coffee.
Top with Whipped Cream.
Sprinkle with crushed Peanut
Brittle.

CAFÉ REGGAE
3/4 oz Dark Rum
3/4 oz Coffee Liqueur
3/4 oz Dark Creme De Cacao
Fill with hot Black Coffee.
Top with Whipped Cream.

CAFÉ ROYALE
2 oz Cognac or Brandy
Fill with hot Black Coffee.
Garnish with Lemon Twist.

CAFÉ THEATRE
1/2 oz Irish Cream
1/2 oz White Creme De Cacao
Fill with hot Black Coffee.
Dash of Hazelnut Liqueur
Dash of Dark Creme De Cacao
Top with Whipped Cream.

CAFÉ VENITZIO
3/4 oz Amaretto
3/4 oz Brandy
3/4 oz Galliano
Fill with hot Black Coffee.

CAFÉ ZURICH
3/4 oz Anisette
3/4 oz Cognac
3/4 oz Amaretto
Fill with hot Black Coffee.
Top with Whipped Cream.
Drizzle with Honey.

CAIPIRINHA
Place 2 Lime wedges and
tsp Sugar in glass and muddle.
Fill glass with ice.
Fill with Cachaca or Rum.
Stir.

CAJUN COFFEE
2 oz Praline Liqueur
Fill with hot Black Coffee.
Top with Whipped Cream.
Garnish with crushed Peanut
Brittle.

CAJUN MARTINI aka CREOLE MARTINI
Fill glass with ice.
2 oz Peppered Vodka
1/2 oz Dry Vermouth
Stir.
Strain into chilled glass.
Garnish with a Jalapeno Pepper.

CALIFORNIA BREEZE aka MADRAS
Fill glass with ice.
2 oz Vodka
Fill with equal parts Orange and
Cranberry Juice.
Stir.
Garnish with Orange or Lime.

CALIFORNIA COOL AID
Fill glass with ice.
2 oz Rum
Fill with equal parts Orange Juice
and Milk.
Shake.

CALIFORNIA COOLER
Fill glass with ice.
2 oz Vodka
Fill with equal parts Orange Juice
And Soda Water.

CALIFORNIA DRIVER
Fill glass with ice.
2 oz Vodka
Fill with equal parts Orange and
Grapefruit Juice.

CALIFORNIA ICED TEA
Fill glass with ice.
1/2 oz Vodka
1/2 oz Gin
1/2 oz Rum
1/2 oz Tequila
1/2 oz Triple Sec
2 oz Grapefruit Juice
Top with Cola.
Garnish with Lemon.

CALIFORNIA LEMONADE
Fill glass with ice.
1/2 oz Vodka
1/2 oz Gin
1/2 oz Brandy
2 oz Sour Mix
2 oz Orange Juice
Dash of Grenadine
Shake.
Garnish with a Lemon.

CALIFORNIA LEMONADE 2
Fill glass with ice.
2 oz Blended Whiskey
1 oz Sour Mix
Dash of Lime Juice
Dash of Grenadine
Fill with Soda Water.
Garnish with Orange and Cherry.

CALIFORNIA MOTHER
Fill glass with ice.
1 oz Brandy
1 oz Coffee Liqueur
Fill with equal parts Milk or Cream
and Cola.

CALIFORNIA ROOT BEER
Fill glass with ice.
1 oz Coffee Liqueur
Fill with Soda Water.
Top with 1/2 oz Galliano.
Dash of Cola or Beer or Milk
(optional).

CALYPSO COFFEE
1 oz Tia Maria
or Dark Creme De Cacao
1 oz Rum
Fill with hot Black Coffee.
Top with Whipped Cream.
Sprinkle with Shaved Chocolate.

CAMPARI AND SODA
Fill glass with ice.
2 oz Campari
Fill with Soda Water.
Garnish with Lemon or Lime.

CAMSHAFT
Fill glass with ice.
3/4 oz Irish Cream
3/4 oz Rootbeer Schnapps
3/4 oz Jaegermeister
Shake.
Strain into shot glass.

CANADA COCKTAIL
Fill glass with ice.
1 1/2 oz Canadian Whiskey
1/2 oz Triple Sec
2 dashes of Bitters
1 tsp Sugar
Shake.
Strain into chilled glass.
Garnish with Orange.

CANADIAN BLACKBERRY FIZZ
1 1/2 oz Canadian Whiskey
1/2 oz Blackberry Brandy
2 oz Sour Mix
Shake.
Fill with Soda Water.

CANADIAN CIDER (frozen)
In Blender:
1/2 cup of Ice
1 oz Canadian Whiskey
1/2 oz Cinnamon Schnapps
3 oz Apple Cider
1/4 ripe Red Apple
Blend until smooth.

CANADIAN COFFEE
2 oz Yukon Jack
Fill with hot Black Coffee.
Top with Whipped Cream.
Dribble 5-6 drops of Creme De
Nouyax on top.

CANCUN (frozen)
In Blender:
1/2 cup ice
3/4 oz Coffee Liqueur
3/4 oz Sambuca
3/4 oz Irish Cream
3 oz cold espresso
Scoop of Vanilla Ice Cream.
Blend until smooth.

CANDY APPLE
Fill glass with ice.
1 oz Apple Brandy
1 oz Cinnamon Schnapps
Fill with Cranberry Juice.
Stir.

CANDY ASS
Fill glass with ice.
3/4 oz Black Raspberry Liqueur
3/4 oz Creme De Cacao
3/4 oz Irish Cream
Shake.

CANDY CANE
Fill glass with ice.
2 oz Peppermint Schnapps
Fill with Milk.
Shake.
Float 1/2 oz Cherry Brandy
on top.

CANDY CANE (floater)
1 1/2 oz Peppermint Schnapps
(bottom)
1/2 oz Creme De Nouyax (top)

CANYON QUAKE
Fill glass with ice.
1 oz Brandy
1 oz Irish Cream
Fill with Milk or Cream.
Shake.

CAPE CODDER
Fill glass with ice.
2 oz Vodka
Fill with Cranberry Juice.
Garnish with Lime.

CAPITAL PUNISHMENT
Fill glass with ice.
1 oz Bourbon
1 oz Amaretto
Stir.
Strain into shot glass.

CAPRI aka BANSHEE
Fill glass with ice.
1 oz Banana Liqueur
1/2 oz White Creme De Cacao
Fill with Milk or Cream.
Shake.

CAPTAIN MARINER
Fill glass with ice.
1 1/2 oz Spiced Rum
1/2 oz Orange Liqueur
Dash of Grenadine
Fill with Orange Juice.
Shake.
Garnish with Orange.

CARA SPOSA aka SEXY
Fill glass with ice.
1 oz Coffee Liqueur
1 oz Orange Liqueur
Fill with Milk or Cream.
Shake.
Garnish with Orange.

CARIBBEAN CHAMPAGNE
1 oz Light Rum
1 oz Banana Liqueur
Stir.
Fill with Champagne.
Garnish with Banana and Cherry.

CARIBBEAN DREAM COFFEE
3/4 oz Dark Rum
3/4 oz Dark Creme De Cacao
3/4 oz Banana Liqueur
Fill with hot Black Coffee.
Garnish with Banana.

CARIBBEAN MADRAS
Fill glass with ice.
2 oz Dark Rum
Fill with equal parts Cranberry and
Orange Juice.

CARIBBEAN SCREW
Fill glass with ice.
3/4 oz Coconut Rum
3/4 oz Banana Liqueur
3/4 oz Peach Schnapps
Fill with equal parts Milk, Orange, and Pineapple Juice.
Shake.

CARIBBEAN SCREW WITH A SUNBURN
Fill glass with ice.
3/4 oz Dark Rum
3/4 oz Coconut Rum
3/4 oz Light Rum
Dash of Grenadine
Fill with Orange Juice.
Shake.

CARIBOU SCREW
Fill glass with ice.
2 oz Yukon Jack or Bourbon
Fill with Orange Juice.

CARROLL COCKTAIL
Fill glass with ice.
1 1/2 oz Brandy
3/4 oz Sweet Vermouth
Stir.
Strain into chilled glass.

CARROT CAKE
Fill glass with ice.
1 oz Irish Cream
1 oz Coffee Liqueur
1 oz Butterscotch Schnapps
1/2 oz Cinnamon Schnapps
Shake. Strain into shot glass.

CARTEL BUSTER (floater)
1 oz Coffee Liqueur (bottom)
1 oz Orange Liqueur
1 oz Gold Tequila (top)

CASABLANCA
Fill glass with ice.
2 oz Rum
1 1/2 tsp Triple Sec
1 1/2 tsp Cherry Liqueur
1 1/2 oz Lime Juice
Shake.
Strain into chilled glass.

CASINO COFFEE
3/4 oz Amaretto
3/4 oz Brandy
3/4 oz Creme De Cacao
Fill with hot Black Coffee.
Top with Whipped Cream.
Sprinkle with Shaved Almonds.

CATFISH
Fill glass with ice.
1 1/2 oz Rum
1/2 oz Triple Sec
Fill with Cola.
Garnish with Lime.

CELTIC COMRADE (floater)
1/2 oz Coffee Liqueur (bottom)
1/2 oz Irish Cream
1/2 oz Vodka
1/2 oz Drambuie (top)

CEMENT MIXER
Fill shot glass with Irish Cream.
Add dash of Lime Juice.
Let set 30 seconds.

CEREBRAL HEMORRHAGE (floater)
Fill glass with ice.
1 oz Coffee Liqueur (bottom)
1 oz Peach Schnapps
1 oz Irish Cream (top)
Add several drops of Grenadine.

CHAIN LIGHTNING
2 oz Gin
1/2 oz Triple Sec
1 oz Fresh Lemon Juice
Shake.
Serve or strain into chilled glass.
Garnish with Lemon.

CHAM CRAN CHAM aka BRUT AND BOGS, SCARLET LETTER
Fill glass 3/4 with ice.
Fill glass 3/4 with Champagne.
Dash of Black Raspberry Liqueur
Fill with Cranberry Juice.

CHAMBERED ROUND
In shot glass:
1 oz Grain Alcohol or Vodka
1 oz Tequila
Garnish with an Olive.

CHAMPAGNE COCKTAIL aka LONDON SPECIAL
In a Champagne glass:
1/2 tsp Sugar or 1 Sugar Cube
2 dashes of Bitters
Fill with Champagne.
Garnish with Lemon or Orange Twist.

CHAMPAGNE SUPER NOVA
Fill glass with ice.
1/2 oz Vodka
1/2 oz Gin
1/2 oz Blue Curacao
Dash of Cranberry Juice
Dash of Sour Mix
Fill with Champagne.

CHANNEL
2 oz Blackberry Brandy
Fill with Beer.
Matt Olga

CHAOS
Fill glass with ice.
1/2 oz 151-Proof Rum
1/2 oz Gin
1/2 oz Sloe Gin
1/2 oz Orange Liqueur
1/2 oz Lime Juice
Shake.
Strain into chilled glass.

C

CHARLIE CHAPLIN
Fill glass with ice.
1 oz Apricot Brandy
1 oz Sloe Gin
1 oz Lemon or Lime Juice
Shake.
Strain into chilled glass.

CHARRO
Fill glass with ice.
1 oz Tequila
1 oz Coffee
1 oz Milk
Stir.
Strain into shot glass.

CHASTITY BELT (floater)
3/4 oz Coffee Liqueur (bottom)
3/4 oz Irish Cream
3/4 oz Hazelnut Liqueur
Top with 1/2 oz Milk (top)

CHEAP SHADES
Fill glass with ice.
1 oz Vodka
1/2 oz Peach Schnapps
1/2 oz Melon Liqueur
Dash of Sour Mix
Dash of Pineapple Juice
Fill with Lemon-Lime Soda.
Garnish with Pineapple.

CHEAP SUNGLASSES
Fill glass with ice.
2 oz Vodka
Fill with equal parts Cranberry
Juice and Lemon-Lime Soda.
Garnish with Lime.

CHERRY BLOSSOM
Fill glass with ice.
1 oz Rum or Brandy
1 oz Cherry Brandy
1 tsp Grenadine
1 tsp Lemon Juice
Shake.
Garnish with Cherry.

CHERRY BOMB aka
EAT THE CHERRY
Place pitted, stemless Cherry in
shot glass.
1 tsp Cherry Juice
Fill with Grain Alcohol or Vodka.

CHERRY COLA
Fill glass with ice.
1 1/2 oz Cherry Brandy
Fill with Cola.
Garnish with Cherry.

CHERRY COLA FROM HELL
In shot glass pour:
1 oz Grain Alcohol
Ignite
Drop into glass containing:
1 oz Cherry Brandy
Filled 3/4 with Cola.

CHERRY HOOKER
Fill glass with ice.
2 oz Cherry Brandy
Fill with Orange Juice.
Shake.
Garnish with Lime.

CHERRY LIFE-SAVOR
Fill glass with ice.
2 oz Amaretto
Fill with Cranberry Juice.

CHERRY PIE
Fill glass with ice.
1 oz Vodka
1/2 oz Brandy
1/2 oz Cherry Brandy
Stir.
Strain into chilled glass.

CHERRY SCREW
Fill glass with ice.
2 oz Cherry Brandy
Fill with Orange Juice.
Shake.
Garnish with Orange and Lime.

CHERRY SWIZZLE
Fill glass with ice.
2 oz Gin
Dash of Cherry Brandy
Fill with Cherry Flavored Spring
Water.
Stir.
Garnish with Cherry.

CHERRY TART
Fill glass with ice.
1 oz Bourbon
1 oz Cherry Brandy
1 oz Sour Mix
tsp Sugar
Shake.
Strain into chilled glass.

CHI-CHI
Fill glass with ice.
1 1/2 oz Rum
1/2 oz Blackberry Brandy
Fill with Pineapple Juice.
Shake.
Garnish with Pineapple.

CHI-CHI (frozen)
In Blender:
1/2 cup of Ice
2 oz Vodka
1/2 oz Blue Curacao
1/2 oz Cream of Coconut
1/2 cup fresh or canned Pineapple
Scoop of Vanilla Ice Cream
Blend until smooth.
If too thick add juice.
If too thin add ice or Ice Cream.
Garnish with Pineapple.

CHICAGO
Fill glass with ice.
1 1/2 oz Brandy
Dash of Curacao or Triple Sec
Dash of Bitters
Shake.
Strain into glass rimmed with sugar.
Fill with Champagne.

CHICKEN SHOT
1 oz Vodka
1 oz Chicken Bouillon
Dash of Worcestershire Sauce
Dash of Salt
Dash of Pepper

CHILES FRITOS
Fill glass with ice.
2 oz Tequila
Dash of Lime Juice
Dash of Celery Salt
Dash of Tabasco Sauce
Dash of Worcestershire Sauce
Dash of Pepper
Dash of Grenadine
Dash of Orange Juice
Shake.
Garnish with 2 Chili Peppers.

CHINA BEACH
Fill glass with ice.
1 oz Vodka
1 oz Ginger Liqueur
Fill with Cranberry Juice.
Stir.

CHINESE COCKTAIL
Fill glass with ice.
1 1/2 oz Dark Rum
1 tsp Triple Sec
1 tsp Cherry Liqueur
1 tsp Grenadine
Dash of Bitters
Shake.
Strain into chilled glass.

CHINESE TORTURE (floater)
1 1/2 oz Ginger Liqueur (bottom)
1/2 oz 151-Proof Rum (top)
Ignite.

CHIQUITA
Fill glass with ice.
1/2 oz Banana Liqueur
1/2 oz Orange Liqueur or Triple Sec
Fill with equal parts Orange Juice
and Milk.
Shake.

CHOCOLATE BANANA FREEZE
(frozen)
In Blender:
1/2 cup of Ice
1 oz Vodka
1 oz Dark Creme De Cacao
1/2 oz Banana Liqueur
1 tbsp Chocolate Syrup
1/2 fresh peeled ripe Banana
Scoop of Chocolate Ice Cream
Blend until smooth.
If too thick add fruit or Milk.
If too thin add ice or Ice Cream.
Garnish with Banana.
Top with Whipped Cream.

CHOCOLATE COLADA (frozen)
In Blender:
1/2 cup of Ice
2 oz Rum
2 tbsp Cream of Coconut
1 oz Chocolate Syrup
Dash of Milk or Cream
Blend until smooth.

CHOCOLATE COVERED BANANA
Fill glass with ice.
3 oz Banana Rum
1 oz White Creme De Cacao
Stir.
Strain into Martini Glass rimmed in
Chocolate then dipped in chopped
Walnuts.
Bill Bona

CHOCOLATE COVERED CHERRY
Fill glass with ice.
1/2 oz Coffee Liqueur
1/2 oz Amaretto
1/2 oz White Creme De Cacao
Shake.
Strain into chilled glass.
Add 1 drop of Grenadine.

CHOCOLATE COVERED CHERRY (frozen)
In Blender:
1/2 cup of Ice
1 1/2 oz Vodka
1/2 oz Dark Creme De Cacao
Dash of Cherry Brandy
4 Maraschino Cherries (no stems)
Scoop of Chocolate Ice Cream
Blend until smooth.
If too thick add Milk.
If too thin add ice or Ice Cream.

CHOCOLATE KISS
1 1/2 oz Peppermint Schnapps
1/2 oz Coffee Liqueur
Fill with Hot Chocolate.
Top with Whipped Cream.
Sprinkle with Shaved Chocolate or
Sprinkles.

C

CHOCOLATE MARTINI
Fill glass with ice.
2 oz Vodka
1/2 oz Creme De Cacao or
Chocolate Liqueur
Dash of Orange Liqueur (optional)
Stir.
Strain into chilled glass or pour
contents (with ice) into short glass.
Garnish with Chocolate-covered
Cherry or any small Chocolate.

CHOCOLATE MESS (frozen)
In Blender:
1/2 cup of ice.
1 oz Creme De Cacao
1 oz Coffee Liqueur
1 oz Black Raspberry Liqueur
Tbsp Powdered Cacao
Scoop of Chocolate Ice Cream
Blend until smooth.
Top with Whipped Cream.
Drizzle Chocolate Syrup on top.

CHOCOLATE RATTLESNAKE
Fill glass with ice.
1 oz Coffee Liqueur
1 oz Irish Cream
1/2 oz Creme De Cacao
1/2 oz Peppermint Schnapps
Stir.
Strain into shot glass.

CHOCOLATE SQUIRREL
Fill glass with ice.
3/4 oz Amaretto
3/4 oz Hazelnut Liqueur
3/4 oz Dark Creme De Cacao
Fill with Milk.
Shake.
Serve or strain into chilled glass.

CHOCOLATE THUNDER
2 oz Vodka
Fill with Ovaltine.

CHRISTIAN'S COFFEE
1 oz Coffee Liqueur
1 oz Irish Cream
1 oz Amaretto
Fill with hot Black Coffee.
Top with Whipped Cream.

CHUPACABRA
Fill glass with ice.
1 oz Tequila
1 oz Jaegermeister
Shake.
Strain into shot glass.

CINCINNATI
Fill glass with equal parts
Beer and Soda Water.

CLAM DIGGER
Fill glass with ice.
2 oz Vodka or Gin
Dash of Tabasco Sauce
Dash of Worcestershire Sauce
Dash of Lime Juice or Sour Mix
Dash of Salt
Dash of Pepper
Dash of Tomato Juice
2 oz Clam Juice
Shake.

CLIMAX
Fill glass with ice.
1/2 oz Vodka
1/2 oz Triple Sec
1/2 oz Amaretto
1/2 oz White Creme De Cacao
1/2 oz Banana Liqueur
Fill with Milk or Cream.
Shake.

CLIMAX 2
Fill glass with ice.
1/2 oz Brandy
1/2 oz Coffee Liqueur
1/2 oz Amaretto
1/2 oz Triple Sec
Fill with Milk or Cream.
Shake.

CLOUDS OVER SCOTLAND
(floater)
1 1/2 oz Green Creme De Menthe
or Melon Liqueur
(bottom)
1/2 oz Irish Cream (top)

CLOUDY NIGHT
Fill glass with ice.
1 1/2 oz Vodka
1/2 oz Tia Maria
Stir.

COBRA aka KAHLUA CLUB
Fill glass with ice.
2 oz Coffee Liqueur
Fill with Soda Water.
Garnish with Lime.

COCA
Fill glass with ice.
3/4 oz Vodka
3/4 oz Southern Comfort
3/4 oz Black Raspberry Liqueur
1 oz Orange Juice
1 oz Cranberry Juice
Shake.
Strain into chilled glass.

COCA 2 aka GRAPE CRUSH
Fill glass with ice.
1 1/2 oz Vodka
1/2 oz Black Raspberry Liqueur
Dash of Sour Mix
Shake.
Fill with Lemon-Lime Soda.

COCA LADY
Fill glass with ice.
1/2 oz Vodka
1/2 oz Rum
1/2 oz Coffee Liqueur
1/2 oz Amaretto or Irish Cream
Fill with Milk or Cream.
Shake.
Dash of Cola

COCO LOCO
Fill glass with ice.
1 oz Dark Rum
1 oz Light Rum
1/2 oz Vodka
1/2 oz Banana Liqueur
1/2 oz Pineapple Juice
1/2 oz Sugar Syrup
1/2 oz Cream of Coconut
Shake.
Strain into chilled glass.

COCOANAPPS aka
ADULT HOT CHOCOLATE,
PEPPERMINT KISS,
SNUGGLER
2 oz Peppermint Schnapps
Fill with Hot Chocolate.
Stir.
Top with Whipped Cream.
Sprinkle with Shaved
Chocolate or Sprinkles.

COCOETTO aka
ALMOND KISS
2 oz Amaretto
Fill with Hot Chocolate.
Stir.
Top with Whipped Cream.
Sprinkle with Shaved Almonds or
Chocolate.

COCONUT CREAM FRAPPE
Fill glass with ice.
1 oz Rum
1 oz Irish Cream
1 tsp Cream of Coconut
Fill with Milk.
Shake.

COCOPUFF
1 oz Coffee Liqueur
1 oz Irish Cream
Fill with Hot Chocolate.
Stir.
Top with Whipped Cream.
Sprinkle with Shaved
Chocolate or Chocolate Syrup.

CODE BLUE aka
ADIOS MOTHER
Fill glass with ice.
1/2 oz Vodka
1/2 oz Gin
1/2 oz Rum
1/2 oz Tequila
1/2 oz Blue Curacao
Fill with Sour Mix.
Shake.

COFFEE ALEXANDER
1 oz Brandy
1 oz Dark Creme De Cacao
Fill with hot Black Coffee.
Top with Whipped Cream.
Sprinkle with Nutmeg.

COFFEE COLADA (frozen)
In Blender:
1/2 cup of Ice
2 oz Coffee Liqueur
1 oz Rum
2 tbsp Cream of Coconut
1/2 cup fresh or canned Pineapple
1 tbsp Vanilla Ice Cream
Blend until smooth.
If too thick add fruit or juice.
If too thin add ice or Ice Cream.

COFFEE LIQUEUR
(type liqueur)
Bring 3 cups water and 4 cups
Granulated Sugar to a boil.
Simmer 20 minutes.
Let cool.
Mix together 2 oz Instant Coffee
and 1 cup boiling Water.
Let cool.
Mix syrups.
Add 1 qt Vodka.
Add 1 Vanilla Bean (cut
lengthwise).
Store in glass container for two
weeks.
Shake for 1 minute everyday.

COFFEE SOMBRERO
Fill glass with ice.
2 oz Coffee Brandy
Fill with Milk or Cream.
Shake.

COLLINS
Fill glass with ice.
2 oz desired Liquor or Liqueur
Fill with Sour Mix.
Shake.
Splash with Soda Water.
Garnish with Orange and Cherry.

COLORADO BULLDOG
Fill glass with ice.
1 oz Vodka
1 oz Coffee Liqueur
Fill with equal parts Milk or Cream
and Cola.
Shake.

COLORADO BULLDOG 2
Fill shot glass with
1 oz Coffee Liqueur
1 oz Irish Cream
Fill chilled glass 3/4 with Beer
Drop shot glass into beer glass.

COLORADO MF
Fill glass with ice.
1/2 oz 151-Proof Rum
1/2 oz Vodka
1/2 oz Dark Rum
1/2 oz Coffee Liqueur
1/2 oz Galliano
Fill with Milk or Cream.
Shake.
Top with Grenadine.

COLORADO MOTHER
Fill glass with ice.
3/4 oz Vodka
3/4 oz Coffee Liqueur
3/4 oz Tequila
Fill with Milk or Cream.
Shake.
Top with Galliano.

COLORADO MOTHER 2
Fill glass with ice.
1 oz Tequila
1 oz Coffee Liqueur
Fill with equal parts Milk or Cream
and Cola.

COMBUSTIBLE EDISON
Fill glass with ice.
1 oz Campari
1 oz Lemon Juice
Shake. Strain into chilled glass.
Heat 2 oz Brandy and Ignite.
Pour Brandy into drink.

COMFORTABLE FUZZY SCREW AGAINST THE WALL
Fill glass with ice.
3/4 oz Southern Comfort
3/4 oz Peach Schnapps
3/4 oz Vodka
Fill with Orange Juice
Shake.
Top with 1/2 oz Galliano.

COMFORTABLE SCREW
Fill glass with ice.
1 oz Southern Comfort
1 oz Vodka
Fill with Orange Juice.

COMMANDO FIX
1 oz Irish Whiskey
Dash of Triple Sec
Dash of Raspberry Schnapps
Dash of Lime Juice
Stir.

CONCORD aka B-51 (floater)
1/2 oz Coffee Liqueur (bottom)
1/2 oz Irish Cream
1/2 oz 151-Proof Rum (top)

CONCORDE
1 1/2 oz Cognac
Dash of Apple Juice or Pineapple
Juice
Fill with Champagne.

CONEY ISLAND
Fill glass with ice.
1 oz Peppermint Schnapps
1 oz Dark Creme De Cacao
Fill with Soda Water.
Stir.

COOKIE MONSTER (floater)
1/2 oz Coffee Liqueur (bottom)
1/2 oz Irish Cream
1/2 oz 100-Proof Peppermint
Schnapps (top)

COOKIES AND CREAM aka OR-E-OH COOKIE (frozen)
In Blender:
1/2 cup of Ice
1 oz Vodka
3/4 oz Dark Creme De Cacao
2 Oreo Cookies
Scoop of Vanilla Ice Cream
Blend until smooth.
If too thick add Milk or Cream. If too
thin add ice or Ice Cream.
Garnish with cookie.

COOL AID
Fill glass with ice.
3/4 oz Vodka
3/4 oz Melon Liqueur or Peach
Schnapps
3/4 oz Amaretto
Fill with Cranberry Juice.
Shake.

COOL AID 2
Fill glass with ice.
1 oz Southern Comfort
1/2 oz Amaretto
1/2 oz Melon Liqueur
Dash of Orange Juice
Dash of Cranberry Juice
Shake.
Fill with Lemon-Lime Soda.

COOL BREEZE
Fill glass with ice.
2 oz Vodka
Fill with equal parts Cranberry and
Grapefruit Juice.
Top with Ginger Ale.
Garnish with Lime.

COPENHAGEN POUSSE-CAFÉ (floater)
1/2 oz Banana Liqueur (bottom)
1/2 oz Cherry Brandy
1/2 oz Cognac or Brandy (top)

COPPERHEAD
Fill glass with ice.
2 oz Vodka
Fill with Ginger Ale.
Garnish with Lime.

CORAL SEA (frozen)
In Blender:
1 cup of Ice
1 1/2 oz Rum
1/2 oz Triple Sec
1 Egg White
1/2 cup fresh or canned
Pineapple
1 tsp Grenadine
Blend until smooth.
If too thick add juice or fruit.
If too thin add ice.
Garnish with Pineapple and Cherry.

CORKSCREW
Fill glass with ice.
1 oz Rum
1/2 oz Peach Schnapps
1/2 oz Dry Vermouth
Stir.
Strain into chilled glass.

CORPSE REVIVER
Fill glass with ice.
3/4 oz Apple Brandy
3/4 oz Cognac or Brandy
1/2 oz Sweet Vermouth
Stir.
Strain into chilled glass.

COSMOPOLITAN
Fill glass with ice.
2 oz Vodka
Dash of Triple Sec
Dash of Lime Juice
Dash of Cranberry Juice
Stir.
Strain into chilled glass.
Garnish with Lime.

COSMOPOLITAN (South Beach)
Fill glass with ice.
2 oz Citrus Vodka
Dash of Black Raspberry Liqueur
Dash of Lime Juice
Dash of Cranberry Juice.
Stir.
Strain into chilled glass.

COUGH DROP
Fill glass with ice.
1 oz Mentholated Schnapps
1 oz Blackberry Brandy
Stir.

COWBOY
Fill glass with ice.
2 oz Bourbon
Fill with Milk.
Shake.

CRAMP RELIEVER
1 oz Blackberry Brandy

CRANAPPLE COOLER
Fill glass with crushed ice.
1 oz Vodka or Rum
1 oz Apple Brandy
Fill with Cranberry Juice.
Stir.
Garnish with Lime.

CRANBERRY LIQUEUR
(type liqueur)
Cook 1 lb Cranberries with
2 cups Sugar and
1 cup Water until berries pop.
Strain out the liquid and mix with 1
qt Vodka.
Store 1 week.
Then add 2 more cups of Sugar.
Store 1 more week.

CRANES BEACH PUNCH
1 gallon Cherry Cool Aid
1 liter cheap Red Wine
1 500ml bottle of Vodka

CRANIUM MELTDOWN
Fill glass with ice.
1/2 oz 151-Proof Rum
1/2 oz Coconut Rum
1/2 oz Black Raspberry Liqueur
1/2 oz Pineapple Juice
Shake.
Strain into chilled glass.

CRANKIN' WANKER
Fill glass with ice.
3/4 oz Vodka
3/4 oz Southern Comfort
3/4 oz Drambuie
Fill with equal parts Orange and
Pineapple Juice.

CRAZY BROAD
Fill glass with ice.
1 oz Vodka
1 oz Amaretto
1 oz Southern Comfort
Fill with equal parts Cranberry
Juice
and Ginger Ale.

CRAZY RED HEAD
Fill glass with ice.
1 oz Jaegermeister
1 oz Peach Schnapps
Fill with Cranberry Juice.
Shake.

CREAM DREAM
1 1/2 oz Dark Creme De Cacao
1 oz Hazelnut Liqueur
Fill with Cream.
Shake.
Tom Lewis

CREAMSICLE
Fill glass with ice.
1 oz Rum
1/2 oz Triple Sec
1/2 oz Vanilla Liqueur
Fill with equal parts Orange Juice
and Cream.
Shake.

CREAMSICLE 2
Fill glass with ice.
1 oz Banana Liqueur
1 oz Triple Sec
Fill with equal parts Orange Juice
and Milk.
Shake.

CREAMSICLE 3
Fill glass with ice.
1 oz Vodka
1/2 oz Hazelnut Liqueur
1/2 oz Galliano
Dash of Milk or Cream.

CREAMSICLE (frozen)
In Blender:
1/2 cup ice
1 oz Rum
1/2 oz Triple Sec
1/2 oz Vanilla Liqueur
1/2 scoop Vanilla Ice Cream
1/2 scoop Orange Sherbet
Blend until smooth.
If too thick add Milk or Orange
Juice.
If too thin add ice or Ice Cream or
sherbet.
Garnish with popsicle stick.

CREATURE FROM THE BLACK LAGOON (floater)
1 oz Jaegermeister (bottom)
1 oz Black Sambuca (top)

CREME DE MENTHE
(type liqueur)
Bring 2 cups water and 2 cups
Sugar to a boil.
Simmer 5 minutes and let cool.
Stir in 1 1/3 cups Vodka,
1/2 tsp Peppermint Extract,
2 tsp of Vanilla Extract,
7 drops of Green Food Coloring
(optional)
Store in glass bottle in dark place
for 1 week.

CREOLE MARTINI aka CAJUN MARTINI
Fill glass with ice.
2 oz Peppered Vodka
1/2 oz Dry Vermouth
Stir.
Strain into chilled glass.
Serve with Jalapeno Peppers.

CRICKET
Fill glass with ice.
1 oz Rum
3/4 oz White Creme De Menthe
3/4 oz Dark Creme De Cacao
Fill with Milk or Cream.
Shake.
Serve or strain into chilled glass.

CRIPPLER
Fill glass with ice.
1 oz Grain Alcohol
1 oz 151-Proof Rum
Dash of Triple Sec
Shake. Strain into shot glass.

CROCODILE COOLER
Fill glass with ice.
1 oz Citrus Vodka or Citrus Rum
1 oz Melon Liqueur
Dash of Sour Mix
Fill with Lemon-Lime Soda.

CRUISE CONTROL
Fill glass with ice.
1 oz Rum
1/2 oz Apricot Brandy
1/2 oz Orange Liqueur or Triple Sec
1/2 oz Sour Mix
Shake.
Fill with Soda Water.
Garnish with Lemon and Orange.

CUBA LIBRA
Fill glass with ice.
2 oz Light Rum
Fill with Cola.
Garnish with Lime.

CUBAN PEACH
Fill glass with ice.
1 1/2 oz Light Rum
1 1/2 oz Peach Schnapps
1/2 oz Lime Juice
Dash of Sugar Syrup
Shake.
Strain into chilled glass.
Garnish with Mint Sprig.

CUDDLER
1 oz Irish Cream
3/4 oz Amaretto
Heat in microwave for 7-8 seconds.

CUPID'S POTION
Fill glass with ice.
1 1/2 oz Amaretto
1/2 oz Triple Sec
Dash of Grenadine
Fill with equal parts Orange Juice
and Sour Mix.
Shake.

CURE-ALL
Fill glass with ice.
1 oz Peppermint Schnapps
1/2 oz Blackberry Brandy
Stir.

CURLEY'S DELIGHT COFFEE
3/4 oz Irish Whiskey
3/4 oz Irish Cream
3/4 oz Orange Liqueur
Fill with hot Black Coffee.
Top with Whipped Cream.
Linda Graham

D.O.A.
3/4 oz Barenjager
3/4 oz Jaegermeister
3/4 oz 100-proof Peppermint
Schnapps
Shake. Strain into shot glass.

DAIQUIRI
Fill glass with ice.
2 oz Rum
2 oz Lime Juice
Dash of Sour Mix
1/2 tsp Sugar
Shake.
Garnish with Lime.

DAIQUIRI (frozen)
In Blender:
1 cup of Ice
2 oz Rum
2 oz Lime Juice
Dash of Sour Mix
1/2 tsp Sugar
Blend until smooth.
Garnish with Lime.

DAISY
Fill glass with ice.
2 oz desired Liquor or Liqueur
1/2 tsp Powdered Sugar
1 tsp Raspberry Syrup
or Grenadine
Shake.
Strain into chilled glass.

DALLAS ALICE aka
ALICE IN WONDERLAND
FIll glass with ice.
3/4 oz Tequila
3/4 oz Orange Liqueur
3/4 oz Coffee Liqueur
Shake.
Strain into shot glass.

DAMN-THE-WEATHER
Fill glass with ice.
1 oz Gin
1/2 oz Sweet Vermouth
1/4 oz Triple Sec
1/2 oz Orange Juice
Shake.
Garnish with Cherry.

DANGEROUS LIAISONS
Fill glass with ice.
2 oz Orange Liqueur
2 oz Coffee Liqueur
1 oz Sour Mix
Shake.
Strain into chilled glass.

DANISH MARY aka
BLOODY HOLLY
Fill glass with ice.
2 oz Aquavit
1 tsp Horseradish
3 dashes of Tabasco Sauce
3 dashes of Worcestershire Sauce
Dash of Lime Juice
3 dashes of Celery Salt
3 dashes of Pepper
1 oz Clam Juice (optional)
Dash of Sherry (optional)
1 tsp Dijon Mustard (optional)
Fill with Tomato Juice.
Pour from one glass to
another until mixed.
Garnish with Lemon and/or Lime,
Celery and/or Cucumber and/or
Cocktail Shrimp.

DARB
Fill glass with ice.
1 oz Gin
1 oz Dry Vermouth
1 oz Apricot Brandy
1/2 oz Sour Mix
1 tsp Sugar
Shake.
Strain into chilled glass.

DARK AND STORMY
Fill glass with ice.(optional)
2 oz Dark Rum
Fill with Ginger Beer.
Garnish with Lime.

DARK EYES
Fill glass with ice.
1 1/2 oz Vodka
1/4 oz Blackberry Brandy
2 tsp Lime Juice
Shake.
Strain into chilled glass.

DARK SECRET
Fill glass with ice.
1 1/4 oz Black Sambuca
Fill with Club Soda.
Stir.

DARK SIDE
Fill glass with ice.
1 1/2 oz Vodka
1 1/2 oz Brandy
1 oz Coffee Liqueur
1/2 oz White Creme De Menthe
Stir.

DARTH VADER
Fill glass with ice.
1/2 oz Vodka
1/2 oz Gin
1/2 oz Rum
1/2 oz Tequila
1/2 oz Triple Sec
1 oz Sour Mix
Top with 1/2 oz Jaegermeister
Garnish with action figure.

DAY AT THE BEACH
Fill glass with ice.
1 oz Amaretto
1 oz Coconut Rum
Dash of Grenadine
Fill with Orange Juice.

DC-10 aka B-54 (floater)
1/2 oz Coffee Liqueur (bottom)
1/2 oz Irish Cream
1/2 oz Amaretto (top)

DE RIGUEUR
Fill glass with ice.
1 1/2 oz Whiskey
3/4 oz Grapefruit Juice
1 tsp Honey
Shake.
Strain into chilled glass.

DEAD NAZI aka
SCREAMING NAZI
Fill glass with ice.
1 oz Jaegermeister
1 oz 100-Proof Peppermint
Schnapps
Stir.
Strain into chilled glass.

DEAD RAT
Fill glass with ice.
1 1/2 oz Scotch
1/2 oz Green Chartreuse
Shake. Strain into shot glass.

DEATH IN THE AFTERNOON
1 oz Pernod
9 oz Champagne

DEATH MINT
1 oz Green Chartreuse
1 oz 100-Proof Peppermint
Schnapps
Stir.

DEATHWISH
Fill glass with ice.
1/2 oz 151-Proof Rum
1/2 oz 100-Proof Bourbon
1/2 oz 100-Proof Peppermint
Schnapps
1/2 oz Grenadine
Shake.
Strain into chilled glass.

DEAUVILLE
Fill glass with ice.
1 1/2 oz Apple Brandy
1/2 oz Triple Sec
Dash of Grenadine
2 oz Sour Mix
Shake.
Strain into chilled glass.

DECEIVER
Fill glass with ice.
1 1/2 oz Tequila
1/2 oz Galliano
Stir.

DEEP DARK SECRET
Fill glass with ice.
1 1/2 oz Dark Rum
1/2 oz Light Rum
1/2 oz Coffee Liqueur
1/2 oz Cream or Milk
Shake. Strain into chilled glass.

DEEP SEA
Fill glass with ice.
1/2 oz Gin
1/2 oz Blue Curacao
1/2 oz Pineapple Juice
1/2 oz Lime Juice
1/2 oz Sugar Syrup
Shake.

DEEP THROAT (floater)
1 oz Coffee Liqueur (bottom)
1 oz Vodka or Orange Liqueur (top)
Top with Whipped Cream.
To drink, place hands behind back
and pick up using only mouth.

DELMONICO
Fill glass with ice.
2 oz Brandy
1/2 oz Sweet Vermouth
Dash of Bitters (optional)
Stir.
Strain into chilled glass or pour
contents (with ice) into short glass.
Garnish with Cherry.

DEPTH BOMB
Fill glass with ice.
1 1/2 oz Apple Brandy
1 1/2 oz Brandy
1/4 tsp Grenadine
1/4 tsp Sour Mix
Shake.
Strain into chilled glass.

DEPTH CHAMBER
In shot glass:
1/2 oz Amaretto
1/2 oz Irish Cream
1/2 oz Coffee Liqueur
Fill chilled glass with Beer leaving
1 inch from top.
Drop shot glass into beer glass.

DEPTH CHARGE
Fill shot glass with Whiskey
or Peppermint Schnapps
or Drambuie.
Fill chilled glass with Beer leaving 1
inch from top.
Drop shot glass into beer glass.

DESERT SUNRISE
Fill glass with ice.
2 oz Tequila
Dash of Sour Mix
Fill with Orange Juice.
Top with 1/2 oz Blue Curacao.

DESIGNER JEANS
Fill glass with ice.
1/2 oz Dark Rum
1/2 oz Irish Cream
1/2 oz Raspberry Schnapps
Shake.
Strain into chilled glass.

DEVIL'S TAIL (frozen)
In Blender:
1/2 cup ice
1 1/2 oz Rum
1 oz Vodka
1/2 oz Apricot Brandy
1 oz Lime Juice
1/2 oz Grenadine
Blend 4-5 seconds.
Garnish with Lime.

DIABLO
Fill glass with ice.
1 1/2 oz Brandy
1/2 oz Triple Sec
1/2 oz Dry Vermouth
2 dashes of Bitters
Stir.
Strain into chilled glass.
Garnish with Lemon Twist.

DIAMOND FIZZ
Fill glass with ice.
1 1/2 oz Gin
Dash of Sour Mix
1 tsp Powdered Sugar
Shake.
Strain into chilled glass.
Fill with Champagne.

DIAMOND HEAD
Fill glass with ice.
1 1/2 oz Gin
1/2 oz Curacao or Triple Sec
2 oz Pineapple Juice
1 tsp Sweet Vermouth
Shake.
Strain into chilled glass.
Garnish with Pineapple.

DICKIE TOECHEESE (floater)
1 oz Blue Curacao (bottom)
1/2 oz Vodka (top)
Either float 1/2 oz Milk or Cream on
Top or squeeze lemon covered with
Bitters.

DIKI DIKI
Fill glass with ice.
1 1/2 oz Apple Brandy
3/4 oz Gin
1 oz Grapefruit Juice
Shake.
Strain into chilled glass.

DINGO
Fill glass with ice.
3/4 oz Rum
3/4 oz Amaretto
3/4 oz Southern Comfort
Dash of Grenadine
Fill with equal parts Sour Mix and
Orange Juice.
Shake.

D

DIRE STRAITS aka
DIRTY M. F.
Fill glass with ice.
1 1/2 oz Brandy
1/2 oz Coffee Liqueur
1/2 oz Galliano
1/2 oz Milk or Cream
Shake.

DIRTY ASHTRAY
Fill glass with ice.
1/2 oz Vodka
1/2 oz Gin
1/2 oz Rum
1/2 oz Tequila
1/2 oz Blue Curacao
Dash of Grenadine
Fill with equal parts Pineapple
Juice and Sour Mix.
Shake.
Garnish with Lemon.

DIRTY BANANA
Fill glass with ice.
1 oz Dark Creme de Cacao
1 oz Banana Liqueur
1 oz Cream or Milk
Shake.
Strain into chilled glass.

DIRTY BIRD
Fill glass with ice.
1 oz Vodka or Tequila
1 oz Coffee Liqueur
Fill with Milk or Cream.
Shake.

DIRTY DOG
Fill glass with ice.
2 oz Vodka or Gin
Fill with Grapefruit Juice.
2 or 3 dashes of bitters

DIRTY G. S.
Fill glass with ice.
1 oz Vodka
1/2 oz Coffee Liqueur
1/2 oz Peppermint Schnapps or
Creme De Menthe
Fill with Milk or Cream.
Shake.

DIRTY HARRY
Fill glass with ice.
1 oz Orange Liqueur
1 oz Coffee Liqueur
Shake.
Strain into shot glass.

DIRTY MARTINI
(*CAUTION:* DRY usually means
Less Vermouth than usual.
EXTRA DRY can mean even less
Vermouth than usual or
No Vermouth at all.)
Fill glass with ice.
2 oz Gin or Vodka
1/2 oz Olive Juice
1/2 oz Dry Vermouth (optional)
Stir.
Strain into chilled glass
or pour contents (with ice)
Into short glass.
Garnish with Olives

DIRTY MONKEY (frozen)
In Blender:
1/2 cup of Ice
3/4 oz Vodka
3/4 oz Coffee Liqueur
3/4 oz Banana Liqueur
1/2 scoop Vanilla Ice Cream
Blend until smooth.

DIRTY MOTHER aka
SEPARATOR
Fill glass with ice.
1 1/2 oz Brandy
3/4 oz Coffee Liqueur
1 oz Cream (optional)
Stir.

DIRTY MOTHER 2
Fill glass with ice.
3/4 oz Tequila
3/4 oz Vodka
3/4 oz Coffee Liqueur
Fill with Milk or Cream.
Shake.

DIRTY M. F. aka DIRE STRAITS
Fill glass with ice.
1 1/2 oz Brandy
1/2 oz Coffee Liqueur
1/2 oz Galliano
1/2 oz Milk or Cream
Shake.

DIRTY SILK PANTIES
Fill glass with ice.
3/4 oz Vodka
3/4 oz Peach Schnapps
Stir.
Strain into chilled glass.
Top with 2 or 3 drops Grenadine.

DIRTY WHITE MOTHER
Fill glass with ice.
1 1/2 oz Brandy
1/2 oz Coffee Liqueur
Float Cream on top.

DIZZY BUDDHA
Fill glass with ice.
1/2 oz Vodka
1/2 oz Dark Rum
1/2 oz Coconut Rum
1/2 oz Southern Comfort
1/2 oz Amaretto
1/2 oz Coffee Liqueur
1/2 oz Melon Liqueur
1/2 oz Banana Liqueur
Dash of Grenadine
Fill with equal parts Orange,
And Pineapple Juice.
Shake.

DOCTOR'S ELIXIR
Fill glass with ice.
1 oz Mentholated Schnapps
1 oz Black Raspberry Liqueur
Stir.

DOG SLED
Fill glass with ice.
2 oz Canadian Whiskey
1 tsp Grenadine
1 tbsp Sour Mix
Fill with Orange Juice.
Shake.

DOG'S NOSE
2 oz Gin
Fill with Beer.

DON JUAN
Fill glass with ice.
1 oz Tequila
1 oz Dark Rum
1 oz Pineapple Juice
1 oz Grapefruit Juice
Shake.
Strain into chilled glass.

DOUBLE-D (D-D)
Fill glass with ice.
3/4 oz Brandy
3/4 oz Southern Comfort
3/4 oz Cherry Brandy
Dash of Sour Mix
Dash of Cranberry Juice
Shake.
Strain into chilled glass.

DOUBLE MINT BJ
In Flute glass.
1 oz Coffee Liqueur
1 oz Peppermint Schnapps
Top with Whipped Cream
To drink, place hands behind back
And pick up using only mouth.

DOUBLE TROUBLE
4 oz Prune Juice
Fill with Beer.

DOWNEASTER aka
HAWAIIAN SEA BREEZE,
BAY BREEZE
Fill glass with ice.
2 oz Vodka
Fill with equal parts Cranberry and
Pineapple Juice.
Garnish with Lime.

DR. FUNK
Fill glass with ice.
1 1/2 oz Dark Rum
2 oz Sour Mix
2 oz Pineapple Juice
Dash of Grenadine
Shake.
Top with 1/2 oz Triple Sec.

DR. FUNK 2
Fill glass with ice.
1/2 oz Light Rum
1/2 oz Dark Rum
1/2 oz Galliano
1/2 oz Triple Sec
1/2 oz Sour Mix
Fill with equal parts Orange and
Pineapple Juice.
Shake.
Garnish with Orange and Cherry.
Float 1/2 oz Cherry Brandy
on top.

DR. J
1 oz Mentholated Schnapps
1 oz Jaegermeister

DR. P.
1/2 oz Amaretto
1/2 oz Light Rum or Brandy
Fill with cold Beer.

DR. P. 2
Fill glass with ice.
1 oz Spiced Rum
1 oz Amaretto
Fill with Cola.

DR. P. FROM HELL
In shot glass pour:
3/4 oz 151-Proof Rum
3/4 oz Amaretto
Ignite.
Drop into glass of Beer 3/4 filled.

DRAGOON
Fill glass with ice.
1/2 oz Coffee Liqueur
1/2 oz Irish Cream
1/2 oz Black Sambuca
Stir.

DRAMBUIE *(type liqueur)*
Mix 1 qt Scotch, 2 cups Honey, and 2
Tbsp Coriander Seeds.
Store 1 month and shake for
1 minute each week.

DREAM COCKTAIL
Fill glass with ice.
1 1/2 oz Brandy
1/2 oz Orange Liqueur or Triple Sec
1/2 tsp Anisette
Stir.
Strain into chilled glass.

DREAMSICLE
Fill glass with ice.
2 oz Amaretto or Licor 43
Fill with equal parts Milk or Cream
and Orange Juice.
Float 1/2 oz Galliano on top
(optional).

DROOLING PASSIONATE LADY
Fill glass with ice.
2 oz Vodka
1 oz Triple Sec
Fill with Pineapple Juice.
Shake.

DRUNKEN WAITER
Fill glass with ice.
Fill with equal parts Red Wine and
cola.

DRY ARROYO
Fill glass with ice.
1 oz Black Raspberry Liqueur
1 oz Coffee Liqueur
1 oz Sour Mix
1 oz Orange Juice
Shake.
Strain into chilled glass.
Fill with Champagne.
Garnish with Orange Twist.

DRY MANHATTAN
(*CAUTION:* DRY can mean make
drink with Dry Vermouth or less
Sweet Vermouth than usual.)
Fill glass with ice.
2 oz Whiskey
1/2 oz Dry Vermouth
or 1/4 oz Sweet Vermouth
Stir.
Strain into chilled glass, or pour
contents (with ice) into short glass.
Garnish with Lemon Twist.

DRY MARTINI
(Caution: DRY means less Dry
Vermouth than usual.
EXTRA DRY means even less or
no Vermouth at all).
Fill glass with ice.
2 oz Gin or Vodka
1/4 oz Dry Vermouth
Stir.
Strain into chilled glass or pour
contents (with ice) into short glass.
Garnish with Lemon Twist or Olives
or Cocktail Onions.

DRY ROB ROY
Fill glass with ice.
2 oz Scotch
1/4 oz Dry Vermouth
Stir.
Strain into chilled glass, or pour
contents (with ice) into short glass.
Garnish with Lemon Twist.

DUBLIN COFFEE
3/4 oz Irish Whiskey
3/4 oz Irish Mist
3/4 oz Coffee Liqueur
Fill with hot Black Coffee.
Top with Whipped Cream.
Drizzle with Green Creme de
Menthe.

DUBONNET COCKTAIL
Fill glass with ice.
1 1/2 oz Gin or Vodka
3/4 oz Dubonnet Rouge
Stir.
Strain into chilled glass.
Garnish with Lemon Twist.

DUBONNET MANHATTAN
Fill glass with ice.
1 1/2 oz Whiskey
3/4 oz Dubonnet Rouge
Shake.
Strain into chilled glass.
Garnish with Cherry.

DUCHESS
Fill glass with ice.
1 oz Pernod
3/4 oz Sweet Vermouth
3/4 oz Dry Vermouth
Shake.
Strain into chilled glass or pour
contents (with ice) into short glass.
Garnish with Cherry.

DUCK FART (floater)
1/2 oz Coffee Liqueur (bottom)
1/2 oz Irish Cream
1/2 oz Blended Whiskey (top)

DUDE
Fill glass with ice.
2 oz Scotch
Dash of Grenadine
Stir.
Float 1/2 oz Sherry on top.

DUNDEE
Fill glass with ice.
1 oz Gin
1/2 oz Drambuie
1/2 oz Scotch
1/2 oz Sour Mix
Shake.
Garnish with Lemon Twist or
Cherry.

DUSTY ROAD (frozen)
In Blender:
1/2 cup of Ice
1 oz Irish Cream
1 oz Black Raspberry Liqueur
1/2 scoop of Vanilla Ice Cream
Blend until smooth.
If too thick add Milk or Cream.
If too thin add ice or Ice Cream.

DUSTY ROSE
Fill glass with ice.
1 oz Irish Cream
1 oz Black Raspberry Liqueur
Stir.
Serve or strain into chilled glass.

DUTCH COFFEE
2 oz Vandermint
Fill with hot Black Coffee.
Top with Whipped Cream.
Sprinkle with Chocolate
shavings or Sprinkles.

DUTCH PIRATE
Fill glass with ice.
1 1/2 oz Vodka
1 oz Vandermint
1/2 oz Dark Rum
Shake.
Strain into chilled glass.
Garnish with Orange.

DUTCH TREAT
2 oz Brandy
Fill with Hot Chocolate.
Top with Whipped Cream.
Sprinkle with Chocolate
shavings or Sprinkles.

DYING NAZI FROM HELL
Fill glass with ice.
1 oz Vodka
1 oz Irish Cream
1 oz Jaegermeister
Strain into shot glass.

E. T. (floater)
1/2 oz Irish Cream (bottom)
1 oz Melon Liqueur
1 oz Vodka (top)

EARTHQUAKE
Fill glass with ice.
3/4 oz Amaretto
3/4 oz Anisette
3/4 oz Southern Comfort
Stir. Strain into shot glass.

EAST INDIA
Fill glass with ice.
1 1/2 oz Brandy
1/2 oz Curacao or Triple Sec
1 oz Pineapple Juice
Dash of Bitters
Shake.
Strain into chilled glass.

EAST INDIAN
Fill glass with ice.
1 oz Brandy
1/2 oz Dark Rum
1/2 oz Triple Sec
Dash of Bitters
1 oz Pineapple Juice
Shake.
Strain into chilled glass.

EAST SIDE
Fill glass with ice.
3/4 oz Rum
3/4 oz Amaretto
3/4 oz Coconut Rum
Fill with Milk or Cream.
Shake.

EAT HOT DEATH
Fill glass with ice.
1 1/2 oz 151-Proof Rum
1/2 oz fresh Lemon Juice or Lime Juice
Stir. Strain into shot glass.

EAT THE CHERRY aka CHERRY BOMB
Place pitted, stemless Cherry in shot glass.
1 tsp Cherry Juice
Fill with Grain Alcohol or Vodka.

ECLIPSE
Place Cherry or ripe Olive in chilled Martini glass and cover with 1/4 oz Grenadine.
Fill separate glass with ice.
1 oz Gin
1 1/2 oz Sloe Gin
Dash of Sour Mix
Shake.
Strain gently into second glass so as not to disturb fruit or Grenadine.

ECLIPSE 2
Fill glass with ice.
2 oz Black Sambuca
Dash of Cream
Stir.
Strain into chilled glass.

ECSTACY
Fill glass with ice.
1 1/2 oz Vodka
1/2 oz Black Raspberry Liqueur
1/2 oz Pineapple Juice
1/2 Cranberry Juice
Shake.
Strain into chilled glass.

EDEN
Fill glass with ice.
2 oz Vodka
Fill with Apple Juice.
Garnish with Cherry.

EDEN ROC FIZZ
Fill glass with ice.
1 1/2 oz Whiskey
Dash of Pernod
Dash of Sugar Syrup
Dash of Sour Mix
1/2 Egg White
Shake.
Fill with Soda Water.

EDITH DAY
Fill glass with ice.
2 oz Gin
tsp Sugar
Fill with Grapefruit Juice.
Shake.

EGGHEAD (frozen)
In Blender:
1/2 cup of Ice
2 oz Vodka
1 Egg
Scoop of Orange Sherbet
Blend until smooth.

EGGNOG
Separate 12 Eggs.
Beat Yolks and 2 cups of Superfine Sugar until thick.
Stir in 2 cups of Cognac or Brandy,
2 cups of Dark Rum,
2 cups of Cream, and
6 cups of Milk.
Refrigerate mixture.
When thoroughly chilled, beat the Egg Whites until stiff.
Carefully fold them into mixture.
Garnish with Nutmeg.

EL CID
Fill glass with ice.
1 1/2 oz Tequila
1/2 oz Orgeat Syrup
1 oz Lime Juice
Shake.
Fill with Tonic Water.
Top with dash of Grenadine.
Garnish with Lime.

EL DIABLO
Fill glass with ice.
1 oz Tequila
1/2 oz Creme De Cassis
Dash of Lime Juice
Fill with Ginger Ale.

EL SALVADOR
Fill glass with ice.
1 1/2 oz Rum
3/4 oz Hazelnut Liqueur
Dash of Grenadine
1/2 oz Lime Juice
Shake.
Strain into chilled glass.

ELECTRIC COOL AID
Fill glass with ice.
1/2 oz Amaretto
1/2 oz Triple Sec
1/2 oz Southern Comfort
1/2 oz Melon Liqueur
1/2 oz Cherry Brandy
1/2 oz Sour Mix
1/2 oz Cranberry juice
Dash of Grenadine
Shake.
Strain into chilled glass.

ELECTRIC LEMONADE
Fill glass with ice.
1/2 oz Vodka
1/2 oz Gin
1/2 oz Rum
1/2 oz Tequila
1/2 oz Triple Sec
Fill with Sour Mix.
Shake.
Top with Lemon-Lime Soda.

ELECTRIC WATERMELON
Fill glass with ice.
1/2 oz Vodka
1/2 oz Rum
1/2 oz Triple Sec
1/2 oz Melon Liqueur
1 oz Orange Juice
1 oz Grenadine
Fill glass with Lemon-Lime Soda.
Shake.

ELMER FUDPUCKER
Fill glass with ice.
1 oz Vodka
1 oz Tequila
Fill with Orange Juice.
Top with Apricot Brandy.
Garnish with Orange.

ELVIRA
Fill glass with ice.
1 1/2 oz Vodka
1/2 oz Blackberry Brandy
Fill with Sour Mix.
Shake.

ELYSEE PALACE
Fill glass with ice.
1 oz Cognac or Brandy
1/2 oz Black Raspberry Liqueur
Fill with Champagne.
Float 1/4 oz Black Raspberry
Liqueur on top.

EMBRYO (floater)
1 oz Coffee Liqueur (bottom)
1/4 oz Cream
1/2 oz 100-proof Vodka (top)

EMERALD FOREST
Fill glass with ice.
1 1/2 oz Gin
1/2 oz Green Creme De Menthe
Stir.

EMPIRE STATE SLAMMER
Fill glass with ice.
1 oz Canadian Whiskey
1/2 oz Sloe Gin
1/2 oz Banana Liqueur
2 oz Orange Juice
Shake.
Strain into chilled glass.

ENERGIZER (floater)
3/4 oz Benedictine (bottom)
3/4 oz Irish Cream
3/4 oz Orange Liqueur (top)

ENGLISH SCREWDRIVER
Fill glass with ice.
2 oz Gin
Fill with Orange Juice.
Garnish with Orange.

ERIE CANAL
Fill glass with ice.
1 1/2 oz Irish Whiskey
1/2 oz Irish Mist
1/2 oz Irish Cream
Stir.

EVERGLADES SPECIAL
Fill glass with ice.
3/4 oz Rum
3/4 oz White Creme De Cacao
1/2 oz Coffee Liqueur
1 oz Cream or Milk
Shake.

EXPRESS
Fill glass with ice.
1 1/2 oz Orange Liqueur
1/2 oz Vodka
Shake.
Strain into chilled glass.
Garnish with Orange.

EYE-OPENER
Fill glass with ice.
1 oz Rum
1/3 oz Triple Sec
1/3 oz White Creme De Cacao
1/3 oz Pernod
1 tsp Sugar Syrup
or Powdered Sugar
1 Egg Yolk
Shake.
Serve or strain into chilled glass.

F-16 (floater)
1 oz Coffee Liqueur (bottom)
1 oz Irish Cream
1 oz Hazelnut Liqueur (top)

F ME HARD
Fill glass with ice.
1/2 oz Vodka
1/2 oz Gin
1/2 oz Rum
1/2 oz Amaretto
1/2 oz Coconut Rum
1/2 oz Melon Liqueur
1/2 oz Peach Schnapps
1/2 oz Sloe Gin
Fill with Orange Juice.
Shake.

F. U.
Fill glass with ice.
2 oz Hazelnut Liqueur
Fill with Lemon-Lime Soda.

FACE ERASER
Fill glass with ice.
1 oz Vodka
1 oz Coffee Liqueur
Fill with Lemon-Lime Soda.
Supposed to be drunk in one shot
through straw.

FACE ERASER 2
Fill glass with ice.
1 1/2 oz Vodka
1/2 oz Coffee Liqueur
1/2 oz Irish Cream
Fill with Soda Water.
Supposed to be drunk in one shot
through straw.

FAHRENHEIT 5
Coat inside of shot glass with hot
sauce.
1 oz Peppered Vodka
1 oz Cinnamon Schnapps

FAIR AND WARMER
Fill glass with ice.
1 1/2 oz Rum
Dash of Triple Sec or Curacao
1/2 oz Sweet Vermouth
Shake.
Serve or strain into chilled glass.
Garnish with Lemon.

FAIRCHILD (floater)
1 oz Melon Liqueur (bottom)
1/2 oz Orange Juice
1/2 oz Irish Whiskey (top)

FALLEN ANGEL
Fill glass with ice.
2 oz Gin
Dash of White Creme De Menthe
Dash of Bitters
2 oz Sour Mix
Shake.
Serve or strain into chilled glass.
Garnish with Cherry.

FANTASIO
Fill glass with ice.
1 1/2 oz Brandy
3/4 oz Dry Vermouth
1 tsp White Creme De Cacao
1 tsp Cherry Liqueur
Shake.
Serve or strain into chilled glass.

FARE-THEE-WELL
Fill glass with ice.
1 1/2 oz Gin
1 oz Dry Vermouth
1/2 oz Triple Sec or Curacao
2 dashes of Sweet Vermouth
Shake.
Strain into chilled glass.

FASCINATION
Fill glass with ice.
1 1/2 oz Dark Rum
3/4 oz Orange Liqueur
1/2 tsp Sugar
1/2 Egg White
Fill with Sour Mix.
Shake.
Strain into chilled glass.

FAT CAT (frozen)
In Blender:
1/2 cup of Ice
3/4 oz Cognac
3/4 oz Galliano
3/4 oz White Creme de Cacao
Scoop of Vanilla Ice Cream
Blend until smooth.
If too thick add Milk.
If too thin add ice or Ice Cream.

FATHER SHERMAN
Fill glass with ice.
1 1/2 oz Brandy
1/2 oz Apricot Brandy
1 oz Orange Juice
Shake.
Strain into chilled glass.

FAVORITE
Fill glass with ice.
3/4 oz Gin
3/4 oz Apricot Brandy
3/4 oz Dry Vermouth
1/4 tsp Sour Mix
Shake.
Strain into chilled glass.

FEDORA
Fill glass with ice.
3/4 oz Dark Rum
3/4 oz Bourbon
3/4 oz Brandy
Dash of Triple Sec
1 oz Sour Mix
Shake.
Strain into chilled glass.
Garnish with Lemon.

F.E.D.X.
Fill glass with ice.
1 1/2 oz Amaretto
1 oz Black Raspberry Liqueur
2 oz Sour Mix
Shake.
Strain into chilled champagne glass.
Fill with Champagne.
Garnish with Lemon Twist.

FERN GULLY
Fill glass with ice.
1 oz Dark Rum
1 oz Light Rum
1/2 oz Creme De Nouyax
or Amaretto
1 oz Orange Juice
1/2 oz Cream of Coconut
1/2 oz Lime Juice
Shake.
Garnish with Lime and Orange.

FERRARI
Fill glass with ice.
1 oz Amaretto
2 oz Dry Vermouth
Stir.
Garnish with Lemon Twist.

FESTERING SLOBOVIAN HUMMER
Fill glass with ice.
1/2 oz 151-Proof Rum
1/2 oz Galliano
1/2 oz Peppermint Schnapps
Shake.
Strain into shot glass.

FESTIVAL
Fill glass with ice.
3/4 oz Dark Creme De Cacao
1 oz Apricot Brandy
1 tsp Grenadine
3/4 oz Cream
Shake.

FIDEL'S MARTINI
Fill glass with ice.
1 1/2 oz Russian Vodka
1/2 oz Banana Liqueur
Stir.
Strain into chilled glass.
Garnish with Banana.

**FIFTH AVENUE aka
LAYER CAKE** (floater)
3/4 oz Dark Creme De Cacao (bottom)
3/4 oz Apricot Brandy
1/2 oz Milk (top)

FIFTY FIFTY (Martini)
Fill glass with ice.
1 1/2 oz Gin
1 1/2 oz Dry Vermouth
Stir.
Strain into chilled glass.
Garnish with Olive.

57 CHEVY
Fill glass with ice.
1 oz Vodka
1 oz White Creme De Cacao
Stir.

57 CHEVY 2
Fill glass with ice.
1/2 oz Vodka
1/2 oz Rum
1/2 oz Amaretto
1/2 oz Southern Comfort
1/2 oz Orange Liqueur
Fill with equal parts Pineapple Juice and Sour Mix.
Shake.
Serve or strain into chilled glass.

57 T-BIRD
Fill glass with ice.
3/4 oz Rum or Vodka
or Southern Comfort
3/4 oz Amaretto
3/4 oz Orange Liqueur
Fill with equal parts Pineapple, Cranberry and Orange Juice.
Shake.

**57 T-BIRD
(with California Plates)**
Fill glass with ice.
3/4 oz Rum or Vodka
or Southern Comfort
3/4 oz Amaretto
3/4 oz Orange Liqueur
Fill with Grapefruit Juice.
Shake.

**57 T-BIRD
(with Florida Plates)**
Fill glass with ice.
3/4 oz Rum or Vodka
or Southern Comfort
3/4 oz Amaretto
3/4 oz Orange Liqueur
Fill with Orange Juice.
Shake.

**57 T-BIRD
(with Hawaiian Plates)**
Fill glass with ice.
3/4 oz Rum or Vodka
or Southern Comfort
3/4 oz Amaretto
3/4 oz Orange Liqueur
Fill with Pineapple Juice.
Shake.

**57 T-BIRD
(with Massachusetts Plates)**
Fill glass with ice.
3/4 oz Rum or Vodka
or Southern Comfort
3/4 oz Amaretto
3/4 oz Orange Liqueur
Fill with Cranberry juice.
Shake.

FIJI FIZZ
Fill glass with ice.
1 1/2 oz Dark Rum
1/2 oz Bourbon
1 tsp Cherry Brandy
3 dashes of Orange Bitters
Shake.
Fill with Cola.
Garnish with Lime.

FILBY
Fill glass with ice.
2 oz Gin
3/4 oz Amaretto
1/2 oz Dry Vermouth
1/2 oz Campari
Stir.
Garnish with Orange.

FINE AND DANDY
Fill glass with ice.
1 1/2 oz Gin
3/4 oz Orange Liqueur or Triple Sec
3/4 oz Sour Mix
Dash of Bitters
Shake.
Strain into chilled glass.
Garnish with Cherry.

FIRE AND ICE (floater)
1 oz Tequila (bottom)
1 oz Peppermint Schnapps or
Creme De Menthe (top)

FIRE-IN-THE-HOLE
Fill shot glass with Ouzo or
Sambuca
Add 3-5 dashes of Tabasco Sauce.

FIREBALL
Fill shot glass with Cinnamon
Schnapps.
Add 4-5 drops of Tabasco Sauce.
Stir.

FIREBALL 2
Fill glass with ice.
1/2 oz Vodka
1/2 oz Cinnamon Schnapps
1/2 oz Cherry Brandy
4-5 drops Tabasco Sauce
Stir.
Strain into shot glass.

FIREBIRD
Fill glass with ice.
2 oz Peppered Vodka
Fill with Cranberry Juice.
Stir.

FIRECRACKER
Fill glass with ice.
2 oz Spiced Rum
1/2 oz Sloe Gin or Grenadine
Fill with Orange Juice
Shake.
Float 1/2 oz 151-Proof Rum on top.
Garnish with Orange.

FIRECRACKER 2
Fill glass with ice.
1 1/2 oz Tequila or Vodka or
Whiskey
1/2 oz Black Raspberry Liqueur
Fill with Sour Mix.
Shake.

FIREFLY
Fill glass with ice.
2 oz Vodka
Dash of Grenadine
Fill with Grapefruit Juice.
Shake.

FIRERY KISS
Rim shot glass with Honey.
Fill with Cinnamon Schnapps
Dash of Amaretto (optional)

FIRESIDE
2 oz Dark Rum
1 tsp Sugar
Fill with hot tea.
Stir.

FIRESTORM
Fill glass with ice.
3/4 oz Cinnamon Schnapps
3/4 oz Peppermint Schnapps
3/4 oz 151-Proof Rum
Shake. Strain into shot glass.

FISH HOUSE PUNCH
Dissolve 3/4 lb Sugar in 1 qt Spring
Water (non-carbonated).
1 1/2 cups Lemon Juice
1/2 cup Peach Schnapps
1 qt Cognac
2 qt Dark Rum
Pour mixture into cold bowl
containing cake of ice.

FIZZ
Fill glass with ice.
2 oz desired Liquor or Liqueur
1 oz Lemon Juice or Sour Mix
1 tsp Powdered Sugar
Shake.
Strain into chilled glass.
Fill with Soda Water.

FJORD
Fill glass with ice.
1 oz Brandy
1/2 oz Aquavit
1 oz Orange Juice
1/2 oz Lime Juice
1 tsp Grenadine
Shake.
Strain into chilled glass.

FLAMING BLUE J.
Fill glass with ice.
1 oz Southern Comfort
1/2 oz Blue Curacao
1/2 oz Peppermint Schnapps
Strain into chilled glass.
Float 1/2 oz 151-Proof Rum on top.
Ignite.

F

FLAMING HOOKER (floater)
1 oz Coffee Liqueur (bottom)
1 oz Ouzo (top)
Ignite.

FLAMING LAMBORGHINI
In straight up glass (martini)
1/2 oz Grenadine (bottom)
1 oz Galliano
1 oz Sambuca
1/2 oz Green Chartreuse
Ignite.
Let burn for 10 seconds
then through straw drink quickly,
while someone pours in
1 oz Blue Curacao
1 oz Irish Cream

FLAMING LAMBORGHINI 2
In shot glass   1 oz Galliano
In another   1 oz Coffee Liqueur
In another   1 oz Blue Curacao
In another   1 oz Milk
In straight up glass (martini)
1 oz Sambuca
Ignite Sambuca, and pour shot
glasses into it.

FLAMING LAMBORGHINI 3
In shot glass float
1 oz Blue Curacao
1/2 oz Milk (top)
In straight up glass (martini) float
1/2 oz Coffee Liqueur
1/2 oz Amaretto
1/2 oz Vodka
1/2 oz Green Chartreuse (top)
Ignite Chartreuse and pour
contents of shot glass into it.

FLAMING NORIEGA (floater)
1/2 oz Strawberry Liqueur
(bottom)
1/2 oz Green Creme De Menthe
1/2 oz Sugar Syrup
1/2 oz 151-Proof Rum (top)
Ignite.

FLAMINGO
Fill glass with ice.
1 1/2 oz Gin
1/2 oz Apricot Brandy
1/2 oz Lime Juice
Dash of Grenadine
Shake.
Strain into chilled glass.

FLAMINGO 2
Fill glass with ice.
2 oz Rum or Vodka
Fill with equal parts Sour Mix,
Pineapple Juice and Orange Juice.
Add Grenadine while stirring until
desired pink color.

FLIM FLAM
Fill glass with ice.
1 1/2 oz Rum
3/4 oz Triple Sec
1/2 oz Sour Mix
1/2 oz Orange Juice
Shake.
Serve or strain into chilled glass.

FLIP
Fill glass with ice.
2 oz desired Liquor or Liqueur
1 raw egg
1 tsp Powdered Sugar
Shake.
Strain into glass.
Garnish with Nutmeg.

FLORIDA
Fill glass with ice.
1/2 oz Gin
1/4 oz Kirschwasser
1/4 oz Triple Sec
2 oz Orange Juice
1/4 oz Sour Mix
Shake.
Serve or strain into chilled glass.
Garnish with Orange.

FLORIDA 2
Fill glass with ice.
1 1/2 oz Light Rum
1/2 oz Green Creme De Menthe
1/2 oz Sugar Syrup
or 1/2 tsp Sugar
1/2 oz Lime Juice
1/2 oz Pineapple Juice
Shake.
Strain into chilled glass.
Fill with Soda Water.
Garnish with mint sprig.

FLORIDA ICED TEA
Fill glass with ice.
1/2 oz Vodka
1/2 oz Gin
1/2 oz Rum
1/2 oz Tequila
1/2 oz Triple Sec
2 oz Orange Juice
Top with Cola.
Garnish with Orange.

FLORIDA PUNCH
Fill glass with ice.
1 1/2 oz Brandy
1/2 oz Dark Rum
Fill glass with equal parts Orange,
and Grapefruit Juice.
Shake.

FLORIDA SUNRISE
Fill glass with ice.
2 oz Rum
Dash of Grenadine
Fill with Orange Juice.
Shake.

FLYING GRASSHOPPER aka VODKA GRASSHOPPER
Fill glass with ice.
1 oz Vodka
3/4 oz Green Creme De Menthe
3/4 oz White Creme De Cacao
Fill with Milk or Cream.
Shake.
Serve or strain into chilled glass.

FLYING GRASSHOPPER (frozen)
In Blender:
1/2 cup of Ice
1 oz Vodka
3/4 oz Green Creme De Menthe
3/4 oz White Creme De Cacao
Scoop of Vanilla Ice Cream
Blend until smooth.
If too thick add Milk or Cream. If too thin add ice or Ice Cream.

FLYING KANGAROO (frozen)
In Blender:
1/2 cup of Ice
3/4 oz Vodka
3/4 oz Rum
3/4 oz Galliano
2 tbsp Vanilla Ice Cream
Blend until smooth.
If too thick add Milk or Cream.
If too thin add ice or Ice Cream.
Garnish with Pineapple and Cherry.

FLYING MADRAS aka RUSSIAN NIGHTS
Fill glass with ice.
2 oz Vodka
2 oz Cranberry Juice
2 oz Orange Juice
Fill with Champagne.
Garnish with Orange.

FLYING SCOT
Fill glass with ice.
1 oz Scotch
1 oz Sweet Vermouth
1/4 oz Sugar Syrup
2-4 dashes of Bitters
Shake.

FOG CUTTER
Fill glass with ice.
1 oz Rum
1 oz Brandy
1 oz Gin
Dash of Creme De Nouyax or Triple Sec
Dash of Sour Mix
Fill with equal parts Orange and Pineapple Juice.
Top with 1/2 oz Sherry.
Shake.

FOG HORN
Fill glass with ice.
2 oz Gin
Fill with Ginger Ale or Ginger Beer.
Garnish with Lemon.

FORBIDDEN JUNGLE
Fill glass with ice.
1 1/2 oz Coconut Rum
1/2 oz Peach Schnapps
Dash of Lime Juice
Fill with Pineapple Juice.
Shake.

FORESTER
Fill glass with ice.
1 1/2 oz Vodka
3/4 oz Cherry Liqueur
1 tsp Sour Mix
Shake.

.44 MAGNUM
Fill glass with ice.
1/2 oz Vodka
1/2 oz Light Rum
1/2 oz Dark Rum
1/2 oz Triple Sec
Dash of Sour Mix
Dash of Pineapple Juice
Shake.
Fill with Lemon-Lime Soda.

FOUR HORSEMEN
Fill glass with ice.
1/2 oz Bourbon
1/2 oz Sambuca
1/2 oz Jaegermeister
1/2 oz 100-proof Peppermint Schnapps
Shake. Strain into shot glass.

FOUR HORSEMEN 2
Fill glass with ice.
1/2 oz Tequila
1/2 oz 151-Proof Rum
1/2 oz 100-proof Peppermint Schnapps
1/2 oz Jaegermeister
Shake. Strain into shot glass.

FOUR HORSEMEN 3
Fill glass with ice.
1/2 oz Jim Beam
1/2 oz Jack Daniels
1/2 oz Johnnie Walker
1/2 oz Jose Cuervo
Stir. Strain into shot glass.

FOURTH OF JULY (floater)
3/4 oz Grenadine (bottom)
3/4 oz Blue Curacao
3/4 oz Rum or Vodka or Milk (top)

FOX RIVER
Fill glass with ice.
1 1/2 oz Whiskey
1/2 oz Dark Creme De Cacao
2 or 3 dashes of Bitters
Stir.
Serve or strain into chilled glass.
Garnish with Lemon Twist.

F

FOX TROT
Fill glass with ice.
1 1/2 oz Rum
1/2 oz Triple Sec
1 oz Lime Juice or Sour Mix
Shake.
Strain into chilled glass.

FOXY LADY
Fill glass with ice.
1 oz Amaretto
1 oz Dark Creme De Cacao
Fill with Cream or Milk.
Shake.

FOXHOUND
Fill glass with ice.
1 1/2 oz Brandy
1 tsp Kummel
Dash of Sour Mix
Dash of Cranberry Juice
Shake.
Garnish with a Lemon.

FRANKENBERRY
Fill glass with ice.
1 oz Currant Vodka
1 oz Black Raspberry Liqueur
Fill with equal parts Sour Mix and
Pineapple Juice.
Shake.
*Frankie Gaul, Hog's Breath
Saloon, Key West*

FRANKENJACK
Fill glass with ice.
1 oz Gin
1/2 oz Triple Sec
1/2 oz Apricot Brandy
1/2 oz Dry Vermouth
Shake.

FRAPPE
Fill large stemmed glass (Red Wine
glass, Champagne saucer) with
crushed ice.
Add 2 oz desired Liquor or Liqueur

FREDDY FUDPUCKER aka
CACTUS BANGER
Fill glass with ice.
1 1/2 oz Tequila
Fill with Orange Juice.
Top with Galliano.
Garnish with Orange.

FREDDY KRUGER (floater)
1 oz Sambuca (bottom)
1 oz Jaegermeister
1 oz Vodka (top)

FREEDOM FIGHTER (floater)
1 1/2 oz Irish Whiskey (bottom)
1/2 oz Irish Cream (top)

FRENCH COFFEE
2 oz Orange Liqueur or Cognac
Fill with hot Black Coffee.
Top with Whipped Cream.
Garnish with Orange and
Cinnamon.

FRENCH CONNECTION
Fill glass with ice.
1 1/2 oz Cognac or Brandy
1/2 oz Amaretto
or Orange Liqueur
Stir.

FRENCH CONNECTION COFFEE
1 1/2 oz Cognac or Brandy
1/2 oz Amaretto
Fill with hot Black Coffee.
Top with Whipped Cream.
Sprinkle with Shaved Almonds.

FRENCH DRAGON
1 oz Brandy or Cognac
1 oz Green Chartreuse
Stir.

FRENCH DREAM
Fill glass with ice.
1 oz Irish Cream
1 oz Black Raspberry Liqueur
1 oz Coffee Liqueur
Stir.

FRENCH ICED COFFEE (frozen)
In Blender:
1/2 cup of Ice
2 oz Cognac or Brandy
Scoop of Vanilla Ice Cream
1/2 cup of Iced Coffee
Blend until smooth.
If too thick add coffee or Milk.
If too thin add ice or Ice Cream.

FRENCH LIFT
Fill glass 1/2 with Champagne.
Dash of Grenadine
Fill with sparkling water.
Garnish with 3 or 4 blueberries.

FRENCH MARTINI
Fill glass with ice.
1 oz Vodka
1/2 oz Black Raspberry Liqueur
1/2 oz Peach Schnapps
Shake.
Strain into chilled glass.
Garnish with Cherry.

FRENCH 95
Fill glass with ice.
1 1/2 oz Bourbon or Gin
1 oz Sour Mix
1 oz Orange Juice
Fill with Champagne.
Float 1/2 oz Brandy on top.
Garnish with Orange or Cherry.

FRENCH 75
Fill glass with ice.
1 1/2 oz Cognac or Brandy
or Gin
1 oz Lemon Juice or Sour Mix
1/2 oz Sugar Syrup
Shake.
Fill with Champagne.
Garnish with Lemon Twist.

FRENCH DREAM
Fill glass with ice.
1 oz Coffee Liqueur
1 oz Black Raspberry Liqueur
1 oz Irish Cream
Stir.

FRENCH SUMMER
Fill glass with ice.
1 oz Black Raspberry Liqueur
Fill with sparkling water
or Soda Water.
Garnish with Orange.

FRENCH TICKLER
Fill glass with ice.
1 oz Orange Liqueur
1 oz 100-proof Cinnamon
Schnapps
Stir.
Strain into shot glass.

FRIAR TUCK
Fill glass with ice.
2 oz Hazelnut Liqueur
2 oz Lemon Juice or Sour Mix
2 dashes of Grenadine
Shake.
Garnish with Orange and Cherry.

FRISCO SOUR
Fill glass with ice.
1 1/2 oz Whiskey
3/4 oz Benedictine
1/2 oz Lemon Juice or Sour Mix
1/2 oz Lime Juice
Shake.
Strain into chilled glass.
Garnish with Orange.

FROG-IN-A-BLENDER (frozen)
In Blender:
1 cup of Ice
2 oz Vodka
4 oz Cranberry Juice
2 Lime wheels
Blend 3-5 seconds.

FROSTBITE
Fill glass with ice.
1 1/2 oz Tequila
1/2 oz White Creme De Cacao
1/2 oz Blue Curacao
Fill with Cream.
Shake.

FROSTBITE (frozen)
In Blender:
1 cup of Ice
1 1/2 oz Yukon Jack
3/4 oz Peppermint Schnapps
2 oz Sour Mix
Blend until smooth.
If too thin add ice.
If too thick add Sour Mix.

FROSTED ROMANCE (frozen)
In Blender:
1/2 cup of Ice
1 oz Black Raspberry Liqueur
1 oz White Creme De Cacao
Scoop of Vanilla Ice Cream
Blend until smooth.
If too thick add Milk or liqueur.
If too thin add ice or Ice Cream.

FROUPE
Fill glass with ice.
1 1/2 oz Brandy
1 1/2 oz Sweet Vermouth
1 tsp Benedictine
Stir.
Strain into chilled glass.

FROZEN BIKINI (frozen)
In Blender:
1 cup of Ice
2 oz Vodka
1 oz Peach Schnapps
3 oz Peach Nectar
2 oz Orange Juice
Whole Peach (no pit, no skin)
Blend until smooth.
Pour into large glass.
Top with Champagne.

FRU FRU
Fill glass with ice.
1 oz Peach Schnapps
1 oz Banana Liqueur
Dash of Lime Juice
1 oz Pineapple Juice
Shake.
Strain into chilled glass.
Garnish with Lime.

FRUITBAR
Fill glass with ice.
1 oz Peach Schnapps
1 oz Dark Creme de Cacao
Stir.

FRUTTI NUEB
Fill glass with ice.
1/2 oz Vodka
1/2 oz Coconut Rum
1/2 oz Melon Liqueur
1/2 oz Black Raspberry Liqueur
Fill with Cranberry Juice.
Shake.

F

FU MANCHU
Fill glass with ice.
1 1/2 oz Dark Rum
1/2 oz Triple Sec
1/2 oz White Creme De Menthe
1/2 oz Lime Juice
Dash of Sugar Syrup
or 1/4 tsp Sugar
Shake.
Strain into chilled glass.

FUBAR
Fill glass with ice.
1/2 oz Vodka
1/2 oz Gin
1/2 oz Rum
1/2 oz Tequila
Fill with Hard Cider

FUDGESICLE (frozen)
In Blender:
1/2 cup of Ice
1 1/2 oz Vodka
1/2 oz Dark Creme De Cacao
1 tbsp Chocolate Syrup
Scoop of Chocolate Ice Cream
Blend until smooth.
If too thick add Milk or Cream.
If too thin add ice or Ice Cream.
Garnish with a popsicle stick.

FUEL-INJECTION
Fill glass with ice
1 1/2 oz Brandy
1/2 oz Mentholated Schnapps
Shake.
Strain into chilled glass.

FULL MOON
Fill glass with ice.
1 oz Orange Liqueur
1 oz Amaretto
Stir.

FUNKY MONKEY (frozen)
In Blender:
1/2 cup of Ice
3/4 oz Rum
3/4 oz White Creme De Cacao
3/4 oz Banana Liqueur
1/2 fresh ripe peeled Banana
Scoop of Vanilla Ice Cream
Blend until smooth.
If too thick add Milk or fruit.
If too thin add ice or Ice Cream.
Garnish with Banana.

FUZZY ASTRONAUT
Fill glass with ice.
1 1/2 oz Vodka
1/2 oz Peach Schnapps
Fill with Tang.

FUZZY BASTARD
Fill glass with ice.
1 oz Dark Rum
1/2 oz 151-Proof Rum
1/2 oz Triple Sec
1/2 oz Syrup
Fill with equal parts Orange Juice
and Sour Mix.
Shake.
Float 1/2 oz Peach Schnapps on
top.

FUZZY FRUIT
Fill glass with ice.
2 oz Peach Schnapps
Fill with Grapefruit Juice.
Stir.

FUZZY GUPPIE
Fill glass with ice.
1 1/2 oz Vodka
1/2 oz Peach Schnapps
1 oz White Wine
Fill with Ginger Ale.
Originally garnished with a fish.
(I don't condone killing an
innocent animal for garnishes.)

FUZZY KAMIKAZE
Fill glass with ice.
2 oz Vodka
2 oz Peach Schnapps
1 oz Lime Juice
Shake.
Serve or strain into chilled glass.
Garnish with Lime.

FUZZY MONKEY
Fill glass with ice.
1 oz Banana Liqueur
1 oz Peach Schnapps
Fill with Orange Juice.
Stir.
Garnish with Orange or Banana.

FUZZY MOTHER
1 1/2 oz Gold Tequila
Top with 1/4 oz 151-Proof Rum.
Ignite.

FUZZY NAVEL
Fill glass with ice.
1 oz Vodka
1 oz Peach Schnapps or
2 oz Peach Schnapps
Fill with Orange Juice.
Garnish with Orange.

FUZZY NAVEL WITH LINT
Fill glass with ice.
1 oz Vodka
1 oz Peach Schnapps
Fill with Orange Juice.
Top with 1/2 oz Irish Cream or Milk.

G AND C
Fill glass with ice.
1 oz Galliano
1 oz Cognac

G-SPOT
Fill glass with ice.
1 oz Vodka
1 oz Orange Liqueur
1 oz Cranberry Juice
Stir.
Strain into chilled glass.

G-STRING
Fill glass with ice.
1 1/2 oz Vodka
1/2 oz Dark Creme De Cacao
1/2 oz Cream or Milk
Shake. Strain into shot glass.

GAELIC COFFEE
3/4 oz Irish Whiskey
3/4 oz Irish Cream
3/4 oz Creme De Cacao
Fill with hot Black Coffee.
Top with Whipped Cream.
Drizzle Green Creme De Menthe
on top.

GALE FORCE
Fill glass with ice.
1 oz Gin
1/2 oz Gold Rum
1/4 oz 151-Proof Rum
Dash of Lime Juice
Fill with Orange Juice.
Shake.

GALE WARNING
Fill glass with ice.
2 oz Scotch
Fill with equal parts Cranberry and
Pineapple Juice.

GALLIANO *(type liqueur)*
Bring 2 cups of Sugar and
2/3 cup water to a boil.
Simmer 10 minutes.
1/2 tsp Anise Extract
1/2 tsp Vanilla Extract
3 tsp Lime Juice
6 drops of Yellow Food Coloring
Let cool.
Add 2 1/2 cups of Vodka.
Put in tightly corked bottle.
Store 6 weeks.

GANDY DANCER
Fill glass with ice.
1 oz Yukon Jack
1 oz Amaretto
1 oz Banana Liqueur
1 oz Pineapple Juice
Shake.
Strain into chilled glass.

GANG BANGER
Fill glass with ice.
1 oz Vodka
1 oz Tequila
1 oz Bourbon
Fill with Lemon-Lime soda

GANGRENE
Fill glass with ice.
1 oz Light Rum
1/2 oz Spiced Rum
1/2 oz Melon Liqueur
1/2 oz Blue Curacao
Fill with Sour Mix.
Shake.

GASOLINE (floater)
1 oz Southern Comfort (bottom)
1 oz Tequila (top)

GAUGIN or GAUGUIN (frozen)
In Blender:
1 cup of Ice
2 oz Rum
1 tsp Passion Fruit Syrup
1 tsp Lime Juice
1 tsp Lemon Juice
Blend until smooth.
Garnish with Cherry and Lemon
Twist.

GENOA
Fill glass with ice.
1 1/2 oz Vodka
3/4 oz Campari
Fill with Orange Juice.
Shake.
Garnish with Orange.

GENTLE BEN
Fill glass with ice.
3/4 oz Vodka
3/4 oz Gin
3/4 oz Rum
Fill with Orange Juice.
Shake.
Garnish with Orange.

GENTLE BULL
Fill glass with ice.
1 1/2 oz Tequila
3/4 oz Coffee Liqueur
Fill with Cream or Milk.
Shake.

GEORGIA PEACH
Fill glass with ice.
2 oz Peach Schnapps
Fill with Cranberry Juice.
Stir.

GERMAN LEG SPREADER
Fill glass with ice.
3/4 oz Jaegermeister
3/4 oz Chocolate Liqueur
3/4 oz 100-proof Peppermint
Schnapps
Shake. Strain into shot glass.

GET LAID
Fill glass with ice.
1 1/2 oz Vodka
1/2 oz Raspberry Liqueur
Dash of Cranberry Juice
Fill with Pineapple Juice.
Shake.

F
G

GHETTO BLASTER (floater)
1/2 oz Coffee Liqueur (bottom)
1/2 oz Brandy
1/2 oz Tequila
1/2 oz Bourbon (top)

GHOSTBUSTER
Fill glass with ice.
1 oz Peach Schnapps
1 oz Melon Liqueur
Shake.
Strain into chilled glass.
Add 3-5 drops of Irish Cream into
center of drink.

GIBSON
(Caution: DRY usually means less
Vermouth than usual.
EXTRA DRY can mean even less
Vermouth than usual, or no
Vermouth at all.)
Fill glass with ice.
2 oz Gin
1/2 oz Dry Vermouth
Stir.
Strain into chilled glass or pour
contents (with ice) into short glass.
Garnish (with Cocktail Onions.

GILLIGAN
Fill glass with ice.
3/4 oz Light Rum
3/4 oz Coconut Rum
3/4 oz Banana Liqueur
Fill with equal parts Pineapple
and Orange Juice.
Shake.

GILLIGAN'S ISLE
Fill glass with ice.
2 oz Rum
Dash of Amaretto
Dash of Maraschino Cherry juice
Dash of Lime Juice
Dash of Grapefruit Juice
Stir.
Strain into chilled glasses.

GIMLET
Fill glass with ice.
2 oz Gin or Vodka
1 oz Lime Juice
Stir.
Strain into chilled glass or pour
contents (with ice) into short glass.
Garnish with Lime.

GIN AND TONIC
Fill glass with ice.
2 oz Gin
Fill with Tonic Water.
Garnish with Lime.

GIN BUCK
Fill glass with ice.
2 oz Gin
Fill with Ginger Ale.
Stir.
Garnish with Lemon.

GIN CASSIS
Fill glass with ice.
1 1/2 oz Gin
1/2 oz Creme De Cassis
1/2 oz Lemon Juice or Sour Mix
Shake.
Serve or strain into chilled glass.

GIN DAISY
Fill glass with ice.
2 oz Gin
1 tsp Sugar
1 tsp Raspberry Syrup
or Grenadine
1 oz Lemon Juice or Sour Mix
Shake.
Fill with Soda Water.
Garnish with Orange and Lemon.

GIN FIZZ
Fill glass with ice.
2 oz Gin
1/2 tsp Sugar
1 oz Sour Mix
Dash of Lime Juice
Shake.
Fill with Soda Water.
Garnish with Cherry.

GIN RICKEY
Fill glass with ice.
2 oz Gin
1 tbsp Lime Juice
Fill with Soda Water.
Garnish with Lime.

GINGERBREAD MAN
Fill glass with ice.
1 oz Cinnamon Schnapps
1 oz Irish Cream
1 oz Butterscotch Schnapps
Shake.
Strain into chilled glass.

GINGERBREAD MAN 2 (floater)
3/4 oz Coffee Liqueur (bottom)
3/4 oz Irish Cream
3/4 oz 100-proof Cinnamon
Schnapps (top)

GINGER SNAP
Fill glass with ice.
2 oz Ginger Brandy
Fill with Ginger Ale.

G. S. COOKIE
Fill glass with ice.
1 oz Peppermint Schnapps or
Creme De Menthe
1 oz Coffee Liqueur
Fill with Milk or Cream.
Shake.

G. S. COOKIE (floater)
1/2 oz Coffee Liqueur (bottom)
1/2 oz Irish Cream
1/2 oz Peppermint Schnapps (top)

G. S. COOKIE (frozen)
In Blender:
1/2 cup of Ice
1 oz Coffee Liqueur
1 oz Peppermint Schnapps or
Creme De Menthe
Scoop of Vanilla Ice Cream
Blend until smooth.
If too thick add Milk or Cream.
If too thin add ice or Ice Cream.
Garnish with Chocolate Shavings
or Sprinkles or a Cookie.

GLAM TRASH
Fill glass with ice.
2 oz Cinnamon Schnapps
Dash of Grenadine
1 oz Beer
Stir. Strain into shot glass.

GLASS TOWER
Fill glass with ice.
1 oz Vodka
1 oz Light Rum
1/2 oz Triple Sec
1/2 oz Peach Schnapps
1/2 oz Sambuca
Fill with Lemon-Lime Soda.
Garnish with Lime.

GLENDA
In Champagne flute
1/2 oz Peach Schnapps
1/2 oz Orange Liqueur
Fill with Champagne.

GLOOMLIFTER
Fill glass with ice.
1 1/2 oz Whiskey
1/2 oz Brandy
1/2 oz Raspberry Syrup
or Black Raspberry Liqueur
1 tsp Sugar
1/2 oz Lemon Juice or Sour Mix
1/2 Egg White
Shake.

GLUEWEIN
In a sauce pan:
5 oz Dry Red Wine
1 Cinnamon Stick (broken up)
2 whole Cloves
1 tsp Honey
Pinch of ground Nutmeg
Heat without boiling.
Pour into mug.
Garnish with Lemon Twist and
Orange.

GO GIRL
Fill glass with ice.
1 oz Vodka
1 oz Black Raspberry Liqueur
Dash of Sour Mix
Shake.
Fill with Soda Water.

GO-GO JUICE
Fill glass with ice.
1/2 oz Vodka
1/2 oz Gin
1/2 oz Rum
1/2 oz Tequila
1/2 oz Blue Curacao
1/2 oz Orange Juice
1 oz Sour Mix
Shake.
Fill with Lemon-Lime Soda.
Garnish with Lemon.

GODCHILD
Fill glass with ice.
1 1/2 oz Vodka
1/2 oz Amaretto
Fill with Milk or Cream.
Shake.

GODCHILD 2
Fill glass with ice.
1 1/2 oz Brandy or Cognac
1/2 oz Amaretto

GODFATHER
Fill glass with ice.
1 1/2 oz Scotch
1/2 oz Amaretto
Stir.

GODMOTHER aka
TAWNY RUSSIAN
Fill glass with ice.
1 1/2 oz Vodka
1/2 oz Amaretto
Stir.

GOLDEN BULL
Fill glass with ice.
1 oz Southern Comfort
1 oz Amaretto
Fill with Orange Juice.
Shake.
Top with Lemon-Lime Soda.
Garnish with Lemon.

GOLDEN CADDIE (frozen)
In Blender:
1 cup of Ice (or 1/2 cup of Ice if
using Ice Cream)
2 oz White Creme De Cacao
1 oz Galliano
3 oz Cream or Milk or
1/2 scoop of Vanilla Ice Cream
Blend 5 seconds on low speed.
Strain and serve.

G

GOLDEN CADDIE WITH DOUBLE BUMPERS (frozen)
In Blender:
Cup of ice (or 1/2 cup if using Ice Cream)
1/2 oz Galliano
1/2 oz White Creme De Cacao
1/2 oz Brandy
1/2 oz Benedictine
3 oz Cream or Milk or
1/2 scoop Vanilla Ice Cream
Blend 5 seconds on low speed.
Strain and serve.

GOLDEN CAPPUCCINO
1 1/2 oz Galliano
Fill with Espresso.
Top with Steamed Milk.
Garnish with Lemon Twist.

GOLDEN DAWN
Fill glass with ice.
1 oz Gin
1 oz Apricot Brandy
1 oz Orange Juice
Shake.
Strain into chilled glass.

GOLDEN DAY
Fill glass with ice.
1 1/2 oz Vodka
1/2 oz Galliano
Stir.

GOLDEN DAZE
Fill glass with ice.
1 1/2 oz Gin
1/2 oz Peach or Apricot Brandy
1 oz Orange Juice
Shake.
Strain into chilled glass.

GOLDEN DRAGON
Fill glass with ice.
1 1/2 oz Yellow Chartreuse
1 1/2 oz Brandy
Stir.
Strain into chilled glass.
Garnish with Lemon Twist.

GOLDEN DREAM
Fill glass with ice.
1 oz Galliano
1/2 oz Triple Sec
Fill with equal parts Orange Juice and Cream or Milk.
Shake.
Serve or strain and serve.
Garnish with Orange.

GOLDEN DREAM (with Double Bumpers)
Fill glass with ice.
1/2 oz Galliano
1/2 oz Triple Sec
1/2 oz Brandy
1/2 oz Benedictine
Fill with equal parts of Orange Juice and Cream or Milk.
Shake.
Serve or strain into chilled glass.

GOLDEN FIZZ
Fill glass with ice.
2 oz Gin
1 Egg Yolk
1 1/2 oz Sour Mix
or Lemon Juice
1 tsp Powdered Sugar
Shake.
Fill with Soda Water.
Garnish with Lemon Wedge.

GOLDEN GATE
Fill glass with ice.
1 oz Rum
1/2 oz Gin
1/2 oz White Creme De Cacao
1 tsp 151-Proof Rum
1 tsp Falernum
1 oz Lemon Juice or Sour Mix
Shake.
Garnish with Orange.

GOLDEN MARGARITA
Fill glass with ice.
1 1/2 oz Gold Tequila
1/2 oz Grand Marnier
or Cointreau or Triple Sec
1/2 oz Lime Juice
3 oz Sour Mix
Dash of Orange Juice
(optional)
Shake.
Rub rim of second glass with Lime and dip in kosher salt.
Strain or pour contents (with ice) into salted glass.
Garnish with Lime.

GOLDEN MARGARITA (frozen)
In Blender:
1 cup of Ice
1 1/2 oz Golden Tequila
1/2 oz Grand Marnier or Orange Liqueur or Triple Sec
1/2 oz Lime Juice
3 oz Sour Mix
Dash of Orange Juice
(optional)
Blend until smooth.
If too thick add juice.
If too thin add ice.
Rub rim of second glass with Lime and dip in kosher salt.
Strain or pour contents (with ice) into salted glass.
Garnish with Lime.

GOLDEN NAIL
Fill glass with ice.
2 oz Drambuie
Fill with Grapefruit Juice.
Stir.

GOLDEN RUSSIAN
Fill glass with ice.
1 1/2 oz Vodka
1 oz Galliano
Stir.
Garnish with Lime.

GOLDEN SCREW aka ITALIAN SCREW
Fill glass with ice.
2 oz Galliano
Fill with Orange Juice.
Shake.

GOLDEN SHOWERS
Uncork bottle of chilled
Champagne or Sparkling Wine.
Cover top with thumb and shake.
Face bottle in direction of unsus-
pecting friend.
Remove thumb.

GOLDEN TORPEDO
Fill glass with ice.
1 oz Amaretto
1 oz Galliano
Fill with Cream or Milk.
Shake.

GOLDRUSH
Fill glass with ice.
1 oz Gold Tequila
1 oz Goldschlager

GOLDRUSH 2
Fill glass with ice.
1 1/2 oz Gold Tequila
1/2 oz Orange Liqueur
1/2 oz Lime Juice
Rub rim of second glass with Lime
and dip into Kosher Salt.
Strain or pour contents (with ice)
into salted glass.

GOLF
Fill glass with ice.
1 1/2 oz Gin
3/4 oz Dry Vermouth
2 dashes of Bitters
Stir.
Strain into chilled glass.
Garnish with Olive.

GOOD AND PLENT-E
1 oz Ouzo or Anisette
1 oz Coffee Liqueur
or Blackberry Brandy

GOOD AND PLENT-E (frozen)
In Blender:
1/2 cup of Ice
1 oz Vodka
1 oz Coffee Liqueur
1/2 oz Anisette
Scoop of Vanilla Ice Cream
Blend until smooth.
If too thick add Milk or Cream.
If too thin add ice or Ice Cream.

GOOD FORTUNE
Fill glass with ice.
1 oz Ginger Liqueur
1 oz Irish Cream
Stir.

GOOMBAY SMASH
Fill glass with ice.
1 oz Rum
1/2 oz Banana Liqueur
1 tsp Cream of Coconut
Dash of Orange Juice
Fill with Pineapple Juice.
Shake.
Top with Dark Rum.

GORILLA
Fill glass with ice.
1 oz Dark Creme De Cacao
1 oz Banana Liqueur
Fill with Orange Juice.

GORILLA FART
Fill glass with ice.
3/4 oz 151-Proof Rum
3/4 oz Bourbon
3/4 oz Southern Comfort or Ouzo
Stir. Strain into shot glass.

GRADEAL SPECIAL
Fill glass with ice.
1 1/2 oz Gin or Rum
3/4 oz Rum or Gin
3/4 oz Apricot Brandy
1 tsp Sugar Syrup
Shake.
Strain into chilled glass.

GRAND ALLIANCE
1 oz Amaretto
Fill with Champagne.

GRAND AM
Fill glass with ice.
1 oz Orange Liqueur
1 oz Amaretto
Stir.

GRAND APPLE
Fill glass with ice.
1 oz Apple Brandy
1/2 oz Cognac or Brandy
1/2 oz Orange Liqueur
Stir.
Strain into chilled glass.
Garnish with Orange and Lemon
Twist.

GRAND MIMOSA
Fill glass with ice.
Fill 3/4 with Champagne.
Dash of Orange Liqueur
Fill with Orange Juice.
Garnish with Orange.

GRAND OCCASION
Fill glass with ice.
1 1/2 oz Rum
1/2 oz Orange Liqueur
1/2 oz White Creme De Cacao
1/2 oz Lemon Juice or Sour Mix
Shake.
Strain into chilled glass.

G

GRAND PASSION
Fill glass with ice.
2 oz Gin
1 oz Passion Fruit Nectar
2 or 3 dashes of Bitters
Shake.
Serve or strain into chilled glass.

GRAND SLAM
Fill glass with ice.
1 1/2 oz Swedish Punch
3/4 oz Dry Vermouth
3/4 oz Sweet Vermouth
Stir.
Strain into chilled glass.

GRAPE APE
Fill glass with ice.
2 oz Vodka
Fill glass with equal parts
Grape Juice and Lemon-Lime
Soda.

GRAPE CRUSH aka COCA
Fill glass with ice.
1 1/2 oz Vodka
1/2 oz Black Raspberry Liqueur
Dash of Sour Mix
Shake.
Fill with Lemon-Lime Soda.

GRAPE NEHI
Fill glass with ice.
1 1/2 oz Vodka
1/2 oz Black Raspberry Liqueur
2 oz Sour Mix
Shake. Strain into shot glass.

GRAPE SOUR BALL
Fill glass with ice.
1 oz Vodka
1 oz Blue Curacao
2 oz Sour Mix
Fill with Cranberry Juice.
Shake.
Strain into chilled glass.

GRASS SKIRT
Fill glass with ice.
1 1/2 oz Gin
1/2 oz Triple Sec
Dash of Grenadine
Fill with Pineapple Juice.
Shake.
Garnish with Cherry.

GRASSHOPPER
Fill glass with ice.
1 oz White Creme De Cacao
1 oz Green Creme De Menthe
Fill with Milk or Cream.
Shake.
Serve or strain into chilled glass.

GRASSHOPPER (frozen)
In Blender:
1/2 cup of Ice
1 oz White Creme De Cacao
1 oz Green Creme De Menthe
Scoop of Vanilla Ice Cream
Blend until smooth.
If too thick add Milk or Cream. If too
thin add ice or Ice Cream.

GRAVEYARD
Fill glass with ice.
1/2 oz Vodka
1/2 oz Gin
1/2 oz 151-Proof Rum
1/2 oz Tequila
1/2 oz Triple Sec
1/2 oz Scotch
1/2 oz Bourbon
Fill with equal parts Beer and
Stout.

GREAT SECRET
Fill glass with ice.
1 1/2 oz Gin
1/2 oz Lillet
Dash of Bitters
Shake.
Strain into chilled glass.
Garnish with Orange.

GREATFUL D.
Fill glass with ice.
1/2 oz Vodka
1/2 oz Gin
1/2 oz Rum
1/2 oz Tequila
1/2 oz Triple Sec
1/2 oz Black Raspberry Liqueur
Fill with Sour Mix
Shake.
Jerry, We miss you!

GREEK COFFEE
1 oz Metaxa
1 oz Ouzo
Fill with hot Black Coffee.
Top with Whipped Cream.

GREEN APPLE
Fill glass with ice.
1 oz Apple Brandy
1 oz Melon Liqueur
1 oz Sour Mix
Stir.

GREEN DEMON
Fill glass with ice.
3/4 oz Vodka
3/4 oz Rum
3/4 oz Melon Liqueur
Fill with Lemonade
Shake.

GREEN DRAGON
Fill glass with ice.
2 oz Vodka
1 oz Green Chartreuse
Shake.
Strain into chilled glass.

GREEN EYES
Fill glass with ice.
1 1/2 oz Vodka
1/2 oz Blue Curacao
Fill with Orange Juice.
Shake.

GREEN GOBLIN
5 oz Hard Cider
5 oz Lager
Float 1/2 oz Blue Curacao on top.

GREEN GODDESS
Fill glass with ice.
1 oz Vodka
1/2 oz Melon Liqueur
1/2 oz Cream of Coconut
Shake.

GREEN HORNET aka
IRISH STINGER
Fill glass with ice.
1 1/2 oz Brandy
1/2 oz Green Creme De Menthe
Stir.
Serve or strain into chilled glass.

GREEN KAMIKAZE
Fill glass with ice.
2 oz Vodka
1/2 oz Melon Liqueur
1 oz Lime Juice
Shake.

GREEN LIZARD
Fill glass with ice.
1/2 oz 151-Proof Rum
1 oz Green Chartreuse
Shake.
Strain into shot glass.

GREEN MEANY
Fill glass with ice.
1 oz Southern Comfort
1 oz Melon Liqueur
1 oz Pineapple Juice
Stir.
Strain into shot glass.

GREEN MOUNTAIN MELON
Fill glass with ice.
1 oz Vodka
1/2 oz Melon Liqueur
1 oz Lime Juice
Fill with Sour Mix.
Shake.
Garnish with Lime.

GREEN RUSSIAN
Fill glass with ice.
1 1/2 oz Vodka
1/2 oz Melon Liqueur
Stir.

GREEN RUSSIAN 2
Fill glass with ice.
1 1/2 oz Vodka
1/2 oz Melon Liqueur
Fill with Milk or Cream.
Shake.

GREEN SNEAKERS
Fill glass with ice.
1 oz Vodka
1/2 oz Melon Liqueur
1/2 oz Triple Sec
2 oz Orange Juice
Shake.
Serve or strain into chilled glass.

GREEN SPIDER
Fill glass with ice.
2 oz Vodka
1 oz Green Creme De Menthe
Stir.
Serve or strain into chilled glass.

GREYHOUND
Fill glass with ice.
2 oz Vodka or Gin
Fill with Grapefruit Juice.
Garnish with Lime.

GROG
2 oz Amber Rum
1 tsp Sugar
Dash of Lemon Juice
3 whole cloves
1 Cinnamon Stick
Fill with boiling water.
Stir.
Garnish with Lemon.

GROUND ZERO aka
MINT CONDITION
Fill glass with ice.
3/4 oz Vodka
1/2 oz Coffee Liqueur
3/4 oz Bourbon
3/4 oz Peppermint Schnapps
Shake.
Serve or strain into chilled glass.

GUANA GRABBER
Fill glass with ice.
3/4 oz Light Rum
3/4 oz Dark Rum
1 oz Coconut Rum
Dash of Grapefruit Juice
Dash of Grenadine
Fill with Pineapple Juice.
Shake.
Garnish with Cherry.

GUILLOTINE
Fill glass with ice.
3/4 oz Vodka
3/4 oz Tequila
3/4 oz Mentholated Schnapps
Shake.
Strain into chilled glass.

GUMBY
Fill glass with ice.
1 oz Vodka
1 oz Melon Liqueur
1 oz Sour Mix
Shake.
Fill with Lemon-Lime Soda.

G

GUMDROP
Fill glass with ice.
1 oz Amaretto or Anisette
1 oz Dark Creme De Cacao
Strain into chilled glass.

GUMMY BEAR
Fill glass with ice.
3/4 oz Southern Comfort
3/4 oz Amaretto
3/4 oz Melon Liqueur
Dash of Grenadine
Fill with equal parts Orange and
Pineapple Juice.
Shake.
Garnish with Candy.

GUN RUNNER COFFEE
1 oz Irish Whiskey
1/2 oz Irish Cream
1/2 oz Coffee Liqueur
Fill with hot Black Coffee.
Top with Whipped Cream.
Sprinkle with Brown Sugar.

GUN RUNNER ICED COFFEE
Fill glass with ice.
1 oz Irish Whiskey
1/2 oz Irish Cream
1/2 oz Coffee Liqueur
Fill with Iced Coffee.
Add sugar or sweetener to taste.

GYPSY
Fill glass with ice.
2 oz Vodka
1/2 oz Benedictine
1 tsp Lemon Juice or Sour Mix
1 tsp Orange Juice
Shake.
Serve or strain into chilled glass.
Garnish with Orange.

H. BAR (frozen)
In Blender:
1/2 cup of Ice
1 1/2 oz Vodka
1 oz Dark Creme De Cacao
1 Toffee Bar
1/2 scoop of Vanilla Ice Cream
Blend until smooth.
If too thick add Milk or Cream.
If too thin add ice or Ice Cream.

H. D. RIDER
1 oz Bourbon
1 oz Tequila or Yukon Jack

HAIRY APE
Fill glass with ice.
1 oz Vodka
1 oz Banana Liqueur
Fill with Orange Juice.
Shake.

HAIRY BITCH
Fill glass with ice.
1 1/2 oz Rum
1/2 oz Triple Sec
Fill with Pineapple Juice.
Shake.

HAIRY MARY
Fill glass with ice.
2 oz Grain Alcohol
Fill with Bloody Mary Mix.

HAIRY NAVEL
Fill glass with ice.
1 oz Vodka
1 oz Peach Schnapps
Fill glass with Orange Juice.
Garnish with Orange.

HAITIAN ASSISTANT
Fill glass with ice.
1 oz Amber Rum
1/2 oz Orange Liqueur
1/2 oz Jaegermeister
1 oz Pineapple Juice
Shake. Strain into shot glass.

HALLEY'S COMFORT aka
HALLEY'S COMET
Fill glass with ice.
1 1/2 oz Southern Comfort
1 1/2 oz Peach Schnapps
Fill glass with Soda Water.

HAMMER aka MEXICAN SCREW
Fill glass with ice.
2 oz Tequila
Fill with Orange Juice.
Garnish with Orange.

HAMMER (floater)
1 1/2 oz Sambuca (bottom)
1/2 oz Brandy (top)

HAMMERHEAD
Fill glass with ice.
1 oz Amber Rum
1 oz Amaretto
1 oz Curacao
1 or 2 dashes of Southern Comfort
Strain into chilled glass.

HAMMERHEAD 2
Fill glass with ice.
1/2 oz Vodka
1/2 oz Light Rum
1/2 oz Spiced Rum
1/2 oz Coconut Rum
Fill with equal parts Pineapple and
Orange Juice.

HAND JOB (floater)
1 oz Peach Schnapps (bottom)
1/2 oz Soda Water
1/2 oz 151-Proof Rum (top)
Ignite.

HAND RELEASE (floater)
1/2 oz Jaegermeister (bottom)
1/2 oz Peppermint Schnapps
1/2 oz 151-Proof Rum (top)

HANGOVER RELIEVER
1 B-Complex Vitamin.
Glass filled with Soda Water,
with 5-10 dashes of Bitters in it.

HAPPY FELLER
Fill glass with ice.
1 1/2 oz Vodka
1/2 oz Black Raspberry Liqueur
1/2 oz Orange Liqueur
Dash of Lime Juice
Strain into chilled glass.

HAPPY JACK
Fill glass with ice.
1 oz Bourbon
1 oz Apple Brandy
Stir.
Strain into chilled glass.

HAPPY SUMMER
Fill glass with ice.
1 1/2 oz Amber Rum
1 1/2 oz Melon Liqueur
Fill with Orange Juice.
Michael T. Duratti

HARBOR LIGHTS (floater)
1 oz Galliano (bottom)
1 oz Brandy (top)
Ignite.

HARBOR LIGHTS 2 (floater)
3/4 oz Coffee Liqueur (bottom)
3/4 oz Tequila
or Southern Comfort
3/4 oz 151-Proof Rum (top)
Ignite.

HARD CANDY
Fill glass with ice.
1 oz Melon Liqueur
1/2 oz White Creme De Menthe or
Peppermint Schnapps
2 oz Sour Mix
Shake. Strain into shot glass.

HARD HAT
Fill glass with ice.
2 oz Rum
Dash of Lime Juice
1 tsp Sugar
Fill with Soda Water.

HARD NIPPLE (floater)
1 oz Irish Cream (bottom)
1 oz Peppermint Schnapps (top)

HARD ON (floater)
3/4 oz Coffee Liqueur (bottom)
3/4 oz Amaretto
3/4 oz Milk (top)

HARDCORE
Fill glass with ice.
1 oz Grain Alcohol
1 oz 151-Proof Rum
1/2 oz Amaretto
1/2 oz Triple Sec
Fill with Cola
Stir.

HARI KARI
Fill glass with ice.
1 1/2 oz Brandy
1/2 oz Triple Sec
1 oz Orange Juice
Shake.
Strain into chilled glass.

HARLEM COCKTAIL
Fill glass with ice.
1 1/2 oz Gin
1 tsp of Cherry Liqueur
1 oz Pineapple Juice
Shake.
Strain into chilled glass.
Garnish with Pineapple.

HARMONY
Fill glass with ice.
1 1/2 oz Ginger Liqueur
1/2 oz Peach Schnapps
Fill with Orange Juice.
Shake.
Garnish with Orange.

HARVARD
Fill glass with ice.
1 1/2 oz Brandy
3/4 oz Sweet Vermouth
1/4 oz Lemon Juice or Sour Mix
1 tsp Grenadine
Dash of Bitters
Shake.
Strain into chilled glass.

HARVEY WALLBANGER
Fill glass with ice.
1 1/2 oz Vodka
Fill with Orange Juice.
Top with 1/2 oz Galliano.
Garnish with Orange.

HARVEY WALLBANGER (frozen)
In Blender:
1/2 cup of Ice
1 1/2 oz Vodka
Dash of Orange Juice
1/2 scoop Orange Sherbet
Blend until smooth.
Top with 1/2 oz Galliano.

HASTA LA VISTA, BABY
Fill glass with ice.
1/2 oz Vodka
1/2 oz Tequila
1/2 oz Triple Sec
1/2 oz Peach Schnapps
1/2 oz Amaretto
1/2 oz B&B
Dash of Dry Vermouth
Dash of Lime Juice
Fill with equal parts of Orange and
Pineapple Juice.
Shake.

HAVANA
Fill glass with ice.
1 1/2 oz Amber Rum
1/2 oz Sherry
1 /1/2 oz Sour Mix
Shake.
Strain into chilled glass.
Garnish with Orange.

HAWAIIAN
Fill glass with ice.
2 oz Gin
1/2 oz Triple Sec
1/2 oz Pineapple Juice
Shake.
Strain into chilled glass.

HAWAIIAN 2
Fill glass with ice.
1 oz Amaretto
1 oz Southern Comfort
Dash of Orange Juice
Dash of Pineapple Juice
Dash of Grenadine
Shake.
Strain into chilled glass.

HAWAIIAN 3
Fill glass with ice.
1 oz Vodka
1 oz Blended Whiskey
1/2 oz Amaretto
Dash of Grenadine
Fill with equal parts Orange Juice
and Pineapple Juice.
Shake.
Garnish with Cherry and Pineapple.

HAWAIIAN COCKTAIL
Fill glass 3/4 with ice.
Fill 3/4 with desired White Wine.
Dash of Pineapple Juice
Dash of Pink Grapefruit Juice

HAWAIIAN EYE (frozen)
In Blender:
1 cup of Ice
3/4 oz Vodka
3/4 oz Coffee Liqueur
1 tsp Bourbon
1 tsp Banana Liqueur
1 Egg White
Dash of Cream
2 oz Pineapple Juice.
Blend until smooth.
If too thick add juice.
If too thin add ice.

HAWAIIAN GARDEN'S SLING
Fill glass with ice.
1 oz Rum
1 oz Sloe Gin
Dash of Grenadine
Fill with Sour Mix.
Shake.

HAWAIIAN MARGARITA (frozen)
In Blender:
1 cup of Ice
1 1/2 oz Tequila
1/2 oz Triple Sec
2 oz fresh or frozen
Strawberries
2 oz fresh or canned
Pineapple
Dash of Sour Mix
Blend until smooth.

HAWAIIAN NIGHTS
Fill glass with ice.
2 oz Rum
Fill with Pineapple Juice.
Float 1/4 oz Cherry Brandy
on top.

HAWAIIAN PUNCHED
Fill glass with ice.
3/4 oz Vodka
3/4 oz Southern Comfort
3/4 oz Amaretto
Dash of Sloe Gin or Grenadine
Fill with Pineapple Juice.
Shake.
Garnish with Pineapple.

HAWAIIAN PUNCHED 2
Fill glass with ice.
1 oz Vodka
1 oz Melon Liqueur
1 oz Amaretto
Dash of Southern Comfort
Fill with Cranberry Juice.
Shake.

HAWAIIAN PUNCHED 3
Fill glass with ice.
1/2 oz Vodka
1/2 oz Southern Comfort
1/2 oz Triple Sec
1/2 oz Amaretto
Dash of Pineapple Juice
Dash of Sour Mix
Dash of Cranberry Juice
Dash of Grenadine
Shake.
Garnish with Cherry and Orange.

HAWAIIAN SEA BREEZE aka BAY BREEZE, DOWNEASTER
Fill glass with ice.
2 oz Vodka
Fill with equal parts Pineapple and
Cranberry Juice.
Garnish with Lime.

HEAD
Fill glass with ice.
1 oz Root Beer Schnapps
1 oz Cream
Shake.

HEAD BANGER
Fill glass with ice.
1 oz 151-Proof Rum
1 oz Sambuca
Dash of Grenadine
Shake. Strain into shot glass.

HEAD ROOM (floater)
1/2 oz Banana Liqueur (bottom)
1/2 oz Melon Liqueur
1/2 oz Irish Cream (top)

HEAD WIND
Fill glass with ice.
1 oz Vodka
1 oz 151-Proof Rum
1 oz Dark Rum
1 oz Brandy
1/2 oz Blue Curacao
Fill with equal parts Orange
and Pineapple Juice and Sour Mix.
Shake.
Garnish with Lime.

HEADHUNTER
Fill glass with ice.
2 oz Rum
1 oz Vodka
1 tbsp Cream of Coconut
Dash of Cream
1 oz Orange Juice
Fill with Pineapple Juice.
Shake.
Garnish with Pineapple.

HEADREST aka
UPSIDE DOWN MARGARITA
Rest head on bar.
Have friend pour ingredients into
mouth.
1 oz Tequila
1/2 oz Triple Sec
Dash of Lime Juice
Dash of Sour Mix
Dash of Orange Juice
Slosh around mouth.
Swallow!

HEART THROB
Fill glass with ice.
2 oz Amaretto
Fill with equal parts Orange and
Cranberry Juice.
Shake.

HEARTBREAK
Fill glass with ice.
2 1/2 oz Blended Whiskey
Fill with Cranberry Juice
Top with 1/2 oz Brandy.

HEATHER COFFEE aka
RUSTY NAIL COFFEE
1 oz Scotch
1 oz Drambuie
Fill with hot Black Coffee.
Top with Whipped Cream.
Sprinkle with Cinnamon.

HEATWAVE
Fill glass with ice.
1 oz Dark Rum
1/2 oz Peach Schnapps
Fill with Pineapple Juice.
Dash of Grenadine
Stir.
Garnish with Cherry and Pineapple.

HELLO NURSE
Fill glass with ice.
1 1/2 oz Vodka
1/2 oz Amaretto
Tbsp Cream of Coconut
1 oz Milk or Cream
Shake.
Strain into chilled glass.

HENRY MORGAN'S GROG
Fill glass with ice.
1 1/2 oz Whiskey
1 oz Pernod
1/2 oz Dark Rum
1 oz Cream
Shake.
Sprinkle ground Nutmeg
on top.

HIGH JAMAICAN WIND (floater)
Fill glass with ice.
1 1/2 oz Dark Rum (bottom)
1/2 oz Coffee Liqueur
1/2 oz Milk or Cream (top)

HIGH ROLLER aka
PRINCE IGOR
Fill glass with ice.
1 1/2 oz Vodka
3/4 oz Orange Liqueur
Dash of Grenadine
Fill with Orange Juice.
Shake.
Garnish with Orange and Cherry.

HIGHBALL
Fill glass with ice.
2 oz Whiskey
Fill with Water or Soda Water
or Ginger Ale.

HIGHLAND COFFEE
1 1/2 oz Scotch
1/2 oz B&B
Fill with hot Black Coffee.
Top with Whipped Cream.

H

HIGHLAND FLING
Fill glass with ice.
1 1/2 oz Scotch
1/2 oz Sweet Vermouth
2-3 dashes of Orange Bitters
Shake.
Strain into chilled glass.
Garnish with Olive.

HILLARY WALLBANGER
Fill glass with ice.
4 oz Dry White Wine
Fill with Orange Juice
Top with 1/2 oz Galliano.

HIT-IT
Fill glass with ice.
1 oz Vodka
1/2 oz Triple Sec
1/2 oz Cherry Brandy
2 oz Orange Juice
2 oz Cranberry Juice
Shake.
Strain into chilled glass.

HOFFMAN HOUSE
Fill glass with ice.
1 1/2 oz Gin
1/2 oz Dry Vermouth
2-3 dashes of Orange Bitters
Stir.
Strain into chilled glass.
Garnish with Olive.

HOG SNORT
Fill glass with ice.
1 oz Coconut Rum
1 oz Blue Curacao
Dash of Sour Mix
Dash of Pineapple Juice
Shake.
Strain into shot glass.

HOGBACK GROWLER
1 oz 151-Proof Rum
1 oz Brandy

HOLE IN ONE (floater)
1 oz Melon Liqueur (bottom)
1 oz Apple Brandy (top)
Add one drop of Cream into center
of drink.

HOLLYWOOD aka
RASPBERRY SMASH
Fill glass with ice.
1 1/2 oz Vodka
1/2 oz Black Raspberry Liqueur
Fill with Pineapple Juice.
Shake.
Garnish with Pineapple.

HOLLYWOOD 2
Fill glass with ice.
1 oz Vodka
1/2 oz Black Raspberry Liqueur
1/2 oz Peach Schnapps
Fill with Pineapple Juice.
Shake.

HOLLYWOOD MARTINI
Fill glass with ice.
2 oz Vodka
1/2 oz Black Raspberry Liqueur
Dash of Pineapple Juice
Shake.
Strain into chilled glass.

HOLY HAIL ROSEMARY
Fill glass with ice.
1 1/2 oz Peppered Vodka
5-7 dashes of Tabasco Sauce
Dash of Tomato Juice
Shake.
Strain into short glass.

HOMECOMING
Fill glass with ice.
1 oz Amaretto
1 oz Irish Cream
Shake.
Strain into chilled glass or pour
contents (with ice) into short glass.

HONEY BEE
Fill glass with ice.
2 oz Rum
1/2 oz Honey
1/2 oz Lemon Juice or Sour Mix
Shake.
Strain into chilled glass.

HONEYDEW
Fill glass with ice.
1 1/2 oz Melon Liqueur
2 oz Sour Mix
1/2 tsp Sugar
Shake.
Fill with Champagne.

HONEYMOON
Fill glass with ice.
3/4 oz Apple Brandy
3/4 oz Benedictine
1 tsp Triple Sec or Curacao
1 oz Lemon Juice or Sour Mix
Shake.
Strain into chilled glass.

HONOLULU
Fill glass with ice.
3/4 oz Gin
3/4 oz Benedictine
3/4 oz Cherry Liqueur
Stir.
Strain into chilled glass.

HONOLULU (frozen)
In Blender:
1 cup of Ice
1 1/2 oz Rum
Dash of Grenadine
Dash of Sour Mix
1/2 cup of fresh or canned
Pineapple
Blend for 3-6 seconds on low
speed.

HOOPLA
Fill glass with ice.
3/4 oz Brandy
3/4 oz Orange Liqueur
3/4 oz Lillet
3/4 oz Lemon Juice
or Sour Mix
Shake.
Strain into chilled glass.
Garnish with Lemon Twist.

HOOSIER ROOSTER aka
RED ROOSTER
Fill 1 shot glass with Gold Tequila.
Fill 1 shot glass with Orange Juice.
Fill 1 shot glass with Bloody Mary mix.
Drink in order given one after the other.
No Reserve Roosters.

HOOT MAN
Fill glass with ice.
1 1/2 oz Scotch
3/4 oz Sweet Vermouth
1 tsp Benedictine
Stir.
Strain into chilled glass.
Garnish with Lemon Twist.

HOOTER
Fill glass with ice.
1 1/2 oz Vodka
1/2 oz Amaretto
Fill with Pineapple Juice.
Shake.

HOP-SKIP-AND-GO-NAKED
Fill glass with ice.
1 oz Vodka
1 oz Gin
Dash of Lime Juice
Fill with Orange Juice (leaving 1/2 inch from top)
Float Beer on top.

HOP TOAD
Fill glass with ice.
1 oz Rum
1 oz Apricot Brandy
1 oz Lime Juice
Stir.
Strain into chilled glass.

HORSE'S NECK
Fill glass with ice.
2 oz Whiskey
Fill with Ginger Ale.
Garnish with Lemon Twist.
(In the original recipe, a whole lemon should be peeled in a continuous spiral for garnish.)

HOT APPLE PIE
2 oz Tuaca
Fill with hot Apple Cider.
Top with Whipped Cream.
Garnish with Cinnamon Stick.

HOT APPLE PIE 2
Fill glass ice.
1 oz Vodka
1 oz Apple Brandy
2 oz Apple Juice
Shake.
Strain into chilled glass.
1 oz Lemon-Lime Soda
Sprinkle with Cinnamon.

HOT APPLE TODDY
2 oz Whiskey or Apple Brandy
1 tsp Honey or Sugar
Fill with hot Apple Cider.
Stir.
Garnish with Lemon, Cinnamon Stick, and 2-3 whole Cloves.

HOT BUTTERED RUM
2 oz Dark Rum
1/2 oz Sugar Syrup
Pinch of Nutmeg
Fill with hot Water.
Garnish with Cinnamon Stick and Pat of Butter.

HOT DOG
Fill glass with ice.
2 oz Peppered Vodka
Fill with Grapefruit Juice.

HOT DOG 2
Rub rim of glass with Lime and dip one side of glass in Kosher Salt.
Fill glass with Beer.
Add 5-7 drops of Tabasco Sauce.

HOT MILK PUNCH
2 oz Bourbon
1/2 oz Sugar Syrup
or 1/2 tsp Sugar
Fill with hot Milk.
Stir.
Sprinkle with Nutmeg.

HOT NAIL
2 oz Scotch
1 oz Drambuie
Dash of Lemon Juice
Fill with boiling Water.
Garnish with Orange, Lemon, and Cinnamon Stick.

HOT PANTS
Fill glass with ice.
1 1/2 oz Tequila
1/2 oz Peppermint Schnapps
Dash of Grenadine
1 oz Grapefruit Juice
Shake and pour contents (with ice) into second glass rimmed with salt).

HOT PEPPERMINT PATTY
1 oz Peppermint Schnapps
1/2 oz Dark Creme De Cacao
1 tsp Creme De menthe
Fill with Hot Chocolate.
Top with Whipped Cream.
Sprinkle with Shaved Chocolate or Sprinkles.

H

HOT RASPBERRY DREAM
1 oz Black Raspberry Liqueur
1 oz Dark Creme De Cacao
4-6 oz steamed Milk
Stir.

HOT SCOTCH
1 oz Scotch
1/4 oz Drambuie
1 oz Lemon Juice
1/2 tsp Sugar
2 oz hot Water
Stir.
Garnish with Lemon.

HOT SEX
1 oz Coffee Liqueur
1 oz Orange Liqueur
Microwave for 10-15 seconds.

HOT TAMALE
Fill glass with ice.
1 1/2 oz Cinnamon Schnapps
1/2 oz Grenadine
Strain into shot glass.
Garnish with Hot Candy.

HOT TODDY
2 oz Whiskey or Rum or Brandy
1 tsp Honey or Sugar
Fill with boiling Water.
Stir.
Garnish with a Lemon,
Cinnamon Stick, and
2-3 whole Cloves.

HOT TUB
Fill glass with ice.
1 1/2 oz Vodka
1/2 oz Black Raspberry Liqueur
Dash of Sour Mix
Dash of Cranberry Juice
Shake.
Fill with Champagne.
Strain into chilled glass.

HOT YOUNG LADY
Fill glass with ice.
1/2 oz Cinnamon Schnapps
1/2 oz Peppermint Schnapps
1/2 oz Coffee Liqueur
1/2 oz Irish Cream
Shake. Strain into shot glass.

HOTEL CALIFORNIA
In Blender:
1/2 cup of ice.
1 oz Tequila or Vodka
1 oz Apricot Brandy
Scoop Orange Sherbet
Blend until smooth.
Float 1/2 oz Grenadine on top.

HOUND DOG
Fill glass with ice.
2 oz Rum
Fill with Grapefruit Juice.
Stir.

HOUNDSTOOTH
Fill glass with ice.
1 oz Vodka
1/2 oz White Creme De Cacao
1/2 oz Blackberry Brandy
Stir.
Serve or strain into chilled glass.

HUDSON BAY
Fill glass with ice.
1 oz Gin
1/2 oz Cherry Brandy
1 1/2 tsp Lime Juice
1 tsp Orange Juice
Shake.
Strain into chilled glass.

HUETCHEN
Fill glass with ice.
2 oz Brandy
Fill with Cola.

HUMMER (frozen)
In Blender:
1/2 cup of Ice
1 oz Dark Rum
1 oz Coffee Liqueur
Scoop of Vanilla Ice Cream
Blend until smooth.
If too thick add Milk or Cream.
If too thin add ice or Ice Cream.

HUNTER'S COCKTAIL
Fill glass with ice.
1 1/2 oz Whiskey
1/2 oz Cherry Brandy
Stir.
Garnish with Cherry.

HUNTRESS COCKTAIL
Fill glass with ice.
1 oz Bourbon
1 oz Cherry Liqueur
1 oz Cream or Milk
Dash of Triple Sec
Shake.
Strain into chilled glass.

HURRICANE
Fill glass with ice.
1 oz Light Rum
1 oz Amber Rum
1/2 oz Passion Fruit Syrup
1/2 oz Lime Juice
Shake.
Strain into chilled glass.
Garnish with Lime.

HURRICANE 2
Fill glass with ice.
1/2 oz Gin
1/2 oz Light Rum
1/2 oz Dark Rum
1/2 oz Amaretto
Dash of Grenadine
Fill with equal parts Pineapple,
Orange and Grapefruit Juice.
Shake.
Garnish with Orange, Lemon, Lime
and Cherry.

HUSSIE
Fill glass with ice.
1 oz Amaretto
1 oz Beer
1 oz Sour Mix
Shake. Strain into shot glass.

I FOR AN I aka
IRISH BROUGUE
Fill glass with ice.
1 1/2 oz Irish Whiskey
1/2 oz Irish Mist
Stir.
Serve or strain into chilled glass.
Garnish with Lemon Twist.

ICE BALL
In Blender:
Cup of ice
1 oz Gin
1 oz Sambuca
1 oz White Creme De Menthe
1 oz Milk or Cream
Blend until smooth.

ICE BOAT
Fill glass with ice.
1 1/2 oz Vodka
1 1/2 oz Peppermint Schnapps
Stir.
Strain into chilled glass.

ICE PICK
Fill glass with ice.
2 oz Vodka or Tequila
Fill with Iced Tea.
Flavor with sugar and/or lemon as desired.
Garnish with Lemon.

ICEBERG
Fill glass with ice.
2 oz Vodka
1 tsp Pernod or Peppermint Schnapps
Shake.
Strain into chilled glass.

ICHBIEN
Fill glass with ice.
2 oz Apple Brandy
1/2 oz Curacao
1 Egg Yolk
2 oz Milk or Cream
Shake.
Strain into chilled glass.
Garnish with Nutmeg.

IDEAL
Fill glass with ice.
1 1/2 oz Gin
1/2 oz Dry or Sweet Vermouth
1 tbsp Grapefruit Juice
1 tsp Cherry Liqueur
Shake.
Strain into chilled glass.
Garnish with Cherry.

IGUANA
Fill glass with ice.
1/2 oz Vodka
1/2 oz Tequila
1/4 oz Coffee Liqueur
1 1/2 oz Sour Mix (optional)
Shake.
Strain into chilled glass.
Garnish with Lime.

IL MAGNIFICO aka
IL PARADISO (frozen)
In Blender:
1 cup of Ice
1 oz Tuaca
1 oz Curacao
1 oz Cream
Blend for 3 or 4 seconds on low speed.

INCIDER
Fill glass with ice.
2 oz Whiskey
Fill with Hard Cider
Stir.

INCOME TAX
Fill glass with ice.
1 oz Gin
Dash of Sweet Vermouth
Dash of Dry Vermouth
Dash of Orange Juice
Dash of Bitters
Shake.
Serve or strain into chilled glass.

INDIAN SUMMER
2 oz Apple Brandy
Pinch of Sugar
Pinch of Cinnamon
Fill with hot Apple Cider.
Stir.
Garnish with Cinnamon Stick.

INDIAN SUMMER 2
Fill glass with ice.
1 oz Vodka
1 oz Coffee Brandy
2 oz Pineapple Juice
Shake.
Strain into shot glass.

INDIAN SUMMER HUMMER
Fill glass with ice.
1 oz Dark Rum
1/2 oz Apricot Brandy
1/2 oz Black Raspberry Liqueur
Fill with Pineapple Juice.
Shake.

INK STREET
Fill glass with ice.
2 oz Whiskey
Fill with equal parts Orange Juice and Sour Mix.
Shake.
Strain into chilled glass.
Garnish with Orange.

INTERNATIONAL INCIDENT
Fill glass with ice.
1/2 oz Vodka
1/2 oz Amaretto
1/2 oz Coffee Liqueur
1/2 oz Irish Cream
Shake. Strain into shot glass.

INTERNATIONAL STINGER
Fill glass with ice.
1 1/2 oz Metaxa
1/2 oz Galliano
Stir.
Serve or strain into chilled glass.

INVERTED NAIL (floater)
1 oz Drambuie (bottom)
1 oz Single Malt Scotch (top)

IRA COCKTAIL
1 1/2 oz Irish Whiskey
1 oz Irish Cream
Stir.

IRISH ANGEL
Fill glass with ice.
1 oz Irish Whiskey
1/2 oz Dark Creme De Cacao
1/2 oz White Creme De Menthe
Fill with Cream.
Shake.

IRISH BROUGUE aka
I FOR AN I
Fill glass with ice.
1 1/2 oz Irish Whiskey
1/2 oz Irish Mist
Stir.
Serve or strain into chilled glass.
Garnish with Lemon Twist.

IRISH BUCK
Fill glass with ice.
2 oz Irish Whiskey
Fill with Ginger Ale.
Garnish with Lemon Twist.

IRISH CAR BOMB (floater)
Fill shot glass with
1 oz Irish Cream (bottom)
1 oz Irish Whiskey (top)
Ignite
Drop shot glass into beer glass
3/4 filled with Stout.

IRISH COFFEE
2 oz Irish Whiskey
Fill with hot Black Coffee.
Top with Whipped Cream.
Dribble 5-6 drops of Green Creme
De Menthe on top.

IRISH COFFEE ROYALE
1 oz Irish Whiskey
1 oz Coffee Liqueur
1/2 tsp Sugar
Fill with hot Black Coffee.
Top with Whipped Cream.
Dribble 5-6 drops of Green Creme
De Menthe on top.

IRISH COW
In a saucepan:
4 oz Irish Cream
4 oz Milk
Warm on low heat
Pour into tempered glass.
Garnish with Nutmeg.

IRISH CREAM SODA
Fill glass with ice.
2 oz Irish Cream
Fill with Soda Water.

IRISH FIX
Fill glass with ice.
2 oz Irish Whiskev
1/2 oz Irish Mist
1 oz Pineapple Juice
1/2 oz Lemon Juice
or Sour Mix
1/2 tsp Sugar Syrup
Shake.
Garnish with Lemon.

IRISH FLAG (floater)
3/4 oz Green Creme De Menthe
(bottom)
3/4 oz Irish Cream
3/4 oz Orange Liqueur or Brandy
(top)

IRISH GENTLEMAN
1 oz Irish Whiskey
1 oz Irish Cream
Fill with hot Black Coffee.
Top with Whipped Cream.
Drizzle Green Creme De Menthe
on top.

IRISH HEADLOCK
1/2 oz Irish Whiskey
1/2 oz Irish Cream
1/2 oz Brandy
1/2 oz Amaretto
Shake.
Strain into chilled glass.

IRISH ICED COFFEE
Fill glass with ice.
2 oz Irish Whiskey
Fill with Iced Coffee.
Add Cream or Milk and sugar or
sweetener to taste.

IRISH ICED TEA
Fill glass with ice.
1/2 oz Vodka
1/2 oz Gin
1/2 oz Rum
1/2 oz Triple Sec
1/2 oz Melon Liqueur
Fill with Lemon-Lime Soda.

IRISH MAIDEN COFFEE
1 oz Irish Whiskey
1 oz Irish Cream
Fill with hot Black Coffee.
Top with Whipped Cream.
Dribble 1/2 oz Green Creme De
Menthe on top.

IRISH MAIDEN ICED COFFEE
Fill glass with ice.
1 oz Irish Whiskey
1 oz Irish Cream
Fill with Iced Coffee.
Sugar to taste.

IRISH MANHATTAN
(Caution: Sweet means use more
Sweet Vermouth than usual.
Dry can either mean make drink
with Dry Vermouth instead of Sweet
Vermouth or less Sweet Vermouth
than usual.
Perfect means use Sweet and Dry
Vermouth.)
Fill glass with ice.
2 oz Irish Whiskey
1/2 oz Sweet Vermouth
Stir.
Strain into chilled glass or pour
contents (with ice) into short glass.
Garnish with Cherry or Lemon
Twist.

IRISH MARIA (floater)
1 oz Tia Maria (bottom)
1 oz Irish Cream (top)

IRISH MOCHA COOLER
Fill glass with ice.
2 oz Irish Whiskey
1 oz Dark Creme De Cacao
Fill with Iced Coffee.

IRISH MONEY COFFEE
1 oz Irish Whiskey
1/2 oz Dark Creme De Cacao
Fill with hot Black Coffee.
Top with Whipped Cream.

IRISH MONK
Fill glass with ice.
1 oz Irish Cream or Irish Whiskey
1 oz Hazelnut Liqueur
Stir.

IRISH MONK COFFEE
1 oz Irish Whiskey or Irish Cream
1 oz Hazelnut Liqueur
Fill with hot Black Coffee.
Top with Whipped Cream.

IRISH ROVER
Fill glass with ice.
1 oz Irish Whiskey
1 oz Irish Cream
1 oz Coffee Liqueur
Shake.

IRISH SKIPPER COFFEE
3/4 oz Irish Mist
3/4 oz Irish Cream
3/4 oz White Creme De Cacao
Fill with hot Black Coffee.
Top with Whipped Cream.

IRISH SPRING
Fill glass with ice.
1 oz Irish Whiskey
1/2 oz Peach Schnapps
1 oz Orange Juice
1 oz Sour Mix
Shake.
Garnish with Orange and Cherry.

IRISH STINGER aka
GREEN HORNET
Fill glass with ice.
1 1/2 oz Brandy
1/2 oz Green Creme De Menthe
Stir.
Serve or strain into chilled glass.

IRON CROSS
Fill glass with ice.
1 oz Apricot Brandy
1 oz Peppermint Schnapps
Stir. Strain into shot glass.

ISRAELI COFFEE
2 oz Sabra Liqueur
Fill with hot Black Coffee.
Top with Whipped Cream.

ITALIAN COFFEE
2 oz Amaretto
Fill with hot Black Coffee.
Top with Whipped Cream.
Sprinkle with Shaved Almonds.

ITALIAN COFFEE 2
2 oz Galliano
Fill with hot Black Coffee.
Top with Whipped Cream.
Sprinkle with Cinnamon.

ITALIAN DELIGHT
Fill glass with ice.
1 oz Amaretto
1/2 oz Orange Juice
1 1/2 oz Cream
Shake.
Strain into chilled glass.
Garnish with Cherry.

ITALIAN ICED COFFEE
Fill glass with ice.
2 oz Amaretto or Galliano
Fill with Iced Coffee.
Add Cream or Milk and
sugar or sweetener to taste.

ITALIAN SCREW aka
GOLDEN SCREW
Fill glass with ice.
2 oz Galliano
Fill with Orange Juice.
Shake.

ITALIAN STALLION
Fill glass with ice.
1 1/2 oz Scotch
1/2 oz Galliano
Stir.

I

ITALIAN STALLION 2
Fill glass with ice.
1 1/2 oz Bourbon
1/2 oz Sweet Vermouth
1/2 oz Campari
Dash of Bitters
Stir.
Strain into chilled glass.
Garnish with Lemon Twist.

ITALIAN STINGER
Fill glass with ice.
1 1/2 oz Brandy
1/2 oz Galliano
Stir.
Serve or strain into chilled glass.

ITALIAN SUNRISE
Fill glass with ice.
2 oz Amaretto
Fill with Orange Juice.
Top with 1/2 oz Creme De Cassis.

ITCHY BITCHY SMELLY NELLY
Fill glass with ice.
1 oz Coconut Rum
1 oz Melon Liqueur
Fill (leaving 1/2 inch from top) with
equal parts Sour Mix and Orange
Juice.
Shake.
Top with Lemon-Lime Soda.
*The Hogettes, Hog's Breath
Saloon, Key West*

IXTAPA
Fill glass with ice.
1 1/2 oz Coffee Liqueur
1/2 oz Tequila
Stir.
Strain into chilled glass.

J. OFF (floater)
1 1/2 oz Bourbon (bottom)
1/2 oz Irish Cream (top)

JACK FROST
Fill glass with ice.
1 oz Bourbon
1 oz Peppermint Schnapps
Stir.

JACK-IN-THE-BOX
Fill glass with ice.
1 1/2 oz Apple Brandy
1 oz Pineapple Juice
Dash of Lemon Juice
2-3 dashes of Bitters
Shake.
Strain into chilled glass.

JACK ROSE
Fill glass with ice.
2 oz Apple Brandy
Dash of Grenadine
Fill with Sour Mix.
Shake.
Garnish with Lemon.

JACKALOPE
Fill glass with ice.
3/4 oz Dark Rum
3/4 oz Coffee Liqueur
3/4 oz Amaretto
3 oz Pineapple Juice
Shake.
Strain into chilled glass.
Top with 1/2 oz Dark Creme De
Cacao.

JACKARITA
Fill glass with ice.
1 1/2 oz Bourbon
1/2 oz Triple Sec
Dash of Lime Juice
3 oz Sour Mix
Dash of Orange Juice (optional)
Shake.
Serve or strain into chilled glass.

JACKHAMMER
Fill glass with ice.
1 1/2 oz Bourbon
1/2 oz Triple Sec
Fill with Sour Mix.
Shake.

JADE
Fill glass with ice.
1 1/2 oz Dark Rum
1/2 tsp Triple Sec or Curacao
1/2 tsp Green Creme De Menthe
Dash of Lime Juice
1 tsp of Powdered Sugar
or Sugar Syrup.
Shake.
Serve or strain into chilled glass.
Garnish with Lime.

JAEGER MONSTER
Fill glass with ice.
1 oz Jaegermeister
1/2 oz Amaretto
Dash of Grenadine
Fill with Orange Juice.
Shake.
Garnish with Orange.

JAEGER SALSA
Fill glass with ice.
2 oz Jaegermeister
2 tsp Salsa
Fill with Bloody Mary Mix.
Shake.
Pour into glass with salted rim
(optional).
Garnish with Lemon and/or Lime
and Celery.

JAEGERITA
Fill glass with ice.
1/2 oz Jaegermeister
1/2 oz Gold Tequila
1/2 oz Orange Liqueur
Dash of Lime Juice
Dash of Sour Mix
Shake.
Strain into chilled glass.

JAMAICA COOLER
Fill glass with ice.
2 oz Dark Rum
1/2 oz Lemon Juice or Sour Mix
2 dashes of Orange Bitters
1 tsp Sugar
Shake until sugar dissolves.
Fill with Lemon-Lime Soda.

JAMAICA ME CRAZY
Fill glass with ice.
1 1/2 oz Dark Rum
1/2 oz Coffee Liqueur
Fill with Pineapple Juice.
Shake.

JAMAICAN
Fill glass with ice.
1 oz Dark Rum
1 oz Coffee Liqueur
1 oz Lime Juice
Dash of Bitters
Fill with Lemon-Lime Soda.

JAMAICAN BOBSLED
Fill glass with ice.
1 1/2 oz Dark Rum
1/2 oz Butterscotch Schnapps
Fill with Root Beer.

JAMAICAN COFFEE
1 oz Tia Maria
1 oz Rum or Brandy
or 2 oz Tia Maria and no second
Liqueur
Fill with hot Black Coffee.
Top with Whipped Cream.
Sprinkle with Cinnamon.

JAMAICAN DELIGHT
Fill glass with ice.
1 oz Amber Rum
3/4 oz Apricot Brandy
3 oz Pineapple Juice
1/2 oz Lime Juice
1/2 oz Sugar Syrup
Shake.

JAMAICAN DUST
Fill glass with ice.
1 oz Dark Rum
1 oz Tia Maria
Fill with Pineapple Juice.
Shake.
Garnish with Lime.

JAMAICAN KISS
Fill glass with ice.
1 oz Amber Rum
1/2 oz Tia Maria
2 oz Milk
1/2 oz Sugar Syrup
Shake.

JAMAICAN MILK SHAKE (frozen)
In Blender:
1/2 cup of Ice
2 oz Bourbon
1 1/2 oz Dark Rum
Scoop of Vanilla Ice Cream
Dash of vanilla extract
Blend until smooth.
If too thick add Milk.
If too thin add ice or Ice Cream.

JAMAICAN MULE
Fill glass with ice.
1 oz Light Rum
1 oz Dark Rum
1/2 oz Amaretto
Fill with Ginger Beer.
Stir.

JAMAICAN PINE
Fill glass with ice.
2 oz Dark Rum
Fill with Pineapple Juice.
Garnish with Lime.

JAMAICAN TEN SPEED
Fill glass with ice.
1/2 oz Vodka
1/2 oz Coconut Rum
1/2 oz Banana Liqueur
1/2 oz Melon Liqueur
1/2 oz Irish Cream
Shake. Strain into shot glass.

JAMAICAN WIND
Fill glass with ice.
1 1/2 oz Dark Rum
1/2 oz Coffee Liqueur
Stir.

JAPANESE FIZZ
Fill glass with ice.
2 oz Whiskey
3/4 oz Port
1/2 oz Lemon Juice
1 tsp Sugar Syrup
1 Egg White (optional)
Shake.
Fill glass with Soda Water.
Garnish with Pineapple and/or
Orange.

JAWBREAKER
Fill shot glass with
Cinnamon Schnapps
Add 4-5 drops of Tabasco Sauce.
Stir.

JAY WALKER
Fill glass with ice.
1 oz Rum
1/2 oz Triple Sec
Fill with Equal parts Sour Mix and
Pineapple Juice.
Shake.
Top with 1/2 oz 151-Proof Rum.

I

J

JELLY BEAN
Fill glass with ice.
1 oz Anisette or Sambuca
1 oz Blackberry Brandy
Stir.

JELLY BEAN (floater)
1/2 oz Blackberry Brandy or
Grenadine (bottom)
1/2 oz Anisette or Sambuca
1/2 oz Southern Comfort (top)

JELLY DOUGHNUT
Fill glass with ice.
1 1/2 oz Irish Cream
1/2 oz Black Raspberry Liqueur
Stir.

JELLY FISH (floater)
1 1/2 oz White Creme De Cacao or
Creme De Menthe (bottom)
1/2 oz Irish Cream
1/2 oz Amaretto (top)
Place 2-3 drops of Grenadine in
center of glass.

JENNY WALLBANGER
Fill glass with ice.
1 1/2 oz Vodka
Fill with equal parts Orange Juice
and Milk or Cream.
Shake.
Top with 1/2 oz Galliano

JEWEL
Fill glass with ice.
3/4 oz Gin
3/4 oz Sweet Vermouth
3/4 oz Green Chartreuse
1-3 dashes of Orange Bitters
Shake.
Serve or strain into chilled glass.
Garnish with a Lemon Twist.

JEWEL OF THE NILE
Fill glass with ice.
2 oz Gin
1/2 oz Green Chartreuse
1/2 oz Yellow Chartreuse
Stir.

JEZEBEL (floater)
1 1/2 oz Southern Comfort (bottom)
1/2 oz Irish Cream (top)

JIGGY COCKFIGHTER
Fill glass with ice.
1 1/2 oz Rum
1/2 oz Gin
1/2 oz Tequila
Fill with equal parts Sour Mix
and Orange Juice.
Shake.

JIZZ
Fill glass with ice.
1 1/2 oz Cognac
1/2 oz Irish Cream
1 oz Cream
Shake. Strain into shot glass.

JOCKEY CLUB
Fill glass with ice.
1 1/2 oz Gin
1/4 oz White Creme De Cacao
1/2 oz Lemon Juice
Dash of Bitters
Shake.
Strain into chilled glass.

**JOE COLLINS aka MIKE
COLLINS, SCOTCH COLLINS**
Fill glass with ice.
2 oz Scotch
Fill with Sour Mix.
Shake.
Dash of Soda Water
Garnish with Cherry and Orange.

JOHN COLLINS
Fill glass with ice.
2 oz Whiskey
Fill with Sour Mix.
Shake.
Dash of Soda Water
Garnish with Cherry and Orange.

JOHNNIE
Fill glass with ice.
1 1/2 oz Sloe Gin
3/4 oz Orange Liqueur or Triple Sec
or Curacao
1 tsp Anisette
Shake.
Strain into chilled glass.

JOLL-E RANCHER
Fill glass with ice.
1 oz Peach Schnapps
1 oz Apple Brandy
Fill with Cranberry Juice.

JOLLY ROGER
Fill glass with ice.
1 oz Rum
1 oz Drambuie
1/2 oz Lime Juice
Dash of Scotch
Shake.
Fill with Soda Water.

JOLLY ROGER 2
Fill glass with ice.
1 oz Dark Rum
1 oz Banana Liqueur
2 oz Lemon Juice
Shake.

JOSÉ WALLBANGER
Fill glass with ice.
1 1/2 oz Tequila
Fill with Orange Juice.
Top with 1/2 oz Galliano.

JUDGE, JR.
Fill glass with ice.
1 oz Gin
1 oz Rum
Dash of Grenadine
1/2 oz Lemon Juice
Shake.
Strain into chilled glass.

JUICY FRUIT
Fill glass with ice.
1 oz Vodka
1/2 oz Peach Schnapps
1/2 oz Melon Liqueur
Fill with Pineapple Juice.
Shake.

JUMP ME
Fill glass with ice.
2 oz Dark Rum
3 dashes of Bitters
Fill with Pineapple Juice.
Squeeze 2 lime wedges over drink.
Stir.

JUMP STARTER
Fill glass with ice.
2 oz Dark Rum
Fill with Jolt Cola.
Stir.

JUMP UP AND KISS ME
Fill glass with ice.
1 1/2 oz Light Rum
1/2 oz Galliano
1/2 oz Apricot Brandy
1/2 Egg White
Dash of Sour Mix
Fill with equal parts Orange and
Pineapple Juice.
Shake.

JUMP UP AND KISS ME 2
Fill glass with ice.
1 1/2 oz Dark Rum
Dash of Bitters
1/2 oz Lime Juice
Fill with Pineapple Juice.
Shake.
Garnish with Pineapple and Lime.

JUMPER CABLE aka SPEEDY
Fill glass with ice.
2 oz 151-Proof Rum
Fill with Jolt Cola
Stir.
Garnish with Lime.

JUNGLE JIM aka
YELLOW RUSSIAN
Fill glass with ice.
1 oz Vodka
1 oz Banana Liqueur
Fill with Milk or Cream.
Shake.

JUNE BUG
Fill glass with ice.
3/4 oz Banana Liqueur
3/4 oz Melon Liqueur
3/4 oz Peach Schnapps
Fill with equal parts Pineapple
and Cranberry Juice.
Shake.

JUPITER COCKTAIL
Fill glass with ice.
1 1/2 oz Gin
1/2 oz Dry Vermouth
1 tsp Parfait Amour
or Creme De Violette
1 tsp Orange Juice
Shake.
Strain into chilled glass.

KABUKI
Fill glass with ice.
1 1/2 oz Sake
1/2 oz Triple Sec
Dash of Lime Juice
1 oz Sour Mix
Shake.
Strain into chilled glass.

KAHLUA CLUB aka COBRA
Fill glass with ice.
2 oz Coffee Liqueur
Fill with Soda Water.
Garnish with Lime.

KAHLUA COFFEE
aka MEXICAN COFFEE
2 oz Coffee Liqueur
Fill with hot Black Coffee
Top with Whipped Cream.
Sprinkle with Shaved
Chocolate or Sprinkles.

KAHLUA SOMBRERO
Fill glass with ice.
2 oz Coffee Liqueur
Fill with Milk or Cream.
Shake.

KAHLUA SOUR
Fill glass with ice.
2 oz Coffee Liqueur
Fill with Sour Mix.
Shake.
Garnish with Cherry and Orange.

KAMIKAZE aka BULLFROG
Fill glass with ice.
2 oz Vodka
1/2 oz Triple Sec
1 oz Lime Juice
Shake.
Serve or strain into chilled glass.
Garnish with Lime.

J
K

KAPPA COLADA (frozen)
In Blender:
1/2 cup of Ice
2 oz Brandy
2 tbsp Cream of Coconut
1/2 cup of fresh or canned
Pineapple
1 tbsp Vanilla Ice Cream
Blend until smooth.
If too thick add fruit or juice.
If too thin add ice or Ice Cream.
Garnish with Pineapple and Cherry.

KATINKA
Fill glass with ice.
1 1/2 oz Vodka
1/2 oz Apricot Brandy
1/2 oz Lime Juice
Stir.
Strain into chilled glass.
Garnish with mint sprig.

KENTUCKY COCKTAIL
Fill glass with ice.
2 oz Bourbon
1 oz Pineapple Juice
Shake.
Strain into chilled glass.

KENTUCKY COFFEE
2 oz Bourbon
1/2 tsp Sugar
Fill with hot Black Coffee.
Top with Whipped Cream
or float high-Proof Bourbon
on top and ignite.

KENTUCKY COLONEL
Fill glass with ice.
1 1/2 oz Bourbon
1/2 oz Benedictine
Stir.
Serve or strain into chilled glass.
Garnish with Lemon Twist.

KENTUCKY COOLER
Fill glass with ice.
1 1/2 oz Bourbon
1/2 oz Brandy
1 oz Sour Mix
2 tsp of Sugar Syrup
Shake.
Fill with Soda Water.
Float 1/4 oz Dark Rum on top.

KENTUCKY ORANGE BLOSSOM
Fill glass with ice.
1 1/2 oz Bourbon
1/2 oz Triple Sec
1 oz Orange Juice
Shake.
Garnish with Lemon.

KENTUCKY SCREWDRIVER
aka BLACK-EYED SUSAN, YELLOW JACKET
Fill glass with ice.
2 oz Bourbon
Fill with Orange Juice.

KENTUCKY SUNRISE
Fill glass with ice.
2 oz Bourbon
Fill with Orange Juice.
Pour 1/2 oz Grenadine down spoon
To bottom of glass.

KENTUCKY SWAMPWATER
Fill glass with ice.
2 oz Bourbon
1/2 oz Blue Curacao
Dash of Sour Mix
Fill with Orange Juice.

KENTUCKY WINDAGE
Fill glass with ice.
2 oz Bourbon
Dash of Lime Juice
Fill with Lemonade.
Shake.

KEOKE CAPPUCCINO
1/2 oz Coffee Liqueur
1/2 oz Cognac or Brandy
1/2 oz Dark Creme De Cacao
Fill with Espresso.
Top with Steamed Milk.
Sprinkle with Powdered Cacao.

KEOKE COFFEE
3/4 oz Coffee Liqueur
3/4 oz Cognac or Brandy
3/4 oz Dark Creme De Cacao
Fill with hot Black Coffee.
Top with Whipped Cream.
Sprinkle with Cinnamon.

KERRY COOLER
Fill glass with ice.
2 oz Irish Whiskey
1 1/2 oz Sherry
1 oz Orgeat Syrup
1 oz Lemon Juice or Sour Mix
Shake.
Fill with Soda Water.

KEY LARGO (frozen)
In Blender:
1/2 cup of Ice
2 oz Dark Rum
1 oz Cream of Coconut
Scoop of Orange Sherbet
Blend until smooth.
Garnish with Orange.

KEY LIME PIE (frozen)
In Blender:
1 cup of Ice
2 oz Light Rum
3 tbsp frozen concentrated
Limeade
Dash of Lime Juice
Blend until smooth.
Garnish with Lime and
a Graham Cracker.

KEY LIME SHOOTER
Fill glass with ice.
1 oz Rum or Vodka
1 oz Licor 43
Dash of Sour Mix
Dash of Cream
Dash of Orange Juice
Dash of Lime Juice
Shake.
Strain into chilled glass.

KEY WEST
Fill glass with ice.
1 oz Dark Rum
1/2 oz Banana Liqueur
1/2 oz Black Raspberry Liqueur
Fill with equal parts Sour Mix and
Orange Juice.
Shake.
Top with Soda Water.
Garnish with Cherry and Orange.

KGB
Fill glass with ice.
1 1/2 oz Gin
1/4 oz Kirschwasser
Dash of Apricot Brandy
Dash of Lemon Juice
Shake.
Strain into chilled glass.
Garnish with Lemon Twist.

KILLER BEE (floater)
1 oz Bärenjägur (bottom)
1 oz Jaegermeister (top)

KILLER COOL AID
Fill glass with ice.
1/4 oz Vodka
1/4 oz Gin
1/4 oz Rum
1/4 oz Black Raspberry Liqueur
Dash of Sour Mix
Fill with Cranberry Juice.

KILLER COOL AID (floater)
2 oz Cranberry Juice (bottom)
1/2 oz Amaretto
1/2 oz Peach Schnapps
1 oz Vodka (top)

KILLER WHALE
Fill glass with ice.
1 oz Vodka
1 oz Rum
1/2 oz Black Raspberry Liqueur
1/2 oz Triple Sec
Fill with equal parts Cranberry
and Orange Juice.
Shake.
Top with Lemon-Lime Soda.

KING ALPHONSE (floater)
2 oz Coffee Liqueur (bottom)
1 oz Cream (top)

KING COBRA
Fill glass with ice.
1 oz Rum
1 oz Coffee Liqueur
Fill with Soda Water.
Garnish with Lime.

KING KONG COFFEE
3/4 oz Cognac or Brandy
3/4 oz Coffee Liqueur
3/4 oz Orange Liqueur
Fill with hot Black Coffee.
Top with Whipped Cream.
Garnish with Orange and
Cinnamon.

KING'S CUP
Fill glass with ice.
1 oz Galliano
1 oz Amaretto
Fill with Milk.
Shake.

KING'S PEG
Fill glass half full with ice.
2 oz Cognac or Brandy
Fill with Champagne.

KINGSTON COFFEE
1/2 oz Dark Rum
1/2 oz Coffee Liqueur
1/2 oz Irish Cream
1/2 oz Chocolate Syrup
Fill with hot Black Coffee.
Top with Whipped Cream.
Drizzle with Chocolate Syrup.

KIOLOA
Fill glass with ice.
1 oz Coffee Liqueur
1/2 oz Amber Rum
1 oz Cream
Shake.

KIR
1/2 oz Creme De Cassis
Fill with White Wine.
Garnish with Lemon Twist.

KIR ROYALE
1/2 oz Black Raspberry Liqueur
Fill with Champagne.
Garnish with Lemon Twist.

KISS
Fill glass with ice.
1 1/2 oz Vodka
1/2 oz Chocolate Liqueur
1/4 oz Cherry Liqueur
3/4 oz Cream or Milk
Shake.
Strain into chilled glass.

KISS IN THE DARK
Fill glass with ice.
3/4 oz Gin
3/4 oz Cherry Brandy
1/2 oz Dry Vermouth
Shake.
Strain into chilled glass.

K

KISS ME QUICK
Fill glass with ice.
2 oz Pernod
1/2 oz Curacao
3 dashes of Bitters
Stir.
Fill with Soda Water.

KISS THE BOYS GOODBYE
Fill glass with ice.
1 oz Sloe Gin
1 oz Brandy
1/4 oz Lemon Juice
1/2 Egg White
Shake.
Strain into chilled glass.

KIWI
Fill glass with ice.
1 oz Banana Liqueur
1 oz Strawberry Liqueur
Fill with Orange Juice.
Shake.

KLONDIKE COOLER
Fill glass with ice.
2 oz Whiskey
Dash of Orange Juice
Fill with Ginger Ale
or Soda Water.
Garnish with Lemon Twist or
Orange Twist.

KNICKERBOCKER
Fill glass with ice.
1 1/2 oz Gin
1/2 oz Dry Vermouth
1 tsp Sweet Vermouth
Stir.
Strain into chilled glass.

KOMANIWANALAYA
Fill glass with ice.
1/2 oz 151-Proof Rum
1/2 oz Amaretto
1 oz Pineapple Juice
1 oz Cranberry Juice
Shake.
Strain into chilled glass.
Top with 1/2 oz Dark Rum.

KOWLOON
Fill glass with ice.
1 oz Orange Liqueur
1 oz Coffee Liqueur
Fill with Orange Juice.
Shake.
Garnish with Orange.

KREMLIN COCKTAIL
Fill glass with ice.
1 oz Vodka
1 oz White Creme De Cacao
1 oz Cream
Shake.
Strain into chilled glass.

KRETCHMA
Fill glass with ice.
1 oz Vodka
1 oz White Creme De Cacao
Dash of Grenadine
1 tbsp Lemon Juice
Shake.
Strain into chilled glass.

KUNG FU
Fill glass with ice.
1oz Jaegermeister
1oz Pisang Ambon
Fill with Cola.

KUWAITI COOLER
Fill glass with ice.
1 oz Melon Liqueur
1 oz Key Largo Schnapps
Dash of Sour Mix
Shake.
Strain into chilled glass.
Fill with Soda Water.

KYOTO
Fill glass with ice.
1 1/2 oz Gin
1/2 oz Dry Vermouth
1/2 oz Melon Liqueur
or Apricot Brandy
1/2 oz Triple Sec
Dash of Lemon Juice (optional)
Shake.
Strain into chilled glass.

L. A. SUNRISE
Fill glass with ice.
1 1/2 oz Vodka
1/2 oz Banana Liqueur
Fill with Equal parts Orange
and Pineapple Juice.
Shake.
Float 1/2 oz Dark Rum on top.

L.A.P.D.
Fill glass with ice.
1 oz Gold Tequila
1/2 oz Blue Curacao
1/4 oz Grenadine
Stir.
Strain into chilled glass.

L. S. D.
Fill glass with ice.
1 oz Scotch
1 oz Drambuie
1 oz Lemonade
Shake.
Strain into chilled glass.

LA BAMBA
Fill glass with ice.
1 1/2 oz Tequila
1/2 oz Orange Liqueur
Fill with equal parts Pineapple and
Orange Juice.
Shake.
Strain into chilled glass.
Top with Grenadine.

LA JOLLA
Fill glass with ice.
1 1/2 oz Brandy
1/2 oz Banana Liqueur
1 tsp Orange Juice
2 tsp Lemon Juice or Sour Mix
Shake.
Strain into chilled glass.

LA MOSCA
Either fill pony glass with Sambuca or
3 oz Sambuca in Brandy snifter.
Add 3 Coffee Beans, for health wealth
and happiness.

LADIES
Fill glass with ice.
1 1/2 oz Whiskey
1 tsp Anisette
1/2 tsp Pernod
2 dashes of Bitters
Shake.
Strain into chilled glass.
Garnish with Pineapple.

LADY BE GOOD
Fill glass with ice.
1 1/2 oz Brandy
1/2 oz White Creme De Menthe
1/2 oz Sweet Vermouth
Shake.
Strain into chilled glass.

LADY LUCK
Fill glass with ice.
3/4 oz Coconut Rum
3/4 oz Black Raspberry Liqueur
3/4 oz Banana Liqueur
Shake.
Strain into chilled glass.

LADYFINGER
Fill glass with ice.
1 oz Gin
1/2 oz Kirschwasser
1/2 oz Cherry Brandy
Shake.
Strain into chilled glass.

LAKE STREET LEMONADE
Fill glass with ice.
1 1/2 oz Vodka
1/2 oz Amaretto
Fill with Lemonade.
Stir.
Garnish with Lemon.

LALLAH ROOKH
Fill glass with ice.
1 1/2 oz Rum
3/4 oz Cognac or Brandy
1/2 oz Creme De Vanilla or Vanilla
Extract
1 tsp Sugar Syrup
Shake.
Top with Whipped Cream.

LAS BRISAS (frozen)
In Blender:
1/2 cup of Ice
1 oz Vodka
1 oz Coconut Rum
1/2 cup fresh or canned Pineapple
1/2 scoop Vanilla Ice Cream
Blend until smooth.

LASER BEAM
Fill glass with ice.
1 oz Bourbon
1 oz Southern Comfort
Fill with Cranberry Juice.
Stir.

LASER BEAM 2
Fill glass with ice.
1/2 oz Bourbon
1/2 oz Tequila
1/2 oz Amaretto
1/2 oz Triple Sec
Fill with Sour Mix.
Shake
Garnish with Lemon and Cherry.

LASER BEAM 3
Fill glass with ice.
1/2 oz Vodka
1/2 oz Southern Comfort
1/2 oz Melon Liqueur
1/2 oz Amaretto
1/2 oz Orange Liqueur
2 oz Sour Mix
Shake.
Fill with Lemon-Lime Soda.

LASKY
Fill glass with ice.
3/4 oz Gin
3/4 oz Swedish Punch
3/4 oz Grape Juice
Shake.
Serve or strain into chilled glass.

LATIN LOVER
Fill glass with ice.
1 1/2 oz Tequila
1/2 oz Amaretto
Stir.

LAWHILL
Fill glass with ice.
1 1/2 oz Whiskey
1/2 oz Dry Vermouth
1/4 oz Pernod
1/4 oz Cherry Liqueur
1/2 oz Orange Juice
Dash of Bitters
Shake.
Strain into chilled glass.

LAYER CAKE aka
FIFTH AVENUE (floater)
3/4 oz Dark Creme De Cacao (bottom)
3/4 oz Apricot Brandy
1/2 oz Milk (top)

K
L

LATIN LOVER
Fill glass with ice.
1 oz Tequila
1 oz Spiced Rum
Dash of Lime Juice
Fill with Pineapple Juice.
Shake.

LEAF
Fill glass with ice.
1 oz Light Rum
1 oz Melon Liqueur
1 oz Cream
Shake.
Strain into chilled glass.

LEAP FROG
Fill glass with ice.
2 oz Gin
1/2 oz Lemon Juice
Fill with Ginger Ale.
Garnish with Lemon.

LEAP YEAR
Fill glass with ice.
1 1/2 oz Gin
1/2 oz Orange Liqueur or Triple Sec
1/2 oz Sweet Vermouth
1 tsp Lemon Juice
Stir.
Strain into chilled glass.

LEAVE IT TO ME
Fill glass with ice.
1 oz Gin
1/2 oz Apricot Brandy
1/2 oz Dry Vermouth
1/4 oz Lemon Juice
1/4 oz Grenadine
Shake.
Strain into chilled glass.

LEBANESE COFFEE
1 oz Apricot Brandy
1 oz Coffee Liqueur
Fill with hot Black Coffee.
Top with Whipped Cream.

'LECTRIC LEMONADE
Fill glass with ice.
1/2 oz Vodka
1/2 oz Gin
1/2 oz Light Rum
1/2 oz Tequila
1/2 oz Triple Sec
2 oz Sour Mix
Shake.
Fill with Lemon-Lime Soda.

LEFT BANK
Fill glass with ice.
1 oz Irish Cream
1 oz Black Raspberry Liqueur
Stir.

LEFT-HANDED SCREWDRIVER
Fill glass with ice.
2 oz Gin
Fill with Orange Juice.
Stir.
Garnish with Orange or Lime.

LEG SPREADER
Fill glass with ice.
1 oz Galliano
1 oz Coffee Liqueur
Strain into chilled glass.

LEG SPREADER 2
Fill glass with ice.
1 oz Grain Alcohol
1 oz Black Raspberry Liqueur
Stir.

LEISURE SUIT
Fill glass with ice.
1 oz Banana Liqueur
1 oz Galliano
Fill with equal parts Orange,
Cranberry and Pineapple Juice.

LEMON DROP
Moisten inside of shot glass with
Lemon Juice.
Coat inside of glass with Sugar.
Fill shot glass with chilled Vodka.

LEMON DROP 2
Fill shot glass with Citrus Vodka.
Coat Lemon wedge with Sugar.

LEMON FRAPPE
Fill large stemmed glass (Red Wine
glass, Champagne saucer) with
crushed ice.
1 oz Tuaca
1 oz Sour Mix

LEMON SLUSH (frozen)
In Blender:
1 cup of Ice
2 oz Vodka
3 tbsp Lemonade concentrate
Blend until smooth.

LEMONADE (modern)
Fill glass with ice.
1 1/2 oz Sloe Gin
1 1/2 oz Sherry
1 oz Sugar Syrup
or 1 tsp Powdered Sugar
2 oz Lemon Juice
Shake.
Top with Soda Water.

LEPRECHAUN
Fill glass with ice.
2 oz Irish Whiskey
Fill with Tonic Water.
Garnish with a Lemon Twist.

LEPRECHAUN 2
Fill glass with ice.
1 oz Vodka
1/2 oz Peach Schnapps
1/2 oz Blue Curacao
Fill with Orange Juice.

LESLIE
3 oz White Wine
3 oz Cranberry juice
3 oz Lemon-Lime Soda
Garnish with Lemon and Lime.

LETHAL INJECTION
Fill glass with ice.
1/2 oz Dark Rum
1/2 oz Spiced Rum
1/2 oz Coconut Rum
1/2 oz Amaretto
or Creme De Nouyax
1 oz Orange Juice
1 oz Pineapple Juice
Shake.
Strain into chilled glass.

LEWINSKY (floater)
1 1/2 oz Jaegermeister (bottom)
1/2 oz Irish Cream (top)

LIBERTY COCKTAIL
Fill glass with ice.
1 1/2 oz Apple Brandy
3/4 oz Rum
1/4 tsp Sugar Syrup
Stir.
Strain into chilled glass.
Garnish with Cherry.

LICORICE STICK
Fill glass with ice.
1 1/2 oz Anisette
Fill with Milk or Cream.
Top with 1/2 oz Galliano.
Stir with Licorice Stick.

LICORICE WHIP (floater)
3/4 oz Coffee Liqueur (bottom)
3/4 oz Irish Cream
3/4 oz Ouzo (top)

LIEBFRAUMILCH
Fill glass with ice.
1 1/2 oz White Creme De Cacao
1 1/2 oz Cream or Milk
1/2 oz Lime Juice
Shake.
Strain into chilled glass.

LIFE LINE
Fill glass with ice.
1 oz Rum
1/2 oz Brandy
1/2 oz Apricot Brandy
1/2 oz Triple Sec
1/2 oz Sweet Vermouth
1/2 oz Lemon juice
Shake.
Strain into chilled glass.

LIFE-SAVER (floater)
1 oz Banana Liqueur (bottom)
1 oz Blackberry Brandy (top)

LIFE-SAVOR
Fill glass with ice.
1/2 oz Triple Sec
1/2 oz Melon Liqueur
1/2 oz Coconut Rum
Fill with Orange Juice.
Shake.

LIFESAVER
Fill glass with ice.
1 1/2 oz Coconut Rum
1/2 oz Melon Liqueur
Fill with Pineapple Juice
Shake.

LIGHTHOUSE
Fill glass with ice.
1/2 oz Tequila
1/2 oz Coffee Liqueur
1/2 oz Peppermint Schnapps
Stir.
Strain into chilled glass.
Top with 1/2 oz 151-Proof Rum.

LILLET NOUYAX
Fill glass with ice.
1 1/2 oz Lillet Blanc
1/2 oz Gin
1 tsp Creme De Nouyax
Shake.
Strain into chilled glass.
Garnish with Orange Twist.

LIMBO
Fill glass with ice.
2 oz Rum
1/2 oz Banana Liqueur
1 oz Orange Juice
Shake.
Strain into chilled glass.

LIME RICKEY
Fill glass with ice.
1 1/2 oz Gin
1/2 oz Lime Juice
Fill with Soda Water.
Stir.
Garnish with Lime.

LINSTEAD
Fill glass with ice.
1 1/2 oz Whiskey
Dash of Pernod
1 oz Pineapple Juice
Dash of Lemon Juice
3 dashes of Bitters (optional)
Shake.
Strain into chilled glass.

LION TAMER
Fill glass with ice.
3/4 oz Southern Comfort
1/4 oz Lime Juice
Stir.
Strain into chilled glass.

L

LIQUID ASPHALT (floater)
1 oz Sambuca (bottom)
1 oz Jaegermeister (top)

LIQUID COCA
Fill glass with ice.
3/4 oz 151-Proof Rum
3/4 oz 100-Proof Peppermint
Schnapps
3/4 oz Jaegermeister
Stir.
Strain into chilled glass.

LIQUID CRACK
Fill glass with ice.
1/2 oz 151-Proof Rum
1/2 oz 100-proof Peppermint
Schnapps
1/2 oz Jaegermeister
1/2 oz Cinnamon Schnapps
Shake. Strain into chilled glass.

LIQUID PANTS REMOVER
Fill glass with ice.
1/2 oz Vodka
1/2 oz Dark Rum
1/2 oz Southern Comfort
1/2 oz Amaretto
1/2 oz Tequila
Fill with Cola.
Garnish with Cherry.

LIQUID VALIUM
Fill glass with ice.
1 oz Vodka
1/2 oz Peppermint Schnapps
Stir.

LITHIUM
Fill glass with ice.
2 oz Vodka
Tbsp Sugar
Fill with Milk.
Shake.

LITTLE DEVIL
Fill glass with ice.
1 oz Gin
1 oz Rum
1/2 oz Triple Sec
1/2 oz Lemon Juice
or Sour Mix
Shake.
Strain into chilled glass.

LITTLE GREEN MEN
1 oz Sambuca
1 oz Melon Liqueur

LITTLE PRINCESS
Fill glass with ice.
1 1/2 oz Rum
1 1/2 oz Sweet Vermouth
Shake.
Strain into chilled glass.

LITTLE PURPLE MEN
1 oz Sambuca
1 oz Black Raspberry Liqueur

LOBOTOMY
Fill glass with ice.
1 oz Amaretto
1 oz Black Raspberry Liqueur
1 oz Pineapple Juice
Shake.
Strain into chilled glass.
Fill with Champagne.

LOCH NESS MONSTER aka NESI
(floater)
1/2 oz Melon Liqueur (bottom)
1/2 oz Irish Cream
1/2 oz Jaegermeister (top)

LOLITA
Fill glass with ice.
1 1/2 oz Tequila
1/4 oz Lime Juice
1 tsp Honey
3-4 dashes of Bitters
Stir.

LOLLIPOP
Fill glass with ice.
3/4 oz Orange Liqueur
3/4 oz Kirschwasser
3/4 oz Green Chartreuse
Dash of Maraschino Liqueur
Shake.

LONDON SOUR
Fill glass with ice.
2 oz Scotch
Dash of Orange Curacao
or Triple Sec
Dash of Orange Juice
Fill with Sour Mix.
Shake.

**LONDON SPECIAL aka
CHAMPAGNE COCKTAIL**
In a Champagne glass:
1/2 tsp Sugar or 1 Sugar Cube
2 dashes of Bitters
Fill with Champagne.
Garnish with Lemon or Orange Twist.

LONDON STINGER
Fill glass with ice.
1 1/2 oz Gin
1/2 oz White Creme De Menthe
Stir.
Serve or strain into chilled glass.

LONE TREE
Fill glass with ice.
3/4 oz Gin
3/4 oz Dry Vermouth
3/4 oz Sweet Vermouth
3 dashes of Orange Bitters
Stir.
Strain into chilled glass.
Garnish with Olive.

LONG BEACH ICED TEA
Fill glass with ice.
1/2 oz Vodka
1/2 oz Gin
1/2 oz Rum
1/2 oz Tequila
1/2 oz Triple Sec
1 oz Orange Juice
Fill with equal parts Sour Mix and
Cranberry Juice.
Top with Cola (optional).
Garnish with Lemon.

LONG COMFORTABLE SCREW AGAINST THE WALL
Fill glass with ice.
3/4 oz Gin
3/4 oz Vodka
3/4 oz Southern Comfort
Fill with Orange Juice.
Shake.
Top with 1/2 oz Galliano

LONG HOT NIGHT
Fill glass with ice.
2 oz Bourbon
Fill with equal parts Pineapple and
Cranberry Juice.

LONG ISLAND ICED TEA
Fill glass with ice.
1/2 oz Vodka
1/2 oz Gin
1/2 oz Rum
1/2 oz Tequila
1/2 oz Triple Sec
1 oz Sour Mix
Top with Cola.
Garnish with Lemon.

LONG ISLAND LEMONADE
Fill glass with ice.
1/2 oz Vodka
1/2 oz Gin
1/2 oz Rum
1/2 oz Tequila
1/2 oz Triple Sec
1 oz Sour Mix
Top with Lemon-Lime Soda.
Garnish with Lemon.

LONG SLOE COMFORTABLE FUZZY SCREW AGAINST THE WALL WITH A KISS
Fill glass with ice.
1/2 oz Gin
1/2 oz Sloe Gin
1/2 oz Southern Comfort
1/2 oz Peach Schnapps
Fill with Orange Juice.
Top with 1/2 oz Galliano.
Dash of Amaretto.

LONG SLOE COMFORTABLE FUZZY SCREW AGAINST THE WALL WITH SATIN PILLOWS THE HARD WAY
Fill glass with ice.
1/2 oz Gin
1/2 oz Sloe Gin
1/2 oz Southern Comfort
1/2 oz Peach Schnapps
Fill with Orange Juice
Shake.
Top with 1/2 oz Galliano
Dash of Frangelico
Dash of Whiskey

LOOK OUT BELOW
Fill glass with ice.
1 1/2 oz 151-Proof Rum
2 tsp Lime Juice
1 tsp Grenadine
Shake.

LOS ANGELES COCKTAIL
Fill glass with ice.
2 oz Whiskey
2-3 dashes of Sweet Vermouth
1/2 oz Lemon Juice
1 oz Sugar Syrup
1/2 raw Egg
Shake.

LOS ANGELES ICED TEA
Fill glass with ice.
1/2 oz Vodka
1/2 oz Gin
1/2 oz Rum
1/2 oz Tequila
1/2 oz Melon Liqueur
2 oz Sour Mix
Fill with Lemon-Lime Soda.
Garnish with Lemon.

LOUDSPEAKER
Fill glass with ice.
1 oz Gin
1 oz Brandy
1/4 oz Orange Liqueur
1/2 oz Lemon Juice
Stir.
Strain into chilled glass.

LOUISIANA SHOOTER aka OYSTER SHOT
In shot glass:
1 raw Oyster
1-3 dashes of Hot Sauce
1/4 tsp Horseradish
Fill with Vodka or Peppermint
Vodka.

LOUNGE LIZARD
Fill glass with ice.
1 1/2 oz Dark Rum
1/2 oz Amaretto
Fill with Cola.
Stir.

L

LOVE
Fill glass with ice.
4 oz Sloe Gin
1 Egg White
1 oz Lemon Juice
1/2 oz Raspberry Syrup or
Grenadine
Shake.
Strain into two chilled glass.

LOVE POTION (frozen)
In Blender:
1 cup of Ice
1 oz Rum
1 oz Banana Liqueur
1/2 oz Triple Sec
1 oz Orange Juice
1 oz Pineapple Juice
1/2 peeled ripe Banana
Blend 2-5 seconds on low
speed.
Garnish with Orange,
Pineapple and Banana.

LOVE POTION #9 (frozen)
In Blender:
1/2 cup of Ice
1 oz Vodka
1/2 oz White Creme De Cacao
1/2 cup fresh or frozen
Strawberries
Scoop of Vanilla Ice Cream
Blend until smooth.
If too thick add berries or Milk.
If too thin add ice or Ice Cream.
Garnish with strawberry.

LUAU
Fill glass with ice.
1 oz Coconut Rum
1 oz Maui Schnapps
Fill with Pineapple Juice.
Shake.
Garnish with Pineapple and Cherry.

LUBE JOB
Fill glass with ice.
1 oz Vodka
1 oz Irish Cream
Stir.

LUGER
Fill glass with ice.
1 oz Brandy
1 oz Apple Brandy
Shake.
Strain into chilled glass.

LYNCHBURG LEMONADE
Fill glass with ice.
2 oz Bourbon
1/2 oz Triple Sec
Dash of Sour Mix (optional)
Fill with Lemon-Lime Soda.

M-16 (floater)
1/2 oz Tia Maria (bottom)
1/2 oz Irish Cream
1/2 oz Cointreau (top)

MAC DADDY
Fill glass with ice.
1 1/2 oz Gin
1/2 oz Cherry Liqueur
Fill with Pineapple Juice.
Shake.

MACAROON
Fill glass with ice.
1 oz Black Raspberry Liqueur
1 oz Cookies and Cream Liqueur
Stir.

MACKENZIE GOLD
Fill glass with ice.
2 oz Yukon Jack
Fill with Grapefruit Juice.

MAD COW
Fill glass with ice.
1 oz 151-Proof Rum or Grain
Alcohol
1 oz Coffee Liqueur
1 oz Milk or Cream
Shake. Strain into shot glass.

MAD MAX
Fill glass with ice.
3 oz Champagne
Dash of Black Raspberry Liqueur
Fill with equal parts Cranberry and
Orange Juice.
Garnish with Orange.

MAD MONK
1 oz Hazelnut Liqueur
1 oz Peppermint Schnapps
Fill with equal parts Hot Chocolate
and hot Coffee.
Top with Whipped Cream.
Sprinkle with Shaved
Chocolate or Sprinkles.

MADEIRA COCKTAIL
Fill glass with ice.
1 1/2 oz Whiskey
1 1/2 oz Madeira
1 tsp Grenadine
Dash of Lemon Juice
Shake.
Garnish with Lemon.

MADRAS aka
CALIFORNIA BREEZE
Fill glass with ice.
2 oz Vodka
Fill with equal parts Orange and
Cranberry Juice.
Stir.
Garnish with Orange or Lime.

MADTOWN MILKSHAKE
In Blender:
1/2 cup of Ice
3/4 oz Irish Cream
3/4 oz Black Raspberry Liqueur
3/4 oz Hazelnut Liqueur
1/2 scoop Vanilla Ice Cream
Blend until smooth.
If too thick add Milk.
If too thin add ice or Ice Cream.

MAGGOT
Pour both liqueurs at the same time on opposite sides of shot glass.
1 oz Irish Cream
1 oz Green Creme De Menthe

MAI TAI (frozen)
In Blender:
1 cup of Ice
1 oz Light Rum
1/2 oz Dark Rum
1/2 oz Apricot Brandy
1/2 cup of fresh or canned Pineapple
Splash of Sour Mix
Splash Orange Juice
Blend for 3-4 seconds on low speed.
Top with Dark Rum.
Garnish with Lime and Orange.

MAIDEN'S BLUSH
Fill glass with ice.
1 1/2 oz Gin
1 tsp Triple Sec or Curacao
1/2 tsp Lemon Juice
1/2 tsp Grenadine
Shake.
Strain into chilled glass.

MAIDEN'S DOWNFALL
Fill glass with ice.
1 oz Vodka
1 oz Rum
1 oz Lime Juice
Dash of Bitters
Fill with Grapefruit Juice.
Shake.

MAIDEN'S PRAYER
Fill glass with ice.
1 1/2 oz Gin
3/4 oz Triple Sec
1/2 oz Lemon Juice
Dash of Orange Juice
Shake.
Strain into chilled glass.

MAINBRACE
Fill glass with ice.
1 1/2 oz Gin
3/4 oz Triple Sec
1 oz Grape Juice
Shake.
Strain into chilled glass.

MAJOR TOM
Fill glass with ice.
1 oz Vodka
1/2 oz Triple Sec
1/2 oz Cherry Brandy
Fill with Orange or Grapefruit Juice.

MALIBU DRIVER
Fill glass with ice.
3 oz Coconut Rum
Fill with Orange Juice.
Stir.
Garnish with Orange.

MALIBU MONSOON
Fill glass with ice.
1 1/2 oz Rum
3/4 oz Malibu Liqueur
Dash of Orange Liqueur
1 oz Pineapple Juice
Dash of Cranberry Juice
Shake.
Add 3 drops of Grenadine.
Garnish with Cherry and Orange.

MALIBU SUNSET
Fill glass with ice.
2 oz Coconut Rum
Fill with Pineapple Juice.
Pour 1/2 oz Creme De Nouyax down spoon to bottom of glass.
Garnish with Pineapple.

MALIBU WAVE
Fill glass with ice.
1 oz Tequila
1/2 oz Triple Sec
1 tsp Blue Curacao
1 1/2 oz Sour Mix
Shake.
Garnish with Lime.

MAMIE TAYLOR
Fill glass with ice.
3 oz Scotch
1/2 oz Lime Juice
Fill with Ginger Ale.
Stir.
Garnish with Lemon.

MAN O'WAR
Fill glass with ice.
2 oz Bourbon
1 oz Orange Curacao
1/2 oz Sweet Vermouth
Dash of Lime Juice
Shake.
Strain into chilled glass.

MANHASSET
Fill glass with ice.
1 1/2 oz Whiskey
1/4 oz Sweet Vermouth
1/4 oz Dry Vermouth
1 oz Lemon Juice
Shake.
Strain into chilled glass.
Garnish with Lemon Twist.

L

M

MANHATTAN
(*CAUTION:* DRY can mean either make drink with Dry Vermouth or less Sweet Vermouth than usual. PERFECT means use equal amounts of Sweet and Dry Vermouth. SWEET means use more Sweet Vermouth than usual. NAKED means no Vermouth at all.)
Fill glass with ice.
2 oz Whiskey
1/2 oz Sweet Vermouth
Stir.
Strain into chilled glass or pour contents (with ice) into short glass.
Garnish with Cherry or Lemon Twist.

MAPLE LEAF
Fill glass with ice.
1 oz Canadian Whiskey
1/4 oz Lemon Juice
1 tsp Maple Syrup
Shake.
Strain into chilled glass.

MAPLE RUSSIAN
Fill glass with ice.
1 oz Vodka
1 oz Coffee Liqueur
1/2 oz Maple Syrup
Fill with Milk or Cream.
Shake.

MARCONI WIRELESS
Fill glass with ice.
1 1/2 oz Apple Brandy
1/2 oz Sweet Vermouth
2-3 dashes of Orange Bitters
Shake.
Strain into chilled glass.

MARGARITA
Fill glass with ice.
1 1/2 oz Tequila
1/2 oz Triple Sec
Dash of Lime Juice
3 oz Sour Mix
Dash of Orange Juice (optional)
Shake.
Rub rim of second glass with Lime and dip into kosher salt.
Pour contents (with ice) or strain into salted glass.
Garnish with Lime.

MARGARITA (frozen)
In Blender:
1 cup of Ice
1 1/2 oz Tequila
1/2 oz Triple Sec
1/2 oz Lime Juice
3 oz Sour Mix
Blend until smooth.
If too thick add juice.
If too thin add ice.
Rub rim of glass with Lime and dip into Kosher Salt.
Pour contents into salted glass.

MARLON BRANDO (floater)
Fill glass with ice.
1 1/2 oz Scotch (bottom)
1/2 oz Amaretto
1/4 oz of Cream (top)

MARMALADE
Fill glass with ice.
1 oz Benedictine
3/4 oz Curacao
Dash of Orange Juice
Fill with Tonic Water.
Stir.
Garnish with Orange.

MARTINEZ
Fill glass with ice.
1 1/2 oz Gin
2 oz Dry Vermouth
2 dashes of Maraschino Liqueur or Triple Sec
2 dashes of Bitters
Shake.
Serve or strain into chilled glass.
Garnish with Cherry.

MARTINI
(*CAUTION:* DRY usually means less Vermouth than usual. EXTRA DRY can mean even less Vermouth than usual or no Vermouth at all.)
Fill glass with ice.
2 oz Gin or Vodka
1/2 oz Dry Vermouth
Stir.
Strain into chilled glass or pour contents (with ice) into short glass.
Garnish with Lemon Twist or Olives or cocktail onions.

MARY GARDEN
Fill glass with ice.
1 1/2 oz Dubonnet
3/4 oz Dry Vermouth
Shake.
Strain into chilled glass.

MARY PICKFORD
Fill glass with ice.
1 1/2 oz Rum
3/4 oz Pineapple Juice
Dash of Grenadine
Shake.
Strain into chilled glass.

MASSACRE
Fill glass with ice.
1 1/2 oz Tequila
1/2 oz Campari
Fill with Ginger Ale.
Stir.

MATADOR
Fill glass with ice.
1 1/2 oz Tequila
1 1/2 oz Pineapple Juice
1/2 oz Lime Juice
1/2 tsp Sugar Syrup
Shake.
Strain into chilled glass.

MAURICE
Fill glass with ice.
1 oz Gin
1/2 oz Dry Vermouth
1/2 oz Sweet Vermouth
1/2 oz Orange Juice
Dash of Bitters
Shake.
Strain into chilled glass.

MAXIM
Fill glass with ice.
1 1/2 oz Gin
1 oz Dry Vermouth
Dash of White Creme De Cacao
Shake.
Strain into chilled glass.

MAXIM'S
In champagne flute
1 oz Brandy
1/2 oz Orange Liqueur
Dash of Orange Juice
Fill with Champagne.

MAXIM'S 2
In champagne flute
3/4 oz Orange Liqueur
3/4 oz Melon Liqueur
3/4 oz Banana Liqueur
Dash of Sour Mix
Shake.
Fill with Champagne.

MAXIM'S A LONDRES
Fill glass with ice.
1 1/2 oz Brandy
Dash of Orange Liqueur
Dash of Orange Juice
Shake.
Strain into chilled glass.
Fill with Champagne.
Garnish with Orange Twist.

MAY BLOSSOM FIZZ
Fill glass with ice.
2 oz Swedish Punch
2 oz Lemon Juice
Dash of Grenadine
Shake.
Fill with Soda Water.

McCLELLAND
Fill glass with ice.
1 1/2 oz Sloe Gin
3/4 oz Triple Sec or Curacao
2 dashes of Orange Bitters
Shake.
Strain into chilled glass.

ME SO HORNEY
1 oz Vodka
1 oz Champagne
Fill with Hard Cider.

MEADOWLARK LEMON
Fill glass with ice.
1 1/2 oz Vodka
1/2 oz Orange Liqueur
1/2 oz Lemon Juice or Sour Mix
Stir.
Strain into chilled glass.
Garnish with Lemon.

MEDITERRANEAN COFFEE
1 1/2 oz Greek Brandy
1/2 oz Galliano
Fill with hot Black Coffee
Top with Whipped Cream.

MEISTER-BATION (frozen)
In Blender:
1 cup of Ice
1 1/2 oz Jaegermeister
1/2 oz Banana Liqueur
1 tbsp Cream of Coconut
2 tbsp Vanilla Ice Cream
1/2 cup fresh or canned Pineapple
Blend until smooth.
Garnish with packaged condom.

MELON BALL
Fill glass with ice.
1 oz Vodka
1 oz Melon Liqueur
Fill with Orange Juice.
Shake.
Garnish with Orange.

MELON BREEZE
Fill glass with ice.
1 oz Vodka
1 oz Melon Liqueur
Fill with equal parts Cranberry and
Pineapple Juice.
Shake.
Garnish with Pineapple and Cherry.

MELON COCKTAIL
Fill glass with ice.
2 oz Gin
1/2 oz Maraschino Liqueur
1/2 oz Lemon Juice
Shake.
Strain into chilled glass.
Garnish with Cherry.

MELON COLADA (frozen)
In Blender:
1 cup of Ice
1 oz Rum
1 oz Melon Liqueur
2 tbsp Cream of Coconut
1/2 cup fresh Honeydew melon or
fresh or canned Pineapple
1 tbsp Vanilla Ice Cream
Blend until smooth.
If too thick add juice or fruit.
If too thin add ice or Ice Cream.
Garnish with melon or Pineapple
and Cherry.

M

MELON GRIND
Fill glass with ice.
3/4 oz Vodka
3/4 oz Rum
3/4 oz Melon Liqueur
Fill with Pineapple Juice.
Shake.

MELON ROYALE
1/2 oz Melon Liqueur
Fill with Champagne.

MELON SOMBRERO
Fill glass with ice.
2 oz Melon Liqueur
Fill with Milk or Cream.
Shake.

MELON SOUR
Fill glass with ice.
2 oz Melon Liqueur
Fill with Sour Mix.
Shake.
Garnish with Orange and Cherry.

MELTDOWN
1 oz Vodka
1/2 oz Peach Schnapps
Stir.

MEMPHIS BELLE
Fill glass with ice.
1 1/2 oz Brandy
3/4 oz Southern Comfort
1/2 oz Lemon Juice
3 dashes of Bitters
Shake.
Strain into chilled glass.

MENAGE a TROIS
Fill glass with ice.
3/4 oz Irish Cream
3/4 oz Black Raspberry Liqueur
3/4 oz Hazelnut Liqueur
Fill with Milk or Cream.
Shake.

MENAGE a TROIS 2
Fill glass with ice.
1 oz Dark Rum
1 oz Triple Sec
1 oz Milk or Cream
Shake. Strain into chilled glass.

MERRY WIDOW
Fill glass with ice.
1 1/4 oz Cherry Brandy
1 1/4 oz Maraschino Liqueur
Shake.
Strain into chilled glass.

METAL HELMET
Fill glass with ice.
1 1/4 oz Banana Liqueur
3/4 oz Vodka
Fill with Milk.
Shake.

METROPOLIS MARTINI
Fill glass with ice.
1 1/2 oz Vodka
1/2 oz Strawberry Liqueur
Stir.
Strain into chilled glass.
Top with 1 oz Champagne.
Garnish with Strawberry.

MEXICAN BLACKJACK
Fill glass with ice.
1/2 oz Tequila
1/2 oz Blended Whiskey
1/2 oz Bourbon
1/2 oz Triple Sec or Curacao
Shake.
Strain into chilled glass.

MEXICAN BOILERMAKER
Fill shot glass with Tequila
Fill chilled glass 3/4 with Beer.
Either drink shot and chase with
Beer or
Drop shot glass into Beer and
drink.

MEXICAN CAPPUCCINO
1 1/2 oz Coffee Liqueur
Fill with espresso.
Top with steamed Milk.
Sprinkle with Powdered Sugar.

MEXICAN COFFEE
2 oz Coffee Liqueur
or 2 oz Tequila
Fill with hot Black Coffee.
Top with Whipped Cream.
Sprinkle with Shaved
Chocolate or Sprinkles.

MEXICAN COFFEE 2
1 oz Tequila
1 oz Coffee Liqueur
Fill with hot Black Coffee.
Top with Whipped Cream.
Sprinkle with Shaved
Chocolate or Sprinkles.

MEXICAN FLAG (floater)
1/2 oz Sloe Gin (bottom)
1/2 oz Vodka
1/2 oz Melon Liqueur (top)

MEXICAN JUMPING BEAN
Fill glass with ice.
3/4 oz Tequila
3/4 oz Coffee Liqueur
3/4 oz Anisette
Stir.

MEXICAN MISSILE
3/4 oz Tequila
3/4 oz Green Chartreuse
Dash of Tabasco Sauce

MEXICAN SCREW aka HAMMER
Fill glass with ice.
2 oz Tequila
Fill with Orange Juice.
Garnish with Orange.

MEXICAN SEABREEZE
Fill glass with ice.
2 oz Tequila
Fill with equal parts Cranberry and
Pineapple Juice.
Garnish with Lime.

MEXICANO
Fill glass with ice.
2 oz Rum
1/2 oz Kummel
1 oz Orange Juice
3 dashes of Bitters
Shake.

MIAMI BEACH
Fill glass with ice.
2 oz Scotch
1 oz Dry Vermouth
1 oz Grapefruit Juice
Shake.
Strain into chilled glass.

MIAMI ICE
Fill glass with ice.
1/2 oz Vodka
1/2 oz Gin
1/2 oz Rum
1/2 oz Peach Schnapps
Dash of Cranberry Juice
Fill with Lemon-Lime Soda.

MIAMI MELON
Fill glass with ice.
1 oz Vodka
1 oz Melon Liqueur
Fill with Milk or Cream.
Shake.

MIAMI VICE
Fill glass with ice.
1 oz Rum
1/2 oz Blackberry Brandy
1/2 oz Banana Liqueur
Dash of Lime Juice
Dash of Grenadine
1 tbsp Cream De Coconut
Fill with Pineapple Juice.
Shake.
Garnish with Pineapple.

MICH
Fill glass with ice.
1 1/2 oz Gin
1/2 oz Sloe Gin
Dash of Lime Juice
Fill with equal parts Sour Mix and
Grapefruit Juice.
Shake.

MICK
Fill glass with ice.
1 1/2 oz Vodka
1/2 oz Banana Liqueur
2 oz Orange Juice
Shake.
Strain into chilled glass.

MIDNIGHT COWBOY
Fill glass with ice.
2 oz Bourbon
1 oz Dark Rum
1 oz Milk or Cream
Shake.
Strain into chilled glass.

MIDNIGHT DREAM
Fill glass with ice.
1 1/2 oz Vodka
1/2 oz Black Raspberry Liqueur
Dash of Cream
Fill with Cranberry Juice.
Shake.

MIDNIGHT MARTINI
Fill glass with ice.
2 oz Vodka
1/4 oz Coffee Liqueur
or Coffee Brandy
Stir.
Strain into chilled glass or pour
contents (with ice) into shot glass.
Garnish with Lemon Twist.

MIDNIGHT SNOWSTORM
2 oz White Creme De Menthe
Fill with Hot Chocolate.
Stir.
Top with Whipped Cream.
Dribble 1/2 oz Green Creme De
Menthe on top.

MIDNIGHT SUN
Fill glass with ice.
2 1/2 oz Vodka
1/2 oz Grenadine
Stir.
Strain into chilled glass.

MIDWAY RAT
Fill glass with ice.
1 oz Rum
1/2 oz Amaretto
1/2 oz Coffee Liqueur
Fill glass with Pineapple Juice.
Shake.
Garnish with Orange, Cherry and a
Black Licorice Whip.

MIKE COLLINS aka JOE COLLINS, SCOTCH COLLINS
Fill glass with ice.
2 oz Scotch
Fill with Sour Mix.
Shake.
Dash of Soda Water
Garnish with Orange and Cherry.

MIKE TYSON
Fill glass with ice.
1 oz Jaegermeister
1 oz Coffee Liqueur
1 oz Anisette or Sambuca
Stir.

M

93

MILANO COFFEE
1 oz Rum
1 oz Amaretto
Fill with hot Black Coffee.
Top with Whipped Cream.
Garnish with Shaved Almonds.

MILLIONAIRE
Fill glass with ice.
1 1/2 oz Bourbon
1/2 oz Pernod
1 tsp Curacao or Triple Sec
1 tsp Grenadine
1/2 Egg White
Shake.
Strain into chilled glass.

MILLIONAIRE'S COFFEE
1/2 oz Coffee Liqueur
1/2 oz Irish Cream
1/2 oz Orange Liqueur
1/2 oz Hazelnut Liqueur
Fill with hot Black Coffee.
Top with Whipped Cream.
Sprinkle with Shaved
Chocolate or Sprinkles.

MIMOSA
Fill glass 3/4 with ice.
Fill 3/4 with Champagne.
Dash of Orange Liqueur
or Triple Sec (optional)
Fill with Orange Juice.
Garnish with Orange.

MIND ERASER
Fill glass with ice.
1 oz Vodka
1 oz Coffee Liqueur
Fill with Soda Water.
Garnish with a Lime.

MIND OBLITERATOR
Fill glass with ice.
1 oz Vodka
1 oz Coffee Liqueur
Fill with Champagne.

MINSTREL FRAPPE
Fill large stemmed glass (Red Wine
glass, Champagne saucer) with
crushed ice.
1/2 oz Vodka
1/2 oz Coffee Liqueur
1/2 oz Brandy
1/2 oz White Creme De Menthe

MINT CHOCOLATE CHIP ICE CREAM
Fill glass with ice.
1/2 oz Vodka
1/2 oz Creme De Cacao
1/2 oz Peppermint Schnapps
1/2 oz Irish Cream
1/2 oz Coffee Liqueur
Fill with Milk or Cream.
Shake.

MINT CONDITION aka GROUND ZERO
Fill glass with ice.
3/4 oz Vodka
1/2 oz Coffee Liqueur
3/4 oz Bourbon
3/4 oz Peppermint Schnapps
Shake.
Serve or strain into chilled glass.

MINT JULEP
Muddle together in a glass:
10-20 Fresh Mint Leaves
1 tsp Sugar
2 tbsp Water
Fill with crushed Ice.
Fill 7/8 with Bourbon.
Float 1/2 oz Rum on top.
Garnish with 3 or 4 leaves.

MISSISSIPPI MUD
1/2 oz Coffee Liqueur
1/2 oz Hazelnut Liqueur
1/2 oz Triple Sec
1/2 oz Rum
Fill with hot Black Coffee.
Top with Whipped Cream.
Sprinkle with Shaved
Chocolate or Sprinkles.

MISSISSIPPI MULE
Fill glass with ice.
1 1/2 oz Gin
1 tsp Creme De Cassis
1 tsp Lemon Juice
Shake.
Garnish with Lemon.

MISSOURI MULE
Fill glass with ice.
2 oz Southern Comfort
Fill with Ginger Beer.
Stir.
Garnish with Lime.

MIST
Is another way to say "On the
rocks," but preferably with Shaved
or crushed ice.

MO FO
Fill glass with ice.
1 1/2 oz Vodka
1/2 oz Peach Schnapps
Dash of Milk or Cream
Fill with Cranberry Juice.
Shake.

MOCHA BERRY FRAPPE (frozen)
In Blender:
1/2 cup of Ice
1 oz Coffee Liqueur
1 oz Black Raspberry Liqueur
1 oz Dark Creme De Cacao
Scoop of Vanilla Ice Cream
Blend until smooth.
If too thick add Milk or Cream.
If too thin add ice or Ice Cream.
Sprinkle with Shaved Chocolate or
Sprinkles.

MOCHA MINT
Fill glass with ice.
3/4 oz Coffee Liqueur
or Coffee Brandy
3/4 oz White Creme De Menthe
3/4 oz White Creme De Cacao
Shake.
Strain into chilled glass.

MOCKINGBIRD
Fill glass with ice.
1 1/2 oz Tequila
1/2 oz White Creme De Menthe
1 oz Lime Juice
Shake.
Strain into chilled glass.

MODERN
Fill glass with ice.
1 1/2 oz Sloe Gin
3/4 oz Scotch
Dash of Pernod
Dash of Grenadine
Dash of Orange Bitters
Shake.

MODERN 2
Fill glass with ice.
3 oz Scotch
Dash of Dark Rum
Dash of Pernod
Dash of Lemon Juice
Dash of Orange Bitters
Shake.
Garnish with Cherry.

MOJITO
Fill glass with ice.
2 oz Light Rum
1 tsp Sugar
Dash of Lime Juice
Fill with Soda Water.
Garnish with Lime and Mint Sprigs.

MOJO
Fill glass with ice.
1 oz Rum
1 oz Cherry Brandy
3 oz Amber Beer or Ale
Fill with equal parts of Orange
Juice, Pineapple Juice,
Cola and Lemon-Lime Soda.

MOLL
Fill glass with ice.
1 oz Gin
1 oz Sloe Gin
1 oz Dry Vermouth
Dash of Orange Bitters
1/2 tsp Sugar (optional)
Shake.
Strain into chilled glass.

MON CHERIE
Fill glass with ice.
1 oz Cherry Brandy
1 oz White Creme De Cacao
1 oz of Milk or Cream.
Shake.

MONGA MONGA (frozen)
In Blender:
1 cup of Ice
1 1/2 oz Brandy
1 oz Dark Rum
1 oz Strawberry Liqueur
1 oz Lime Juice
1/2 cup fresh or frozen Strawberries
Blend until smooth.
If too thick add fruit.
If too thin add ice.
Garnish with Lime.

MONGOLIAN MOTHER
Fill glass with ice.
Dash of Vodka
Dash of Gin
Dash of Rum
Dash of Tequila
Dash of Triple Sec
Dash of Peach Schnapps
Dash of Amaretto
Dash of Sloe Gin
Dash of Southern Comfort
Dash of 151-Proof Rum
Dash of Grenadine
Fill with equal parts Cranberry
and Orange Juice.
Shake.
Garnish with Orange, Lime, Lemon
and Cherry.

MONK JUICE
Fill glass with ice.
2 oz Hazelnut Liqueur
Fill with Milk or Cream.
Shake.
Michele Cooke

MONK SLIDE (floater)
1/2 oz Coffee Liqueur (top)
1/2 oz Irish Cream
1/2 oz Hazelnut Liqueur
(bottom)

MONK'S COFFEE
1 oz Benedictine
1 oz Orange Liqueur
Fill with hot Black Coffee.
Top with Whipped Cream.
Garnish with Orange.

MONKEY JUICE
Fill glass with ice.
1 1/2 oz Dark Rum
1/2 oz Irish Cream
1/2 oz Banana Liqueur
Stir.

MONKEY SPECIAL (frozen)
In Blender:
1 cup of Ice
1 oz Dark Rum
1 oz Light Rum
1/2 ripe peeled Banana
1/2 scoop Vanilla Ice Cream
Blend until smooth.
If too thick add Milk or Cream. If too
thin add ice or Ice Cream.
Sprinkle with Shaved Chocolate.

M

MONKEY WRENCH
Fill glass with ice.
2 oz Rum
Fill with Grapefruit Juice.

MONKEY WRENCH 2
Fill glass with ice.
1 oz Vodka
1 oz Amaretto
1 oz Orange Juice
Strain into shot glass.

MONTANA
Fill glass with ice.
1 1/2 oz Brandy
1 oz Port
1/2 oz Dry Vermouth
Stir.

MONTE CARLO
Fill glass with ice.
1 1/2 oz Whiskey
1/2 oz Benedictine
3 dashes of Bitters
Shake.

MONTE CRISTO COFFEE
1 oz Coffee Liqueur
1 oz Orange Liqueur
Fill with hot Black Coffee.
Top with Whipped Cream.
Garnish with Orange.

MONTEGO BAY COFFEE
1/2 oz Dark Rum
1/2 oz Coffee Liqueur
Fill with hot Black Coffee.
Top with Whipped Cream.
Garnish with Banana.

MONTMARTE
Fill glass with ice.
1 1/2 oz Gin
1/2 oz Sweet Vermouth
1/2 oz Triple Sec
Stir.
Strain into chilled glass.

MONTREAL CLUB BOUNCER
Fill glass with ice.
1 1/2 oz Gin
1 oz Pernod

MOODY BLUE
Fill glass with ice.
3/4 oz Vodka
3/4 oz Peach Schnapps
3/4 oz Blue Curacao
Fill with Pineapple Juice.
Shake.

MOON CHASER
In Blender:
1/2 cup of ice
3/4 oz Dark Rum
3/4 oz Coconut Rum
3/4 oz Amaretto
Scoop Orange Sherbet
Blend until smooth.

MOON RACKER
Fill glass with ice.
1 1/2 oz Tequila
1/2 oz Blue Curacao
Fill with Pineapple Juice
Shake.

MOONBEAM
Fill glass with ice.
1 oz Amaretto
1 oz White Creme De Cacao
Fill with Milk or Cream.

MOONLIGHT
Fill glass with ice.
2 oz Apple Brandy
1 oz Lemon Juice
1 tsp Powdered Sugar
or Sugar Syrup
Shake.
Splash of Soda Water (optional)
Garnish with Lemon Twist.

MOONPIE (frozen)
In Blender:
1 cup of Ice
1 oz Amber Rum
Dash of Peach Schnapps
Dash of Banana Liqueur
1/2 a ripe Banana
1/2 ripe peeled Peach
Dash of Orange Juice
Blend until smooth.
Garnish with Banana.

MOOSE MILK
In a large mixing bowl:
20 oz Dark Rum
10 oz Tia Maria
40 oz Milk
1/2 gallon Vanilla Ice Cream
Stir until smooth.
Serves 20 people.

MOOSEBERRY
Fill glass with ice.
1 oz Vodka
1 oz Amaretto
2 oz Cranberry Juice
2 oz Sour Mix
Shake.
Strain into chilled glass.
Top with 1/2 oz Orange Liqueur.

MORNING
Fill glass with ice.
1 oz Brandy
1 oz Dry Vermouth
Dash of Triple Sec or Curacao
Dash of Maraschino Liqueur
Dash of Pernod
2 dashes of Orange Bitters
Stir.

MORNING GLORY
Fill glass with ice.
1 oz Scotch
1 oz Brandy
Dash of Pernod
2 dashes of Curacao
2 dashes of Bitters
Shake.
Top with Soda Water.
Stir with a spoon dipped in water
and coated with sugar.

MOSCOW MIMOSA
Fill glass with ice.
1/2 oz Vodka
Fill with equal parts Champagne
and Orange Juice.

MOSCOW MULE
Fill glass with ice.
2 oz Vodka
Fill with Ginger Beer.
Stir.
Garnish with Lime.

MOTHER LOVE
Fill glass with ice.
1 1/2 oz Canadian Whiskey
1/2 oz Peppermint Schnapps
Stir.

MOTHER SHERMAN
Fill glass with ice.
1 1/2 oz Apricot Brandy
1 oz Orange Juice
3-4 dashes of Orange Bitters
Shake.
Garnish with Orange.

MOULIN ROUGE
Fill glass with ice.
1 1/2 oz Sloe Gin
1/2 oz Sweet Vermouth
3 dashes of Bitters
Shake.
Strain into chilled glass.

MOUND BAR
2 oz Coconut Rum
Fill with Hot Chocolate.
Top with Whipped Cream.
Sprinkle with Shaved Chocolate.

MOUND BAR 2
Fill glass with ice.
3/4 oz Coconut Rum
3/4 oz Dark Creme De Cacao
3/4 oz Irish Cream
3/4 oz Milk or Cream
Shake.
Strain into chilled glass.

MOUNT FUJI
Fill glass with ice.
1 1/2 oz Gin
1/2 oz Lemon Juice
1/2 oz Heavy Cream
1 tsp Pineapple Juice
1 Egg White
3 dashes of Maraschino Liqueur
Shake.

MOUNT VESUVIUS
Fill glass with ice.
1 oz Coconut Rum
1 oz Triple Sec
Dash of Grenadine
Fill with Orange Juice.
Shake.
Top with 151-Proof Rum.

MOUNTAIN RED PUNCH
Fill glass with ice.
1/2 oz Amaretto
1/2 oz Brandy
1/2 oz Cherry Brandy
2 oz Ginger Ale
Fill with Red Wine.

MUDSLIDE
Fill glass with ice.
1 oz Coffee Liqueur
1 oz Irish Cream
1 oz Vodka
Shake.

MUDSLIDE 2
Fill glass with ice.
1 oz Vodka
1 oz Coffee Liqueur
1 oz Irish Cream
Fill with Milk or Cream.

MUDSLIDE 3
Fill glass with ice.
1 oz Dark Creme De Cacao
1 oz Irish Cream
Shake.

MUDSLIDE (floater)
1/2 oz Coffee Liqueur (bottom)
1/2 oz Irish Cream
1/2 oz Vodka (top)

MUDSLIDE (frozen)
In Blender:
1/2 cup of Ice
1 oz Coffee Liqueur
1 oz Irish Cream
1 oz Vodka
Scoop of Vanilla Ice Cream
Blend until smooth.
If too thick add Milk or Cream.
If too thin add ice or Ice Cream.
Sprinkle with Shaved Chocolate or
Sprinkles.

MUDSLING
1/2 oz Coffee Liqueur
1/2 oz Irish Cream
1/2 oz Vodka
Fill with Hot Chocolate.
Top with Whipped Cream.
Sprinkle with Shaved Chocolate.

MUFF DIVER
Fill glass with ice.
1 oz Amaretto
1 oz White Creme De Cacao
Dash of Lime Juice or Lemon Juice
1 oz Milk or Cream
Shake. Strain into shot glass.

M

MULE SKINNER
1 1/2 oz Bourbon
1/2 oz Blackberry Brandy

MULE'S HIND LEG
Fill glass with ice.
3/4 oz Gin
3/4 oz Apple Brandy
3/4 oz Benedictine
3/4 oz Apricot Brandy
3/4 oz Maple Syrup
Shake.

MULLED CIDER
Place 2 smashed Cinnamon Sticks,
10 whole Cloves,
and 1 tsp Allspice Berries into
cheese cloth bag.
In saucepan on low heat, stir
together 1/2 gallon of Apple Cider,
and 1/2 cup Brown Sugar.
After sugar dissolves, place bag
containing spices in and keep heat-
ing for 5 minutes, then serve.
Garnish with Cinnamon Stick and
Dried Apple Ring.
(serves 10-15 people)

MULTIPLE ORGASM
Fill glass with ice.
1/2 oz Vodka
1/2 oz Amaretto
1/2 oz Irish Cream
1/2 oz Orange Liqueur
1/2 oz Coffee Liqueur
1 oz Milk
Shake
Strain into chilled glass.
Garnish with 2 or more Cherries.

MUSCLE BEACH
Fill glass with ice.
1 1/2 oz Vodka
1/2 oz Triple Sec
Fill with Pink Lemonade.

MUTUAL ORGASM
Fill glass with ice.
3/4 oz Vodka
3/4 oz Amaretto
3/4 oz Creme De Cacao
1 oz Milk or Cream
Shake.
Strain into chilled glass.

NAKED G S (floater)
1 oz Chocolate Liqueur (bottom)
1 oz 100-proof Peppermint
Schnapps (top)

NAKED LADY
Fill glass with ice.
1 oz Rum
1 oz Apricot Brandy
Dash of Grenadine
1 oz Sour Mix
Shake.
Strain into chilled glass.

NAKED LADY 2
Fill glass with ice.
3/4 oz Vodka
3/4 oz Gin
3/4 oz Brandy
1/2 oz Apricot Brandy
1/2 oz Blackberry Brandy
Fill with equal parts Orange
and Pineapple Juice.
Shake.
Top with tsp Grenadine.

NANTUCKET BREEZE
Fill glass with ice.
1 oz Vodka
1 oz Cranberry Liqueur
Fill with Grapefruit Juice.
Garnish with Lime.

NANTUCKET RED aka
POINSETTIA
Fill glass 3/4 with ice.
Fill 3/4 with Champagne.
Fill with Cranberry Juice.
Garnish with Lime.

NAPOLEON
Fill glass with ice.
1 oz Gin
1 oz Orange Liqueur
1 oz Dubonnet Rouge
Stir.
Strain into chilled glass.
Garnish with Orange Twist.

NARRAGANSETT
Fill glass with ice.
1 1/2 oz Bourbon
1 oz Sweet Vermouth
Dash of Anisette
Stir.
Garnish with Lemon Twist.

NASTY GIRL
Fill glass with ice.
3/4 oz Dark Rum
1/4 oz Coconut Rum
1/4 oz Amaretto
1/4 oz Banana Liqueur
1/4 oz Peach Schnapps
Dash of Cranberry Juice
Dash of Pineapple Juice
Shake. Strain into shot glass.

NAUGHTY HULA PIE
Fill glass with ice.
1 oz Amaretto
1 oz Dark Creme De Cacao
Dash of Pineapple Juice
2 oz Cream or Milk
Shake.
Strain into chilled glass.

NAVY GROG
Fill glass with ice.
1 oz Light Rum
1 oz Dark Rum
1/2 oz Orange Juice
1/2 oz Guava Nectar
1/2 oz Pineapple Juice
1/2 oz Lime Juice
1/2 oz Orgeat Syrup
Shake.
Garnish with Lime and Mint Sprig.

NEGRONI
Fill glass with ice.
1 oz Gin
1 oz Campari
1 oz Dry or Sweet Vermouth
Stir.
Strain into chilled glass.
Garnish with Lemon Twist.

NELSON'S BLOOD
Fill glass with ice.
2 oz Pusser's Rum
Dash of Lime Juice
Fill with Ginger Beer.

NELSON'S BLOOD 2
1 oz Tawny Port
Fill with Champagne.

NEON
Fill glass with ice.
1 oz Citrus Vodka
1/2 oz Melon Liqueur
1/2 oz Blue Curacao
Dash of Lime Juice.
Fill with Sour Mix.
Shake.

NERVOUS BREAKDOWN
Fill glass with ice.
1 1/2 oz Vodka
1/2 oz Black Raspberry Liqueur
Fill with Soda Water.
Top with splash of Cranberry Juice.
Garnish with Lime.

NESI aka LOCH NESS MONSTER
(floater)
1/2 oz Melon Liqueur (bottom)
1/2 oz Irish Cream
1/2 oz Jaegermeister (top)

NETHERLAND
Fill glass with ice.
1 oz Brandy
1 oz Triple Sec
Dash of Orange Juice
Shake.
Serve or strain into chilled glass.

NEUTRON BOMB (floater)
1/2 oz Coffee Liqueur (bottom)
1/2 oz Irish Cream
1/2 oz Butterscotch Schnapps (top)

NEVINS
Fill glass with ice.
1 1/2 oz Bourbon
1 oz Apricot Brandy
1 oz Grapefruit Juice
1 tsp Lemon Juice
3 dashes of Bitters
Shake.

NEW WORLD
Fill glass with ice.
1 1/2 oz Whiskey
1/2 oz Lime Juice
1 tsp Grenadine
Shake.
Serve or strain into chilled glass.
Garnish with Lime.

NEW YORK COCKTAIL
Fill glass with ice.
1 1/2 oz Whiskey
1/2 oz Lime Juice
1 tsp Sugar Syrup or Powdered Sugar
Dash of Grenadine
Shake.
Garnish with Orange Twist.

NEW YORK SLAMMER
Fill glass with ice.
1 oz Blended Whiskey
1/2 oz Banana Liqueur
1/2 oz Sloe Gin
Fill with Orange Juice.
Shake.

NEW YORK SOUR
Fill glass with ice.
2 oz Whiskey
Fill with Sour Mix.
Shake.
Top with 1/2 oz Red Table Wine.
Garnish with Cherry and Lemon.

NEWBURY
Fill glass with ice.
1 oz Gin
1 oz Sweet Vermouth
3 dashes of Curacao
Stir.
Strain into chilled glass.
Garnish with Orange and Lemon Twist.

NIAGARA FALLS
Fill glass with ice.
1 1/2 oz Whiskey
1/2 oz Irish Mist
1/2 oz Heavy Cream
Shake.
Strain into chilled glass.

NIGHT TRAIN (frozen)
In Blender:
1/2 cup of Ice
1 oz Rum
1/2 oz Cherry Brandy
1/2 oz White Creme De Cacao
1 oz Cream of Coconut
Dash of Pineapple Juice
Scoop of Vanilla Ice Cream
Blend until smooth.
Garnish with Cherry.

M
N

NIGHTINGALE
Fill glass with ice.
1 oz Banana Liqueur
1/2 oz Curacao
1 oz Cream
1/2 Egg White
Shake.
Strain into chilled glass.
Garnish with Cherry.

NIGHTMARE
Fill glass with ice.
1 oz Gin
1 oz Dubonnet
1/2 oz Cherry Brandy
1 oz Orange Juice
Shake.
Strain into chilled glass.

NINE-ONE-ONE or 911 aka 24 KARAT NIGHTMARE
1 oz 100-Proof Cinnamon Schnapps
1 oz 100-Proof Peppermint Schnapps

NINETEEN
Fill glass with ice.
2 oz Dry Vermouth
1/2 oz Gin
1/2 oz Kirschwasser
Dash of Pernod
1 tsp Sugar Syrup
Shake.
Strain into chilled glass.

NINETEEN PICK-ME-UP
Fill glass with ice.
1 1/2 oz Pernod
3/4 oz Gin
3 dashes of Sugar Syrup
3 dashes of Bitters
3 dashes of Orange Bitters
Shake.
Top with Soda Water.

NINJA (floater)
1/2 oz Dark Creme De Cacao (bottom)
1/2 oz Melon Liqueur
1/2 oz Hazelnut Liqueur (top)

NINJA TURTLE
Fill glass with ice.
1 1/2 oz Gin
1/2 oz Blue Curacao
Fill with Orange Juice.
Stir.

NINJA TURTLE 2
Fill glass with ice.
1 oz Coconut Rum
1 oz Melon Liqueur
1 oz Pineapple Juice
Shake.
Strain into chilled glass.
Garnish with Cherry.

NINOTCHKA
Fill glass with ice.
1 1/2 oz Vodka
1/2 oz White Creme De Cacao
1 tsp Lemon Juice
Shake.
Serve or strain into chilled glass.

NO PROBLEM
Fill glass with ice.
1 oz Coconut Rum
1 oz Cherry Brandy
1 1/2 oz Apple Juice
1/2 oz Orange Juice
1/2 oz Lime Juice
1/2 oz Sugar Syrup
Shake.

NO TELL MOTEL
Fill glass with ice.
1 oz Bourbon
1 oz Mentholated Schnapps
Stir.
Strain into chilled glass.

NOCTURNAL
Fill glass with ice.
2 oz Bourbon
1 oz Dark Creme De Cacao
Fill with Cream or Milk.
Shake.

NORTHERN LIGHTS
Fill glass with ice.
2 oz Yukon Jack
Dash of Peach Schnapps (optional)
Fill with equal parts of Orange and Cranberry Juice.
Stir.

NORTHERN LIGHTS 2
1 oz Yukon Jack
1 oz Orange Liqueur
Fill with hot Black Coffee.
Top with Whipped Cream.

NUCLEAR KAMIKAZE aka BLUE KAMIKAZE
Fill glass with ice.
2 oz Vodka
1/2 oz Blue Curacao
Dash of Lime Juice
Shake.
Serve or strain into chilled glass.
Garnish with Lime.

NUCLEAR MELTDOWN aka THREE MILE ISLAND
Fill glass with ice.
1/2 oz Vodka
1/2 oz Gin
1/2 oz Rum
1/2 oz Tequila
1/2 oz Triple Sec
Fill with Sour Mix
or Pineapple Juice.
Shake.
Top with 1/2 oz Melon Liqueur.

NUT AND HONEY (frozen)
In Blender:
1/2 cup of Ice
1 1/2 oz Vodka
1/2 oz Hazelnut Liqueur
1 tbsp Honey
Scoop of Vanilla Ice Cream
Blend until smooth.
If too thick add Milk.
If too thin add ice or Ice Cream.

NUTCRACKER
Fill glass with ice.
1 oz Vodka
1 oz Coffee Liqueur
1 oz Irish Cream
Shake.

NUTCRACKER 2
Fill glass with ice.
1 oz Vodka
1/2 oz Irish Cream
1/2 oz Amaretto
1/2 oz Hazelnut Liqueur
Shake.

NUTCRACKER (frozen)
In Blender:
1/2 cup of Ice
1 oz Vodka
1/2 oz Irish Cream
1/2 oz Amaretto
1/2 oz Hazelnut Liqueur
Scoop of Vanilla Ice Cream
Blend until smooth.
If too thick add Milk or Cream.
If too thin add ice or Ice Cream.

NUTS AND BERRIES
Fill glass with ice.
3/4 oz Black Raspberry Liqueur
3/4 oz Hazelnut Liqueur
3/4 oz Coffee Liqueur
Fill with Cream.
Shake.

NUTS AND BERRIES 2
Fill glass with ice.
1/2 oz Vodka
1/2 oz Irish Cream
1/2 oz Black Raspberry Liqueur
1/2 oz Hazelnut Liqueur
Shake.
Strain into chilled glass.

NUTS AND CREAM
Fill glass with ice.
1 oz Amaretto
1 oz Hazelnut Liqueur
1 oz Cream
Shake.
Strain into chilled glass.

NUTTY BITCH
Fill glass with ice.
1 oz Vodka
1 oz Coffee Liqueur
1/2 oz Peppermint Schnapps
1/2 oz Irish Cream
Dash of Cola
Fill with Milk or Cream.
Shake.
Top with 1/2 oz Hazelnut Liqueur.

NUTTY CHINAMAN
Fill glass with ice.
1 oz Ginger Liqueur
1 oz Irish Cream
1 oz Hazelnut Liqueur
Stir.
Strain into chilled glass.

NUTTY COLADA (frozen)
In Blender:
1/2 cup of Ice
1 oz Amaretto
1 oz Rum
2 tbsp Cream of Coconut
1/2 cup fresh or canned Pineapple
1 tbsp Vanilla Ice Cream (optional)
Blend until smooth.
If too thick add fruit or juice.
If too thin add ice or Ice Cream.
Garnish with Pineapple, Cherry and
Shaved Almonds.

NUTTY IRISH COOLER
Fill glass with ice.
1 oz Irish Cream
1 oz Hazelnut Liqueur
Fill with Iced Coffee.
Shake.
Top with Whipped Cream.

NUTTY IRISHMAN
Fill glass with ice.
1 oz Irish Cream
1 oz Hazelnut Liqueur
Stir.

NUTTY IRISHMAN 2
Fill glass with ice.
1 oz Irish Whiskey
1 oz Hazelnut Liqueur
Fill with Milk or Cream.
Shake.

NUTTY IRISHMAN COFFEE
1 oz Irish Cream or Irish Whiskey
1 oz Hazelnut Liqueur
Fill with hot Black Coffee.
Top with Whipped Cream.
Sprinkle with Shaved Chocolate.

NUTTY JAMAICAN
Fill glass with ice.
1 oz Dark Rum
1 oz Hazelnut Liqueur
Stir.
Strain into chilled glass.

N

NUTTY RUSSIAN
Fill glass with ice.
1 oz Vodka
1 oz Hazelnut Liqueur
Fill with Milk or Cream.
Shake.

OATMEAL COOKIE
Fill glass with ice.
1/2 oz Jaegermeister
1/2 oz Cinnamon Schnapps
1/2 oz Irish Cream
1/2 oz Butterscotch Schnapps
Shake.
Strain into chilled glass.

OATMEAL COOKIE 2
Fill glass with ice.
3/4 oz Coffee Liqueur
3/4 oz Irish Cream
3/4 oz Cinnamon Schnapps
Dash of Milk or Cream
Shake.
Strain into chilled glass.

OCEAN VIEW SPECIAL
Fill glass with ice.
1 oz Vodka
1 oz Galliano
1 oz Green Creme De Menthe
Fill with Orange Juice.
Shake.

ODD McINTYRE
Fill glass with ice.
1 oz Brandy
1 oz Triple Sec
1 oz Lillet Blanc
1/2 oz Lemon Juice
Shake.
Strain into chilled glass.

OH, HENRY
Fill glass with ice.
1 1/2 oz Whiskey
1/4 oz Benedictine
3 oz Ginger Ale
Stir.
Garnish with Lemon.

OIL SLICK
Fill glass with ice.
1 oz Vodka
1 oz White Creme De Cacao
1 oz Milk
Shake.
Float 1 oz Dark Rum on top.

OIL SLICK 2
1 oz Peppermint Schnapps
1/2 oz Blue Curacao
Stir.
Float 1/2 oz Jaegermeister
on top.

OLD FASHIONED
Muddle together in glass:
Stemless Maraschino Cherry,
Orange Slice, 1/2 tsp Sugar,
4-5 dashes of Bitters.
Fill glass with ice.
2 oz Whiskey
Splash with Soda Water.
Stir.

OLD GROANER
Fill glass with ice.
1 1/2 oz Whiskey
1/2 oz Amaretto
Stir.

OLD GROANER'S WIFE
Fill glass with ice.
1 1/2 oz Whiskey
1/2 oz Amaretto
Fill with Cream or Milk.
Shake.

OLIVER TWIST
Fill glass with ice.
2 oz Gin or Vodka
1/2 oz Dry Vermouth
Stir.
Strain into chilled glass or pour
contents (with ice) into shot glass.
Garnish with Lemon Twist and
Olives.

OLYMPIC
Fill glass with ice.
1 oz Brandy
1 oz Curacao or Triple Sec
1 oz Orange Juice
Shake.

ONE SEVENTY
1 oz Brandy
Fill with Champagne.

OOM PAUL
Fill glass with ice.
1 oz Apple Brandy
1 oz Dubonnet Rouge
3 dashes of Bitters
Shake.

OPEN GRAVE
Fill glass with ice.
1/2 oz 151-Proof Rum
1/2 oz Dark Rum
1/2 oz Vodka
1/2 oz Southern Comfort
1/2 oz Peach Schnapps
Fill with equal parts Sour Mix,
Orange, Grapefruit, Pineapple
and Cherry Juice.

OPENING
Fill glass with ice.
1 1/2 oz Whiskey
1 tsp Sweet Vermouth
1 tsp Grenadine
Stir.
Strain into chilled glass.

OPERA
Fill glass with ice.
1 1/2 oz Gin
1/2 oz Dubonnet
1/2 oz Maraschino Liqueur
Stir.
Strain into chilled glass.
Garnish with Orange Twist.

ORAL SEX ON THE BEACH
Fill glass with ice.
1 oz Vodka
1/2 oz Black Raspberry Liqueur
1/2 oz Melon Liqueur
Fill with Orange Juice.
Shake.

ORANGE BLOSSOM
Fill glass with ice.
1 oz Gin
1 oz Orange Juice
1/4 tsp Sugar Syrup
or Powdered Sugar
Shake.
Strain into chilled glass.
Garnish with Orange.

ORANGE BUCK
Fill glass with ice.
1 1/2 oz Gin
1 oz Orange Juice
1 tbsp Lime Juice
Shake.
Strain into chilled glass.
Top with Ginger Ale.

ORANGE DROP
Moisten inside of shot glass with
Orange Juice, then coat inside of
glass with Sugar.
Fill shot glass with chilled Vodka.

ORANGE DROP 2
Fill shot glass with Orange Vodka
Coat Orange wedge with Sugar.

ORANGE FREEZE (frozen)
In Blender:
1/2 cup of Ice
2 oz Vodka
Scoop of Orange Sherbet
Dash of Orange Juice
Blend until smooth.
If too thick add orange juice.
If too thin add sherbet.

ORANGE JULIUS (frozen)
In Blender:
1/2 cup of Ice
1 1/2 oz Vodka
1/2 oz Triple Sec or Curacao
Scoop of Orange Sherbet
1 Egg White
Blend until smooth.
If too thick add orange juice.
If too thin add ice or sherbet.

ORANGE KRUSH
Fill glass with ice.
1 1/2 oz Vodka
1/2 oz Triple Sec
1 oz Orange Juice
1 oz Lemon-Lime Soda
Stir.
Serve or strain into short glass.

ORANGE LIQUEUR
(type liqueur)
Mix together:
40 Coffee Beans
1 mashed ripe Orange
1 qt Vodka
1 1/2 cups Sugar
Store for 3 months.
Strain through cheesecloth.

ORANGE MARGARITA (frozen)
In Blender:
1/2 cup of Ice
1 1/2 oz Tequila
1/2 oz Triple Sec
or Orange Liqueur
Dash of Lime Juice
Scoop of Orange Sherbet
Blend until smooth.
If too thick add juice.
If too thin add ice or sherbet.
Garnish with Orange and Lime.

ORANGE OASIS
Fill glass with ice.
1 1/2 oz Gin
1/2 oz Cherry Brandy
4 oz Orange Juice
Stir.
Top with Ginger Ale.

ORANGE WHIP
In Blender:
1/2 cup of Ice
1 Egg White
Scoop of Orange Sherbet
2 oz Orange Juice
Blend until smooth.
If too thick add juice.
If too thin add sherbet or ice.

OR-E-OH COOKIE aka
COOKIES AND CREAM (frozen)
In Blender:
1/2 cup of Ice
1 oz Vodka
3/4 oz Dark Creme De Cacao
2 cookies
Scoop of Vanilla Ice Cream
Blend until smooth.
If too thick add Milk or Cream.
If too thin add ice or Ice Cream.
Garnish with a cookie.

ORIENT EXPRESS
Fill glass with ice.
3/4 oz Ginger Liqueur
1 tsp Sugar
Fill with espresso.

N
O

ORIENTAL
Fill glass with ice.
1 oz Whiskey
1/2 oz Triple Sec
1/2 oz Sweet Vermouth
1/2 oz Lime Juice
Shake.
Strain into chilled glass.

ORGASM aka
BURNT ALMOND,
ROASTED TOASTED ALMOND
Fill glass with ice.
1 oz Vodka
1 oz Coffee Liqueur
1 oz Amaretto
Fill with Cream or Milk.
Shake.

ORGASM 2
Fill glass with ice.
1/2 oz Vodka
1/2 oz Triple Sec
1/2 oz Amaretto
1/2 oz White Creme De Cacao
1 oz Cream
Shake.
Serve or strain into short glass.

ORGASM 3
Fill glass with ice.
3/4 oz Coffee Liqueur
3/4 oz Amaretto
3/4 oz Irish Cream
Fill with equal parts Milk or Cream
and Soda Water.

ORSINI (frozen)
In Blender:
1/2 cup of Ice
1 1/2 oz Gin
1/2 oz Triple Sec
Dash of Sour Mix
Dash of Orange Juice
Scoop of Vanilla Ice Cream.
Blend until smooth.
If too thick add Milk or Cream. If too
thin add ice or Ice Cream.

OSTEND FIZZ
Fill glass with ice.
1 oz Kirschwasser
1 oz Creme De Cassis
Stir.
Top with Soda Water.
Garnish with Lemon Twist.

OUT OF THE BLUE
Fill glass with ice.
1/4 oz Vodka
1/4 oz Blue Curacao
1/4 oz Blueberry Schnapps
Dash of Sour Mix
Shake.
Top with Soda Water.

OUTRIGGER
Fill glass with ice.
1 oz Light Rum
1/2 oz Amaretto
Fill with equal parts of Cranberry
and Pineapple Juice.
Top with Dark Rum.

OXBEND
Fill glass with ice.
1 oz Southern Comfort
1/2 oz Tequila
Dash of Grenadine
Fill with Orange Juice.
Stir.

OYSTER SHOT aka
LOUISIANA SHOOTER
In a shot glass:
1 raw oyster
1-3 dashes of Tabasco Sauce
1/4 tsp Horseradish
Fill with Vodka or Peppered Vodka.

OZARK MOUNTAIN PUNCH
Fill glass with ice.
1/2 oz Vodka
1/2 oz Gin
1/2 oz Tequila
1/2 oz Bourbon
Dash of Orgeat Syrup
Fill with Orange Juice.
Shake.
Top with 151-Proof Rum.

P. M. S.
Fill glass with ice.
3/4 oz Peach Schnapps
3/4 oz Coconut Rum
3/4 oz Russian Vodka
Stir.
Strain into chilled glass.

PACIFIC PACIFIER
Fill glass with ice.
1 oz Orange Liqueur or Triple Sec
1/2 oz Banana Liqueur
1/2 oz Cream
Shake.

PADDY COCKTAIL
Fill glass with ice.
1 1/2 oz Irish Whiskey
3/4oz Sweet Vermouth
3 dashes of Bitters
Shake.
Strain into chilled glass.

PAGO PAGO
Fill glass with ice.
1 1/2 oz Amber Rum
1/2 tsp White Creme De Cacao
1/2 tsp Green Chartreuse
1/2 oz Pineapple Juice
1/2 oz Lime Juice
Shake.

PAIN IN THE ASS (frozen)
In Blender:
1 cup of Ice
2 oz Rum
1/2 oz Banana Liqueur
1/2 oz Blackberry Brandy
Dash of Lime Juice
Dash of Grenadine
Dash of Cream of Coconut
1/2 cup fresh or canned Pineapple
Blend.

PAINT BALL
Fill glass with ice.
1/2 oz Southern Comfort
1/2 oz Triple Sec
1/2 oz Irish Cream
1/2 oz Banana Liqueur
1/2 oz Blue Curacao
Shake. Strain into shot glass.

PAIR OF JACKS (floater)
1 oz Yukon Jack (bottom)
1 oz Bourbon (top)

PAISLEY MARTINI
Fill glass with ice.
2 oz Gin
1/2 tsp Dry Vermouth
1/2 tsp Scotch
Shake.
Strain into chilled glass.

PALL MALL
Fill glass with ice.
1 oz Gin
1 oz Dry Vermouth
1 oz Sweet Vermouth
1 tsp White Creme De Menthe
2 dashes of Orange Bitters
Stir.

PALM BEACHER
Fill glass with ice.
1 1/2 oz Dark Rum
1/2 oz Amaretto
Fill with Orange Juice.
Shake.

PALMETTO
Fill glass with ice.
1 1/2 oz Rum
1 oz Sweet Vermouth
2 dashes of Bitters
Stir.
Serve or strain into chilled glass.
Garnish with Lemon Twist.

**PAN GALACTIC GARGLE
BLASTER**
Fill glass with ice.
3/4 oz Vodka
3/4 oz Rum
3/4 oz Melon Liqueur
Dash of Sour Mix
Dash of Lime Juice
Shake.
Strain into chilled glass.
Fill with Lemon-Lime Soda.

**PAN GALACTIC GARGLE
BLASTER 2**
Fill glass with ice.
1 1/2 oz Vodka
1/2 oz Triple Sec
Dash of Grenadine
4 oz Pineapple Juice
Shake
Strain into chilled glass.
Fill with Lemon-Lime Soda.

**PAN GALACTIC GARGLE
BLASTER 3**
Fill glass with ice.
1 1/2 oz Vodka
1/2 oz Blue Curacao
4 oz Champagne
Stir (gently).
Strain into chilled glass.
Garnish with Bitters soaked Sugar
cube
and a cocktail onion.

PANABRAITOR
Fill glass with ice.
1 oz Southern Comfort
1/2 oz Black Raspberry Liqueur
1/2 oz Triple Sec
Fill with equal parts Sour Mix and
Orange Juice.
Shake.

PANAMA
Fill glass with ice.
1 oz Dark Rum or Brandy
3/4 oz White Creme De Cacao
3/4 oz Cream
Shake.
Serve or strain into chilled glass.
Garnish with Nutmeg.

PANAMA JACK
Fill glass with ice.
2 oz Yukon Jack
Fill with equal parts Pineapple and
Cranberry Juice.

PANAMA RED
Fill glass with ice.
1 1/2 oz Gold Tequila
1/2 oz Triple Sec
Dash of Grenadine
Dash of Sour Mix
Shake.
Strain into chilled glass.

PANCHO VILLA
Fill glass with ice.
1 oz Rum
1 oz Gin
1 oz Apricot Brandy
1 tsp Cherry Brandy
1 tsp Pineapple Juice
Shake.

O

P

PANDA BEAR (frozen)
In Blender:
1/2 cup of Ice
1 oz Amaretto
1/2 oz White Creme De Cacao
1/2 oz White Creme De Menthe
Scoop of Vanilla Ice Cream
2-3 dashes of vanilla extract
Blend until smooth.
If too thick add Milk or Cream.
If too thin add ice or Ice Cream.
Dribble Chocolate Syrup on the
inside of glass before pouring in
drink.

PANTHER
Fill glass with ice.
2 oz Tequila
2 oz Sour Mix
Shake.

PANTOMIME
Fill glass with ice.
1 1/2 oz Dry Vermouth
3 drops of Orgeat Syrup
Dash of Grenadine
1/2 an Egg White
Shake.
Strain into chilled glass.

PANTY BURNER
Fill glass with ice.
3/4 oz Amaretto
3/4 oz Hazelnut Liqueur
3/4 oz Coffee Liqueur
Shake. Strain into shot glass.

PANTY DROPPER
Fill glass with ice.
1 oz Vodka
1 oz Coffee Liqueur
1 oz Sloe Gin
Fill with Milk.
Shake.
Garnish with Cherry.

PARADISE
Fill glass with ice.
1 oz Gin
1 oz Apricot Brandy
1 oz Orange Juice
Stir.
Strain into chilled glass.

PARADISE PUNCH
Fill glass with ice.
1 oz Amber Rum
1 oz Dark Rum
1 oz Sour Mix
1 oz Cream of Coconut
1 oz Cream or Milk
Shake.

PARANOIA
Fill glass with ice.
1 oz Coconut Rum
1 oz Amaretto
Fill with equal parts Orange and
Pineapple Juice.
Shake.
Garnish with Pineapple or Orange.

PARFAIT
In Blender:
1/2 cup of Ice
2 oz Desired Liqueur
Scoop of Vanilla Ice Cream
Blend until smooth.
If too thick add Liqueur or Milk.
If too thin add ice or Ice Cream.

PARIS MATCH aka
PARIS IS BURNING
1 oz Cognac or Brandy
1 oz Black Raspberry Liqueur
Heat in microwave 10-15
seconds.

PARISIAN
Fill glass with ice.
1 oz Gin
1 oz Dry Vermouth
1 oz Creme De Cassis
Stir.
Strain into chilled glass.

PARISIAN BLONDE
Fill glass with ice.
1 oz Dark Rum
1 oz Triple Sec or Curacao
1 oz Cream
Shake.
Strain into chilled glass.

PARISIAN FRAPPE
Fill large stemmed glass (Red Wine
glass, Champagne saucer) with
crushed ice.
3/4 oz Dark Rum
3/4 oz Orange Liqueur
3/4 oz Cream

PARK AVENUE
Fill glass with ice.
1 1/2 oz Gin
1/2 oz Sweet Vermouth
1 oz Pineapple Juice
2-3 drops of Curacao (optional)
Stir.
Strain into chilled glass.

PARROT HEAD
Fill glass with ice.
1 1/2 oz Spiced Rum
1/2 oz Black Raspberry Liqueur
Fill with Pineapple Juice.
Shake.

PASSIONATE POINT
Fill glass with ice.
3/4 oz Amber Rum
3/4 oz Peach Schnapps
3/4 oz Orange Liqueur
2 oz Orange Juice
2 oz Cranberry Juice
Shake.
Strain into chilled glass.

PASSIONATE SCREW
Fill glass with ice.
1 oz Vodka
1 oz Coconut Rum
1 oz Black Raspberry Liqueur
Dash of Grenadine
Fill with equal parts Orange and
Pineapple Juice.
Shake.
Garnish with Cherry and Orange or
Pineapple.

PEACH ALEXANDER (frozen)
In Blender:
1/2 cup of Ice
1 oz Peach Schnapps
1/2 oz White Creme De Cacao
1/2 fresh or canned Peach
1 1/2 oz Cream
or 1/2 scoop Vanilla Ice Cream
Blend until smooth.
If too thick add juice or Milk.
If too thin add ice or Ice Cream.

PEACH BLASTER
Fill glass with ice
2 oz Peach Schnapps
Fill with Cranberry Juice.
Stir.

PEACH BLOW FIZZ
Fill glass with ice.
2 oz Gin
1 oz Cream
1 tsp Sugar Syrup
or Powdered Sugar
1 oz Lemon Juice
1/4 fresh ripe Peach (mashed with
no skin or pit)
Shake.
Top with Soda Water.

PEACH BREEZE
Fill glass with ice.
1 oz Vodka
1 oz Peach Schnapps
Fill with equal parts Cranberry and
Grapefruit Juice.
Shake.

PEACH BUCK
Fill glass with ice.
1 1/2 oz Vodka
1/2 oz Peach Schnapps
1/2 oz Lemon Juice
Shake.
Top with Ginger Ale.
Garnish with peach.

PEACH BULLDOG
Fill glass with ice.
1 oz Vodka
1 oz Peach Schnapps
Fill with Cranberry Juice.
Stir.

PEACH COBBLER
1 oz Rum
1 oz Peach Schnapps
Dash of Cinnamon Schnapps
Fill with hot Apple Cider.
Stir.
Top with Whipped Cream.

PEACH COLADA (frozen)
In Blender:
1/2 cup of Ice
2 oz Light Rum
2 tbsp Cream of Coconut
1 cup of fresh or canned Peaches
1 tbsp Vanilla Ice Cream (optional)
Blend until smooth.
If too thick add fruit or juice.
If too thin add ice or Ice Cream.
Garnish with Peach and Cherry.

PEACH DAIQUIRI (frozen)
In Blender:
1 cup of Ice
1 oz Peach Schnapps
1 oz Rum
1/2 cup of fresh or canned Peaches
Dash of Lime Juice
Blend until smooth.

PEACH FUZZ
Fill glass with ice.
2 oz Peach Schnapps
Fill with equal parts Milk and
Cranberry Juice.
Shake.
Serve or strain into chilled glass.

PEACH MIMOSA
Fill glass with ice.
Fill 3/4 with Champagne.
Splash of Peach Schnapps
Fill with Orange Juice.
Garnish with Orange.

PEACH VELVET (frozen)
In Blender:
1/2 cup of Ice.
1 1/2 oz Peach Schnapps
1/2 oz White Creme De Cacao
1 scoop of Vanilla Ice Cream
1/2 fresh or canned Peach
Blend until smooth.

PEACHES AND CREAM
Fill glass with ice.
1 oz Irish Cream
1 oz Peach Schnapps
Splash of Cream
Shake.
Top with Soda Water.

PEANUT BUTTER AND JELLY
Fill glass with ice.
1 oz Hazelnut Liqueur
1 oz Black Raspberry Liqueur
Shake. Strain into shot glass.
Garnish with 3 or 4 peanuts.

P

PEANUT BUTTER AND JELLY

(frozen)
In Blender:
1/2 cup of Ice
1 oz Black Raspberry Liqueur
1 oz Hazelnut Liqueur
Dash of Irish Cream
3 tbsp Cocktail Peanuts
3 tbsp Grape Jelly
Scoop of Vanilla Ice Cream.
Blend until smooth.
If too thick add Milk.
If too thin add ice or Ice Cream.

PEARL DIVER

Fill glass with ice.
1 1/2 oz Vodka
1/2 oz Orange Juice
Strain into chilled glass.
Dash of Grenadine
Splash of Lemon-Lime Soda
Garnish with stemless Cherry.

PEARL HARBOR

Fill glass with ice.
1 oz Vodka
1 oz Melon Liqueur
Fill with Pineapple Juice.
Shake.
Garnish with Cherry and Pineapple.

PEARL HARBOR (frozen)

In Blender:
1/2 cup of Ice
1 oz Vodka
1 oz Melon Liqueur
1/2 cup of fresh or canned
Pineapple
Scoop of Vanilla Ice Cream
Blend until smooth.
If too thick add fruit or juice.
If too thin add ice or Ice Cream.
Garnish with Cherry and Pineapple.

PEARL NECKLACE aka

BLOW JOB (floater)
1/2 oz Cream (bottom)
1/2 oz White Creme De Cacao
1/2 oz Vodka (top)
Contents should mix slightly.
To drink, place hands behind back
and pick up using only mouth.

PECKERHEAD

Fill glass with ice.
1 oz Yukon Jack or Southern
Comfort
1 oz Amaretto
1 oz Pineapple Juice
Shake.
Strain into chilled glass.

PEDRO COLLINS

Fill glass with ice.
2 oz Rum
Fill with Sour Mix.
Shake.
Splash of Soda Water
Garnish with Orange and Cherry.

PEGU CLUB

Fill glass with ice.
1 1/2 oz Gin
3/4 oz Orange Curacao
1 tsp Lime Juice
Dash of Bitters
Dash of Orange Bitters
Shake.
Strain into chilled glass.

PENDENNIS CLUB

Fill glass with ice.
1 1/2 oz Gin
3/4 oz Apricot Brandy
1/2 oz Lime Juice
1 tsp Sugar Syrup
3 dashes of Peychaud's Bitters
Shake.
Strain into chilled glass.

PENSACOLA (frozen)

In Blender:
1 cup of Ice
1 1/2 oz Rum
1/2 oz Guava Nectar
1/2 oz Orange Juice
1/2 oz Lemon Juice
Blend until smooth.
If too thick add juice.
If too thin add ice.

PEPPER MARTINI

Fill glass with ice.
2 oz Peppered Vodka
1/2 oz Dry Vermouth
Stir.
Strain into chilled glass or pour
contents (with ice) into short glass.
Garnish with a Jalapeno Pepper.

PEPPERMINT KISS aka
SNUGGLER, COCOANAPPS,
ADULT HOT CHOCOLATE

2 oz Peppermint Schnapps
Fill with Hot Chocolate.
Top with Whipped Cream.
Sprinkle with Shaved
Chocolate or Sprinkles.

PEPPERMINT PATTIE

Fill glass with ice.
1 oz White Creme De Cacao or
Dark Creme De Cacao
1 oz White Creme De Menthe
Stir.

PEPPERMINT PATTY

Fill glass with ice.
1 oz Peppermint Schnapps
1 oz Dark Creme De Cacao
2 oz Cream
Shake.

PEPPERMINT STINGER

Fill glass with ice.
1 1/2 oz Brandy
1/2 oz Peppermint Schnapps
Stir.
Serve or strain into chilled glass.

PERFECT MANHATTAN
Fill glass with ice.
2 oz Whiskey
1/4 oz Dry Vermouth
1/4 oz Sweet Vermouth
Stir.
Strain into chilled glass or pour
contents (with ice) into short glass.
Garnish with Cherry or Lemon
Twist.

PERNOD COCKTAIL
Fill glass with ice.
2 oz Pernod
3 dashes of Bitters
3 dashes of Sugar Syrup
1/2 oz Water
Stir.
Serve or strain into chilled glass.

PERNOD FLIP
Fill glass with ice.
1 oz Pernod
1/2 oz Orange Liqueur or Triple Sec
1/2 oz Lemon Juice
1 1/2 tsp Sugar Syrup
1 Egg
Shake.

PERNOD FLIP (frozen)
In Blender:
1 cup of Ice
1 1/2 oz Pernod
1 oz Heavy Cream
1/2 oz Sugar Syrup
or Orgeat Syrup
1 Egg
Blend until smooth.
Garnish with Nutmeg.

PERNOD FRAPPE
Fill glass with ice.
1 1/2 oz Pernod
1/2 oz Anisette
3 dashes of Bitters
Shake.
Strain into chilled glass.

PERSUADER
Fill glass with ice.
1 oz Brandy
1 oz Amaretto
Fill glass with Orange Juice.
Shake.

PETRIFIER
Fill glass with ice.
2 oz Vodka
2 oz Gin
2 oz Cognac
2 oz Triple Sec
3 dashes of Bitters
Dash of Grenadine
Shake.
Strain into chilled glass.
Fill with Ginger Ale.
Garnish with Orange and Cherry.

PEZ
Fill glass with ice.
1 oz Spiced Rum
1 oz Black Raspberry Liqueur
1 oz Sour Mix
Shake. Strain into shot glass.

PHANTOM
Fill glass with ice.
1 1/2 oz Black Raspberry Liqueur
1/2 oz Black Sambuca
Stir.
Serve or strain into chilled glass.

PHOEBE SNOW
Fill glass with ice.
1 1/2 oz Cognac or Brandy
1 1/2 oz Dubonnet Rouge
2 dashes of Bitters
Stir.
Serve or strain into chilled glass.
Garnish with Lemon Twist.

PICKLED BRAIN (floater)
3/4 oz Irish Cream (bottom)
3/4 oz Vodka
1/2 oz Green Creme De Menthe
(top)

PICON FIZZ
Fill glass with ice.
1 1/2 oz Amer Picon
1/4 oz Grenadine
3 oz Soda Water
Float 1/2 oz Cognac or Brandy on
top.

PICON ORANGE
Fill glass with ice.
2 oz Amer Picon
2 oz Orange Juice
Shake.
Fill with Soda Water.
Garnish with Orange.

PICON SOUR
Fill glass with ice.
1 1/2 oz Amer Picon
1 oz Sour Mix or Lemon Juice
1/2 tsp Powdered Sugar
or Sugar Syrup
Shake.
Strain into chilled glass.

PIERRE COLLINS
Fill glass with ice.
2 oz Cognac or Brandy
Fill with Sour Mix
Shake.
Splash with Lemon-Lime Soda.
Garnish with Orange and Cherry.

PILE DRIVER
Fill glass with ice.
2 oz Vodka
Fill with prune juice.
Stir.

P

PILOT BOAT
Fill glass with ice.
1 1/2 oz Dark Rum
1 oz Banana Liqueur
1 1/2 oz Sour Mix
Dash of Lime Juice
Shake.
Strain into chilled glass.

PIMLICO SPECIAL
Fill glass with ice.
1 1/2 oz Brandy
1/2 oz Amaretto
1/2 oz White Creme De Cacao
Shake.
Strain into chilled glass.

PIMM'S CUP
Fill glass with ice.
2 oz Pimm's cup No. 1
Fill with Lemon-Lime Soda.
Garnish with Lemon and/or
Cucumber.

PIÑA
Fill glass with ice.
1 1/2 oz Tequila
3 oz Pineapple Juice
1 oz Lime Juice
1 tsp Honey or Sugar Syrup
Shake.
Garnish with Lime.

PIÑA COLADA (frozen)
In Blender:
1/2 cup of Ice
2 oz Light Rum
2 tbsp Cream of Coconut
1/2 cup fresh or canned Pineapple
1 tbsp Vanilla Ice Cream (optional)
Blend until smooth.
If too thick add fruit or juice.
If too thin add ice or Ice Cream.
Garnish with Pineapple and Cherry.

PIÑATA
Fill glass with ice.
1 1/2 oz Tequila
1 oz Banana Liqueur
1 oz Lime Juice
Shake.
Serve or strain into chilled glass.

PINEAPPLE BOMB
Fill glass with ice.
1 1/2 oz Rum
1/2 oz Amaretto
Fill with Pineapple Juice.
Shake.

PINEAPPLE BOMBER
Fill glass with ice.
1 oz Spiced Rum
1 oz Southern Comfort
1 oz Amaretto
Fill with Pineapple Juice.
Shake.

PINEAPPLE BOMBER 2
Fill glass with ice.
1 oz Yukon Jack
1 oz Amaretto
Fill with Pineapple Juice.
Shake.

PINEAPPLE DAIQUIRI (frozen)
In Blender:
1/2 cup of Ice
1 2 oz Rum
1/2 oz Lime Juice
1/2 cup of fresh or canned
Pineapple
Blend until Smooth.
If too thick add juice.
If too thin add ice.

PINEAPPLE MARGARITA (frozen)
In Blender:
1 cup of ice
2 oz Tequila
1/2 oz Lime Juice
3/4 cup Fresh or canned Pineapple
(with juice)
Blend until smooth. If too thick add
juice.
If too thin add ice.
Garnish with Pineapple.

PINEAPPLE MARTINI
Fill glass with ice.
2 tbsp Crushed Pineapple
3 oz Vodka or Gin
Dash of Simple Syrup or pinch
Sugar
Shake.
Strain into chilled glass.

PINEAPPLE PASSION
Fill glass with ice.
1 1/2 oz Rum
1 oz Orange Curacao
2 oz Pineapple Juice
1 oz Passion Fruit Juice
Shake.

PINK ALMOND
Fill glass with ice.
1 oz Whiskey
1/2 oz Creme De Nouyax
1/2 oz Amaretto
1/2 oz Kirschwasser
1/2 oz Lemon Juice
Shake.
Garnish with Lemon.

PINK CADDIE
Fill glass with ice.
1 1/2 oz Rum Tequila
1/2 oz Triple Sec
Fill with equal parts Sour Mix and
Cranberry Juice.
Shake.

PINK FLOYD (frozen)
In Blender:
1/2 cup of Ice
1 oz Vodka
1 oz Sloe Gin
1/2 cup fresh or canned Pineapple
Blend until smooth.
Top with Soda Water.
Garnish with Pineapple.

PINK GATOR
Fill glass with ice.
1 oz Light Rum
1 oz Amber Rum
1/2 oz Grenadine
Dash of Sour Mix
Fill with equal parts Orange and
Pineapple Juice.

PINK GIN
Fill glass with ice.
2 oz Gin
2 dashes of Bitters
Stir.
Serve or strain into chilled glass.

PINK HOTEL
Fill glass with ice.
1 oz Vodka
1/2 oz Creme De Noyaux
Shake. Strain into short glass.
Dash of Ginger Ale
Fill with Beer.

PINK LADY
Fill glass with ice.
1 1/2 oz Gin
1 1/2 oz Cream
1 tsp Grenadine
Shake.
Strain into chilled glass.

PINK LEMONADE
Fill glass with ice.
1 1/2 oz Vodka or Rum
1 oz Cranberry Juice
2 oz Sour Mix
Shake.
Fill with Lemon-Lime Soda.
Garnish with Lemon.

PINK LEMONADE 2
Fill glass with ice.
2 oz Citrus Vodka
Dash of Grenadine
Shake.
Strain into chilled glass.

PINK MISSILE
Fill glass with ice.
1 1/2 oz Vodka
1/2 oz Black Raspberry Liqueur
Dash of Grenadine
Dash of Cranberry Juice
Fill with equal parts Grapefruit
Juice and Ginger Ale.
Stir.

PINK PANTHER
Fill glass with ice.
3/4 oz Gin
3/4 oz Dry Vermouth
1/2 oz Creme De Cassis
1/2 oz Orange Juice
1/2 Egg White
Shake.
Strain into chilled glass.

PINK PANTHER 2
Fill glass with ice.
2 oz Rum
Dash of Lemon Juice
Dash of Cream
Dash of Grenadine
Shake.
Strain into chilled glass.

PINK PANTHER 3
Fill glass with ice.
2 oz Gin
2 oz Apple Juice
Dash of Grenadine
Fill with Grapefruit Juice.
Shake.

PINK PANTY PULLDOWN
Fill glass with ice.
2 oz Grain Alcohol
Fill with Pink Lemonade
Garnish with Lemon.

PINK PARADISE
Fill glass with ice.
1 oz Coconut Rum
1 oz Amaretto
2 oz Pineapple Juice
Fill with Cranberry Juice.
Stir.

PINK PUSSYCAT
Fill glass with ice.
1 1/2 oz Gin or Vodka
1/2 oz Grenadine
Fill with Pineapple or Grapefruit Juice.
Shake.

PINK ROSE
Fill glass with ice.
1 1/2 oz Gin
1 tsp Lemon Juice
1 tsp Heavy Cream
1 Egg White
3 dashes of Grenadine
Shake.
Strain into chilled glass.

PINK SLIP
1 oz Coconut Rum
1 oz Cranberry juice
Fill with Champagne.

PINK SQUIRREL
Fill glass with ice.
1 oz Creme De Nouyax.
1 oz White Creme De Cacao
1 oz Cream or Milk
Shake.
Strain into chilled glass.

P

PINK VERANDA
Fill glass with ice.
1 oz Amber Rum
1/2 oz Dark Rum
1 1/2 oz Cranberry Juice
1/2 oz Lime Juice
1 tsp Sugar
1/2 Egg White
Shake.

PINK WHISKERS
Fill glass with ice.
1 oz Apricot Brandy
1/2 oz Dry Vermouth
1 oz Orange Juice
1 tsp Grenadine
3 dashes of White Creme De
Menthe
Shake.
Float 1 oz Port on top.

PISCO PUNCH
Fill glass with ice.
3 oz Brandy
1 tsp Lime Juice
1 tsp Pineapple Juice
2 oz cold Water (optional)
Stir.
Garnish with Pineapple.

PISCO SOUR
Fill glass with ice.
2 oz Brandy
1 oz Sour Mix
1/2 Egg White
Dash of Lime Juice
Shake.
Strain into chilled glass.
2-3 dashes of Bitters

PITBULL ON CRACK
Fill glass with ice.
3/4 oz Tequila
3/4 oz Jaegermeister
3/4 oz 100-proof Peppermint
Schnapps
Shake. Strain into shot glass.

PIXIE STICK
Fill glass with ice.
1 oz Gin or Vodka
1 oz Melon Liqueur
Fill with Lemon-Lime Soda.

PIXIE STICK 2
Fill glass with ice.
1 oz Southern Comfort
1 oz Blackberry Brandy
Fill with Lemonade.
Shake.

PLAID
Fill glass with ice.
1 1/2 oz Gin
1/2 oz Peach Schnapps
Fill with Ginger Ale.
Stir.

PLANTER'S PUNCH
Fill glass with ice.
1 1/2 oz Light Rum
Dash of Grenadine
Fill with equal parts Sour Mix and
either Orange or Pineapple Juice.
Shake.
Top with 1/2 oz Dark Rum.
Garnish with Orange and Cherry.

PLANTER'S PUNCH 2
Fill glass with ice.
1 oz Dark Rum
1 oz Amber Rum
Dash of Grenadine
Dash of Sweet Vermouth
Dash of Bitters
1 tsp of Cherry Juice
or Grenadine
Fill with equal parts Sour Mix and
Pineapple Juice.
Shake.

PLATINUM BLOND
Fill glass with ice.
1 1/2 oz Rum
3/4 oz Orange Liqueur or Curacao
or Triple Sec
Fill with Milk or Cream.
Shake.

PLAYBOY COOLER
Fill glass with ice.
1 oz Rum
1 oz Coffee Liqueur
Dash of Lime Juice
Fill with Pineapple Juice.
Shake.
Dash of Cola.

PLAZA
Fill glass with ice.
3/4 oz Gin
3/4 oz Dry Vermouth
3/4 oz Sweet Vermouth
1 tbsp Pineapple Juice (optional)
Shake.
Strain into chilled glass.

PLEASURE DOME (floater)
3/4 oz Brandy (bottom)
3/4 oz White Creme De Cacao
3/4 oz Benedictine (top)

POINSETTIA aka
NANTUCKET RED
Fill glass 3/4 with ice.
Fill 3/4 with Champagne.
Fill with Cranberry Juice.
Garnish with Lime.

POINT (floater)
3/4 oz Drambuie (bottom)
3/4 oz White Creme De Menthe
3/4 oz Irish Cream (top)

POKER
Fill glass with ice.
1 1/2 oz Amber Rum
1 oz Dry Vermouth
Stir.
Strain into chilled glass.
Garnish with Orange Twist.

POLISH BUTTERFLY
1 oz Grain Alcohol
1 oz Blue Curacao
Dash of Grenadine

POLLYANNA
Fill glass with ice.
1 1/2 oz Gin
1/4 oz Sweet Vermouth
1/4 oz Grenadine
Shake.
Strain into chilled glass.

POLLY'S SPECIAL
Fill glass with ice.
1 1/2 oz Scotch
1/2 oz Triple Sec
1/2 oz Grapefruit Juice
Shake.

POLO
Fill glass with ice.
1 1/2 oz Gin
1 tbsp Orange Juice
1 tbsp Lemon or Grapefruit Juice
Stir.
Serve or strain into chilled glass.

POLYNESIAN
Fill glass with ice.
1 1/2 oz Vodka
3/4 oz Cherry Brandy
3/4 oz Lime Juice
Shake.
Rub rim of second glass with Lime
and dip rim in Powdered Sugar.
Strain into second glass.

POND SCUM
Fill glass with ice.
2 oz Vodka
Fill with Soda Water.
Float 1/4oz Irish Cream on top.

POOP DECK
Fill glass with ice.
1 oz Blackberry Brandy
1/2 oz Brandy
1/2 oz Port
Shake.
Strain into chilled glass.

PONTIAC
Fill glass with ice.
2 oz Amaretto
Fill with Soda Water.

POP-SICLE
Fill glass with ice.
2 oz Amaretto
Fill with equal parts Cream
and Orange Juice.
Shake.

POP-SICLE 2
Fill glass with ice.
1 1/2 oz Southern Comfort
1/2 oz Amaretto
Dash of Grenadine
1 oz Orange Juice
Fill with Lemon-Lime Soda.

POP-SICLE 3
Fill glass with ice.
1 1/2 oz Vodka
1/2 oz Triple Sec
Dash of Milk or Cream
Fill with Orange Juice.
Shake.

POPPER
In shot glass:
1 oz Desired Liqueur or Liquor
1 oz Ginger Ale
or Lemon-Lime Soda
Cover glass with napkin and hand,
then slam on bar top.
Drink while foaming.

PORCH CLIMBER
Fill glass with ice.
1 oz Rum
1/2 oz Apricot Brandy
1/2 oz Cherry Brandy
Fill with Sour Mix.
Shake.

PORT IN A STORM
Fill glass with ice.
1 oz Brandy or Cognac
2 oz Port
Fill with Red Wine
Strain.
Garnish with mint sprig.

PORT AND STARBOARD (floater)
1 oz Green Creme De Menthe
(bottom)
1 oz Grenadine (top)

PORT ANTONIO
Fill glass with ice.
1 oz Amber Rum
1/2 oz Dark Rum
1/2 oz Lime Juice
1/2 oz Tia Maria
1 tsp Falernum
Shake.
Garnish with Lime.

PORT PELICAN
Fill glass with ice.
1 oz Rum
1/2 oz Banana Liqueur
1/2 oz Galliano
Fill with Orange Juice.
Shake.

P

PORT SANGAREE
Fill glass with ice.
2 oz Port
1/2 tsp Powdered Sugar
1 oz Water
Fill with Soda Water.
Stir.
Float 1 tsp Brandy on top (optional).

POUSSE CAFÉ
A glass of liqueurs arranged
in layers.

POUSSE CAFÉ (floater)
Layer ingredients in order and in
equal amounts.
1/4 oz Grenadine (bottom)
1/4 oz Coffee Liqueur
1/4 oz White Creme De Cacao
1/4 oz Blue Curacao
1/4 oz Galliano
1/4 oz Green Chartreuse
1/4 oz Brandy (top)

PRADO
Fill glass with ice.
1 1/2 oz Tequila
1/2 oz Maraschino Liqueur
3/4 oz Lime Juice
1/2 Egg White
1 tsp Grenadine
Shake.
Garnish with Cherry.

PRAIRIE CHICKEN
In shot glass:
1 oz Tequila
1 raw egg yolk
2-10 dashes of Tabasco.

PRAIRIE FIRE aka
BURNING BUSH
2 oz Tequila
Add Tabasco Sauce until pink.

PRAIRIE OYSTER
1 oz Brandy or Whiskey
1 unbroken Egg Yolk
Dash of Wine Vinegar
Dash of Tabasco Sauce
1 tsp Worcestershire Sauce
2 oz Tomato Juice
Pinch of Salt
Stir gently.

PREAKNESS
Fill glass with ice.
1 1/2 oz Whiskey
1/4 oz Benedictine
1/4 oz Sweet Vermouth
Dash of Bitters
Stir.
Strain into chilled glass.
Garnish with Lemon Twist.

PRESIDENTE
Fill glass with ice.
1 1/2 oz Rum
1/2 oz Dry Vermouth
1/2 oz Curacao
Dash of Grenadine
Shake.
Serve or strain into chilled glass.
Garnish with Lemon Twist.

PRESS
Fill glass with ice.
2 oz Whiskey
Fill with equal parts Ginger Ale and
Soda Water.

PRIMAL SCREAM
Fill glass with ice.
1 oz Tequila or Grain Alcohol
1 oz Coffee Liqueur
Fill with Soda Water.

PRINCE EDWARD
Fill glass with ice.
1 1/2 oz Scotch
1/2 oz Lillet Blanc
1/4 oz Drambuie
Shake.
Serve or strain into chilled glass.
Garnish with Orange.

PRINCE IGOR aka
HIGH ROLLER
Fill glass with ice.
1 1/2 oz Vodka
3/4 oz Orange Liqueur
Dash of Grenadine
Fill with Orange Juice.
Shake.
Garnish with Orange and Cherry.

PRINCE OF WALES
Fill glass with ice.
1 oz Brandy
1 oz Madeira
or any sweet Red Wine
1/4 oz Curacao
3 dashes of Bitters
Shake.
Strain into wine glass.
Fill with Champagne.
Garnish with Orange.

PRINCE'S SMILE
Fill glass with ice.
1 oz Gin
1/2 oz Apricot Brandy
1/2 oz Apple Brandy
1/4 oz Lemon Juice
Shake.
Strain into chilled glass.

PRINCESS MARY'S PRIDE
Fill glass with ice.
1 1/2 oz Apple Brandy
3/4 oz Dubonnet Rouge
1/2 oz Dry Vermouth
Shake.
Strain into chilled glass.

PRINCETON
Fill glass with ice.
1 1/2 oz Gin
3/4 oz Port
3 dashes of Orange Bitters
Shake.
Strain into chilled glass.
Garnish with Lemon Twist.

PRISON BITCH
Fill glass with ice.
1 1/2 oz Vodka
1/2 oz Triple Sec
1/2 oz Amaretto
Fill with equal parts Orange
and Cranberry Juice.
Shake.

PROFESSOR AND MARYANN
Fill glass with ice.
1 1/2 oz Vodka
1/2 oz Apricot Brandy
Dash of Lime Juice
Fill with Soda Water.
Stir.
Garnish with Lime.

PROVINCETOWN
Fill glass with ice.
2 oz Vodka
2 oz Cranberry Juice
2 oz Grapefruit Juice
Strain into chilled glass.
Fill with Soda Water.
Garnish with Lemon wedge.

PTERODACTYL
Fill glass with ice.
1/2 oz Vodka
1/2 oz Rum
1/2 oz Triple Sec
1/2 oz Amaretto
1/2 oz Southern Comfort
Dash of Grenadine
Fill with Orange Juice.
Shake.
Garnish with Orange.

PUCCINI
Fill glass with ice.
1 1/2 oz Vodka
1 oz Melon Liqueur
1/2 oz Tuaca
Fill with Orange Juice.
Shake.

PUERTO RICAN SCREW
Fill glass with ice.
2 oz Rum
Fill with Orange Juice.

PUMPKIN PIE (floater)
1/2 oz Coffee Liqueur (bottom)
1/2 oz Irish Cream
1/2 oz Cinnamon Schnapps (top)

PUNT E MES NEGRONI
Fill glass with ice.
1/2 oz Gin or Vodka
1/2 oz Punt e Mes
1/2 oz Sweet Vermouth
Shake.
Strain into chilled glass.
Garnish with Orange Twist.

PURPLE ALASKAN
Fill glass with ice.
1/2 oz Bourbon
1/2 oz Southern Comfort
1/2 oz Amaretto
1/2 oz Black Raspberry Liqueur
1/2 oz Orange Juice
Shake. Strain into shot glass.

PURPLE ARMADILLO
Fill glass with ice.
1 1/2 oz Rum
1/2 oz Blue Curacao
Fill with equal parts Sour Mix and
Cranberry Juice.
Shake.
Top with Lemon-Lime Soda.

PURPLE BUNNY
Fill glass with ice.
1 oz Cherry Brandy
1/2 oz White Creme De Cacao
1 oz Cream or Milk
Shake.
Strain into chilled glass.

PURPLE DREAM
Fill glass with ice.
1 oz Black Raspberry Liqueur
1 oz White Creme De Cacao
Fill with Milk or Cream.
Shake.

PURPLE FLIRT
Fill glass with ice.
1 1/2 oz Amber Rum
1/2 oz Blue Curacao
Dash of Pineapple Juice
Dash of Cranberry Juice
Dash of Sour Mix
Dash of Grenadine
Shake.
Strain into chilled glass.

PURPLE HAZE
Fill glass with ice.
1 1/2 oz Vodka
1/2 oz Black Raspberry Liqueur
Fill with equal parts Sour Mix,
Cranberry, and Pineapple Juice.
Shake.

PURPLE HAZE 2
Fill glass with ice.
1 oz Vodka
1 oz Black Raspberry Liqueur
1 oz Cranberry Juice
Stir.
Strain into chilled glass.

P

PURPLE HEATHER
Fill glass with ice.
1 1/2 oz Scotch
1/2 oz Creme De Cassis
Fill with Soda Water.

PURPLE HELMETED WARRIOR
Fill glass with ice.
1/2 oz Gin
1/2 oz Southern Comfort
1/2 oz Peach Schnapps
1/2 oz Blue Curacao
Dash of Grenadine
Dash of Lime Juice
Shake. Strain into shot glass.

PURPLE HOOTER or
PURPLE KAMIKAZE,
RASPBERRY GIMLET
Fill glass with ice.
2 oz Vodka
1/2 oz Black Raspberry Liqueur
1/2 oz Lime Juice
Stir.
Strain into shot glass.

PURPLE JESUS
1 oz Canadian Whiskey
1 oz Blackberry Brandy
1 oz Peppermint Schnapps
Dash of Tabasco
Stir.

PURPLE MARGARITA
Fill glass with ice.
1 oz Tequila
1/2 oz Sloe Gin
1/2 oz Blue Curacao
Dash of Lime Juice
3 oz Sour Mix
Shake.

PURPLE MATADOR
Fill glass with ice.
1 1/2 oz Amaretto
1 oz Black Raspberry Liqueur
1/2 oz Pineapple Juice
Shake.
Strain into chilled glass.

PURPLE NASTY
1/2 oz Creme De Cassis
Fill with equal parts Hard Cider and Ale.

PURPLE NIPPLE (floater)
1/2 oz Black Raspberry Liqueur
(bottom)
1/2 oz Irish Cream (top)

PURPLE PASSION aka
TRANSFUSION
Fill glass with ice.
2 oz Vodka
Fill with equal parts Grape Juice
and Ginger Ale or Soda Water.

PURPLE PASSION 2
Fill glass with ice.
2 oz Vodka
Fill with Grape Cool Aid.

PURPLE RAIN
Fill glass with ice.
1/2 oz Vodka
1/2 oz Gin
1/2 oz Rum
1/2 oz Tequila
1/2 oz Triple Sec
Fill with Sour Mix.
Shake.
Top with Black Raspberry Liqueur.
Garnish with Lime.

PURPLE RAIN 2
Fill glass with ice.
1 1/2 oz Vodka
1/2 oz Blue Curacao
1 oz Cranberry Juice
Stir.
Strain into chilled glass.

PURPLE RUSSIAN
Fill glass with ice.
1 1/2 oz Vodka
1/2 oz Black Raspberry Liqueur
Stir.

PURPLE THUNDER
Fill glass with ice.
1 oz Light Rum
1 oz Amber Rum
1/2 oz Blue Curacao
Fill with equal parts Grape and
Cranberry Juice.
Shake.
Strain into chilled glass.
Fill with Soda Water.

PUSSER'S PAINKILLER
Shake without ice.
2 oz Pusser's Rum
1 oz Cream of Coconut
1 oz Orange Juice
4 oz Pineapple Juice
Pour over ice.
Garnish with a pinch of
Cinnamon and Nutmeg.

PUSSY GALORE (floater)
1/2 oz Banana Liqueur
(bottom)
1 oz White Creme De Cacao
1/2 oz Irish Cream (top)

QUAALUDE
Fill glass with ice.
1/2 oz Vodka
1/2 oz Coffee Liqueur
1/2 oz Hazelnut Liqueur
1/2 oz Dark Creme De Cacao
1/2 oz Orange Liqueur
Fill with Milk or Cream.
Shake.

QUAALUDE 2
Fill glass with ice.
1 oz Southern Comfort
1 oz Bourbon
Splash of Orange Juice
Fill with Pineapple Juice.
Shake.

QUAKER
Fill glass with ice.
1 1/2 oz Brandy
3/4 oz Rum
1/2 oz Lemon Juice
1/2 oz Raspberry Syrup
Shake.
Strain into chilled glass.
Garnish with Lemon Twist.

QUAKER CITY COOLER
Fill glass with ice.
1 oz Vodka
3 oz Chablis
1/2 oz Sugar Syrup
1/2 oz Lemon Juice
3 dashes of Vanilla Extract
Stir.
Top with 1/4 oz Grenadine.

QUARTER DECK
Fill glass with ice.
1 1/2 oz Rum
1/3 oz Sherry
1 tsp Lime Juice
Shake.
Serve or strain into chilled glass.

QUEBEC
Fill glass with ice.
1 1/2 oz Canadian Whiskey
1/2 oz Amer Picon
1/2 oz Maraschino Liqueur
1/2 oz Dry Vermouth
Shake.
Strain into chilled glass.

QUEEN
Muddle 1/2 cup Pineapple in glass.
Fill glass with ice.
1 1/2 oz Gin
1/2 oz Dry Vermouth
Stir.
Strain into chilled glass.

QUEEN ELIZABETH
Fill glass with ice.
1 oz Gin
1/2 oz Orange Liqueur
1/2 oz Lemon Juice
1 tsp Pernod
Stir.
Strain into chilled glass.

QUEEN ELIZABETH WINE
Fill glass with ice.
1 1/2 oz Benedictine
3/4 oz Dry Vermouth
3/4 oz Lemon Juice
Shake.
Strain into chilled glass.

QUELLE VIE
Fill glass with ice.
1 1/2 oz Brandy
3/4 oz Kummel
Stir.
Strain into chilled glass.

QUICK F (floater)
3/4 oz Coffee Liqueur (bottom)
3/4 oz Melon Liqueur
3/4 oz Irish Cream (top)

QUICKIE
Fill glass with ice.
1 oz Bourbon
1 oz Rum
1/4 oz Triple Sec
Stir.
Strain into chilled glass.

QUIET NUN
Fill glass with ice.
1 oz Benedictine
1 oz Tripe Sec
1 oz Cream or Milk
Shake.
Strain into chilled glass.

R. ROGERS
Fill glass with ice.
Fill with Cola.
Dash of Grenadine
Garnish with Cherry.

R. ROYCE
Fill glass with ice.
1 1/2 oz Gin
1/2 oz Dry Vermouth
1/2 oz Sweet Vermouth
Stir.
Strain into chilled glass.

RACQUET CLUB
Fill glass with ice.
1 1/2 oz Gin
3/4 oz Dry Vermouth
Dash of Bitters
Stir.
Strain into chilled glass.

RADIOACTIVE ICED TEA
Fill glass with ice.
1/2 oz Vodka
1/2 oz Gin
1/2 oz Rum
1/2 oz Coconut Rum
1/2 oz Tequila
1/2 oz Triple Sec
1/2 oz Melon Liqueur
1 oz Sour Mix
Top with Cola.
Garnish with Lemon.

RAGNAR
Fill glass with ice.
2 oz Citrus Vodka or Currant Vodka
Squeeze in tsp fresh Lime Juice.
Fill with Lemonade or Lemon-Lime Soda.
Stir.

RAIN MAN
Fill glass with ice.
1 oz 151-Proof Rum
1 oz Melon Liqueur
Fill with Orange Juice.
Shake.

RAINBOW (floater)
1/2 oz Dark Creme De Cacao
(bottom)
1/2 oz Creme De Violette
1/2 oz Yellow Chartreuse
1/2 oz Maraschino Liqueur
1/2 oz Benedictine
1/2 oz Green Chartreuse
1/2 oz Cognac (top)

RAINBOW 2 (floater)
1/2 oz Creme De Nouyax
(bottom)
1/2 oz Melon Liqueur
1/2 oz White Creme De Cacao
(top)

RAINFOREST (frozen)
In Blender:
1 cup of Ice
1 oz Dark Rum
1 oz Melon Liqueur
1 tbsp Cream of Coconut
1 oz Passion Fruit Liqueur
Blend until smooth.

RAMOS FIZZ
Fill glass with ice.
1 1/2 oz Gin
1/2 oz Cream
1 1/2 oz Sour Mix
1 Egg White
1 tsp Triple Sec or Curacao
or Orange Juice
Shake.
Strain into chilled glass.
Fill with Soda Water.

**RANCH VALENCIA
RUM PUNCH**
Fill glass with ice.
1 oz Light Rum
1 oz Amber Rum
2 dashes of Bitters
Fill with equal parts Orange and
Pineapple Juice.
Shake.
Strain into glass.
Float 1/2 oz Dark Rum on top.
Garnish with Orange and/or
Pineapple.

RASBARETTA (frozen)
In Blender:
1/2 cup of Ice
1 oz Raspberry Liqueur
1 oz Amaretto
Scoop of Vanilla Ice Cream
Blend until smooth.
If too thick add liqueur or Milk. If too
thin add ice or Ice Cream.

RASPBERRY BERET
Fill glass with ice.
1 oz Vodka
1 oz Black Raspberry Liqueur
Dash of Milk or Cream
Shake.
Strain into shot glass.
Top with Soda Water.

RASPBERRY COLADA (frozen)
In Blender:
1/2 cup of Ice
1 oz Rum
1 oz Black Raspberry Liqueur
2 tbsp Cream of Coconut
1/2 cup fresh or frozen Raspberries
1 tbsp Vanilla Ice Cream (optional)
Blend until smooth.

RASPBERRY DAIQUIRI
(frozen)
In Blender:
1 cup of Ice
1 1/2 oz Rum
3/4 oz Raspberry Liqueur
Dash of Lime Juice
1/2 cup of fresh or frozen
Raspberries
or 2 tbsp Raspberry Jam
Blend until smooth.
If too thick add berries.
If too thin add ice.
Garnish with Lime.

**RASPBERRY GIMLET aka
PURPLE HOOTER, PURPLE
KAMIKAZE**
Fill glass with ice.
2 oz Vodka
1/2 oz Black Raspberry Liqueur
1/2 oz Lime Juice
Stir.
Strain into shot glass.

RASPBERRY KISS
Fill glass with ice.
1 oz Black Raspberry Liqueur
1 oz Dark Creme De Cacao
1 oz Milk or Cream
Shake.
Strain into chilled glass.

RASPBERRY LIME RICKEY
Fill glass with ice.
1 1/2 oz Vodka or Gin or Rum or
Whiskey
1/2 oz Black Raspberry Liqueur
Dash of Lime Juice
Fill with Soda Water
Garnish with Lime.

RASPBERRY MARGARITA
(frozen)
In Blender:
1/2 cup of Ice
1 1/2 oz Tequila
1/2 oz Black Raspberry Liqueur
1/2 cup fresh or frozen
Raspberries or 2 tbsp of Raspberry
Jam
Dash of Lime Juice
Blend until smooth.
If too thick add juice or alcohol.
If too thin add ice.
Garnish with Lime.

RASPBERRY SHERBET
Fill glass with ice.
1 1/2 oz Vodka
1/2 oz Black Raspberry Liqueur
Dash of Grenadine
Dash of Orange Juice
Dash of Lime Juice
Fill with Sour Mix.
Shake.
Nick G. Zeroulias

RASPBERRY SMASH aka HOLLYWOOD
Fill glass with ice.
1 1/2 oz Vodka
1/2 oz Black Raspberry Liqueur
Fill with Pineapple Juice.
Garnish with Pineapple.
Shake.

RASPBERRY SODA
Fill glass with ice.
2 oz Vodka
1/2 oz Black Raspberry Liqueur
Fill with Raspberry Flavored
Sparkling Water.
Garnish with Orange.

RASPBERRY SOMBRERO
Fill glass with ice.
2 oz Black Raspberry Liqueur
Fill with Milk or Cream.
Shake.

RASPBERRY TORTE
Fill glass with ice.
1 oz Vodka
1 oz Black Raspberry Liqueur
Stir.

RASPBERRY VODKA
(type liqueur)
In a screw top jar mix together:
1 qt Vodka
1 lb fresh Raspberries
2 cups of Sugar (optional)
Store in cool dark place for
2 months (optional)
Stir weekly.
Strain when ready.

RASTA MAN (floater)
1/2 oz Coffee Liqueur (bottom)
1/2 oz Myer's Rum Cream
1/2 oz Chocolate Liqueur (top)

RATTLER
Fill glass with ice.
1 1/2 oz Tequila
1/2 oz Triple Sec
Fill with Grapefruit Juice.
Garnish with Lime.

RATTLESNAKE
Fill glass with ice.
1 1/2 oz of Whiskey
1/2 Egg White
1/4 tsp Pernod
1 tsp Powdered Sugar
or Sugar Syrup
1 tsp Lemon Juice
Shake.

RATTLESNAKE 2
Fill glass with ice.
1 1/2 oz Southern Comfort
or Yukon Jack
1/2 oz Blackberry Brandy
1/4 oz Sugar Syrup
Stir.

RATTLESNAKE 3
Fill glass with ice.
1/2 oz Coffee Liqueur
1/2 oz Irish Cream
1/2 oz Peppermint Schnapps
Stir.
Strain into chilled glass.

RAZORBACK HOGCALLER
Fill glass with ice.
1 oz 151- Proof Rum
1 oz Green Chartreuse
Strain into chilled glass.

REAR BUSTER
Fill glass with ice.
1 oz Tequila
1 oz Coffee Liqueur
Fill with Cranberry Juice.
Shake.

REAR ENTRY
2 oz Vodka
Fill with Chocolate Yoo Hoo.

REBEL RUSSIAN
Fill glass with ice.
1 oz Southern Comfort
1 oz Coffee Liqueur
Fill with Milk or Cream.
Shake.

REBEL YELL
Fill glass with ice.
1 1/2 oz Bourbon
1/2 oz Triple Sec
1 oz Lime Juice
Shake. Strain into shot glass.

RED APPLE
Fill glass with ice.
1 oz Vodka
1 oz Apple Juice
1/2 oz Lemon Juice
3-4 dashes of Grenadine
Shake.
Serve or strain into chilled glass.

R

RED BARON
Fill glass with ice.
2 oz Gin
Dash of Grenadine
Fill with equal parts Sour Mix
and Orange Juice.
Shake.

RED BEER
2 oz Tomato Juice
Fill with Beer.
Add Salt to taste.

RED BEER SHOOTER
In shot glass:
Dash of Tabasco
Dash of Tomato Juice
Fill with Beer.

RED CLOUD
Fill glass with ice.
1 1/2 oz Gin
1/2 oz Apricot Liqueur
1/2 oz Lemon Juice
1 tsp Grenadine
Dash of Bitters
Shake.
Strain into chilled glass.

RED DEATH
Fill glass with ice.
1/2 oz Vodka
1/2 oz Southern Comfort
1/2 oz Amaretto
1/2 oz Triple Sec
1/2 oz Sloe Gin
1/2 oz Lime Juice
Fill with Orange Juice.
Shake.

RED DEATH 2
Fill glass with ice.
1/2 oz Vodka
1/2 oz 151-Proof Rum
1/2 oz Yukon Jack
1/2 oz Cinnamon Schnapps
Stir.
Strain into chilled glass.

RED DEVIL
Fill glass with ice.
1/2 oz Vodka
1/2 oz Southern Comfort
1/2 oz Sloe Gin
1/2 oz Triple Sec
1/2 oz Peach Schnapps or Banana
Liqueur
Dash of Lime Juice or Grenadine
Fill with Orange Juice.
Shake.

RED DWARF
Fill glass with ice.
1 oz Rum
1 oz Peach Schnapps
1 oz Lemon Juice or Sour Mix
2 oz Orange Juice
Shake.
Strain into chilled glass.
Pour 1/2 oz Creme De Cassis
down spoon to bottom of drink.

RED EYE
1 1/2 oz Vodka
1 Egg
2 oz Bloody Mary Mix
Fill with cold Beer.
Shake.

RED LION
Fill glass with ice.
1 oz Gin
1 oz Orange Liqueur
1/2 oz Orange Juice
1/2 oz Lemon Juice
Shake.
Strain into chilled glass.

RED NEEDLE
2 oz Tequila
Fill to 1/2 inch from top with Ginger
Ale.
Top with Cranberry Juice.
Garnish with Lime.

RED PANTIES
Fill glass with ice.
1 1/2 oz Vodka
1/2 oz Peach Schnapps
Dash of Grenadine
1 oz Orange Juice
1 oz Cranberry Juice
Shake.
Strain into chilled glass.

RED ROOSTER aka
HOOSIER ROOSTER
Fill 1 shot glass with Gold Tequila.
Fill 1 shot glass with Orange Juice.
Fill 1 shot glass with Bloody Mary mix.
Drink in order given, one after the
other.

RED RUBY
Fill glass with ice.
2 oz Amaretto
2 tsp Grenadine
1 1/2 oz Orange Juice
1 1/2 oz Cranberry Juice
Fill with Ginger Ale.

RED RUM SONIC
Fill glass with ice.
2 oz Amber Rum
2 oz Cranberry Juice
Fill with equal parts Soda Water
and Tonic Water.
Garnish with a Lemon.
Orville Giddings

RED RUSSIAN aka
SNOWBERRY
Fill glass with ice.
1 oz Vodka
1 oz Strawberry Liqueur
Fill with Milk or Cream.
Shake.

RED SILK PANTIES
Fill glass with ice.
1 1/2 oz Vodka
1/2 oz Peach Schnapps
1 oz Cranberry Juice
Stir.
Strain into chilled glass.

RED SNAPPER
Fill glass with ice.
2 oz Gin
1 tsp of Horseradish
3 dashes of Tabasco Sauce
3 dashes of Worcestershire Sauce
Dash of Lime Juice
3 dashes of Celery Salt
3 dashes of Pepper
1 oz Clam Juice (optional)
Fill with Tomato Juice.
Shake.
Garnish with Lemon or Lime,
Celery or Cucumber and/or
Cocktail Shrimp.

RED TIDE
Fill glass with ice.
3/4 oz Light Rum
3/4 oz Dark Rum
3/4 oz Banana Liqueur
Dash of Pineapple Juice
Dash of Sour Mix
Fill with Cranberry Juice.

RED WINE COOLER
Fill glass 3/4 with ice.
Fill 3/4 with desired Red Wine.
Fill with Lemon-Lime Soda or
Ginger Ale.
Stir.
Garnish with Lime.

RED ZIPPER
Fill glass with ice.
1 oz Vodka
1 oz Galliano
Fill with Cranberry Juice.
Stir.
Garnish with Lime.

REFORM
Fill glass with ice.
1 1/2 oz Dry Sherry
3/4 oz Dry Vermouth
1-2 dashes of Orange Bitters
Stir.
Strain into chilled glass.

RELEASE VALVE
Fill glass with ice.
1 oz Vodka
1 oz Rum
Fill with Pineapple Juice.
Top with 1/2 oz Grenadine.

RENAISSANCE COCKTAIL
Fill glass with ice.
1 1/2 oz Gin
1/2 oz Dry Sherry
1 tbsp Cream
Shake.
Strain into chilled glass.
Sprinkle with Nutmeg.

RENDEZVOUS
Fill glass with ice.
1 1/2 oz Gin
1/2 oz Kirschwasser
1/2 oz Campari
Shake.
Strain into chilled glass.
Garnish with Lemon Twist.

RESTORATION
Fill glass with ice.
1 oz Brandy
1 oz Black Raspberry Liqueur
Dash of Sour Mix
Fill with Red Wine.
Shake.
Strain into wine glass.
Garnish with Lemon Twist.

REVEREND
Fill glass with ice.
2 oz Bourbon
2 oz Sour Mix
Shake and strain.
Fill with Beer.

RHETT BUTTLER
Fill glass with ice
1 1/2 oz Southern Comfort
1 tsp Curacao
1/2 oz Lime Juice
1/2 oz Lemon Juice
1 tsp Sugar
Shake.
Strain into chilled glass.

RHODE ISLAND ICED TEA
Fill glass with ice.
3/4 oz Brandy
3/4 oz Vodka
3/4 oz Coffee Liqueur
Fill with Milk or Cream.
Shake.

RICKEY
Fill glass with ice.
2 oz Desired Liquor or Liqueur
Dash of Lime Juice
Fill with Soda Water.
Stir.

RIGOR MORTIS
Fill glass with ice.
1 1/2 oz Vodka
1 oz Amaretto
Fill with equal parts Orange and
Pineapple Juice.
Shake.

R

RISING SUN
Fill glass with ice.
4 oz Sake
Fill with Orange Juice.
Pour 1/2 oz Grenadine down spoon
to bottom of drink.

RITZ FIZZ
Fill glass with ice.
1 oz Amaretto
1/2 oz Blue Curacao
1 oz Sour Mix
Shake.
Strain into chilled glass.
Fill with Champagne.
Garnish with Orange.

RITZ PICK-ME-UP
1 oz Cognac or Brandy
1 oz Orange Liqueur
2 oz Orange Juice
Fill with Champagne.

RIVER BERRY
Fill glass with ice.
1 oz Vodka
1 oz Wildberry Schnapps
4 oz Sour Mix
Shake.
Drop of Grenadine
Splash of Soda Water

RIVIERA
Fill glass with ice.
3/4 oz Rum
3/4 oz Orange Liqueur
3/4 oz Black Raspberry Liqueur
Stir.

ROASTED TOASTED ALMOND
aka BURNT ALMOND, ORGASM
Fill glass with ice.
1 oz Vodka
1 oz Coffee Liqueur
1 oz Amaretto
Fill with Milk or Cream.
Shake.

ROASTED TOASTED ALMOND
(frozen)
In Blender:
1/2 cup of Ice
1 oz Vodka
1 oz Coffee Liqueur
1 oz Amaretto
Scoop of Vanilla Ice Cream
Blend until smooth.
If too thick add Milk or Cream.
If too thin add ice or Ice Cream.

ROB ROY
(*CAUTION:* DRY can mean either
make drink with Dry Vermouth or
less Sweet Vermouth than usual.
PERFECT means use equal
amounts of Sweet and Dry
Vermouth. SWEET means use
more Sweet Vermouth than usual.)
Fill glass with ice.
2 oz Scotch Whiskey
1/2 oz Sweet Vermouth
Stir.
Strain into chilled glass or pour
contents (with ice) into short glass.
Garnish with Cherry or Lemon
Twist.

ROBSON
Fill glass with ice.
1 1/2 oz Jamaican Rum
1 tbsp Orange Juice
1 1/2 tsp Lemon Juice
1 tsp Grenadine
Shake.
Serve or strain into chilled glass.

ROCK LOBSTER (frozen)
In Blender:
1 cup of Ice
1 oz Coconut Rum
1/2 oz Banana Liqueur
Dash of Grenadine
1/2 ripe peeled Banana
Dash of Pineapple and Orange
Juice
Blend until smooth.
Top with Dark Rum.

ROCKAWAY BEACH
Fill glass with ice.
1 1/2 oz Light Rum
1/2 oz Dark Rum
1/2 oz Tequila
1 oz Orange Juice
1/2 oz Pineapple Juice
1/2 oz Cranberry Juice
1 tsp Creme De Nouyax
Shake.
Garnish with Cherry.

ROCKET
Fill glass with ice.
2 oz Yukon Jack
Fill with Lemonade.
Float 1/2 oz 151-Proof Rum
on top.

ROCKY MOUNTAIN ROOTBEER
Fill glass with ice.
1 1/2 oz Vodka
1/2 oz Galliano
Fill with Cola.
Stir.

ROCKY ROAD
Fill glass with ice.
1 oz Hazelnut Liqueur
1 oz Creme De Cacao
Fill with Milk or Cream.
Shake.

ROMAN CANDLE
Fill glass with ice.
1 oz Sambuca
1 oz Amaretto
Dash of Grenadine
Fill with Orange Juice.
Shake.
Top with Soda Water.

ROMAN CAPPUCCINO
1 1/2 oz Sambuca
Fill with Espresso.
Top with steamed Milk.
Garnish with 3 Coffee Beans.

ROMAN CAPPUCCINO (frozen)
In Blender:
1/2 cup of Ice
2 oz Sambuca
3 oz Espresso
Scoop of Vanilla or Coffee Ice Cream
Blend until smooth.

ROMAN COFFEE
2 oz Sambuca
Fill with hot Black Coffee.
Top with Whipped Cream.
Garnish with 3 Coffee Beans.

ROMAN HOLIDAY
Fill glass with ice.
3/4 oz Amaretto
3/4 oz Sambuca
3/4 oz Blackberry Brandy
Fill with Milk.
Shake.

ROMAN ICED TEA
Fill glass with ice.
1/2 oz Vodka
1/2 oz Gin
1/2 oz Rum
1/2 oz Triple Sec
1/2 oz Amaretto
Fill with equal parts Cranberry
Juice and Sour Mix.
Shake.
Top with Lemon-Lime Soda.

ROMAN RASTA COFFEE
1 oz Sambuca
1 oz Dark Rum
Fill with hot Black Coffee.
Top with Whipped Cream.

ROMAN RIOT
Fill glass with ice.
3/4 oz Amaretto
3/4 oz Sambuca
3/4 oz Galliano
Shake.
Strain into chilled glass.

ROOT BEER
Fill glass with ice.
3/4 oz Vodka
3/4 oz Coffee Liqueur
3/4 oz Galliano
Fill with Cola.
Stir.

ROOT BEER FLOAT
Fill glass with ice.
1 oz Vodka
1 oz Root Beer Schnapps
1 oz Cream
Shake.
Top with 2 oz Cola.

ROOT BEER FLOAT 2
Place a scoop of Vanilla Ice Cream
in large glass.
2 oz Dark Rum
Fill with Root Beer.

ROSÉ COOLER
Fill glass 3/4 with ice.
Fill 3/4 with Rosé Wine.
Fill with Ginger Ale
or Lemon-Lime Soda.
Garnish with Lime.

ROSE HALL
Fill glass with ice.
1 1/2 oz Dark Rum
1/2 oz Banana Liqueur
1 oz Orange Juice
1 tsp Lime Juice
Shake.
Serve or strain into chilled glass.
Garnish with a Lime.

ROSÉ SPRITZER
Fill glass 3/4 with ice.
Fill glass 3/4 with Rosé Wine.
Fill with Soda Water.
Garnish with Lime.

ROSY DAWN
Fill glass with ice.
1 oz Vodka or Rum
1 oz Gin
Dash of Grenadine
Dash of Lime Juice
Fill with Grapefruit Juice.
Shake.

ROXANNE
Fill glass with ice.
1 oz Vodka
1/2 oz Peach Schnapps
1/2 oz Amaretto
Fill with equal parts Orange Juice
and Cranberry Juice.
Shake.
Strain into chilled glass.

ROYAL CANADIAN
Fill glass with ice.
1/2 oz Canadian Whiskey
1/2 oz Coffee Liqueur
1/2 oz Amaretto
Strain into chilled glass.

R

ROYAL GIN FIZZ
Fill glass with ice.
2 oz Gin
1/2 oz Orange Liqueur
1 Egg
1 oz Lemon Juice or Sour Mix
1 tsp Sugar Syrup
Shake.
Fill with Soda Water.

ROYAL SCREW
Fill glass 3/4 with ice.
2 oz Cognac
2 oz Orange Juice
Fill with Champagne.

ROYAL SHEET COFFEE
1 oz Amaretto
1 oz Coffee Liqueur
Fill with hot Black Coffee.
Top with Whipped Cream.
Sprinkle with Shaved Almonds.

ROYAL SMILE
Fill glass with ice.
1 oz Apple Brandy
1/2 oz Gin
1/2 oz Lemon Juice
1 tsp Grenadine
Shake.
Strain into chilled glass.

ROYAL SPRITZER
Fill glass 3/4 with ice.
1 oz Black Raspberry Liqueur
Fill 3/4 with Champagne.
Fill with Soda.
Garnish with Lime.

RUBY FIZZ
Fill glass with ice.
2 1/2 oz Sloe Gin
1/2 oz Egg White
1 tsp Grenadine
1 tsp Sugar Syrup
or Powdered Sugar
1 oz Lemon Juice
Shake.
Fill with Soda Water.

RUBY RED
Fill glass with ice.
1 1/2 oz Vodka
1/2 oz Grenadine or Campari
Fill with Grapefruit Juice.
Shake.

RUDDY MIMOSA
1/2 oz Peach Schnapps
1 oz Orange Juice
1 oz Cranberry Juice
Fill with Champagne.
Garnish with Orange.

RUM AND COKE
Fill glass with ice.
2 oz Rum
Fill with Cola.
Garnish with Lime.

RUM-LACED CIDER
1 oz Dark Rum
1 oz Spiced Rum
Fill with hot Apple Cider.
Float Pat of Butter on top.
Sprinkle Cinnamon and whole
Cloves on top.

RUM MADRAS aka
BOG FOG
Fill glass with ice.
2 oz Rum
Fill with equal parts Orange and
Cranberry Juice.
Garnish with Lime.

RUM PUNCH
Fill glass with ice.
2 oz Rum
Dash of Grenadine
Fill with equal parts Orange and
Pineapple Juice.
Shake
Splash with Lemon-Lime Soda.
Garnish with Lime.

RUM RUNNER
Fill glass with ice.
1/2 oz Light Rum
1/2 oz Dark Rum
1/2 oz Banana Liqueur
1/2 oz Blackberry Brandy
Dash of Grenadine
Dash of Sour Mix
Dash of Orange Juice
Shake.
Float 1/2 oz 151-Proof Rum
on top.

RUM RUNNER (frozen)
In Blender:
1 cup of Ice
1 oz Rum
1 oz Banana Liqueur
1/2 oz Blackberry Brandy
Dash of Grenadine
Dash of Lime Juice
Blend until smooth.
If too thick add liqueur or juice.
If too thin add ice.

RUMBALL
1 oz Dark Rum
1 oz Chocolate Liqueur
Stir.

RUMPLESTILTSKIN
1 oz 100-Proof Peppermint Schnapps
1 oz Bourbon

RUN, SKIP AND GO NAKED
Fill glass with ice.
1/2 oz Gin
1/2 oz Rum
1/2 oz Brandy
1/2 oz Triple Sec
Fill with Sour Mix (leaving 1/2 inch
from top).
Shake.
Top with Beer.

RUPTURED DUCK
Fill glass with ice.
1 oz Banana Liqueur
1 oz Creme De Nouyax
1 oz Cream
Shake.
Strain into chilled glass.

RUSSIAN
Fill glass with ice.
3/4 oz Vodka
3/4 oz Gin
3/4 oz White Creme De Cacao
Shake.
Strain into chilled glass.

RUSSIAN BANANA
Fill glass with ice.
3/4 oz Vodka
3/4 oz Banana Liqueur
3/4 oz Dark Creme De Cacao
1 oz Cream or Milk
Shake.
Strain into chilled glass.

RUSSIAN BEAR
Fill glass with ice.
1 oz Vodka
1 oz Dark Creme De Cacao
1 oz Heavy Cream
Shake.
Strain into chilled glass.

RUSSIAN COFFEE
2 oz Vodka
Fill with hot Black Coffee.
1/2 tsp of Sugar (optional)
Stir.
Top with Whipped Cream.
Garnish with Orange.

RUSSIAN NIGHTS aka
FLYING MADRAS
Fill glass with ice.
2 oz Vodka
2 oz Cranberry Juice
2 oz Orange Juice
Fill with Champagne.
Garnish with Orange.

RUSSIAN PUSSY
Fill glass with ice.
1 1/2 oz Vodka
1/2 oz White Creme De Cacao
1 oz Milk or Cream
Shake. Strain into chilled glass.

RUSSIAN QUAALUDE
Fill glass with ice.
1 oz Vodka
1 oz Irish Cream
1 oz Hazelnut Liqueur
Fill with Milk.
Shake.

RUSSIAN QUAALUDE 2
Fill glass with ice.
1/2 oz Vodka
1/2 oz Coffee Liqueur
1/2 oz Amaretto
1/2 oz Hazelnut Liqueur
1/2 oz Irish Cream
1 oz Milk (optional)
Shake.

RUSSIAN QUAALUDE (floater)
1 oz Hazelnut Liqueur (bottom)
1 oz Irish Cream
1 oz Vodka (top)

RUSSIAN QUAALUDE (frozen)
In Blender:
1/2 cup of Ice
1/2 oz Vodka
1/2 oz Coffee Liqueur
1/2 oz Irish Cream
1/2 oz Hazelnut Liqueur
1/2 oz Tia Maria
1/2 oz Amaretto
Scoop of Vanilla Ice Cream
Blend until smooth.
If too thick add Milk or Cream.
If too thin add ice or Ice Cream.
Garnish with Shaved Chocolate or
Sprinkles.

RUSSIAN ROSE
Fill glass with ice.
2 oz Vodka
1/2 oz Grenadine
Dash of Orange Bitters
Shake.
Strain into chilled glass.

RUSSIAN ROULETTE
Fill glass with ice.
1 oz Vodka
1/2 oz Drambuie
1/2 oz Galliano
Fill with equal parts Sour Mix and
Orange Juice.
Shake.
Garnish with Lemon.

RUSSIAN ROULETTE 2
Fill glass with ice.
1/2 oz Vodka
1/2 oz Brandy or Cognac
1/2 oz Banana Liqueur
1 oz Sour Mix
1 oz Orange Juice
Shake.
Strain into chilled glass.

RUSSIAN SUNRISE
Fill glass with ice.
2 oz Vodka
Fill with Orange Juice.
Pour 1/2 oz Grenadine down spoon
to bottom of glass.
Garnish with Orange.

R

RUSTY NAIL
Fill glass with ice.
1 1/2 oz Scotch
1/2 oz Drambuie
Stir.

RUSTY NAIL COFFEE aka
HEATHER COFFEE
1 oz Scotch
1 oz Drambuie
Fill with hot Black Coffee.
Top with Whipped Cream.
Sprinkle with Cinnamon.

S. O. B.
1/3 oz Orange Liqueur or Triple Sec
1/3 oz Brandy
1/3 oz 151-Proof Rum

S. O. B. 2 (floater)
1 oz Orange Liqueur (bottom)
1 oz Southern Comfort (top)
Serve with Lemon or Lime wedge.
Bite fruit before drinking.

S. O. M. F. (floater)
1/2 oz Coffee Liqueur (bottom)
1/2 oz Irish Cream
1/2 oz Hazelnut Liqueur (top)

S. O. M. F. 2 (floater)
1/2 oz Blackberry Brandy
(bottom)
1/2 oz Amaretto
1/2 oz Triple Sec
1/2 oz Lime Juice (top)

S. O. S.
Fill glass with ice.
1 1/2 oz Vodka
1/2 oz Black Raspberry Liqueur
Fill with equal parts Cranberry
and Orange Juice.
Shake.

ST. PETERSBURG SUNDAE
(frozen)
In Blender: 1/2 cup of ice.
1 1/2 oz Vanilla Vodka
1/2 oz Amaretto
Scoop of Chocolate Ice Cream
Blend until smooth.
If too thick add Milk or Cream.
If too thin add ice or Ice Cream.
Garnish with Shaved Almonds.

SAINT MORITZ (floater)
1/2 oz Black Raspberry Liqueur
(bottom)
1/2 oz Milk or Cream (top)

SAKETINI
Fill glass with ice.
2 oz Gin or Vodka
1/2 oz Sake
Stir.
Strain into chilled glass
or pour contents (with ice)
into short glass.
Garnish with Lemon Twist
or Olives.

SALTY BULL
Fill glass with ice.
2 oz Tequila
Fill with Grapefruit Juice.
Rub rim of second glass with Lime.
Dip rim in Kosher Salt.
Pour contents of first glass into salt-
ed glass.
Garnish with Lime.

SALTY DOG
Fill glass with ice.
2 oz Gin or Vodka
Fill with Grapefruit Juice.
Rub rim of second glass with Lime.
Dip rim in kosher salt.
Pour contents of first glass into salt-
ed glass.
Garnish with Lime.

SALTY DOGITRON
Fill glass with ice.
2 oz Citrus Vodka
Dash of Grenadine
Fill with Grapefruit Juice.

SALTY JOHN
Fill glass with ice.
2 oz Whiskey
Fill with Grapefruit Juice.
Stir.
Pour into glass with salted rim.

SAMARI
Fill glass with ice.
1 1/2 oz Citrus Vodka
1/2 oz Triple Sec
Stir.
Garnish with a Lemon.

SAN FRANCISCO
Fill glass with ice.
3/4 oz Sloe Gin
3/4 oz Dry Vermouth
3/4 oz Sweet Vermouth
Dash of Bitters
Dash of Orange Bitters
Shake.
Strain into chilled glass.

SAN JUAN (frozen)
In Blender:
1 cup of Ice
1 1/2 oz Amber Rum
1 oz Grapefruit Juice
1 oz Lime Juice
1/2 oz Cream of Coconut
Blend until smooth.
If too thick add juice.
If too thin add ice.
Float tsp 151-Proof Rum
on top.
Garnish with Lime.

SAN JUAN SUNSET
Fill glass with ice.
2 oz Rum
Fill with Orange Juice.
Float 1/2 oz Cherry Brandy
on top.

SAN SEBASTIAN
Fill glass with ice.
1 oz Gin
1 1/2 tsp Rum
1/2 tsp Triple Sec
1 tbsp Grapefruit Juice
1 tbsp Lemon Juice
Shake.
Strain into chilled glass.

SANCTUARY
Fill glass with ice.
1 1/2 oz Dubonnet Rouge
3/4 oz Amer Picon
3/4 oz Orange Liqueur
Shake.
Serve or strain into chilled glass.

SAND BLASTER
Fill glass with ice.
1 oz Rum
1 oz Jaegermeister
Fill with Cola.
Stir.
Garnish with Lime.

SAND FLEA
Fill glass with ice.
1 oz Rum
1/2 oz Apricot Brandy
1/2 oz Orange Liqueur
Dash of Grenadine.
Fill with equal parts Orange Juice
and Sour Mix.

SAND IN YOUR BUTT
Fill glass with ice.
1 oz Southern Comfort
1 oz Melon Liqueur
1 oz Pineapple Juice
Shake. Strain into shot glass.

SANGRIA 1
(Chill all ingredients prior to mixing.)
In a large punch bowl with a cake
of ice in it, mix:
2 750ml bottles of desired Red Wine
3 oz Curacao or Triple Sec
2 oz Brandy
1/2 cup Orange Juice
1/4 cup Lemon Juice
1/4 cup Sugar
2 oz Water
Stir until sugar dissolves.
Add an Orange and a Lemon sliced
thinly.
Add 1 qt Soda Water.

SANGRIA 2
Fill glass with ice.
1 oz Orange Liqueur
1/2 oz Brandy
Dash of Sour Mix
Dash of Orange Juice
Pinch Sugar
Fill with desired Red Wine.
Shake.
Splash with Soda Water.
Garnish with Orange and Lemon.

SANTA SHOT (floater)
3/4 oz Grenadine (bottom)
3/4 oz Green Creme De Menthe
3/4 oz Peppermint Schnapps (top)

SANTIAGO
Fill glass with ice.
1 oz Light Rum
1 oz Dark Rum
1 oz Triple Sec
1 oz Sour Mix
1/2 oz Lime Juice
2-3 dashes of Bitters
Shake.
Strain into chilled glass.
Garnish with Lime.

SANTIAGO 2
Fill glass with ice.
3/4 oz Light Rum
3/4 oz Dark Rum
3/4 oz Triple Sec
1 oz Sour Mix
1/2 oz Lime Juice
2-3 dashes of Bitters
Shake.
Strain into tall chilled glass.
Fill with Champagne.
Garnish with Lime.

SARATOGA
Fill glass with ice.
2 oz Brandy
1 oz crushed fresh or canned
Pineapple
1/2 tsp Maraschino Liqueur
2 or 3 dashes of Bitters
Shake.
Strain into chilled glass.

SATURN'S RING (floater)
1/2 oz Anisette (bottom)
1/2 oz Grenadine
1/2 oz Southern Comfort (top)

SAUCY SUE
Fill glass with ice.
2 oz Apple Brandy
1/2 tsp Apricot Brandy
1/2 tsp Pernod
Stir.
Strain into chilled glass.

SAVANNAH
Fill glass with ice.
2 oz Gin
1 Egg White
1 oz Orange Juice
Shake.
Strain into chilled glass.
Top with 1/2 oz White Creme De Cacao.

SAVE THE PLANET
Fill glass with ice.
1 oz Vodka
1 oz Melon Liqueur
1/2 oz Blue Curacao
Shake.
Strain into chilled glass.
Float 1/2 oz Green Chartreuse on top.

SAVOY HOTEL (floater)
1/2 oz White Creme De Cacao (bottom)
1/2 oz Benedictine
1/2 oz Brandy (top)

SAVOY TANGO
Fill glass with ice.
1 1/2 oz Apple Brandy
1 oz Sloe Gin
Stir.
Strain into chilled glass.

SAZERAC
Fill glass with ice.
2 oz Bourbon
1 tsp Sugar
2 dashes of Bitters
Stir until sugar dissolves.
Coat inside of second glass with Pernod.
Strain mixture into coated glass.
Garnish with Lemon Twist.

SCARLET LETTER aka CHAM CRAN CHAM, BRUT AND BOGS
Fill glass 3/4 with ice.
Fill glass 3/4 with Champagne.
Dash of Black Raspberry Liqueur
Fill with Cranberry Juice.

SCARLET O'HARA
Fill glass with ice.
2 oz Southern Comfort
Dash of Lime Juice (optional)
Fill with Cranberry Juice.
Garnish with Lime.

SCHOOL BUS
Fill glass glass with ice.
2 oz Amaretto
Fill with equal parts Beer and Orange Juice.
Stir.
Garnish with unused number 2 pencil.

SCOOBY SNACK
Fill glass with ice.
1 oz Coconut Rum
1 oz Melon Liqueur
Dash of Pineapple Juice
Dash of Milk
Shake. Strain into shot glass.
Top with Whipped Cream.

SCORPION (frozen)
In Blender:
1/2 cup of Ice
1 oz Light Rum
1 oz Gin
1 oz Brandy
1 oz Orange Juice
1 oz White wine
1 oz Lemon Juice
1/2 oz Creme De Nouyax or Orgeat Syrup
Blend until smooth.
Float 1/2 oz Dark Rum on top.
Garnish with gardenia.

SCORPION (floater)
1/2 oz Grenadine (bottom)
1 oz Blackberry Brandy
1/2 oz Vodka (top)

SCOTCH BIRD
1 1/2 oz Scotch
1/2 oz Triple Sec
Tsp powdered Sugar
Fill with Milk or Cream.
Shake.

SCOTCH COLLINS aka JOE COLLINS, MIKE COLLINS
Fill glass with ice.
2 oz Scotch
Fill with Sour Mix.
Shake.
Splash with Soda Water.
Garnish with Orange and Cherry.

SCOTCH SOUR
Fill glass with ice.
2 oz Scotch
Fill with Sour Mix.
Shake.
Garnish with Orange and Cherry.

SCOTTI WAS BEAMED UP
Fill glass with ice.
1 1/2 oz Tequila
1/2 oz Galliano
Shake. Strain into shot glass.

SCOTTISH COFFEE
2 oz Drambuie or Scotch
or 1 oz of each
Fill with hot Black Coffee.
Top with Whipped Cream.
Sprinkle with Shaved Chocolate.

SCREAMER
Fill glass with ice.
1 1/2 oz Greek Brandy
1/2 oz Green Chartreuse
Stir.
Strain into chilled glass.

SCREAMING BANSHEE
Fill glass with ice.
1 oz Vodka
1 oz Banana Liqueur
1/2 oz White Creme De Cacao
Fill with Milk or Cream.
Shake.

SCREAMING BLUE MESSIAH
(floater)
1 1/2 oz 100-proof Goldschlager
(bottom)
1/2 oz Blue Curacao (top)

SCREAMING DEAD NAZI
DIGGING FOR GOLD
Fill glass with ice.
1/2 oz Grain Alcohol
1/2 oz 100-proof Peppermint
Schnapps
1/2 oz Jaegermeister
1/2 oz Yellow Chartreuse
Shake. Strain into shot glass.

SCREAMING NAZI aka
DEAD NAZI
Fill glass with ice.
1 oz 100-Proof Peppermint
Schnapps
1 oz Jaegermeister
Stir.
Strain into chilled glass.

SCREAMING O.
Fill glass with ice.
1/2 oz Vodka
1/2 oz Coffee Liqueur
1/2 oz Amaretto or Orange Liqueur
1/2 oz Irish Cream
Fill with equal parts Milk
or Cream and Soda Water.

SCREAMING VIKING aka
SKYSCRAPER
Fill glass with ice.
2 oz Bourbon
2-3 dashes of Bitters
1/2 oz Lime Juice
Fill with Cranberry Juice.
Stir.
Garnish with Cucumber.

SCREAMING YELLOW
MONKEY
Fill glass with ice.
1 oz Vodka
1 oz Banana Liqueur
1/2 oz White Creme De Cacao
Fill with Milk or Cream.
Shake.

SCREW-UP
Fill glass with ice.
2 oz Vodka
Splash of Orange Juice
Fill with Lemon-Lime Soda.
Garnish with Orange.

SCREWDRIVER
Fill glass with ice.
2 oz Vodka
Fill with Orange Juice.
Garnish with Orange or Lime.

SCUMBUCKET
Fill glass with ice.
1 oz Beer
Dash of Bourbon
Dash of Sambuca
Dash of Red Wine
Dash Irish Cream
Shake. Strain into shot glass.

SEA BREEZE aka
CAPE GRAPE
Fill glass with ice.
2 oz Vodka
Fill with equal parts Cranberry and
Grapefruit Juice
Garnish with Lime.

SEA MONKEYS
In shot glass:
1 1/2 oz Goldschlager
1/2 oz Blue Curacao
Stir.

SEDUCTION (floater)
3/4 oz Hazelnut Liqueur (bottom)
3/4 oz Banana Liqueur
3/4 oz Irish Cream (top)

SELF-STARTER
Fill glass with ice.
1 oz Gin
1/2 oz Lillet Blanc
1 tsp Apricot Brandy
2-3 dashes of Pernod
Shake.
Strain into chilled glass.

SEPARATOR aka
DIRTY MOTHER
Fill glass with ice.
1 1/2 oz Brandy
3/4 oz Coffee Liqueur
1 oz Cream (optional)
Stir.

S

SEPTEMBER MORN
Fill glass with ice.
2 1/2 oz Rum
1/2 oz Lime Juice
1 tsp Grenadine
1 Egg White
Shake.
Strain into chilled glass.

SEVEN AND SEVEN
Fill glass with ice.
2 oz Seagram's 7 Whiskey
Fill with 7-up.
Garnish with Lemon.

727
Fill glass with ice.
1/2 oz Vodka
1/2 oz Coffee Liqueur
1/2 oz Irish Cream
1/2 oz Orange Liqueur
Shake.

747 (floater)
1/2 oz Coffee Liqueur (bottom)
1/2 oz Irish Cream
1/2 oz Hazelnut Liqueur (top)

SEVENTH AVENUE
Fill glass with ice.
1 oz Amaretto
1 oz Drambuie
1 oz Chocolate Liqueur
Fill with Milk or Cream.
Shake.

SEVENTH HEAVEN
Fill glass with ice.
1 1/2 oz Whiskey
1/2 oz Amaretto
Fill with Orange Juice.
Stir.

SEVILLA
Fill glass with ice.
1 oz Dark Rum
1 oz Sweet Vermouth
Shake.
Strain into chilled glass.
Garnish with Orange Twist.

SEVILLA 2
Fill glass with ice.
1 1/2 oz Rum
1 1/2 oz Port
1 egg
1/2 tsp Powdered Sugar
or Sugar Syrup
Shake.
Sprinkle Nutmeg on top.

SEWER RAT
Fill glass with ice.
1 oz Vodka
1/2 oz Peach Schnapps
1/2 oz Coffee Liqueur
Fill with Orange Juice.

SEX
Fill glass with ice.
1 oz Coffee Liqueur
1 oz Orange Liqueur
Stir.
Garnish with Orange.

SEX AT MY HOUSE
Fill glass with ice.
1 oz Amaretto
1 oz Black Raspberry Liqueur
Fill with Pineapple Juice.
Shake.
Garnish with Pineapple.

SEX AT THE BEACH
Fill glass with ice.
1/2 oz Vodka
1/2 oz Southern Comfort
1/2 oz Peach Schnapps
1/2 oz Apple Brandy
1/2 oz Orange Liqueur
1/2 oz Orange Juice
1/2 oz Cranberry Juice
1/2 oz Milk or Cream
Shake.
Strain into chilled glass.

SEX IN A BUBBLEGUM FACTORY
Fill glass with ice.
1 oz Light Rum
2/3 oz Apricot Brandy
1/2 oz Banana Liqueur
1/2 oz Blue Curacao
Fill with Lemon-Lime Soda.

SEX IN A HOT TUB
Fill glass with ice.
1 oz Vodka
1/2 oz Peach Schnapps
1/2 oz Black Raspberry Liqueur
Dash of Cranberry Juice
Dash of Pineapple Juice
Shake.
Fill with Champagne.

SEX IN THE PARKING LOT
Fill glass with ice.
1 oz Vodka
1/2 oz Black Raspberry Liqueur
1/2 oz Apple Brandy
Fill with equal parts Orange
and Cranberry Juice.
Shake.

SEX IN THE WOODS
Fill glass with ice.
1 oz Vodka
1/2 oz Amaretto
1/2 oz Coffee Liqueur
Fill with Pineapple Juice.
Shake.

SEX MACHINE
Fill glass with ice.
3/4 oz Vodka
3/4 oz Coffee Liqueur
3/4 oz Orange Liqueur
Float 1/2 oz Milk or Cream on top.

SEX ON A BOAT
Fill glass with ice.
1 1/2 oz Spiced Rum
1/2 oz Banana Liqueur
Fill with Orange Juice
Shake.

SEX ON THE BEACH
Fill glass with ice.
1 1/2 oz Vodka
1/2 oz Peach Schnapps
Fill with equal parts Cranberry and
Orange or Pineapple Juice.
Garnish with Orange or Pineapple.

SEX ON THE BEACH 2
Fill glass with ice.
1 oz Vodka
1/2 oz Melon Liqueur
1/2 oz Black Raspberry Liqueur
Fill with Pineapple Juice or equal
parts Pineapple and Cranberry
Juice.
Shake.
Garnish with Pineapple.

SEX ON THE BEACH 3
Fill glass with ice.
1 oz Vodka
1/2 oz Coffee Liqueur
1/2 oz Black Raspberry Liqueur
Fill with Pineapple Juice.
Shake.

SEX ON THE BEACH (Australian)
Fill glass with ice.
1 oz Blue Curacao
1 oz Pisang Ambon
Dash of Grenadine
Fill with Orange Juice.
Shake.

SEX ON THE BEACH IN WINTER
Fill glass with ice.
1 oz Vodka
1 oz Peach Schnapps
1/2 tsp Cream of Coconut
Fill with equal parts Pineapple and
Cranberry Juice.
Shake.

SEX ON THE POOL TABLE
Fill glass with ice.
1 oz Vodka
1/2 oz Melon Liqueur
1/2 oz Blue Curacao
Fill with equal parts Orange
and Pineapple Juice.
Shake.

SEXY aka CARA SPOSA
Fill glass with ice.
1 oz Coffee Liqueur
1 oz Orange Liqueur
Fill with Milk or Cream.
Shake.
Garnish with Orange.

SHADY LADY
Fill glass with ice.
1 oz Tequila
1 oz Melon Liqueur
Fill with Grapefruit Juice.

SHANGHAI
Fill glass with ice.
1 1/2 oz Dark Rum
1/2 oz Sambuca or Anisette
1/2 oz Lemon Juice
1 tsp Grenadine
Shake.
Strain into chilled glass.

SHANTE'GAF
Fill glass 3/4 with Ale or Beer.
Fill with Ginger Beer or
Lemon-Lime Soda.

SHARK ATTACK
Fill glass with ice.
2 oz Light Rum
Fill with Lemonade.
Float 1/2 oz Blue Curacao
on top.

SHARK BITE
Fill glass with ice.
2 oz Dark Rum
Dash of Grenadine
Fill with Orange Juice.
Shake.
Garnish with Orange and Cherry.

SHARK'S TOOTH
Fill glass with ice.
1 1/2 oz Dark Rum
1/2 oz Lime Juice
1/2 oz Lemon Juice
1/4 oz Grenadine
Shake.
Fill with Soda Water.

SHARK'S TOOTH 2
Fill glass with ice.
2 oz Dark Rum
Fill with Sour Mix.
Shake.
Top with 1/2 oz Grenadine.

SHARKY PUNCH
Fill glass with ice.
1 1/2 oz Apple Brandy
1/2 oz Whiskey
1 tsp Sugar Syrup
Shake.
Fill with Soda Water.

SHAVED BUSH
Fill glass with ice.
1/2 oz Light Rum
1/2 oz Coffee Liqueur
1/2 oz White Creme De Cacao
1 oz Amaretto
1 oz Milk or Cream
Shake. Strain into shot glass.

S

SHERRY COCKTAIL
Fill glass with ice.
2 1/2 oz Cream Sherry
Dash of Bitters
Stir.
Strain into chilled glass.
Garnish with Orange Twist.

SHERRY TWIST
Fill glass with ice.
3 oz Sherry
1 oz Brandy
1 oz Dry Vermouth
1/2 tsp Curacao or Triple Sec
3 dashes of Lemon Juice
Shake.
Strain into chilled glass.
Sprinkle with Cinnamon.

SHILLELAGH aka BUSHWACKER
Fill glass with ice.
1 oz Irish Whiskey or Irish Mist
1 oz Irish Cream
Stir.

SHINEY NAVEL
Fill glass with ice.
2 oz Apple Brandy
Fill with Orange Juice.

SHIPWRECK
Fill glass with ice.
2 oz Coconut Rum
Fill with Pineapple Juice.
Top with 1/2 oz 151-Proof Rum.
Garnish with Pineapple.

SHIRLEY TEMPLE
Fill glass with ice.
Fill with Ginger Ale or
Lemon-Lime Soda.
Dash of Grenadine
Garnish with Cherry.

SHIVER SHOT
Find an attractive, desirable, ample
bust.
Ask permission to use it.
If yes, fill shot glass with Tequila.
Lick upper chest, and salt
moistened location.
Place Lime wedge between desired
lips.
Place shot glass in cleavage.
Lick salt, drink shot, take Lime.
(No Hands)

SHOGUN
1 1/2 oz Citrus Vodka
1/2 oz Orange Liqueur
1 oz Lime Juice or Sour Mix
Shake.

SHOT IN THE DARK
1/2 oz Yukon Jack
1/2 oz Orange Liqueur
1/2 oz hot Black Coffee

SIBERIAN
Fill glass with ice.
1 1/2 oz Vodka
1/2 oz Coffee Liqueur
1/2 oz Brandy
Stir.

SICILIAN COFFEE
1 oz Southern Comfort
1 oz Amaretto
Fill glass with hot Black Coffee.
Top with Whipped Cream.
Sprinkle with Shaved Almonds.

SICILIAN KISS
Fill glass with ice.
1 1/2 oz Southern Comfort
1/2 oz Amaretto
Stir.

SIDECAR
Fill glass with ice.
1 1/2 oz Brandy
1/2 oz Triple Sec
Fill with Sour Mix.
Shake.
Garnish with Orange and Cherry.

SILK PANTIES
Fill glass with ice.
3/4 oz Peach Schnapps
3/4 oz Sambuca or Vodka
Stir.
Strain into chilled glass.

SILK PANTIES 2 aka
WOO WOO
Fill glass with ice.
3/4 oz Vodka
3/4 oz Peach Schnapps
1 oz Cranberry Juice
Stir.
Strain into chilled glass.

SILK SHORTS
3/4 oz Vodka
3/4 oz Peach Schnapps
Stir.

SILKEN VEIL
Fill glass with ice.
1 oz Vodka
1 oz Dubonnet Rouge
Stir.
Garnish with twist.

SILVER BULLET
Fill glass with ice.
1 1/2 oz Tequila
1/2 oz White Creme De Menthe
Stir.
Serve or strain into chilled glass.

SILVER CLOUD
Fill glass with ice.
1/2 oz Vodka
1/2 oz Coffee Liqueur
1/2 oz White Creme De Cacao
1/ oz Amaretto
Fill with Milk.
Shake.
Top with Whipped Cream.

SILVER FIZZ
Fill glass with ice.
2 oz Gin
1 Egg White
2 oz Sour Mix
Shake.
Strain into chilled glass.
Fill with Soda Water.

SILVER FIZZ 2
Fill glass with ice.
2 oz Gin
1 Egg White
1/2 oz Sugar Syrup
or 1 tsp Sugar
1 oz Sour Mix
2 oz Cream or Milk
Shake.
Strain into chilled glass.
Splash with Soda Water.
Garnish with Orange and Cherry.

SILVER KING
Fill glass with ice.
1 1/2 oz Gin
1 Egg White
1 oz Lemon Juice
1/2 tsp Sugar Syrup
or Powdered Sugar
2 dashes of Orange Bitters
Shake.
Serve or strain into chilled glass.

SILVER SPIDER
Fill glass with ice.
1/2 oz Vodka
1/2 oz Light Rum
1/2 oz Triple Sec
1/2 oz White Creme De Menthe
Stir.
Serve or strain into chilled glass.

SILVERADO
Fill glass with ice.
1 1/2 oz Vodka
1/2 oz Campari
Fill with Orange or Grapefruit Juice.
Shake.

SIMPLY BONKERS
Fill glass with ice.
1 oz Rum
1 oz Black Raspberry Liqueur
1 oz Cream or Milk
Shake. Strain into shot glass.

SIMPLY EXQUISITE
Fill glass with ice.
3/4 oz Orange Liqueur
3/4 oz Banana Liqueur
3/4 oz Hazelnut Liqueur
Fill with Milk or Cream.
Shake.
Garnish with Orange and Banana.

SINGAPORE SLING
Fill glass with ice.
2 oz Gin
Splash Sloe Gin
3 oz Sour Mix
Shake.
Splash of Soda Water
Top with Cherry Brandy.
Garnish with Cherry and Lemon.

SINGAPORE SLING 2
Fill glass with ice.
1 1/2 oz Gin
1/2 oz Triple Sec
Dash of Lime Juice
Fill with equal parts Orange,
Pineapple Juice and Sour Mix.
Shake.
Top with Cherry Brandy
Garnish with Orange and Cherry.

SINK OR SWIM
Fill glass with ice.
1 1/2 oz Brandy
1/2 oz Sweet Vermouth
3 dashes of Bitters
Shake.
Strain into chilled glass.

SINNER
Fill glass with ice.
2 oz Vodka
Dash of Sour Mix
Fill with Lemon-Lime Soda.

SIR WALTER
Fill glass with ice.
1 1/2 oz Brandy
3/4 oz Light Rum
1 tsp Curacao
1 tsp Grenadine
1 tsp Lemon or Lime Juice
Shake.
Serve or strain into chilled glass.

69ER
Fill glass with ice.
1 1/2 oz Rum
1/2 oz Peach Schnapps
Fill with Cola.

SIZZLER
Fill glass with ice.
1 oz Vodka
1 oz Bourbon
1 oz Beer
1 oz Lemonade
Stir. Strain into shot glass.

S

SKI LIFT
1 oz Peach Schnapps
1 oz Coconut Rum
Fill with Hot Chocolate.
Top with Whipped Cream.
Sprinkle with Shredded Coconut.

SKID MARK
Fill glass with ice.
3/4 oz Coffee Liqueur
3/4 oz Peppermint Schnapps
3/4 oz Jaegermeister
Shake.
Strain into shot glass.

SKINNY DIPPING
Fill glass with ice.
1 1/2 oz Vodka
1/2 oz Peach Schnapps
1/2 oz Amaretto
Fill with equal parts Orange and
Cranberry Juice.
Stir.
Garnish with Orange.

SKIP AND GO NAKED
Fill glass with ice.
2 oz Gin
Fill with Orange Juice or Sour Mix
(leaving 1/2 inch from top).
Float Beer on top.
Garnish with Orange.

SKIP AND GO NAKED 2
Fill glass with ice.
2 oz Gin or Vodka
Dash of Grenadine
Fill with Sour Mix
(leaving 1/2 inch from top).
Float Beer on top.
Garnish with Lemon.

SKULL CRACKER
Fill glass with ice.
4 oz Rum
1 oz White Creme De Cacao
1 oz Pineapple Juice
1 oz Lemon Juice
Shake.
Garnish with Lime.

SKYLAB FALLOUT
Fill glass with ice.
1/2 oz Vodka
1/2 oz Gin
1/2 oz Rum
1/2 oz Tequila
1/2 oz Blue Curacao
1/2 oz Pineapple Juice
Shake. Strain into shot glass.

SKYSCRAPER aka
SCREAMING VIKING
Fill glass with ice.
2 oz Bourbon
2-3 dashes of Bitters
1/2 oz Lime Juice
Fill with Cranberry Juice.
Stir.
Garnish with Cucumber.

SLEDGEHAMMER
Fill glass with ice.
1 oz Brandy
1 oz Apple Brandy
1 oz Dark Rum
2 dashes of Pernod
Shake.
Strain into chilled glass.

SLEDGEHAMMER 2
Fill glass with ice.
1 oz Gin
1 oz Coconut Rum
Dash of Grenadine
Fill with equal parts Pineapple and
Orange Juice.
Shake.

SLEDGEHAMMER (floater)
1 oz Sambuca (bottom)
1 oz Cognac or Brandy (top)

SLEEPY HEAD
Fill glass with ice.
3 oz Brandy
Fill with Ginger Ale.
Garnish with Orange Twist.

SLIM JIM
Fill glass with ice.
2 oz Vodka
Fill with Diet Soda.
Garnish with Lime.

SLIMEBALL
Make Lime Flavored Gelatin.
Replace 1 cup of water in the
recipe with:
6 oz Vodka
2 oz Melon Liqueur
Chill until it coagulates.

SLIPPERY BLACK NIPPLE
(floater)
1 1/2 oz Black Sambuca
(bottom)
1/2 oz Irish Cream (top)
Carefully drip a single drop of
Grenadine in center (optional).

SLIPPERY DICK (floater)
1 1/2 oz Banana Liqueur
(bottom)
1/2 oz Irish Cream (top)

SLIPPERY NIPPLE
Fill glass with ice.
1 1/2 oz Sambuca
1/2 oz Irish Cream
Shake.

SLIPPERY NIPPLE (floater)
1 1/2 oz Sambuca (bottom)
1/2 oz Irish Cream (top)
Carefully drop a single drop of
Grenadine in center (optional).

SLIPPERY NIPPLE 2 (floater)
1 1/2 oz Peppermint Schnapps
1/2 oz Irish Cream
Carefully drip a single drop of
Grenadine in center (optional).

SLOE BALL
Fill glass with ice.
1 oz Sloe Gin
1/2 oz Vodka
1/2 oz Gin
Dash of Sour Mix
1 oz Orange Juice
Shake.
Strain into chilled glass.

SLOE BOAT TO CHINA
Fill glass with ice.
1 1/2 oz Ginger Liqueur
1/2 oz Sloe Gin
Stir.
Fill with Lemon-Lime Soda.

SLOE BRANDY
Fill glass with ice.
2 oz Brandy
1/2 oz Sloe Gin
1 tsp Lemon Juice
Shake.
Strain into chilled glass.
Garnish with Lemon Twist.

**SLOE COMFORTABLE FUZZY
SCREW AGAINST THE WALL**
Fill glass with ice.
1/2 oz Sloe Gin
1/2 oz Southern Comfort
1/2 oz Peach Schnapps
1/2 oz Vodka
Fill with Orange Juice.
Shake.
Top with 1/2 oz Galliano.

**SLOE COMFORTABLE MEXICAN
SCREW AGAINST THE WALL**
Fill glass with ice.
1/2 oz Sloe Gin
1/2 oz Southern Comfort
1/2 oz Tequila
1/2 oz Vodka
Fill with Orange Juice.
Shake.
Top with 1/2 oz Galliano.

SLOE COMFORTABLE SCREW
Fill glass with ice.
1 oz Vodka
1 oz Southern Comfort
1/2 oz Sloe Gin
Fill with Orange Juice.
Garnish with Orange.

**SLOE COMFORTABLE SCREW
AGAINST THE WALL**
Fill glass with ice.
1 oz Vodka
1 oz Southern Comfort
1/2 oz Sloe Gin
Fill with Orange Juice.
Shake.
Top with Galliano.
Garnish with Orange.

SLOE DOG
Fill glass with ice.
1 1/2 oz Vodka
1/2 oz Sloe Gin
Fill with Grapefruit Juice.
Shake.

SLOE GIN FIZZ
Fill glass with ice.
2 oz Sloe Gin
Fill with Sour Mix.
Shake.
Splash with Soda Water.
Garnish with Lemon.

SLOE POKE
Fill glass with ice.
2 oz Sloe Gin
Fill with Cola.

SLOE SCREW
Fill glass with ice.
1 1/2 oz Sloe Gin
or 3/4 oz Vodka
and 3/4 oz Sloe Gin
Fill with Orange Juice.
Stir.
Garnish with Orange.

SLOE TEQUILA
Fill glass with ice.
1 1/2 oz Tequila
1/2 oz Sloe Gin
1 tsp Lime Juice
Shake.
Strain into chilled glass.
Garnish with Cucumber Peel.

SLOPPY JOE
Fill glass with ice.
3/4 oz Rum
3/4 oz Dry Vermouth
1/4 oz Triple Sec
1/4 oz Grenadine
1 oz Lime Juice
Shake.
Serve or strain into chilled glass.

SLOPPY JOE'S
Fill glass with ice.
1 oz Brandy
1 oz Port
1/2 tsp Triple Sec
1 oz Pineapple Juice
1/2 tsp Grenadine
Shake.
Strain into chilled glass.

S

SMELLY CAT
Fill glass with ice.
1 1/2 oz Citrus Vodka
1/2 oz Peach Schnapps
Dash of Cranberry Juice
Shake.
Strain into chilled glass.

SMITH AND KERNS
Fill glass with ice.
2 oz Coffee Liqueur
1 oz Cream
Shake.
Fill with Soda Water.

SMOOTH DRIVER
Fill glass with ice.
2 oz Vodka
Fill with Orange Juice.
Float 1/2 oz Orange Liqueur on top.

SMOOTH OPERATOR
In Blender: cup of ice
3/4 oz Coffee Liqueur
3/4 oz Hazelnut Liqueur
3/4 oz Irish Cream
1/2 ripe peeled banana
Dash of Milk or Cream
Blend until smooth.

SMURF P.
Fill glass with ice.
1 oz Light Rum
1/2 oz Blueberry Schnapps
1/2 oz Blue Curacao
1 oz Sour Mix
Shake.
Strain into chilled glass.
Splash with Lemon-Lime Soda.

SNAKE BITE
Fill glass with ice.
2 oz Yukon Jack
Dash of Lime Juice
Shake.
Serve or strain into chilled glass.
Garnish with Lime.

SNAKE BITE 2
Fill glass with ice.
1 1/2 oz Bourbon
or Canadian Whiskey
1/2 oz Peppermint Schnapps
Stir.
Strain into chilled glass.

SNAKE BITE 3
Fill glass 3/4 with Hard Cider.
Fill glass with Ale.

SNEAKY PETE
Fill glass with ice.
2 oz Tequila
1/2 oz White Creme De Menthe
1 oz Pineapple Juice
Dash of Lime Juice
Shake.
Strain into chilled glass.
Garnish with Lime.

SNICKER
Fill glass with ice.
1 oz Hazelnut Liqueur
1 oz Irish Cream
1 oz Dark Creme De Cacao
Fill with Milk or Cream.
Shake.

SNICKER AT THE BAR (frozen)
In Blender:
1/2 cup of Ice
3/4 oz Coffee Liqueur
3/4 oz Irish Cream
3/4 oz Hazelnut Liqueur
1/4 cup peanuts
1 scoop of Vanilla Ice Cream
Blend until smooth.
If too thick add Milk.
If too thin add ice or Ice Cream.

SNO CAP (frozen)
In Blender: cup of ice.
1 oz Coffee Liqueur
3/4 oz Vodka
3/4 oz Irish Cream
Blend until smooth.
Garnish with non perils.
Bill Bona

SNOWBALL
Fill glass with ice.
1 oz Gin
1/2 oz White Creme De Menthe
1/2 oz Anisette
Fill with Milk or Cream.
Shake.

SNOWBALL 2
Fill glass with ice.
3/4 oz Brandy
3/4 oz Peppermint Schnapps
3/4 oz White Creme De Cacao
Shake.
Strain into shot glass.

SNOWBALL 3
Fill glass with ice.
1 oz Sambuca
1 oz White Creme De Cacao
1 oz Cream
Shake.
Strain into chilled glass.

SNOWBERRY aka
RED RUSSIAN
Fill glass with ice.
1 oz Vodka
1 oz Strawberry Liqueur
Fill with Milk or Cream.
Shake.

SNOWBLOWER
Fill glass with ice.
1 oz Rum
1 oz Cranberry Liqueur
Fill with Orange Juice.
Shake.

SNOWBLOWER 2
Fill glass with ice.
1 oz Gin
3/4 oz Peppermint Schnapps
2 oz Cream of Coconut
Fill with Pineapple Juice.
Shake.

SNOWCAP (floater)
3/4 oz Tequila (bottom)
3/4 oz Irish Cream (top)

SNOWSHOE GROG
Fill glass with ice.
1 1/2 oz Bourbon or Brandy
1/2 oz Peppermint Schnapps
Stir.

SNUGGLER aka COCOANAPPS, ADULT HOT CHOCOLATE, PEPPERMINT KISS
2 oz Peppermint Schnapps
Fill with Hot Chocolate.
Top with Whipped Cream.
Sprinkle with Shaved Chocolate or
Chocolate Sprinkles.

SOMBRERO
Fill glass with ice.
2 oz Coffee Liqueur
or Coffee Brandy
Fill with Milk or Cream.
Shake.

SONIC
Fill glass with ice.
1 oz desired Liquor or Liqueur
Fill with equal parts Soda Water
and Tonic Water.

SOUL KISS
Fill glass with ice.
1 oz Whiskey
1 oz Dry Vermouth
1/2 oz Dubonnet
3/4 oz Orange Juice
Shake.
Serve or strain into chilled glass.

SOUR
Fill glass with ice.
2 oz desired liquor or liqueur
Fill with Sour Mix.
Shake.
Garnish with Orange and Cherry.

SOUR BALL
Fill glass with ice.
1 oz Vodka
1 oz Apricot Brandy
Fill with equal parts Sour Mix and
Orange Juice.
Shake.
Garnish with Orange and Cherry.

SOUR GRAPES
Fill glass with ice.
3/4 oz Vodka
3/4 oz Black Raspberry Liqueur
3/4 oz Sour Mix
Shake.
Strain into chilled glass.

SOUR MIX
In Blender:
1 Egg White
1 cup of Water
1 cup of Lemon Juice
3 tbsp Sugar
Blend until sugar is liquefied.

SOUTH FORK COFFEE
1 oz Bourbon
1 oz Creme De Cacao
Fill with hot Black Coffee
Top with Whipped Cream.
Drizzle with Chocolate Syrup.

SOUTH OF FRANCE
Fill glass with ice.
1 oz Rum
1 oz B&B
1 tbsp Cream of Coconut
Fill with Pineapple Juice.
Shake.

SOUTH OF THE BORDER
Fill glass with ice.
1 1/2 oz Tequila
1/2 oz Coffee Liqueur
1oz Lime Juice
Shake.
Strain into chilled glass.

SOUTH PACIFIC
Fill glass with ice.
1 1/2 oz Dark Rum
1/2 oz Coconut Rum
Fill with equal parts Orange,
Cranberry, and Pineapple Juice.
Shake.
Garnish with Cherry and Orange.

SOUTHERN BEACH
Fill glass with ice.
1 oz Southern Comfort
1/2 oz Peach Schnapps
1/2 oz Amaretto
Dash of Pineapple Juice
Dash of Cranberry Juice
1 oz Orange Juice
Shake.
Strain into chilled glass.

SOUTHERN BELLE
Fill glass with ice.
1 oz Southern Comfort
1 oz Irish Cream

S

SOUTHERN BELLE 2
Fill glass with ice.
1 1/2 oz Bourbon or Southern Comfort
1/2 oz Triple Sec
Dash of Grenadine
Fill with equal parts Pineapple Juice
and Orange Juice or Sour Mix.
Shake.

SOUTHERN BRIDE
1 1/2 oz Gin
1 oz Grapefruit Juice
Dash of Grenadine
Shake.
Strain into chilled glass.

SOUTHERN BRIDE 2
Fill glass with ice.
2 oz Gin
1/2 tsp Triple Sec or Curacao
2 dashes of Orange Bitters
Stir.
Strain into chilled glass.
Garnish with Lemon Twist.

SOUTHERN BULLDOG
Fill glass with ice.
1 oz Southern Comfort
1 oz Coffee Liqueur
Fill with Milk or Cream.
Shake.

SOUTHERN COMFORT MANHATTAN
Fill glass with ice.
2 oz Southern Comfort
1/2 oz Dry Vermouth
Stir.
Strain into chilled glass or pour contents (with ice) into short glass.
Garnish with Cherry or Lemon Twist.

SOUTHERN COMFORT OLD FASHIONED
Muddle together in glass:
Stemless Maraschino Cherry
Orange Slice
1/2 tsp Sugar
4 or 5 dashes of Bitters
Fill glass with ice.
2 oz Southern Comfort
Splash of Soda Water
Stir.

SOUTHERN MAIDEN
Fill glass with ice.
1 1/2 oz Bourbon
1/2 oz Triple Sec
2 oz Orange Juice
Fill with Pineapple Juice.
Shake.

SOUTHSIDE
Muddle together in glass:
6 Mint Leaves
1 tsp Sugar
Dash of Water
1 tbsp Lemon Juice.
Fill glass with crushed ice.
2 oz Bourbon
Fill with Spring Water.
Stir vigorously.

SOVEREIGN COFFEE
1 oz Black Raspberry Liqueur
1 oz Dark Creme De Cacao
Fill with hot Black Coffee.
Top with Whipped Cream.
Sprinkle with Shaved Chocolate or Sprinkles.

SOVIET COCKTAIL
Fill glass with ice.
1 1/2 oz Vodka
1/2 oz Amontillato Sherry
1/2 oz Dry Vermouth
Shake.
Serve or strain into chilled glass.
Garnish with Lemon Twist.

SPANISH COFFEE aka SUPER COFFEE
1 oz Coffee Liqueur
1 oz Cognac or Brandy
Fill with hot Black Coffee.
Top with Whipped Cream.
Garnish with Orange.

SPANISH COFFEE 2
3/4 oz Coffee Liqueur
3/4 oz Brandy
3/4 oz Orange Liqueur
Fill with hot Black Coffee.
Top with Whipped Cream.
Garnish with Orange.

SPANISH COFFEE 3
2 oz Tequila
Fill with hot Black Coffee.
Top with Whipped Cream.
Garnish with Lime.

SPANISH DYNAMITE
Fill glass with ice.
1 oz Tequila
1/2 oz Licor 43
1/2 oz Orange Liqueur or Triple Sec
Shake.
Strain into chilled glass.
Garnish with Cinnamon Stick.

SPANISH FLY
Fill glass with ice.
1 oz Tequila
1 oz Amaretto
Stir.

SPANISH ICED COFFEE
Fill glass with ice.
1 oz Coffee Liqueur
1 oz Cognac or Brandy
Fill with Iced Coffee.
Add Cream or Milk and sugar or
sweetener to taste.

SPANISH MOSS
Fill glass with ice.
1 1/2 oz Tequila
1 oz Coffee Liqueur
or Coffee Brandy
Shake.
Strain into chilled glass.
Add 3 drops of Green Creme De
Menthe.

SPARKS
Fill glass 3/4 full with ice.
1 oz Peppered Vodka
Fill with Champagne.

SPATS
Fill glass with ice.
1 1/2 oz Rum
1/2 oz Melon Liqueur
Fill with equal parts Orange and
Pineapple Juice.
Shake.
Float 1/2 oz Sloe Gin on top.
Garnish with Orange or Pineapple
and Cherry.

SPECIAL ROUGH
Fill glass with ice.
1 1/2 oz Brandy
1 1/2 oz Apple Brandy
2 dashes of Pernod
Stir.
Strain into chilled glass.

SPEEDY aka JUMPER CABLE
Fill glass with ice.
2 oz 151-Proof Rum
Fill with Jolt Cola
Stir.
Garnish with Lime.

SPEEDY GONZALAS
Fill glass with ice.
2 oz 151-Proof Rum
Dash of Lime Juice
Fill with Jolt Cola.
Stir.
Garnish with Lime.

SPERM WHALE (floater)
1 1/2 oz Tequila (bottom)
1/2 oz Irish Cream (top)

SPERM WHALE AT THE BANK
(floater)
1/2 oz Irish Cream (bottom)
1/2 oz White Creme De Cacao
1/2 oz Amaretto (top)
Place 1 drop of Grenadine in center
of glass.

SPHINX
Fill glass with ice.
2 oz Gin
2 tsp Dry Vermouth
2 tsp Sweet Vermouth
Stir.
Strain into chilled glass.

SPIKE
Fill glass with ice.
2 oz Tequila
Fill with Grapefruit Juice.
Stir.
Garnish with Lime.

SPILT MILK
1/2 oz Light Rum
1/2 oz Blended Whiskey
1/2 oz Irish Cream
1/2 oz Creme De Nouyax
or Amaretto
1 oz Milk or Cream
Shake.
Strain into chilled glass.

SPLEEF
Fill glass with ice.
2 oz Dark Rum
2 oz Orange Juice
Fill with Pineapple Juice.
Stir.
Garnish with Lime.

SPOOGE
Fill glass with ice.
1 oz Coconut Rum
1 oz Coffee Liqueur
1 oz Cream
Shake. Strain into shot glass.

SPRING ACTION
Fill glass with ice.
3/4 oz Southern Comfort
3/4 oz Apricot Brandy
3/4 oz Sloe Gin
Fill with Orange Juice.
Shake.

SPRING BREAK
Fill glass with ice.
2 oz Coconut Rum
Fill with equal parts Cranberry
Juice and Lemon-Lime Soda.

SPRING FLING
Fill glass with ice.
1/2 oz Vodka
1/2 oz Triple Sec
1/2 oz Apricot Brandy
Fill with equal parts Orange Juice
and Sour Mix.
Shake.

SPRING THAW (floater)
1 1/4 oz Yukon Jack (bottom)
1/2 oz Irish Cream
1/4 oz Vodka (top)
Nick G. Zeroulias

S

SPRITZER
Fill glass 3/4 with ice.
Fill 3/4 with desired Wine.
Fill with Soda Water.
Garnish with Lime.

SPY'S DEMISE
Fill glass with ice.
1/2 oz Vodka
1/2 oz Gin
1/2 oz Rum
1/2 oz Sloe Gin
1 oz Sour Mix
Shake.
Strain into chilled glass.
Fill with Lemon-Lime Soda.

SQUID INK
Fill glass with ice.
1 oz Black Sambuca
1 oz Black Raspberry Liqueur
Stir.

STAR
Fill glass with ice.
1 1/2 oz Apple Brandy
1 1/2 oz Sweet Vermouth
2 dashes of Bitters
Stir.
Strain into chilled glass.

STAR WARS
Fill glass with ice.
3/4 oz Vodka
3/4 oz Southern Comfort
3/4 oz Orange Liqueur
Fill with Orange Juice.
Dash of Grenadine
Shake.
Garnish with Orange.

STARBOARD TACK
Fill glass with ice.
1 oz Spiced Rum
1 oz Coconut Rum
Fill with equal parts Cranberry
and Orange Juice.
Garnish with Orange.

STARLIGHT
Fill glass with ice.
1 1/2 oz Vodka
1/2 oz Black Sambuca
Stir.
Strain into chilled glass.
Garnish with Lemon Twist.

STARS AND STRIPES (floater)
1 oz Grenadine (bottom)
1 oz Heavy Cream
1 oz Blue Curacao (top)

STEALTH (floater)
1/2 oz Coffee Liqueur (bottom)
1/2 oz Banana Liqueur
1/2 oz Irish Cream
1/2 oz Orange Liqueur (top)

STEEL HELMET
Fill glass with ice.
1 oz Vodka
1 oz Coffee Liqueur
Fill with Milk or Cream.
Shake.
Top with Galliano.

STEEPLE JACK
Fill glass with ice.
2 oz Apple Brandy
2 oz Apple Cider
or Apple Juice
Dash of Lime Juice
Shake.
Strain into chilled glass.
Fill with Soda Water.
Garnish with Cinnamon Stick and
Lime.

STEVIE RAY VAUGHAN
Fill glass with ice.
1 oz Bourbon
1 oz Southern Comfort
1/2 oz Triple Sec
Dash of Sour Mix
Fill with Orange Juice.
Shake.

STILETTO
Fill glass with ice.
1 oz Rum
1/2 oz Amaretto
1/2 oz Banana Liqueur
Fill with equal parts Orange Juice
and Pineapple Juice.
Shake.

STINGER
Fill glass with ice.
1 1/2 oz Brandy
1/2 oz White Creme De Menthe
Stir.
Serve or strain into chilled glass.

STOCK MARKET ZOO
Fill glass with ice.
1/2 oz Gin
1/2 oz Rum
1/2 oz Tequila
1/2 oz Bourbon
Dash of Grenadine
Dash of Orange Juice
Fill with Pineapple Juice.
Shake.
Strain into chilled glass.

STONE FENCE
Fill glass with ice.
2 oz Apple Brandy or Scotch
2 dashes of Bitters
Fill glass with cold cider.

STONEWALL
Fill glass with ice.
1 oz Dark Rum
2 oz Apple Cider
Stir.

STORM CLOUD
Fill glass with ice.
1 oz 151-Proof Rum
1 oz Coffee Liqueur
Stir.

STRAIGHT LAW
Fill glass with ice.
2 oz Dry Sherry
1 oz Gin
Stir.
Strain into chilled glass.
Garnish with Lemon Twist.

STRAWBERRY BLONDE (frozen)
In Blender:
1/2 cup of Ice
1 oz Strawberry Liqueur
1 oz White Creme De Cacao
1/2 cup fresh or frozen
Strawberries
Scoop of Vanilla Ice Cream
Blend until smooth.
If too thick add Milk or berries. If too
thin add ice or Ice Cream.

STRAWBERRY COLADA
(frozen)
In Blender:
1/2 cup of Ice
2 oz Rum
2 tbsp Cream of Coconut
1/2 cup fresh or frozen
Strawberries
1 tbsp Vanilla Ice Cream
Blend until smooth.
If too thick add fruit or juice.
If too thin add ice or Ice Cream.
Garnish with strawberry.

STRAWBERRY DAIQUIRI
(frozen)
In Blender:
1 cup of Ice
1 1/2 oz Rum
1/2 oz Strawberry Liqueur
1/2 oz Lime Juice
1/2 cup fresh or frozen
Strawberries
Blend until smooth.
If too thick add berries or juice.
If too thin add ice.
Garnish with Lime and/or strawberry.

STRAWBERRY LIQUEUR
(type liqueur)
Bring 2 cups of Water and
2 cups Granulated Sugar
to a boil.
Simmer for 5 minutes.
Let cool.
Add: 1 1/3 cups Vodka
2 tsp Strawberry Extract
6 drops of Red Food Coloring
Store in a glass jar in the dark for 1
week.

STRAWBERRY MARGARITA
(frozen)
In Blender:
1 cup of Ice
1 1/2 oz Tequila
1/2 oz Triple Sec
1/2 oz Lime Juice
1/2 cup fresh or frozen
Strawberries
Blend until smooth.
If too thick add juice or berries.
If too thin add ice.
Garnish with Lime and/or Strawberry.

STRAWBERRY SHORTCAKE
(frozen)
In Blender:
1/2 cup of Ice
1 oz Vodka
1 oz Strawberry Liqueur
1/2 cup fresh or frozen
Strawberries
Scoop of Vanilla Ice Cream
Blend until smooth.
If too thick add fruit or Milk.
If too thin add ice or Ice Cream.
Top with Whipped Cream.
Garnish with strawberry.

STREGA SOUR
Fill glass with ice.
1 1/2 oz Gin
1/2 oz Strega
2 oz Sour Mix
Shake.
Strain into chilled glass.

STUFFED TOILET (floater)
1/2 oz Coffee Liqueur (bottom)
1/2 oz Irish Cream
1/2 oz Tuaca (top)

STUMBLING F.
Fill glass with ice.
1 oz 151-Proof Rum
1 oz Jaegermeister
1 oz 100-Proof Peppermint
Schnapps
Stir.
Strain into shot glass.

STUMP BUSTER
Fill glass with ice.
1/2 oz Vodka
1/2 oz Gin
1/2 oz Rum
1/2 oz Tequila
Dash of Grenadine
Fill with Orange Juice.
Shake.
Garnish with Orange.

S

STUPID CUBE
Fill glass with ice.
1/2 oz Light Rum
1/2 oz Spiced Rum
1/2 oz Dark Rum
1/2 oz Amber Rum
Fill with equal parts Orange,
Grapefruit and Cranberry Juice.
Garnish with Lime, Lemon, Orange
and Cherry.

SUFFERING BASTARD
Fill glass with ice.
1 1/2 oz Dark Rum
1 oz 151-Proof Rum
1/2 oz Orange Curacao
or Triple Sec
1/2 oz Orgeat Syrup
Fill with equal parts Orange and
Lemon Juice.
Shake.
Garnish with Lime.

SUFFRAGETTE CITY
Fill glass with ice.
2 oz Rum
1 oz Orange Liqueur
Dash of Grenadine
Dash of Lime Juice
Shake.
Strain into chilled glass.

SUGAR DADDY
Fill glass with ice.
1 oz Butterscotch Schnapps
1 oz Irish Cream
Dash of Coffee Liqueur
1 oz Milk
Shake.

SUGAR SYRUP
Mix 1 part Water
with 2 parts Sugar
(Works much better with hot water
and superfine sugar.)

SUICIDAL TENDENCIES
Fill glass with ice.
1 oz Grain Alcohol
1 oz Absinthe
Stir.

SUISSESSE
Fill glass with ice.
1 1/2 oz Pernod
2 oz Sour Mix
Shake.
Strain into chilled glass.
Fill with Soda Water.
Garnish with Lemon and Cherry.

SUMMER BREEZE
Fill glass with ice.
2 oz Rum
Fill with equal parts Cranberry and
Grapefruit Juice.
Garnish with Lime.

SUMMER SHARE
Fill glass with ice.
1 oz Vodka
1 oz Rum
1/2 oz Tequila
1 oz Orange Juice
1 oz Cranberry Juice
Dash of Apricot Brandy
Shake.
Fill with Lemon-Lime Soda.
Garnish with Orange.

SUMMER SOLSTICE SUNRISE
Fill glass with ice.
1 oz Vodka
1 oz Rum
Fill glass leaving 1/4 inch from top
with Orange, Pineapple and
Cranberry Juice.
Top with 1/2 oz Cherry Brandy.

SUN STROKE
Fill glass with ice.
1 1/2 oz Vodka
1/4 oz Orange Liqueur
Fill with Grapefruit Juice.
Shake.

SUNBURST
Fill glass with ice.
1 1/2 oz Vodka
1/2 oz Triple Sec
Fill with Grapefruit Juice.
Dash of Grenadine
Shake.

SUNDOWNER
Fill glass with ice.
2 oz Rum
Dash of Triple Sec
1 tsp Grenadine
3/4 oz Sour Mix
Shake.
Strain into chilled glass.
Fill with Tonic Water.

SUNKEN TREASURE (floater)
1 oz Irish Cream (bottom)
1 oz Spiced Rum (top)

SUNNY DAY DREAM
Fill glass with ice.
2 oz Southern Comfort
Fill with Iced Tea.
Garnish with Lemon.
Mary Beth Dallas

SUNSPOT
Fill glass with ice.
1 1/2 oz Rum
1/2 oz Triple Sec
tsp Fresh Lemon Juice
Fill with Orange Juice.
Shake.

SUNTAN
Fill glass with ice.
2 oz Coconut Rum
Fill with Iced Tea.
Garnish with Lemon and Lime.

SUPER COFFEE aka SPANISH COFFEE
1 oz Coffee Liqueur
1 oz Cognac or Brandy
Fill with hot Black Coffee.
Top with Whipped Cream.
Garnish with Orange.

SURF RAT
Fill glass with ice.
3/4 oz Spiced Rum
3/4 oz Banana Liqueur
3/4 oz Coconut Rum
Fill with equal parts Orange,
Cranberry and Pineapple Juice.
Shake.

SURF'S UP
Fill glass with ice.
1 oz Coconut Rum
1/2 oz Banana Liqueur
1/2 oz White Creme De Cacao
Fill with equal parts Milk
and Pineapple Juice.
Shake.

SURFER ON ACID
Fill glass with ice.
1 oz Coconut Rum
1 oz Jaegermeister
Fill with Pineapple Juice.
Shake.

SUSIE TAYLOR
Fill glass with ice.
2 oz Light Rum
1/2 oz Lime Juice
Fill with Ginger Ale.
Stir.
Garnish with Lemon.

SWAMP WATER
Fill glass with ice.
2 oz Rum
1/4 oz Blue Curacao
1 oz Orange Juice
1/2 oz Lemon Juice
Shake.

SWAMP WATER 2
Fill glass with ice.
2 oz Green Chartreuse
Fill with Pineapple Juice or
Grapefruit Juice.
Shake.

SWEATY MEXICAN LUMBERJACK
Fill glass with ice.
1 oz Tequila
1 oz Yukon Jack
3 dashes of Tabasco Sauce
Strain into shot glass.

SWEET CREAM (floater)
1 1/2 oz Coffee Liqueur (bottom)
1/2 oz Irish Cream (top)

SWEET PATOOTIE
Fill glass with ice.
1 oz Gin
1/2 oz Triple Sec
1/2 oz Orange Juice
Shake.
Strain into chilled glass.

SWEET RELEASE
Fill glass with ice.
1 oz Vodka
1 oz Rum
Fill with Pineapple Juice.
Top with Sloe Gin.

SWEET TART
Fill glass with ice.
1 1/2 oz Vodka
1/2 oz Black Raspberry Liqueur
2 oz Sour Mix
2 oz Cranberry Juice
Shake.
Fill with Lemon-Lime Soda.

SWEET TART 2
Fill glass with ice.
1 oz Vodka
1/2 oz Orange Liqueur
1/2 oz Amaretto
Dash of Grenadine
Dash of Lime Juice
Fill with equal parts Sour Mix and
Lemon-Lime Soda.
Shake.

SWEDISH B J (floater)
1/2 oz Coffee Liqueur (bottom)
1/2 oz Banana Liqueur
1/2 oz Irish Cream
1/2 oz Swedish Vodka (top)
Top with Whipped Cream.
To drink, place hands behind back
and pick up using only mouth.

SWEDISH BEAR
Fill glass with ice.
1 1/2 oz Vodka
1/2 oz Dark Creme De Cacao
Fill with Milk or Cream.
Shake.

SWEDISH LULLABY
Fill glass with ice.
1 1/2 oz Swedish Punch
1 oz Cherry Liqueur
1/2 oz Lemon juice
Shake.
Strain into chilled glass.

T-BIRD
Fill glass with ice.
1/2 oz Vodka
1/2 oz Orange Liqueur
1/2 oz Amaretto
2 oz Pineapple Juice
Dash of Cream (optional)
Shake.
Strain into chilled glass.

S
T

T L C
Fill glass with ice.
2 oz Tequila
Fill with Cola .
Garnish with Lime.

T. K. O.
Fill glass with ice.
2 oz Tequila
1 oz Coffee Liqueur
1 oz Ouzo
Stir.

T. N. T.
Fill glass with ice.
2 oz Tequila
Fill with Tonic Water.
Garnish with Lime.

T.N.T. can also mean a Tangueray
Gin and Tonic

TAHITI CLUB
Fill glass with ice.
2 oz Amber Rum
1/2 oz Lime Juice
1/2 oz Lemon Juice
1/2 oz Pineapple Juice
1/4 oz Maraschino Liqueur
Shake.
Garnish with Orange.

TAHITIAN APPLE
Fill glass with ice.
2 oz Light Rum
Fill with Apple Juice.

TAHITIAN ITCH
Fill glass with ice.
1 oz Bourbon
1 oz Rum
1/2 oz Orange Liqueur
2 oz Pineapple Juice
2 tbsp Lime Sherbet
Fill with Ginger Ale.

TAM-O-SHANTER
Fill glass with ice.
1 oz Irish Whiskey
1 oz Coffee Liqueur
Fill with Milk or Cream.
Shake.

TAMPA BAY SMOOTHIE
Fill glass with ice.
1 1/2 oz Vodka
1/2 oz Orange Liqueur
Dash of Grenadine
1 oz Orange Juice
Shake.
Strain into chilled glass.
Garnish with Orange and Cherry.

TANGERINE
Fill glass with ice.
2 oz Gin
1 tsp Grenadine
1 tsp Lime Juice
Fill with Sour Mix.

TANGERINE 2
Fill glass with ice.
1 oz Vodka
1/2 oz Orange Liqueur
1/2 oz Amaretto
Dash of Grenadine
Fill with Orange Juice.
Shake.

TANGO
Fill glass with ice.
1 1/2 oz Gin
1/4 oz Dry Vermouth
1/4 oz Sweet Vermouth
1/2 tsp Curacao or Triple Sec
3/4 oz Orange Juice
Shake.
Serve or strain into chilled glass.
Garnish with Orange.

TANTALUS
Fill glass with ice.
1 oz Brandy
1 oz Forbidden Fruit
1 oz Lemon Juice
Shake.
Strain into chilled glass.

TARANTULA
Fill glass with ice.
3/4 oz Whiskey
3/4 oz Amaretto
3/4 oz Irish Cream
Stir.

TARNISHED BULLET
Fill glass with ice.
1/2 oz Tequila
1/2 oz Green Creme De Menthe
Stir.

TAWNY RUSSIAN aka GODMOTHER
Fill glass with ice.
1 1/2 oz Vodka
1/2 oz Amaretto
Stir.

TEACHER'S PET aka AGGRAVATION
Fill glass with ice.
1 oz Scotch
1 oz Coffee Liqueur
or Coffee Brandy
Fill with Milk or Cream.
Shake.

TEAR DROP
3 oz White Zinfandel
1 oz Peach Schnapps
Dash of Sour Mix
Fill with Soda Water.
Garnish with Lemon.

TEMPTATION
Fill glass with ice.
1 1/2 oz Whiskey
1/4 oz Triple Sec or Curacao
1/4 oz Dubonnet Rouge
1/4 oz Pernod
Shake.
Strain into chilled glass.
Garnish with Orange Twist and
Lemon Twist.

TEMPTER
Fill glass with ice.
1 1/2 oz Apricot Brandy
1 1/2 oz Port
Shake.
Serve or strain into chilled glass.

TENNESSEE
Fill glass with ice.
2 oz Whiskey
3/4 oz Maraschino Liqueur
1/2 oz Lemon Juice
Shake.

TENNESSEE LEMONADE
Fill glass with ice.
2 oz Bourbon
Fill with Lemonade.
Shake.

TENNESSEE MUD
1 oz Bourbon
1 oz Amaretto
Fill with hot Black Coffee.
Top with Whipped Cream.
Sprinkle with Brown Sugar.

TENNESSEE TEA
Fill glass with ice.
1/2 oz Bourbon
1/2 oz Dark Creme De Cacao
Fill with Cranberry Juice.
Stir.
Garnish with Lemon.

TEQUILA COLLINS
Fill glass with ice.
2 oz Tequila
Fill with Sour Mix.
Shake.
Splash of Soda Water
Garnish with Cherry and Orange.

TEQUILA GIMLET
Fill glass with ice.
2 oz Tequila
1 oz Lime Juice
Stir.
Serve or strain into chilled glass.
Garnish with Lime.

TEQUILA MANHATTAN
Fill glass with ice.
2 oz Tequila
1/2 oz Sweet Vermouth
Stir.
Strain into chilled glass or pour
contents (with ice) into short glass.
Garnish with Cherry.

TEQUILA MARTINI aka TEQUINI
Fill glass with ice.
2 oz Tequila
1/2 oz Dry Vermouth
Stir.
Strain into chilled glass
or pour contents (with ice)
into short glass.
Garnish with Lemon Twist or
Orange Twist.

TEQUILA OLD FASHIONED
Muddle together in glass:
Stemless Maraschino Cherry
Orange Slice
1/2 tsp Sugar
4-5 dashes of Bitters
Fill glass with ice.
2 oz Tequila
Fill with Soda Water.
Stir.

TEQUILA POPPER
In shot glass:
1 oz Tequila
1 oz Ginger Ale or Lemon-Lime
Soda
Cover glass with napkin and hand,
then slam on bar top.
Drink while foaming.

TEQUILA QUENCHER
Fill glass with ice.
2 oz Tequila
Fill with equal parts Orange Juice
and Soda Water.
Garnish with Lime.

TEQUILA ROSE
Fill glass with ice.
2 oz Tequila
1/2 oz Lime Juice
Fill with Grapefruit Juice.
Shake.
Float 1/2 oz Grenadine on top.

TEQUILA SCREW-UP
Fill glass with ice.
2 oz Tequila
Splash Orange Juice
Fill with Lemon-Lime Soda
Garnish with Orange.

TEQUILA SHOOTER
Fill shot glass with Tequila.
Lick hand and pour small amount
of salt on moistened skin.
Have wedge of Lime or Lemon
ready.
1. Lick off salt
2. Drink shot
3. Bite and suck fruit wedge

T

TEQUILA SLAMMER

In Shot glass:
1 oz Tequila
1/2 tsp Cream of Coconut
1/2 tsp Strawberries in syrup
Fill with Ginger Ale.
Place hand and/or napkin over
glass. Slam on bar to make foam.
Drink.

TEQUILA SOUR

Fill glass with ice.
2 oz Tequila
Fill with Sour Mix.
Shake.
Garnish with Cherry and Orange.

TEQUILA STINGER

Fill glass with ice.
1 1/2 oz Tequila
1/2 oz White Creme De Menthe
Stir.
Strain into chilled glass.

TEQUILA SUNRISE

Fill glass with ice.
2 oz Tequila
Fill with Orange Juice.
Pour 1/2 oz Grenadine down
spoon to bottom of glass.
Garnish with Orange.

TEQUILA SUNSET

Fill glass with ice.
2 oz Tequila
Fill with Orange or Grapefruit Juice.
Pour 1/2 oz Blackberry Brandy
down spoon to bottom of glass.

TEQUINI aka
TEQUILA MARTINI

Fill glass with ice.
2 oz Tequila
1/2 oz Dry Vermouth
Stir.
Strain into chilled glass
or pour contents (with ice)
into short glass.
Garnish with Lemon Twist or
Orange Twist.

TERMINAL ICED TEA

Fill glass with ice.
1/2 oz Premium Vodka
1/2 oz Premium Gin
1/2 oz Premium Rum
1/2 oz Premium Tequila
1/2 oz Premium Orange Liqueur
2 oz Sour Mix
Top with Cola.
Garnish with Lemon.

TERMINATOR

Fill glass with ice.
1 oz Yukon Jack
1 oz Amaretto
1/2 oz Coconut Rum
1/2 oz Blue Curacao
Dash of Orange Juice
Shake.
Fill with Lemon-Lime Soda.

TEST-TUBE BABE

Fill glass with ice.
1 oz Tequila
or Southern Comfort
1 oz Amaretto
Strain into chilled glass.
Add 3-4 drops of Irish Cream or
Milk.

TEXAS MARY

Fill glass with ice.
2 oz Vodka
1 oz Steak Sauce
tsp Horseradish
3 dashes of Tabasco Sauce
3 dashes of Worcestershire Sauce
Dash of Lime Juice
3 dashes of Celery Salt
3 dashes of Pepper
Fill with Tomato Juice.
Shake.

TEXAS TEA

Fill glass with ice.
1 oz Tequila
1/2 oz Vodka
1/2 oz Rum
1/2 oz Triple Sec
1 oz Sour Mix
Splash with Cola.
Garnish with Lemon.

THANKSGIVING

Fill glass with ice.
3/4 oz Gin
3/4 oz Dry Vermouth
3/4 oz Apricot Brandy
1/4 oz Lemon Juice
Shake.
Strain into chilled glass.
Garnish with Cherry.

THEY KILLED KENNY

Fill glass with ice.
1 1/2 oz Bourbon
1/2 oz Apple Brandy
1 oz Apple Juice
Fill with Lemon-Lime Soda.
Stir.

THIRD DEGREE

Fill glass with ice.
1 1/2 oz Gin
1/2 oz Dry Vermouth
1/2 tsp Pernod
Stir.
Strain into chilled glass.

THIRD RAIL
Fill glass with ice.
3/4 oz Brandy
3/4 oz Apple Brandy
3/4 oz Light Rum
1/4 tsp Pernod
Shake.
Strain into chilled glass.

38TH PARALLEL COFFEE
1/2 oz Brandy
1/2 oz Irish Cream
1/2 oz Dark Creme De Cacao
1/2 oz Black Raspberry Liqueur
Fill with hot Black Coffee.
Top with Whipped Cream.
Drizzle Chocolate Syrup on top.

THISTLE
Fill glass with ice.
1 1/2 oz Scotch
3/4 oz Sweet Vermouth
3 dashes of Bitters
Stir.
Strain into chilled glass.

THREE AMIGOS
Fill glass with ice.
3/4 oz Jose Cuervo
3/4 oz Ron Bacardi
3/4 oz Jack Daniels
Stir.
Strain into shot glass.

THREE KINGS (floater)
3/4 oz Coffee Liqueur (bottom)
3/4 oz Galliano
3/4 oz Cognac (top)

THREE MILES
Fill glass with ice.
1 oz Brandy
1 oz Rum
1 tsp Grenadine
1/4 tsp Lemon Juice
Shake.
Strain into chilled glass.

THREE MILE ISLAND aka NUCLEAR MELTDOWN
Fill glass with ice.
1/2 oz Vodka
1/2 oz Gin
1/2 oz Rum
1/2 oz Tequila
1/2 oz Triple Sec
Fill with Sour Mix
or Pineapple Juice.
Shake.
Top with 1/2 oz Melon Liqueur.

THREE STORY HOUSE ON FIRE (floater)
1/2 oz Creme De Nouyax (bottom)
1/2 oz Banana Liqueur
1/2 oz Melon Liqueur
1/2 oz 151-Proof Rum (top)
Ignite.

THREE STRIPES
Fill glass with ice.
1 oz Gin
1/2 oz Dry Vermouth
1/2 oz Orange Juice
Shake.
Strain into chilled glass.

THREE WISE MEN
Fill glass with ice.
3/4 oz Johnnie Walker
3/4 oz Jim Beam
or Jack Daniels
3/4 oz Ron Bacardi
Stir.
Strain into chilled glass.

THREE WISE MEN 2
Fill glass with ice.
3/4 oz 100-proof Peppermint
Schnapps
3/4 oz Jaegermeister
3/4 oz 100-proof Cinnamon
Schnapps
Stir. Strain into shot glass.

THREE WISE MEN AND THE MEXICAN PORTER
Fill glass with ice.
1/2 oz Johnnie Walker
1/2 oz Jim Beam
1/2 oz Jack Daniels
1/2 oz Jose Cuervo
Shake. Strain into shot glass.

THUG HEAVEN
Fill glass with ice.
1 oz Vodka
1 oz Alize
Stir.

THUG PASSION
2 oz Cognac or Alize
Fill with Champagne.

THUMPER
Fill glass with ice.
1 1/2 oz Cognac or Brandy
1/2 oz Tuaca
Stir.
Garnish with Lemon Twist.

THUNDER
Fill glass with ice.
1 1/2 oz Brandy
1 tsp Sugar Syrup
or Powdered Sugar
1 Egg Yolk
1 pinch Cayenne Pepper
Shake.
Serve or strain into chilled glass.

THUNDER AND LIGHTNING
In shot glass:
1 oz 151-Proof Rum
1 oz 100-Proof Peppermint
Schnapps

T

TIA TIA
Fill glass with ice.
1 oz Rum
1/2 oz Dark Rum
1/2 oz Dark Creme De Cacao
2 oz Pineapple Juice
1/2 oz Lime Juice
1/2 oz Sugar Syrup
Shake.

TIC TAC
Fill glass with ice.
1 oz Peppermint Schnapps
1 oz Anisette or Sambuca
Stir.
Strain into chilled glass.

TIDAL WAVE
Fill glass with ice.
1 oz Coconut Rum
1 oz Blackberry Brandy
Dash of Grenadine
Fill with Pineapple Juice.
Shake.

TIDAL WAVE 2
Fill glass with ice.
1 oz Vodka
1 oz Light Rum
1 oz Spiced Rum
1 oz Sour Mix
Fill with Cranberry Juice.
Shake.

TIDAL WAVE (frozen)
In Blender:
1/2 cup of Ice
3/4 oz Vodka
3/4 oz Gin
3/4 oz Southern Comfort
Dash of Grenadine
Scoop of Orange Sherbet
Blend until smooth.
If too thick add orange juice.
If too thin add ice or sherbet.

TIDBIT (frozen)
In Blender:
1/2 cup of Ice
1 oz Gin
1/4 oz Dry Sherry
Scoop of Vanilla Ice Cream
Blend until smooth.
If too thick add Milk.
If too thin add ice or Ice Cream.

TIE ME TO THE BEDPOST
Fill glass with ice.
1 oz Citrus Vodka
1 oz Coconut Rum
1 oz Melon Liqueur
1 oz Sour Mix
Shake.
Strain into chilled glass.

TIE ME TO THE BEDPOST BABY
Fill glass with ice.
1/2 oz Vodka
1/2 oz Southern Comfort
1/2 oz Melon Liqueur
1/2 oz Black Raspberry Liqueur
1/2 oz Sloe Gin
1/2 oz Cranberry Juice
1/2 oz Pineapple Juice
Shake.
Strain into chilled glass.

TIGER BALLS
Fill glass with ice.
1 oz Bourbon
1 oz Grain Alcohol
1 oz Beer
Shake. Strain into shot glass.

TIGER'S MILK
Fill glass with ice.
1 oz Amber or Dark Rum
1 oz Cognac or Brandy
4 oz Cream
1/4 oz Sugar Syrup
Shake.
Garnish with grated Nutmeg or
Cinnamon.

TIGER'S MILK 2
Fill glass with ice.
2 oz Tuaca
Fill with Milk.
Shake.

TIGER'S TAIL
Fill glass with ice.
1 1/2 oz Pernod or Ricard
Dash of Curacao
or Triple Sec
Fill with Orange Juice.
Stir.
Garnish with Lime.

TIGHT SNATCH
Fill glass with ice.
1 1/2 oz Light Rum
1/2 oz Peach Schnapps
Fill with Pineapple Juice.
Shake.

TIJUANA BULLDOG
Fill glass with ice.
1 1/2 oz Tequila
1/2 oz Coffee Liqueur
Fill with equal parts Milk and Cola.
Shake.

TIJUANA SUNRISE
Fill glass with ice.
2 oz Tequila
Fill with Orange Juice.
Stir.
Pour 1/4 oz Bitters down spoon to
bottom of glass.

TIJUANA TITTY TICKLER
Fill glass with ice.
3/4 oz Tequila
3/4 oz Triple Sec
3/4 oz Tuaca
Shake. Strain into shot glass.

TIKI BOWL
Fill glass with ice.
3/4 oz Light Rum
3/4 oz Dark Rum
1/2 oz Cherry Brandy
Fill with equal parts Orange and
Pineapple Juice.
Shake.

TINTORETTO
Puree 1/2 cup of fresh or canned
pears.
Pour into glass.
1/2 oz Pear Brandy
Fill with chilled Champagne.

TINY BOWL
1 1/2 oz Vodka
1 or 2 drops Blue Curacao
Garnish with 2 Raisins.

TIPPERARY
Fill glass with ice.
3/4 oz Irish Whiskey
3/4 oz Sweet Vermouth
3/4 oz Green Chartreuse
Stir well.
Strain into chilled glass.

TIVOLI
Fill glass with ice.
1 1/2 oz Bourbon
1/2 oz Aquavit
1/2 oz Sweet Vermouth
Dash of Campari
Shake.
Strain into chilled glass.

TO HELL YOU RIDE
Fill shot glass with Vodka
7-10 dashes of hot sauce

TOASTED ALMOND
Fill glass with ice.
1 oz Coffee Liqueur
1 oz Amaretto
Fill with Milk or Cream.
Shake.

TOASTED ALMOND (frozen)
In Blender:
1/2 cup of Ice
1 oz Coffee Liqueur
1 oz Amaretto
Scoop of Vanilla Ice Cream
Blend until smooth.
If too thick add Milk or Cream.
If too thin add ice or Ice Cream.

TOASTED MARSHMALLOW
Fill glass with ice.
3/4 oz Amaretto
3/4 oz Galliano
3/4 oz Banana Liqueur
Fill with Milk or Cream.
Shake.
Top with Soda Water.

TOBLERONE
Fill glass with ice.
3/4 oz Hazelnut Liqueur
3/4 oz Irish Cream
3/4 oz Coffee Liqueur
Tsp Honey
Fill with Milk or Cream.
Shake.

TOBLERONE (frozen)
In Blender:
1/2 cup of ice
3/4 oz Hazelnut Liqueur
3/4 oz Irish Cream
3/4 oz Coffee Liqueur
tsp Honey
Scoop Vanilla Ice Cream
Blend until smooth.

TOKYO EXPRESS (frozen)
In Blender:
1 cup of Ice
2 oz Dark Rum
1 oz Peach Schnapps
Dash of Grenadine
1 oz Sour Mix
2 oz Orange Juice
Blend 3-6 seconds on low speed.
Garnish with Orange, Lemon and
Cherry.

TOKYO ROSE
Fill glass with ice.
2 oz Dry Sake
1 oz Peach Schnapps
Fill with equal parts Orange
and Cranberry Juice.
Shake.

TOM AND JERRY
Beat an Egg White and an Egg Yolk
separately.
Fold together and place into mug.
1/2 oz Sugar Syrup
or 1 tsp Powdered Sugar
1 oz Dark Rum
1 oz Cognac or Brandy
Fill with hot Milk or hot Water.
Stir.
Garnish with Nutmeg.

TOM COLLINS
Fill glass with ice.
2 oz Gin
Fill with Sour Mix.
Shake.
Splash of Soda Water
Garnish with Orange and Cherry.

T

TOM MIX HIGH
Fill glass with ice.
2 oz Blended Whiskey
Dash of Grenadine
Dash of Bitters
Fill with Soda Water.
Garnish with Lemon.

TOOL
Fill glass with ice.
1 1/2 oz Tequila
Dash of Grenadine
Fill with Orange Juice.
Shake.
Float 1/2 oz Southern Comfort
on top.

TOOTSIE
Fill glass with ice.
2 oz Coffee Liqueur or Sabra
or Dark Creme De Cacao
Fill with Orange Juice.
Shake.
Garnish with Orange.

TOP BANANA
Fill glass with ice.
1 oz Vodka
1 oz Banana Liqueur
Fill with Orange Juice.
Shake.

TOP GUN
Fill glass with ice.
Dash of Vodka
Dash of Dark Rum
Dash of Coconut Rum
Dash of Southern Comfort
Dash of Peach Schnapps
Dash of Amaretto
Dash of Triple Sec
Fill with equal parts Orange and
Cranberry Juice.
Shake.

TOP HAT
Fill glass with ice.
1 oz Orange Liqueur
1 oz Cherry Liqueur
Stir.

TOREADOR
Fill glass with ice.
1 1/2 oz Tequila
1/2 oz White Creme De Cacao
1/2 oz Cream
Shake.
Strain into chilled glass.
Top with Whipped Cream.
Sprinkle with Cocoa or Shaved
Chocolate.

TOREADOR 2
Fill glass with ice.
2 oz Brandy
1 oz Coffee Liqueur
1/2 Egg White
Shake.

TORONTO ORGY
Fill glass with ice.
1/2 oz Vodka
1/2 oz Coffee Liqueur
1/2 oz Orange Liqueur
1/2 oz Irish Cream
Shake.
Strain into shot glass.

TORPEDO
Fill glass with ice.
1 1/2 oz Apple Brandy
3/4 oz Brandy
Shake.
Strain into chilled glass.

TORQUE WRENCH
1 oz Melon Liqueur
1 oz Orange Juice
Fill with Champagne.
Garnish with Orange.

TONGUE STROKE
Fill glass with ice.
1 1/2 oz Brandy
Fill with equal parts Hard Cider
and Ginger Ale.
Stir.

TOVARICH
Fill glass with ice.
1 1/2 oz Vodka
3/4 oz Kummel
1/4 oz Lime Juice
Shake.
Strain into chilled glass.

TOXIC JELLYBEAN
Fill glass with ice.
3/4 oz Sambuca
3/4 oz Blackberry Brandy
3/4 oz Jaegermeister
Shake. Strain into shot glass.

TOXIC SHOCK
Fill glass with ice.
1/2 oz Vodka
1/2 oz Citrus Vodka
1/2 oz Gin
1/2 oz Rum
1/2 oz Spiced Rum
1/2 oz Tequila
Fill with Sour Mix.
Shake.
Top with Lemon-Lime Soda

TOXIC WASTE
Fill glass with ice.
1/2 oz Coffee Liqueur
1/2 oz Galliano
1/2 oz Apricot Brandy
Fill with Orange Juice
(leaving 1/2 inch from top).
Shake.
Top with Cream.

TRADE WIND
Fill glass with ice.
1/2 oz Rum
1/2 oz Galliano
1/2 oz Apricot Brandy
1/2 oz Orange Liqueur
Fill with Milk or Cream.
Shake.

TRADE WINDS (frozen)
In Blender:
1/2 cup of Ice
2 oz Amber Rum
1/2 oz Plum Brandy
1/2 oz Lime Juice
2 tsp Sugar Syrup
Blend until smooth.

TRAFFIC LIGHT
In three separate shot glasses.
1. 1 oz Vodka
   1/2 oz Melon Liqueur
2. 1 oz Vodka
   1/2 oz Orange Juice
3. 1 oz Vodka
   1/2 oz Cranberry Juice

TRAFFIC LIGHT 2 (floater)
1/2 oz Creme De Nouyax
(bottom)
1/2 oz Galliano
1/2 oz Melon Liqueur (top)

TRAFFIC LIGHT (floater)
1/2 oz Green Creme De Menthe
(bottom)
1/2 oz Banana Liqueur
1/2 oz Sloe Gin (top)

TRAIN WRECK
In Beer glass:
4 oz Mad Dog
Fill with Beer.

TRANSFUSION aka
PURPLE PASSION
Fill glass with ice.
2 oz Vodka
Fill with equal parts
Grape Juice and Ginger Ale
or Soda Water.

TRAPPIST FRAPPE
Fill large stemmed glass (Red Wine
glass, Champagne saucer) with
crushed ice.
3/4 oz Coffee Liqueur
3/4 oz Hazelnut Liqueur
3/4 oz Irish Cream

TRAPPIST MONK
3/4 oz Coffee Liqueur
3/4 oz Hazelnut Liqueur
3/4 oz Irish Cream
Fill with hot Black Coffee.
Top with Whipped Cream.

TREE CLIMBER
Fill glass with ice.
1 oz Rum
1/2 oz Amaretto
1/2 oz White Creme De Cacao
Fill with Milk or Cream.
Shake.

TREE SMACKER
Fill glass with ice.
1 oz Rum
1/2 oz Peach Schnapps
1/2 oz Apple Brandy
Dash of Grenadine
Fill with equal parts Sour Mix,
Pineapple,
And Orange Juice.
Shake.
Top with 1/2 oz 151-Proof Rum.

TRILBY
Fill glass with ice.
1 1/2 oz Bourbon
1/2 oz Sweet Vermouth
2 dashes of Orange Bitters
Stir.
Strain into chilled glass.

TRIP TO THE BEACH
Fill glass with ice.
3/4 oz Vodka
3/4 oz Coconut Rum
3/4 oz Peach Schnapps
Fill with Orange Juice.
Shake.

TROIKA
Fill glass with ice.
1 oz Peach Vodka
1/2 oz Amaretto
1/2 oz Sloe Gin
Fill glass with Sour Mix.
Shake.

TROIS RIVIERES
Fill glass with ice.
1 1/2 oz Canadian Whiskey
3/4 oz Dubonnet Rouge
1/2 oz Triple Sec
Shake.
Serve or strain into chilled glass.
Garnish with Orange Twist.

TROLLEY
Fill glass with ice.
2 oz Bourbon
Fill with equal parts Cranberry and
Pineapple Juice.
Stir.

TROPHY ROOM COFFEE
1/2 oz Amaretto
1/2 oz Vandermint
1/2 oz Dark Rum
Fill with hot Black Coffee.
Top with Whipped Cream.
Dribble Coffee Liqueur on top.

T

TROPICAL BREEZE (frozen)
In Blender:
1/2 cup of Ice
1 1/2 oz Banana Liqueur
1 1/2 oz Creme De Nouyax
1/2 cup fresh or frozen Strawberries
Scoop of Vanilla Ice Cream
Blend until smooth.
If too thick add berries or juice.
If too thin add ice or Ice Cream.
Top with Whipped Cream.

TROPICAL COCKTAIL
Fill glass with ice.
3/4 oz White Creme De Cacao
3/4 oz Maraschino Liqueur
3/4 oz Dry Vermouth
Dash of Bitters
Stir.
Strain into chilled glass.

TROPICAL GOLD
Fill glass with ice.
1 1/2 oz Rum
1/2 oz Banana Liqueur
Fill with Orange Juice.
Shake.

TROPICAL HOOTER
Fill glass with ice.
1 1/2 oz Coconut Rum
1/2 oz Melon Liqueur
Dash of Cranberry Juice
Dash of Pineapple Juice
Shake.
Strain into chilled glass.

TROPICAL LIFESAVER
Fill glass with ice.
3/4 oz Citrus Vodka
3/4 oz Coconut Rum
3/4 oz Melon Liqueur
Dash of Sour Mix
Fill with Pineapple Juice.
Shake.
Top with Lemon-Lime Soda

TROPICAL MOON (frozen)
In Blender:
1/2 cup of Ice
1 oz Dark Rum
1 oz coconut Rum
1/2 cup fresh or canned Pineapple
Scoop of Vanilla Ice Cream
Blend until smooth.
Float 1/2 oz Amaretto on top.
Garnish with Pineapple.

TROPICAL SCREW
Fill glass with ice.
2 oz Coconut Rum
Fill with Orange Juice.

TROPICAL STORM
Fill glass with ice.
1/2 oz Vodka
1/2 oz Gin
1/2 oz Rum
1/2 oz Tequila
1/2 oz Triple Sec
Dash of Cherry Brandy
Dash of Sour Mix
Shake.

TROPICAL STORM 2
Fill glass with ice.
1 1/2 oz Rum
1/2 oz Blackberry Brandy
Fill with Grapefruit Juice.
Shake.
Garnish with Lime.

TROPICAL STORM 3
Fill glass with ice.
1 oz Dark Rum
1/4 oz Amber Rum
1/4 oz Coconut Rum
1/4 oz Galliano
1/4 oz Grenadine
Fill with equal parts Sour Mix,
Pineapple and Orange Juice.
Shake.
Garnish with Orange and Cherry.

TTT
Fill glass with ice.
1 1/2 oz Tequila
1/2 oz Triple Sec
Fill with Tonic Water.

TUACA COCKTAIL
Fill glass with ice.
1 oz Vodka
1 oz Tuaca
2 tbsp Lime Juice
Shake.
Strain into chilled glass.

TULIP
Fill glass with ice.
3/4 oz Apple Brandy
3/4 oz Sweet Vermouth
1 1/2 tsp Apricot Brandy
1 1/2 tsp Lemon Juice
Shake.
Strain into chilled glass.

TUMBLEWEED
Fill glass with ice.
1/2 oz Coffee Liqueur
1/2 oz Brandy
1/2 oz White Creme De Cacao
1/2 oz Hazelnut Liqueur
Fill with Milk.
Shake.

TUMBLEWEED (frozen)
In Blender:
1/2 cup of Ice
1/2 oz Coffee Liqueur
1/2 oz Brandy
1/2 oz White Creme De Cacao
1/2 oz Hazelnut Liqueur
Scoop of Vanilla Ice Cream
Blend until smooth.
If too thick add Cream or Milk.
If too thin add ice or Ice Cream.
Top with Whipped Cream.
Sprinkle with Shaved Chocolate
or Sprinkles.

TURF
Fill glass with ice.
1 oz Gin
3/4 oz Dry Vermouth
1/4 oz Maraschino Liqueur (optional)
1/4 oz Anisette
1/4 oz Bitters
Stir.
Strain into chilled glass.

TURKEY SHOOT (floater)
3/4 oz 101-Proof Bourbon (bottom)
1/4 oz White Creme De Menthe
(top)

TURTLE DOVE
Fill glass with ice.
1 1/2 oz Dark Rum
1/2 oz Amaretto
Fill with Orange Juice.
Shake.

TUXEDO
Fill glass with ice.
2 oz Fino Sherry
1/2 oz Anisette
1/4 oz Maraschino Liqueur
1/4 oz Bitters
Stir.
Strain into chilled glass.

24 KARAT NIGHTMARE aka 911
Fill glass with ice.
1 oz 100-Proof Cinnamon
Schnapps
1 oz 100-Proof Peppermint
Schnapps
Stir.

TWIN HILLS
Fill glass with ice.
1 1/2 oz Whiskey
2 tsp Benedictine
1 1/2 tsp Lemon Juice
1 1/2 tsp Lime Juice
1 tsp Sugar Syrup
or Powdered Sugar
Shake.
Strain into chilled glass.

TWIN SIX
Fill glass with ice.
1 oz Gin
1/2 oz Sweet Vermouth
1 tsp Grenadine
1 tbsp Orange Juice
1 Egg White
Shake.
Strain into chilled glass.

TWISTER
Fill glass with ice.
2 oz Vodka
1/2 oz Lime Juice
Fill with Lemon-Lime Soda.
Stir.
Garnish with Lime.

252 (floater)
1 oz 101-proof Bourbon (bottom)
1 oz 151-Proof Rum (top)

TYPHOON
Fill glass with ice.
1/2 oz Gin
1/2 oz Sambuca
Dash of Lime Juice
Fill with Champagne.
Garnish with Lime.

UGLY DUCKLING
Fill glass with ice.
2 oz Amaretto
Fill with equal parts Milk or Cream
and Soda Water.
Stir.

ULANDA
Fill glass with ice.
1 1/2 oz Gin
3/4 oz Orange Liqueur or Triple Sec
1/4 tsp Pernod
Shake.
Strain into chilled glass.

UNCLE SAM
1 oz Bourbon
1 oz Peach Schnapps
Dash of Lime Juice
Stir.

UNDER THE COVERS
Fill glass with ice.
1 oz Vodka or Sambuca
1 oz Irish Cream
1 oz Peach Schnapps
Shake.

UNION JACK
Fill glass with ice.
1 1/2 oz Gin
3/4 oz Sloe Gin
1/2 tsp Grenadine
Shake.
Strain into chilled glass.

T
U

UNION JACK 2
Fill glass with ice.
1 1/2 oz Gin
1/4 oz Creme De Yvette
Stir.
Strain into chilled glass.

UNION LEAGUE
Fill glass with ice.
1 1/2 oz Gin
1 oz Port
2-3 dashes of Orange Bitters
Stir.
Strain into chilled glass.
Garnish with Orange Twist.

UNIVERSAL
Fill glass with ice.
3/4 oz Vodka
3/4 oz Amaretto
3/4 oz Melon Liqueur
Fill with Grapefruit
or Pineapple Juice.
Shake.

UNPUBLISHED HEMINGWAY
2 oz Cognac
1/2 oz Orange Liqueur

UPSIDE DOWN MARGARITA aka HEAD REST
Rest head on bar.
Have friend pour ingredients into mouth.
1 oz Tequila
1/2 oz Triple Sec
Dash of Lime Juice
Dash of Sour Mix
Dash of Orange Juice
Slosh around mouth.
Swallow!

URINALYSIS
Fill glass with ice.
1 1/2 oz Southern Comfort
1/2 oz Peppermint Schnapps
Stir.
Strain into chilled glass.

URINE SAMPLE
Fill glass with ice.
2 oz Amber Rum
1 oz Sour Mix
1 oz Pineapple Juice
Fill with Lemon-Lime Soda.

UZI (floater)
1/2 oz Coffee Liqueur (bottom)
1/2 oz Apricot Brandy
1/2 oz Ouzo (top)

VACATION
Fill glass with ice.
1 oz Spiced Rum
1 oz Coconut Rum
Fill with equal parts Cranberry,
And Pineapple Juice.
Shake.

VALENCIA
Fill glass with ice.
2 oz Apricot Brandy
1 oz Orange Juice
2-3 dashes of Orange Bitters
Shake.
Strain into chilled glass.
Add 3 oz chilled Champagne (optional).

VAMPIRE
Fill glass with ice.
1 1/2 oz Vodka
1/2 oz Black Raspberry Liqueur
Fill with Cranberry Juice.
Shake.

VANCOUVER
Fill glass with ice.
2 oz Canadian Whiskey
1 oz Dubonnet Rouge
1/2 oz Lemon Juice
1/2 oz Egg White
1/2 tsp Maple or Sugar Syrup
3 dashes of Orange Bitters
Shake.

VANDERBILT
Fill glass with ice.
1 1/2 oz Brandy
3/4 oz Cherry Brandy
1 tsp Sugar Syrup
2 dashes of Bitters
Stir.
Strain into chilled glass.

VANITY FAIR
Fill glass with ice.
1 1/2 oz Apple Brandy
1/2 oz Cherry Brandy
1/2 oz Cherry Liqueur
Shake.
Float 1 tsp Creme De Nouyax or
Amaretto on top.

VATICAN COFFEE
1 oz Cognac or Brandy
1 oz Hazelnut Liqueur
Fill with hot Black Coffee.
Top with Whipped Cream.

VEGAS B J
Fill glass with ice.
3/4 oz Rum
3/4 oz Jaegermeister
3/4 oz Banana Liqueur
3/4 oz Orange Juice
3/4 oz Pineapple Juice
Shake. Strain into shot glass.

VELVET DRESS
Fill glass with ice.
1 oz Brandy
1/2 oz Coffee Liqueur
1/2 oz Triple Sec
Fill with Milk or Cream
Shake.

VELVET GAF
Fill glass 1/2 with Porter.
Fill glass 1/2 with Champagne.

VELVET GLOVE
Fill glass with ice.
1 oz Sloe Gin
1 oz White Creme De Menthe
1 oz Cream or Milk
Shake.
Strain into chilled glass.

VELVET HAMMER
Fill glass with ice.
1 oz Triple Sec or Curacao
1 oz White Creme De Cacao
1 oz Cream or Milk
Shake.
Strain into chilled glass.

VELVET HAMMER (frozen)
In Blender:
1/2 cup of Ice
1 oz Triple Sec or Curacao
1 oz White Creme De Cacao
Scoop of Vanilla Ice Cream
Blend until smooth.
If too thick add Milk or Cream.
If too thin add ice or Ice Cream.
Sprinkle with Shaved Chocolate.
Garnish with Orange.

VELVET KISS
Fill glass with ice.
1 oz Gin
1/2 oz Banana Liqueur
1/2 oz Pineapple Juice
1 oz Cream
Dash of Grenadine (optional)
Shake.
Strain into chilled glass.

VENETIAN COFFEE
1 oz Brandy
1/2 oz Galliano
1/2 oz Triple Sec
Fill with hot Black Coffee.
Top with Whipped Cream.
Sprinkle with Cinnamon.

VENETIAN FRAPPE
Fill large stemmed glass (Red
Wine glass, Champagne saucer)
with crushed ice.
3/4 oz Brandy
3/4 oz Galliano
3/4 oz Triple Sec

VENETIAN SUNRISE
Fill glass with ice.
1 1/2 oz Grappa or Brandy
Fill with Orange Juice.
Pour 1/2 oz Campari down spoon
to bottom of glass.
Garnish with Orange.

VERMOUTH CASSIS
Fill glass with ice.
2 oz Sweet or Dry Vermouth
1 oz Creme De Cassis
Fill with Soda Water.
Stir.
Garnish with Lemon Twist.

VERONA
Fill glass with ice.
1 oz Gin
1 oz Amaretto
1/2 oz Sweet Vermouth
1 or 2 dashes of Lemon Juice
Shake.
Garnish with Orange.

VERY JOLL-E RANCHER
Fill glass with ice.
1 oz Vodka
1/2 oz Apple Brandy
1/2 oz Peach Schnapps
Fill with Cranberry Juice.
Shake.

VIA VENETO
Fill glass with ice.
1 1/2 oz Brandy
1/2 oz Sambuca
1/2 oz Lemon Juice
1 tsp Sugar Syrup
1/2 Egg White
Shake.

VIBRATOR (floater)
1 1/2 oz Southern Comfort (bottom)
1/2 oz Irish Cream (top)

VICTOR
Fill glass with ice.
1 1/2 oz Gin
1/2 oz Brandy
1/2 oz Sweet Vermouth
Shake.
Strain into chilled glass.

VICTORY
Fill glass with ice.
1 1/2 oz Pernod
3/4 oz Grenadine
Shake.
Fill with Soda Water.

VIKING
Fill glass with ice.
1 1/2 oz Swedish Punch
1 oz Aquavit
1 oz Lime Juice
Shake.

VIRGIN
Fill glass with ice.
1 oz Gin
1/2 oz White Creme De Menthe
1 oz Forbidden Fruit
Shake.
Strain into chilled glass.
Garnish with Cherry.

VIRGIN BANANA ORANGE FROSTIE
In Blender:
1 cup of Ice.
1/2 ripe peeled Banana
1/2 peeled Orange
Dash of Grenadine
2 oz Milk or Cream
Blend until smooth.

U

V

VIRGIN MARY

Fill glass with ice.
1 tsp Horseradish
3 dashes of Tabasco Sauce
3 dashes of Worcestershire Sauce
Dash of Lime Juice
3 dashes of Celery Salt
3 dashes of Pepper
1 oz Clam Juice (optional)
Fill with Tomato Juice.
Pour from one glass to another until mixed.
Garnish with Lemon and/or Lime, Celery and /or Cucumber and /or Cocktail Shrimp.

VIRGIN PIÑA COLADA

(frozen)
In Blender:
1 cup of Ice
2 tbsp Cream of Coconut
1 cup fresh or canned Pineapple
1 tsp Vanilla Ice Cream (optional)
Blend until smooth.
If too thick add fruit or juice.
If too thin add ice.
Garnish with Pineapple and Cherry.

VIRGIN STRAWBERRY DAIQUIRI

(frozen)
In Blender:
1 cup of Ice
Dash of Lime Juice
1 cup of fresh or frozen Strawberries
Blend until smooth.
If too thick add berries or juice.
If too thin add ice.
Garnish with Strawberry and/or Lime.

VISITOR

Fill glass with ice.
1 oz Vodka
1/2 oz Orange Liqueur
1/2 oz Banana Liqueur
Fill with Orange Juice.
Shake.

VODKA COLLINS

Fill glass with ice.
2 oz Vodka
Fill with Sour Mix.
Shake.
Splash with Soda Water.
Garnish with Orange and Cherry.

VODKA COOLER

Fill glass with ice.
2 oz Vodka
1/2 oz Sweet Vermouth
Dash of Sour Mix
1/2 oz Sugar Syrup
or Powdered Sugar
Shake.
Fill with Soda Water.

VODKA GIBSON

(*CAUTION:* DRY usually means less Vermouth than usual.
EXTRA DRY can mean even less Vermouth than usual or
no Vermouth at all.)
Fill glass with ice.
2 oz Vodka
1/2 oz Dry Vermouth
Stir.
Strain into chilled glass
or pour contents (with ice)
into short glass.
Garnish with Cocktail Onion.

VODKA GIMLET

Fill glass with ice.
2 oz Vodka
1/2 oz Lime Juice
Stir.
Strain into chilled glass
or pour contents (with ice)
into short glass.
Garnish with Lime.

VODKA GRAND MARNIER

Fill glass with ice.
1 1/2 oz Vodka
1/2 oz Orange Liqueur
1/2 oz Lime Juice
Shake.
Strain into chilled glass.
Garnish with Orange.

VODKA GRASSHOPPER aka FLYING GRASSHOPPER

Fill glass with ice.
1 oz Vodka
3/4 oz Green Creme De Menthe
3/4 oz White Creme De Cacao
Fill with Milk or Cream.
Shake.
Serve or strain into chilled glass.

VODKA MARTINI

(*CAUTION:* DRY usually means less Vermouth than usual.
EXTRA DRY can mean even less Vermouth than usual or
no Vermouth at all.)
Fill glass with ice.
2 oz Vodka
1/2 oz Dry Vermouth
Stir.
Strain into chilled glass
or pour contents (with ice)
into short glass.
Garnish with Lemon Twist or Olives.

VODKA SAKETINI

Fill glass with ice.
2 oz Vodka
1/2 oz Sake
Stir.
Strain into chilled glass
or pour contents (with ice)
into short glass.
Garnish with Lemon Twist or Olives or Cocktail Onions.

VODKA SLING
Fill glass 1/2 way with ice.
Place 2 fresh Sliced Pitted Cherries
around the inside of the glass.
2 oz Vodka
1/2 oz Lime Juice
Fill glass with crushed ice.
Top with 1/2 oz Cherry Brandy.

VODKA SODA
Fill glass with ice.
2 oz Vodka
Fill with Soda Water.
Garnish with Lemon or Lime.

VODKA SONIC
Fill glass with ice.
2 oz Vodka
Fill with equal parts Soda and Tonic
Water.
Garnish with Lemon or Lime.

VODKA SOUR
Fill glass with ice.
2 oz Vodka
Fill with Sour Mix.
Shake.
Garnish with Cherry and Orange.

VODKA STINGER
Fill glass with ice.
1 1/2 oz Vodka
1/2 oz White Creme De Menthe
Stir.
Serve or strain into chilled glass.

VODKA TONIC
Fill glass with ice.
2 oz Vodka
Fill with Tonic Water.
Garnish with Lime.

VOLCANO
Fill glass with ice.
1 1/2 oz Brandy
1 oz Orange Juice
1 oz Pineapple Juice
1 oz Sour Mix
Dash of Grenadine
Dash of Lime Juice
Shake.
Top with 1/2 oz 151-Proof Rum.
Ignite.
Pour in 1/2 oz Champagne.

VOLGA BOATMAN
Fill glass with ice.
1 1/2 oz Vodka
1 oz Cherry Liqueur
1 oz Orange Juice
Shake.
Strain into chilled glass.
Garnish with Cherry.

VOLGA COOLER
Fill glass with ice.
1 oz Vanilla Vodka
1/2 oz Banana Liqueur
1/2 oz Triple Sec
Fill with Lemon-Lime Soda.
Stir.

VOO DOO (floater)
1/2 oz Coffee Liqueur (bottom)
1/2 oz Irish Cream
1/2 oz Dark Rum (top)

VOO DOO 2 (floater)
1/2 oz Coffee Liqueur (bottom)
1/2 oz Dark Rum
1/2 oz 151-Proof Rum (top)

VULCAN
Fill glass with ice.
1/2 oz Vodka
1/2 oz Gin
1/2 oz Coconut Rum
1/2 oz Southern Comfort
Fill with equal parts Grapefruit
Juice and Lemon-Lime Soda.
Stir.

VULCAN BLOOD
Fill glass with ice.
1 oz Vodka
1 oz Blue Curacao
Fill with Orange Juice.
Shake.

VULCAN MIND MELD
1 oz Sambuca
1 oz 151-Proof Rum
Ignite.

VULCAN MIND PROBE
Fill glass with ice.
1/2 oz Vodka
1/2 oz Gin
1/2 oz Coconut Rum
1/2 oz Melon Liqueur
Dash of Lime Juice
Shake.
Strain into chilled glass.

VULCAN MIND PROBE 2
Fill glass with ice.
1/2 oz Gin
1/2 oz Rum
1/2 oz Brandy
1/2 oz Triple Sec or Curacao
Fill with equal parts Sour Mix and Beer.

W. W. II
Fill glass with ice.
1 oz Vodka
1 oz Triple Sec
1 oz Melon Liqueur
Dash of Lime Juice
Fill with Pineapple Juice.
Shake.

WADKINS GLEN
Fill glass with ice.
1 oz Vodka
1/2 oz Black Raspberry Liqueur
1/2 oz Banana Liqueur
Dash of Orange Juice
Dash of Cranberry Juice
Dash of Pineapple Juice
Shake.
Strain into chilled glass.
Garnish with Lime.

V

W

WAGON WHEEL
Fill glass with ice.
2 oz Southern Comfort
1 oz Cognac or Brandy
1 oz Sour Mix
1/2 oz Grenadine
Shake.
Strain into chilled glass.

WAIKIKI BEACHCOMBER
Fill glass with ice.
1 1/2 oz Gin
1/2 oz Triple Sec
Fill with Pineapple Juice
Shake.

WALDORF
Fill glass with ice.
1 1/2 oz Bourbon
3/4 oz Pernod
1/2 oz Sweet Vermouth
Dash of Bitters
Stir.
Strain into chilled glass.

WALL STREET LIZARD
Fill glass with ice.
1/2 oz Vodka
1/2 oz Gin
1/2 oz Rum
1/2 oz Melon Liqueur
1/2 oz Blue Curacao
Stir.
Serve or strain into chilled glass.

WALLY WALLBANGER
Fill glass with ice.
1 oz Vodka
1/2 oz Galliano
Fill with Orange Juice.
Shake.
Top with 1/2 oz 151-Proof Rum.

WALTZING MATILDA
Fill glass with ice.
2 oz Vodka
1 tsp Horseradish
3 dashes of Tabasco Sauce
3 dashes of Worcestershire Sauce
Dash of Lime Juice
3 dashes of Celery Salt
3 dashes of Pepper
1 oz Clam Juice (optional)
Fill with Tomato Juice.
Pour from one glass to
another until mixed.
Garnish with Lemon and/or Lime,
Celery and/or Cucumber
and/or Cocktail Shrimp.

WANDERING MINSTREL
Fill glass with ice.
1/2 oz Vodka
1/2 oz Coffee Liqueur
1/2 oz Brandy
1/2 oz White Creme De Menthe
Stir.
Strain into chilled glass.

WANNA PROBE YA
Fill glass with ice.
1 oz Spiced Rum
1 oz Coconut Rum
Fill with equal parts Pineapple and
Cranberry Juice.
Stir.
Garnish with Lime.

WARD EIGHT
Fill glass with ice.
2 oz Whiskey
Dash of Grenadine
Fill with Sour Mix.
Shake.
Garnish with Cherry and Orange.

WARDAY'S COCKTAIL
Fill glass with ice.
1 oz Gin
1 oz Sweet Vermouth
1 oz Apple Brandy
1 tsp Yellow Chartreuse
Shake.
Strain into chilled glass.

WARM CREAMY BUSH
1 oz Irish Whiskey
1 oz Irish Cream
1 oz hot Coffee

WARSAW
Fill glass with ice.
1 1/2 oz Vodka
1/2 oz Blackberry Liqueur
1/2 oz Dry Vermouth
1/4 oz Lemon Juice
Shake.
Strain into chilled glass.
Garnish with Lemon Twist.

WASHINGTON
Fill glass with ice.
1 1/2 oz Dry Vermouth
3/4 oz Brandy
1/2 tsp Sugar Syrup
2-3 dashes of Bitters
Stir.
Strain into chilled glass.

WATERBURY COCKTAIL
Fill glass with ice.
2 oz Cognac or Brandy
1/2 oz Lemon Juice
1 tsp Sugar Syrup
1/2 Egg White
2-3 dashes of Bitters
Shake.
Strain into chilled glass.

WATERFALL
Fill shot glass with desired Liquor
or Liqueur. (Tequila, Peppermint
Schnapps, Jaegermeister, Whiskey)
Fill shot glass with desired chaser.
(beer, soda, juice, water, espresso)
Hold 1st glass between thumb and
forefinger. Hold 2nd glass between
forefinger and middle finger. Drink
from first glass and let second
glass flow into first glass.

WATERGATE COFFEE
1 oz Coffee Liqueur
1 oz Orange Liqueur
Fill with hot Black Coffee.
Top with Whipped Cream.

WATERMELON
Fill glass with ice.
1 oz Southern Comfort
1/2 oz Sloe Gin
Dash of Orange Juice
Fill with Pineapple Juice.
Shake.

WATERMELON 2
Fill glass with ice.
1 oz Vodka or Amaretto
1 oz Melon Liqueur
Fill with Cranberry Juice.
Stir.

WATERMELON 3
Fill glass with ice.
1 oz Vodka
1 oz Strawberry Liqueur
1 oz Sour Mix
1 oz Orange Juice
Shake.

WEDDING BELLE
Fill glass with ice.
3/4 oz Gin
3/4 oz Dubonnet Rouge
1/2 oz Cherry Brandy
1/2 oz Orange Juice
Shake.
Serve or strain into chilled glass.

WEDDING CAKE
Fill glass with ice.
1 1/2 oz Amaretto
1/2 oz White Creme De Cacao
Fill with equal parts Milk
and Pineapple Juice.
Shake.

WEEK ON THE BEACH
Fill glass with ice.
1 oz Rum
1/2 oz Peach Schnapps
1/2 oz Apple Brandy
Fill with equal parts Orange,
Cranberry and Pineapple Juice.
Shake.

WEEKEND AT THE BEACH
Fill glass with ice.
1 oz Rum
1 oz Peach Schnapps
Fill with equal parts Pineapple and
Orange Juice.
Shake.

WEEP NO MORE
Fill glass with ice.
3/4 oz Brandy
3/4 oz Dubonnet
3/4 oz Lime Juice
1/4 tsp Cherry Liqueur (optional)
Shake.
Strain into chilled glass.

WELL RED RHINO (frozen)
In Blender:
1 cup of Ice
1 oz Vodka
1 oz Rum
1 oz Cream of Coconut
1 oz fresh or frozen
Strawberries
Dash of Cranberry, Lime and
Pineapple Juice
Blend until smooth.

WEMBLEY
Fill glass with ice.
1 1/2 oz Gin
3/4 oz Dry Vermouth
1/2 oz Apple Brandy
1/4 oz Apricot Brandy (optional)
Stir.
Strain into chilled glass.

WENCH
Fill glass with ice.
1 oz Spiced Rum
1 oz Amaretto
Shake. Strain into shot glass.

WEST INDIAN FRAPPE
Fill large stemmed glass (Red Wine
glass, Champagne saucer) with
crushed ice.
3/4 oz Light Rum
3/4 oz Banana Liqueur
3/4 oz Orange Liqueur

WEST INDIES YELLOWBIRD
Fill glass with ice.
1 oz Rum
1 oz Banana Liqueur
Splash Galliano
1/2 tsp Sugar
Dash of Cream
Fill with equal parts Orange and
Pineapple Juice.
Shake.

WET CROTCH
Fill glass with ice.
3/4 oz Irish Cream
3/4 oz Triple Sec
3/4 oz Black Raspberry Liqueur
Shake. Strain into shot glass.

WET DREAM
1 oz Vodka
1/2 oz Black Raspberry Liqueur
1/2 oz Banana Liqueur
Fill with equal parts of Orange
Juice and Milk.
Shake.

W

WHALE'S TAIL
Fill glass with ice.
1 oz Vodka
1 oz Spiced Rum
1/2 oz Blue Curacao
1 oz Sour Mix
Fill with Pineapple Juice.
Shake.

WHARF RAT
Fill glass with ice.
1 oz Rum
1/2 oz Apricot Brandy
Dash of Grenadine
2 oz Sour Mix
Fill with Orange Juice.
Shake.
Garnish with Lime and Black
Licorice Whip.

WHEN HELL FREEZES OVER
(frozen)
In Blender:
1 cup of Ice
1 oz Cinnamon Schnapps
1 oz Banana Liqueur
1/2 ripe peeled Banana
Dash of Orange Juice
Dash of Cranberry Juice
Pinch ground Cinnamon
Blend until smooth.

WHIP COCKTAIL
Fill glass with ice.
1 1/2 oz Brandy
3/4 oz Sweet Vermouth
3/4 oz Dry Vermouth
1/2 tsp Curacao or Triple Sec
1/4 tsp Pernod
Stir.
Strain into chilled glass.

WHIPPET
Fill glass with ice.
1 1/2 oz Whiskey
1/2 oz Peppermint Schnapps
1/2 oz White Creme De Cacao
Shake.
Strain into chilled glass.

WHIRLAWAY
Fill glass with ice.
1 1/2 oz Bourbon
3/4 oz Curacao
2-3 dashes of Bitters
Shake.
Top with Soda Water.

WHISKEY AND WATER
Fill glass with ice.
2 oz Whiskey
Fill with Water.
Stir.

WHISKEY COLLINS
Fill glass with ice.
2 oz Whiskey
Fill with Sour Mix.
Shake.
Splash with Soda Water.
Garnish with Cherry and Orange.

WHISKEY DAISY
Fill glass with ice.
2 oz Whiskey
1 tsp Raspberry Syrup
or Grenadine or Red Currant Syrup
1/2 oz Lemon Juice
Shake.
Fill with Soda Water.
Float 1 tsp Yellow Chartreuse on
top.
Garnish with Lemon wedge.

WHISKEY FIX
Fill glass with ice.
2 oz Blended Whiskey
or Blended Scotch Whiskey
1 oz Lemon Juice
1 tsp Powdered Sugar
Stir.
Garnish with Lemon.

WHISKEY HIGHBALL
Fill glass with ice.
2 oz Whiskey
Fill with Water or Soda Water
or Ginger Ale.

WHISKEY RICKEY
Fill glass with ice.
1 1/2 oz Whiskey
1/2 oz Lime Juice
1 tsp Sugar Syrup (optional)
Fill with Soda Water.
Stir.
Garnish with Lime.

WHISKEY SOUR
Fill glass with ice.
2 oz Whiskey
Fill with Sour Mix.
Shake.
Garnish with Cherry and Orange.

WHISKEY ZIPPER
Fill glass with ice.
1 1/2 oz Whiskey
Dash of Drambuie
Dash of Cherry Liqueur
Squeeze and drop Lemon Wedge
into drink.

WHISPER (frozen)
In Blender:
1/2 cup of Ice
1/2 oz Coffee Liqueur
1/2 oz Creme De Cacao
1/2 oz Brandy
Scoop of Vanilla Ice Cream
Blend until smooth.
If too thick add Cream or Milk.
If too thin add ice or Ice Cream.
Sprinkle with Shaved Chocolate.

WHITE BABY
Fill glass with ice.
1 oz Gin
1 oz Triple Sec
1 oz Heavy Cream
Shake.
Strain into chilled glass.

WHITE BULL aka AMIGO
Fill glass with ice.
1 oz Tequila
1 oz Coffee Liqueur
Fill with Milk or Cream.
Shake.

WHITE CADILLAC
Fill glass with ice.
2 oz Scotch
Fill with Milk or Cream.
Stir.

WHITE CADILLAC 2
Fill glass with ice.
1 oz Triple Sec
1 oz White Creme De Cacao
1 oz Milk or Cream
Shake.
Strain into chilled glass.

WHITE CARGO (frozen)
In Blender:
1/2 cup of Ice
2 1/2 oz Gin
1/2 oz Maraschino Liqueur
1/2 oz Dry White Wine
Scoop of Vanilla Ice Cream
Blend until smooth.
If too thick add Milk or Cream.
If too thin add ice or Ice Cream.

WHITE CLOUD
Fill glass with ice.
2 oz Sambuca
Fill with Soda Water.
Stir.

WHITE DEATH
Fill glass with ice.
1 oz Vodka
1/2 oz White Creme De Cacao
1/2 oz Raspberry Schnapps
Stir.
Strain into chilled glass.

WHITE ELEPHANT
Fill glass with ice.
1 oz Vodka
1 oz White Creme De Cacao
Fill with Milk.
Shake.

WHITE GHOST (frozen)
In Blender:
1 cup of Ice
1 1/2 oz Hazelnut Liqueur
3/4 oz White Creme De Cacao
1/4 oz Black Raspberry Liqueur
2 oz Cream
Blend.

WHITE HEART
Fill glass with ice.
1/2 oz Sambuca
1/2 oz White Creme De Cacao
2 oz Cream or Milk
Shake.
Strain into chilled glass.

WHITE HEAT
Fill glass with ice.
1 oz Gin
1/2 oz Triple Sec
1/2 oz Dry Vermouth
1 oz Pineapple Juice
Shake.

WHITE JAMAICAN
Fill glass with ice.
1 oz Rum
1 oz Coffee Liqueur
Fill with Milk or Cream.
Shake.

WHITE KNIGHT
Fill glass with ice.
3/4 oz Scotch
3/4 oz Drambuie
3/4 oz Coffee Liqueur
Fill with Milk or Cream.
Shake.

WHITE LADY
Fill glass with ice.
1 1/2 oz Gin
1/4 oz Cream
1 tsp Sugar Syrup
or Powdered Sugar
1/2 Egg White
Shake.
Strain into chilled glass.

WHITE LADY 2
Fill glass with ice.
1 oz Gin
1 oz Triple Sec
1 oz Cream or Milk
Shake.
Strain into chilled glass.

WHITE LILY
Fill glass with ice.
1 oz Gin
1 oz Rum
1 oz Triple Sec
1/4 tsp Pernod
Shake.
Serve or strain into chilled glass.

WHITE LION
Fill glass with ice.
1 1/2 oz Rum
3/4 oz Lemon juice
1 tsp Powdered Sugar
1/2 tsp Grenadine
2-3 dashes of Bitters
Shake.
Strain into chilled glass.

WHITE MINK
Fill glass with ice.
1 oz Vodka
1/2 oz White Creme De Menthe
1/2 oz Galliano
Fill with Cream or Milk.
Shake.

WHITE MINK 2
Fill glass with ice.
1 oz Galliano
1 oz Triple Sec
1 oz Cream or Milk
Shake.
Strain into chilled glass.

WHITE MINNESOTA
Fill glass with ice.
2 oz White Creme De Menthe
Fill with Soda Water.
Stir.

WHITE OUT
Fill glass with ice.
1 1/2 oz Gin
1 oz White Creme De Cacao
Fill with Milk.
Shake.

WHITE ROMAN
Fill glass with ice.
1 oz Sambuca
1 oz Coffee Liqueur
Fill with Milk or Cream.
Shake.

WHITE ROSE
Fill glass with ice.
1 1/2 oz Gin
3/4 oz Cherry Liqueur
2 oz Orange Juice
1/2 oz Lime Juice
1 tsp Sugar Syrup
1/2 Egg White
Shake.
Strain into chilled glass.

WHITE RUSSIAN
Fill glass with ice.
1 oz Vodka
1 oz Coffee Liqueur
Fill with Milk or Cream.
Shake.

WHITE RUSSIAN (frozen)
In Blender:
1/2 cup of Ice
1 oz Vodka
1 oz Coffee Liqueur
Scoop of Vanilla Ice Cream
Blend until smooth.
If too thick add Milk or Cream.
If too thin add ice or Ice Cream.
Sprinkle with Shaved Chocolate or
Sprinkles.

WHITE SPANIARD
Fill glass with ice.
1 oz Brandy
1 oz Coffee Liqueur
Fill with Milk or Cream.
Shake.

WHITE SPIDER
Fill glass with ice.
2 oz Vodka
1 oz White Creme De Menthe
Shake.
Strain into chilled glass.

WHITE SWAN
Fill glass with ice.
2 oz Amaretto
2 oz Milk or Cream
Shake.

WHITE TRASH
Fill glass with ice.
2 oz Southern Comfort
Fill with Milk.

WHITE WATER
Fill glass with ice.
1/2 oz Triple Sec
1 oz Pineapple Juice
Fill with White Wine.
Top with Lemon-Lime Soda.

WHITE WAY
Fill glass with ice.
2 oz Gin
1/2 oz White Creme De Menthe
Stir.
Strain into chilled glass.

WHITE WITCH
Fill glass with ice.
1 oz Light Rum
1/2 oz White Creme De Cacao
1/2 oz Triple Sec
Squeeze 1/2 Lime into drink.
Fill with Soda Water.
Garnish with Mint Sprigs
dusted with Powdered Sugar.

WHY NOT
Fill glass with ice.
1 oz Gin
1 oz Apricot Brandy
or Dry Vermouth
1/2 oz Dry Vermouth
or Apricot Brandy
1 tsp Lemon Juice
Shake.
Strain into chilled glass.

WIDOW'S DREAM
Fill glass with ice.
2 oz Benedictine
1 Egg
Shake.
Strain into chilled glass.
Float 1 oz Cream on top.

WIDOW'S KISS
Fill glass with ice.
1 oz Brandy
1/2 oz Benedictine
1/2 oz Yellow Chartreuse
Dash of Bitters
Shake.
Strain into chilled glass.

WIKI WAKI WOO
Fill glass with ice.
1/2 oz Vodka
1/2 oz 151-Proof Rum
1/2 oz Tequila
1/2 oz Triple Sec
1/2 oz Amaretto
Fill with equal parts Orange,
Cranberry,
and Pineapple Juice.
Shake.

WILD FLING
Fill glass with ice.
2 oz Wildberry Schnapps
Splash of Cranberry Juice
Fill with Pineapple Juice.
Stir.

WILD IRISH ROSE
Fill glass with ice.
1 1/2 oz Irish Whiskey
1 1/2 tsp Grenadine
1/2 oz Lime Juice
Stir.
Fill with Soda Water.

WILD THING
Fill glass with ice.
1 oz Vodka
1/2 oz Rum
1/2 oz Triple Sec
Dash of Lime Juice
Dash of Sour Mix
Shake.
Fill with Cranberry Juice.

WILL ROGERS
Fill glass with ice.
1 1/2 oz Gin
1/2 oz Dry Vermouth
Dash of Triple Sec
1 tbsp Orange Juice
Shake.
Strain into chilled glass.

WIND JAMMER
Fill glass with ice.
1 oz Dark Rum
1/2 oz White Creme De Cacao
2 oz Pineapple Juice
1 oz Cream
Shake.
Garnish with Pineapple.

WIND SURF
4 oz White Wine
Dash of Triple Sec
Fill with equal parts Pineapple
Juice and Soda Water.
Stir.

WINDEX
Fill glass with ice.
1 1/2 oz Vodka
1/4 oz Blue Curacao
Strain into shot glass.
Splash with Soda Water.

WINDEX 2
Fill glass with ice.
1 oz Vodka
1 oz Rum
1/2 oz Blue Curacao
Dash of Lime Juice
Fill with Lemon-Lime Soda
Use paper towel as coaster.

WINDY CITY
Fill glass with ice.
1 1/4 oz Whiskey
Dash of Triple Sec
2 oz water
Garnish with Lemon Twist.

WINE COOLER
Fill glass 3/4 with ice.
Fill 3/4 with desired Wine.
Fill with Ginger Ale
or Lemon-Lime Soda.
Garnish with Lime.

WINE SPRITZER
Fill glass 3/4 with ice.
Fill 3/4 with desired Wine.
Fill with Soda Water.
Garnish with Lime.

WINTER FROST (frozen)
In Blender:
1/2 cup of Ice
3/4 oz Brandy
3/4 oz White Creme De Cacao
3/4 oz White Creme De Menthe
Scoop of Vanilla Ice Cream
Blend until smooth.

WOLFHOUND
Fill glass with ice.
1 oz Irish Whiskey
3/4 oz Dark Creme De Cacao
1 oz Milk or Cream
Shake.
Top with 1 oz Soda Water.

WOMBAT
Pulverize 6 oz of Fresh Watermelon
(minus seeds) in glass.
2 oz Dark Rum
1/2 oz Strawberry Liqueur
3 oz Orange Juice
3 oz Pineapple Juice
Shake well.

WOO WOO aka
SILK PANTIES 2
Fill glass with ice.
1 1/2 oz Vodka
1/2 oz Peach Schnapps
2 oz Cranberry Juice
Stir.
Serve or strain into chilled glass.

WOODEN SHOE
2 oz Vandermint
Fill with Hot Chocolate.
Top with Whipped Cream.
Drizzle Chocolate Syrup on top.

W

WYOMING SWING COCKTAIL
Fill glass with ice.
1 1/2 oz Sweet Vermouth
1 1/2 oz Dry Vermouth
3 oz Orange Juice
1/2 oz Sugar Syrup
Shake.

WYOOTER HOOTER
Fill glass with ice.
2 oz Bourbon
Dash of Grenadine
Fill with Lemon-Lime Soda.

XALAPA PUNCH
In Sauce Pan over low heat:
2 cups of Hot Black Tea
Add rind of 2 Oranges (use carrot peeler or cheese grater)
Heat for 5 minutes.
Let cool.
Add 1 cup of Honey or Sugar (stir until dissolved)
Pour into punch bowl with ice.
Add:
1 Quart Amber Rum
1 Quart Apple Brandy
1 Quart Dry Red Wine
Diced Orange and Lemon
Serves 40

XANADU (floater)
1/2 oz Galliano (bottom)
1/2 oz Orange Liqueur
1/2 oz Amaretto (top)

XANGO
Fill glass with ice.
1 1/2 oz Rum
1/2 oz Triple Sec
1 oz Grapefruit Juice
Shake.
Strain into chilled glass.

XANTHIA
Fill glass with ice.
3/4 oz Gin
3/4 oz Cherry Brandy
3/4 oz Yellow Chartreuse
Shake.
Serve or strain into chilled glass.

XAVIER
Fill glass with ice.
3/4 oz Coffee Liqueur
3/4 oz Creme De Nouyax
3/4 oz Orange Liqueur
Fill with Milk or Cream.
Shake.

XERES
Fill glass with ice.
2 oz Dry Sherry
Dash of Orange Bitters
Stir.
Strain into chilled glass.

XYLOPHONE (frozen)
In Blender:
1/2 cup of Ice
1 1/2 oz Tequila
1 oz White Creme De Cacao
1 oz Sugar Syrup
Scoop of Vanilla Ice Cream
Blend until smooth.
If too thick add Milk or Cream.
If too thin add ice or Ice Cream.

XYZ
Fill glass with ice.
1 1/2 oz Rum
1/2 oz Triple Sec
1/2 oz Lemon Juice
Shake.
Strain into chilled glass.

Y 2 K
Fill glass with ice.
1 1/2 oz Yukon Jack
1/2 oz Coffee Liqueur
Shake. Strain into shot glass.

Y. I.
Fill glass with ice.
1/2 oz Vodka
1/2 oz Coconut Rum
1/2 oz Melon Liqueur
1/2 oz Black Raspberry Liqueur
Dash of Pineapple and Cranberry Juice
Shake.
Strain into shot glass.

YALE COCKTAIL
Fill glass with ice.
1 1/2 oz Gin
1/2 oz Dry Vermouth
1 tsp Blue Curacao
or Cherry Brandy
Dash of Bitters
Stir.

YARD OF FLANNEL
In sauce pan over low heat:
2 pints of Ale (do not boil)
Blend in a separate bowl:
4 oz Amber Rum
3 oz Super Fine Sugar
1/2 tsp ground Nutmeg
4 Eggs
1/2 tsp Ginger or Cinnamon
Beat well.
Pour mixture in heated pitcher.
Slowly add hot ale.
Stir constantly.
Serves 4.

YASHMAK
Fill glass with ice.
1 1/2 oz Rye Whiskey
3/4 oz Dry Vermouth
1/2 oz Pernod
3 dashes of Bitters
1/2 tsp Sugar Syrup
Shake.

YELLOW BIRD
Fill glass with ice.
3/4 oz Vodka
3/4 oz White Creme De Cacao
3/4 oz Orange Juice
3/4 oz Cream
1/2 oz Galliano
Shake.
Strain into chilled glass.

YELLOW BIRD (frozen)
In Blender:
1 cup of Ice
1 oz Rum
1/2 oz Coffee Liqueur
1/2 oz Banana Liqueur
2 tbsp Cream of Coconut
1/2 cup fresh or canned Pineapple
Blend until smooth.

YELLOW FEVER
Fill glass with ice.
2 oz Vodka
Fill with Lemonade.
Stir.
Garnish with Lemon.

YELLOW JACKET aka KENTUCKY SCREWDRIVER, BLACK-EYED SUSAN
Fill glass with ice.
2 oz Bourbon
Fill with Orange Juice.

YELLOW JACKET 2
Fill glass with ice.
1/2 oz Jaegermeister
1/2 oz Bärenjäger
1/2 oz Coffee Liqueur
Stir.
Strain into chilled glass.

YELLOW PARROT
Fill glass with ice.
1 oz Apricot Brandy
1 oz Pernod
1 oz Yellow Chartreuse
Shake.
Strain into chilled glass.

YELLOW RATTLER
Fill glass with ice.
1 oz Gin
1 oz Dry Vermouth
1 oz Sweet Vermouth
3 oz Orange Juice
Shake.
Strain into chilled glass.

YELLOW RUSSIAN aka JUNGLE JIM
Fill glass with ice.
1 oz Vodka
1 oz Banana Liqueur
Fill with Milk or Cream.
Shake.

YELLOW SNOW
Fill glass with ice.
2 oz Vodka
Fill with equal parts Pineapple
Juice and Milk.
Shake.

YELLOW SUBMARINE
Fill glass with ice.
1 oz Peach Schnapps
1 oz Banana Liqueur
Fill with equal parts Orange and
Pineapple Juice.
Shake.

YO MAMA
Fill glass with ice.
2 oz Orange Vodka
Fill with Soda Water.
Float 1/2 oz Orange Juice on top.

YODEL
Fill glass with ice.
2 oz Fernet Branca
2 oz Orange Juice
Stir.
Fill with Soda Water.
Garnish with Orange.

YOG
Fill glass with ice.
2 oz Yukon Jack
Fill with equal parts Orange and
Grapefruit Juice.
Shake.

YOKOHAMA MAMA
Fill glass with ice.
1 1/2 oz Brandy
1/2 oz Melon Liqueur
Dash of Amaretto
Dash of Grenadine
Fill with equal parts Orange
and Pineapple Juice.
Shake.

YORSH
2 oz Vodka
Fill with Beer.

ZAMBOANGA HUMMER
Fill glass with ice.
1/2 oz Amber Rum
1/2 oz Gin
1/2 oz Brandy
1/2 oz Curacao or Triple Sec
2 oz Orange Juice
2 oz Pineapple Juice
1/2 oz Lemon Juice
1 tsp Brown Sugar
Shake.

W
X
Y
Z

ZANZIBAR
Fill glass with ice.
2 1/2 oz Dry Vermouth
1 oz Gin
1/2 oz Lemon Juice
1 tsp Sugar Syrup
3 dashes of Bitters
Shake.
Strain into chilled glass.
Garnish with a Lemon Twist.

ZAZA
Fill glass with ice.
1 1/2 oz Gin
1 1/2 oz Dubonnet
1/2 oz Triple Sec
2 oz Orange Juice
Shake.
Strain into chilled glass.

ZAZARAC
Fill glass with ice.
1 oz Whiskey
1/4 oz Rum
1/4 oz Anisette
1/4 oz Sugar Syrup
3 dashes of Bitters
1 oz Water
Stir.
Garnish with Lemon.

ZHIVAGO STANDARD
Fill glass with ice.
1 1/2 oz Vodka
1/2 oz Kummel
1/2 oz Lime Juice
Stir.
Strain into chilled glass.
Garnish with Olive.

ZIPPER
1 oz Tequila
1 oz Orange Liqueur or Triple Sec
1/2 oz Milk or Cream
Shake.
Strain into shot glass.

ZIPPER HEAD
Fill glass with ice.
1 1/2 oz Vodka
1/2 oz Black Raspberry Liqueur
Fill with Soda Water.

ZOMBIE
Fill glass with ice.
1 oz Light Rum
1 oz Dark Rum
1/2 oz Triple Sec or Curacao or
Apricot Brandy
Dash of Creme De Nouyax
or Grenadine
2 oz Orange Juice
2 oz Sour Mix
or Pineapple Juice
Shake.
Top with 1/2 oz 151-Proof Rum.
Garnish with Lemon, Orange and
Cherry.

ZONKER
Fill glass with ice.
1 oz Vodka
1 oz Triple Sec
1 oz Amaretto
1 oz Cranberry Juice
Shake.
Strain into chilled glass.

ZOO
Fill glass with ice.
1/2 oz Gin
1/2 oz Rum
1/2 oz Tequila
1/2 oz Bourbon
Dash of Grenadine
Fill with equal parts Orange and
Pineapple Juice.
Shake.

ZOOM
Fill glass with ice.
1 1/2 oz Brandy
1/4 oz Honey
1/2 oz Cream
Shake.
Strain into chilled glass.

ZUMA BUMA
Fill glass with ice.
1 1/2 oz Citrus Vodka
1/2 oz Black Raspberry Liqueur
Fill with Orange Juice.
Splash of Cranberry Juice

A SALUTE TO THE BIG APPLE!

BIG APPLE MARTINIS

APPLE MARTINI
Fill glass with ice.
4 oz Apple Vodka
Dash Dry Vermouth or Apple Vodka (optional)
Stir
Strain into chilled glass or
Pour contents (with ice) into short glass.
Garnish with apple slice.

CARMEL APPLE MARTINI
Fill glass with ice.
3 1/2 oz Vodka
Dash Apple Cider or Apple Juice
Shake
Dip rim of chilled glass in carmel or
Drizzle onto side of glass.
Strain into chilled glass.

DIRTY SOUR MARTINI
Place 1/4 diced skinless Granny Smith Apple
in mixing glass and mash.
Fill glass with ice.
3 1/2 oz Sour Apple Liqueur
Shake vigorously.
Strain into chilled glass.

SOUR APPLE MARTINI
Fill glass with ice.
3 1/2 oz Vodka
1/2 oz Sour Apple Liqueur
Stir
Strain into chilled glass.
Garnish with cherry.

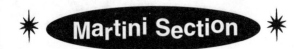

MARTINI FAVORITES

Below is an index of Martini recipes which
can be found in alphabetical order in this book.

Martini Section

SPHINX
TANGO
TEQUILA MARTINI
THANKSGIVING
THIRD DEGREE
THREE STRIPES
TURF
TWIN SIX
ULANDA
UNION JACK
VELVET KISS
VERONA
VICTOR

VIRGIN
VOLGA BOATMAN
WARSAW
WEMBLEY
WHITE HEAT
WHITE WAY
WHY NOT
WILL ROGERS
WOO WOO
YALE COCKTAIL
YELLOW RATTLER
ZANZIBAR

BEER

ALES

Ale: A fermented beverage containing malt and hops, similar to but heavier than lagers. Ale can vary from blond to black in color.

Alt: Means "old" in German and refers to a traditional brewing process.

Barley Wine: A strong ale, copper to amber colored. Should be sipped like brandy. A great winter warmer with complex sweetness and bitterness. Wide spectrum of tastes from maple to prune. Can improve with age. Serve at 55-60°F.

Biere de Garde: From northwest France, it is medium to strong in alcohol content and straw to copper colored. Biere de Garde is generally in the ale family, but some lagers also exist. Both types are conditioned and often fruity. Serve at 50-55°F.

Bitter: Straw, gold, or copper in color. Ordinary bitter is low to medium in alcohol content, while Extra Special Bitter is medium to high. Low to medium bitterness with low carbonation. Serve at 50-55°F.

Black & Tan: A mixture of stout or porter with a light or pale ale. A layered drink when made from scratch, a mixture when bottled.

Brown Ale: Color ranges from light amber to very dark brown; low to medium alcohol content. Usually bitter tasting with either a nutty or chocolatey flavor. Serve at 50-55°F.

Hefe: Means "yeast" in German. An unfiltered wheat beer, cloudy and bottle-conditioned with yeast. Can taste of clove or citrus. Pour to evacuate the sediment out of the bottom; squeeze a lemon wedge into the creamy head.

Imperial: Dark copper to very black, created for export to frozen Russian climates. It is heavy, fruity, and rich, coffee-like, with a burnt currant flavor. Serve at 60°F.

India Pale Ale: Created to endure voyages from England to India during British rule. Pale or golden to deep copper in hue. Quite hoppy, with nuances of fruit and/or flowers. Alcohol strength is evident.

Lambic: Wheat beer with fruit or sugar added. Very sweet, often tart. Types include: Kriek (cherry), Framboise (raspberry), Peche (peach), Faro (candy sugar), and Gueuze (A blend of different Lambics). Serve at 45-50°F

Old Ale: This term describes a medium to strong dark ale often consumed in winter. Originally referred to 17th-century English ales aged for up to 12 months.

Pale Ale: Color ranges from gold to amber to copper-brown. Low to medium maltiness. Medium to high hop flavor; hop bitterness can be fruity with a hint of caramel.

Porter: Medium brown to black, usually very hoppy and malty. Can be sharp with a hint of burnt charcoal flavor. Originated in 18th-century London.

Scotch Ale: Amber to red to dark brown color. Sweet and rich with a creamy head. Also Known as "Wee Heavy".

Stout: Very dark to black. Origins in 18th-century London. Tastes range from charcoal and molasses to malty sweet and bitter sweet. Serve warm at 55°F.

Trappist: This fruity and heavily sedimented ale is dark, rich, and strong. True Trappist is brewed at Trappist monasteries in the Netherlands (especially) and throughout Europe (as well) under centuries-old guidelines. Serve mild to warm 55-60°F.

Wheat Beer: A general term for beer made with wheat malts. Pale straw to deep copper or brown, clear, or cloudy. Usually highly carbonated. Yeasty and tart, with overtones such as apple, banana, orange, and honey. Serve at 45-50ºF

White Beer: Originates from Belgium and is a form of wheat beer. Color varies from pale to golden with a creamy head. Flavors can vary from fruity, with orange or banana, to spicy, with cinnamon, nutmeg or clove.

LAGERS

Lager: Bottom fermented beer, named for the German word *lager,* "to store". It is aged at cool temperatures that give it a smooth refined taste.

Amber: Pale or golden to deep brown. Generally light-bodied with mild malt flavor and a hint of hop aroma. Mainly American, but stronger European ones do exist. Usually rather effervescent.

Bock: Traditionally brewed in Germany in the spring. It is a stronger lager with a malty finish.

Doppelbock: Doublebock, very full-bodied and strong. Can be amber, red amber, dark brown. Often sweet and creamy, sometimes fruity or tangy. Serve at 50-55°F.

Dry Beer: Brewed with enzymes that convert more of the malt into alcohol, making a drier tasting beer.

Dunkel: Refers to any dark lager from deep red to black. Full-bodied with heavy malt character. Clean and crisp with caramel undertones. It is of average strength and slightly bitter.

Ice Beer: A medium lager filtered through an ice chamber to remove ice crystals, rendering a higher alcohol content.

Light Beer: A pale and watery, low-calorie, low-strength, pilsner style beer. An American original.

Malt Liqueur: An American term. Generally pale but strong and not very malty. High in alcohol content, usually consumed fast for a quick high.

Marzen: Amber to pale copper in color. Very malty and medium to strong in potency. Brewed in March to be ceremoniously drunk in late September and early October.

Plilsner: Origins in Pilsner, Czechoslovakia. Pale to golden, elegantly dry, and crisp with a fragrant, flowery finish. The most copied and widely brewed beer style in the world.

Vienna: Amber to copper; toasted malt flavor with rich, malty taste. Medium to strong in potency. Brewed in spring to be ceremoniously drunk in the fall.

CIDERS

Hard Cider: Actually apple wine, produced from fermented apples. Platinum to deep yellow to deep copper in color, 2.5% to 14% alcohol by volume. Flavors vary, featuring melon, citrus, herbs, caramel, spices and flowers.

Hard Lemonade: Made from fermented lemons. A sparkling sweet drink geared to the younger crowed. From Australia, England, U.S. 4%-10%. Apparently at least one brewer adds vodka in their product.

Perry: A sparkling alcoholic pear flavored drink. Pear Cider. English.

Clear Carbonated Alcoholic Beverage: Beer that has been filtered until it is colorless and tasteless, and then reflavored. 4.7%.

COGNAC

Cognac (kon yak) is a brandy produced in the vicinity of Cognac in western France. Cognacs are aged in wooden barrels and will improve in quality until they are 50 or 60 years old. Cognacs do not age in the bottle. Therefore a bottle of cognac bottled in 1990 at age 20, is still age 20 in the year 2000. The alcohol content of bottled cognacs range from 80-94 proof.

Below are listed some of the various grades of cognac.

V.S. 3 Star: (Very Special) 4-8 years old.

V.S.O.P.: (Very Superior Old Pale) or V.O. (Very Old) No brandy in the blend. May be less than 4 years 6 months old.

Napoleon: 6-25 years old.

X.O.: (Extra Old) May be 10-70 years old.

Reserve: 20-25 year old.

Extra: 20-50 years old.

Rare: 35-40 years old.

Remember these are guidelines and not rules.

Listed below are some of the major cognac houses and their finest products:

Beaulon	Cognac Rare
Camus	Extraordinaire
CCG	Meukow X.O.
Chabasse	Bowen Extra
Courvoisier	Collection Erte
Dor	Reserve No.11
Duboigalant	Tres Rare Grande Champagne
Dupuy	Rochas X.O. Fine Champagne
Pierre Frapin	Cuvee Rabelais
Gautier	Tradition Rare
Paul Giraud	Tres Rare
Hennessy	Richard Hennessy
Hine	Family Reserve Grande Champagne
Guy Lheraud	Tres Vieille Reserve Du Paradis
Martell	Creation
Moyet	Grande Champagne Tres Vieille
Normandin-Mercier	Grande Champagne Vieille 43 degrees
Paulet	Lalique
Remy Martin	Louie XIII

WINES

Serving Wines
Temperature
    Whites and Rosé- 40-55°
    Reds- 55-65° (exception: Red Beaujolais- 40-55°)
Note: When room temperature is suggested, it means European room temperature (approximately 60°).
If you enjoy white wines warm and red wines chilled by all means, serve it as you like it.

Opening
    There are two methods of getting at the cork.
      1. Using a knife, cut around the top of the bottle above the raised lip, but below the mouth.
      2. Using a knife, remove the foil capsule leaving the neck naked.
Note: The latter is favored because of lead toxins which can occur if the foil contains lead, and dripped wine sits for any length of time in the minute crevice created by using step one. (Newer wine foils do not contain lead).
Before uncorking insure the top of the cork and lip of the bottle are free of mildew which commonly occurs. Wipe with clean damp cloth.

Removing the cork
Place bottle on flat surface. Insert tip of corkscrew slightly off center, so that spiral will penetrate the center of the cork. Insure the spirals completely penetrate the cork, lessening chance of breaking cork.

Opening Champagne
Remove foil to expose wire fastener. Take a clean cloth and grip cork and fastener firmly and untwist fastener. Slowly twist cork and bottle in separate directions. Cork may want to rifle out of bottle, but control cork so it releases slowly.

Types of Wines

Beaujolais-(Bow-show-lay) (primarily red) (France, U.S.)
Should be drunk young, and served chilled.

Bordeaux-(Bore-doe) (primarily red) (France)
Many types exist. All wines from this seaport are entitled to the name.

Burgundy-(Bur-gun-dee) (red, white and rosé) (France, U.S.)
True French ones are better than average wines. Americans use the name as a word meaning generic red wine.

Cabernet Savignon-(Cab-air-nay So-veen-yaw) (red) (France, U.S.)
A superb grape. Took very well to American soil. A kaleidoscope of flavors, undertones, and nuances.

Chablis-(Shab-lee) (white) (France, U.S.)
In France it is strictly made with Chardonnay grapes by a certain process. In the U.S. it's name is used as a term for any white wine.

Champagne-(Sham-pain) (white) (France, U.S.)
Made from a mixture of different grapes. Before final bottling, sugar, wine and even Brandy are added for flavor. Brut means up to 1 1/2% added. Dry means up to 4% added.

Chardonnay-(Shar-doe-nay) (white) (France, U.S.)
Probably the best U.S. grown white table wines. Globally considered one of the finest white grapes.

Chateauneuf-du-Pape-(Shot-toe-nuff-dew Pop) (primarily red) (France)
A mixture of different grapes. Best between 5 and 10 years old.

Chenin Blanc-(Shay-nan Blaw) (white) (France, U.S.)
A grape of excellent quality. The grape transplanted to American soil took very well.

Chianti-(Key-ahnt-tee) (red) (Italy)
Properly drunk young. The elegant straw wrapped bottles are often worth more money than the contents, although the contents are sometimes excellent.

Cotes-du-Rhone-(Coat dew Rone) (primarily red) (France)
Moderately priced, fair to good table wine from the Rhone Valley.

Dubonnet-(Due-bawn-nay) (red, white) (France, U.S.).
Wine laced with herbs, and quinine. Usually served as an apertif.

Fumé Blanc-(Foo-may-Blaw) (white) (France, U.S.)
A dry, crisp, popular wine. Made with Sauvignon grapes.

Gewurztraminer-(Ge-vertz-tram-mener) (white, pink) (Germany, France, U.S.).
A spicy, highly prized, heavy scented wine.

Graves-(Grahv) (red, white) (France)
The reds age very well. The best whites come from Leognan.

Liebfraumilch-(Leeb-frau-milsh) (white) (Germany)
"Milk of the Blessed Mother". Almost always Rhine wine.

Madeira-(Ma-day-rah) (red) (Portugal)
Made world famous by American settlers. In modern day it is primarily used as cooking wine.

Marsala-(Mar-sahl-la) (red, amber) (Italy)
High alcohol content due to the fact it is fortified with high proof brandy. Popular for cooking.

Medoc-(May-dawk) (red) (France)
A superior red, even the lesser of the Medocs.

Merlot-(Mair-lo) (red) (U.S., Italy, Switzerland)
Much like a Cabernet in taste, but simpler and fruitier. It is a short lived wine.

Muscadet-(Mus-cad-day) (white) (France, U.S.)
An agreeable, fresh, fruity early maturing wine.

Muscatel-(Mus-cat-tel) (red, white) (U.S., Portugal, Spain, France, Italy)
Range from poor to excellent quality.

Petite Sirah-(Peh-teet See-rah) (red) (U.S.)
An American wine made from Syrah grapes transplanted from the Rhone Valley.

Piesport-(Peas-port) (white) (Germany)
From one of the most famous yet smallest wine producing villages.

Pinot Blanc-(Pee-no Blaw) (white) (U.S., Italy)
A light white.

Pinot Noir-(Pee-no Nwahr) (red) (U.S. France)
One of the main grapes of Champagne. A mainstay of Burgundies.

Pommard-(Po-mar) (red) (France)
Probably the most popular Burgundy. It is soft, well-balanced and fruity.

Port-(Port) (red, tawny, white) (Portugal, U.S.)
Fortified with Brandy. The most celebrated dessert wine.

Pouilly Fuisse-(Poo-ye Fwee-say) (white) (France)
Made from the Chardonnay grape. It does not improve past the age of 3 years.

Rhine-(Rine) (white) (Germany, U.S.)
Refers to the Rhine Valley. Can be any of several wines, Reisling being the most common.

Riesling-(Reece-ling) (white) (Italy, Switzerland, Chile, Austria, Germany, U.S.)
There are many types with many flavors. It is probably the most famous grape in the world.

Rosé-(Ro-zay) (pink) (France, Italy, U.S.)
It should be chilled and drunk young. Excellent domestic ones are available.

St. Emilion-(Sant A-me-lee-aw) (red) (France)
This wine is primarily Merlot.

Saké-(Sa-kay) (beer) (Japan)
Made from fermented rice and served warm. It is actually a beer and not a wine.

Sauvignon Blanc-(So-veen-yaw Blaw) (white) (France, U.S.)
This is the same wine as Fumé Blanc. A dry, crisp popular wine.

Semillon-(Say-me-yaw) (white) (France, U.S., Australia)
A prominent grape in white Bordeaux. Usually mixed with
Sauvignon Blanc to make Sauternes.

Sherry-(Shar-ee) (red) (Spain, U.S., Australia, South Africa)
The finest apertif as well as an excellent dessert wine. Made from
raisin or table grapes, and fortified with Brandy.

Soave-(So-ah-veh) (white) (Italy)
This wine should be drunk 3 to 4 years old.

Spumante-(Spoo-mahn-teh) (white) (Italy)
This is a sparkling or foaming wine.

Valpolicella-(Vahl-po-lee-chel-la) (red) (Italy)
Should be drunk 4 to 7 years old.

Vermouth-(Ver-mooth) (red, white) (France, Argentina, Italy, U.S.)
Wine fortified with herbs, barks, seeds and spices.

Vouvray-(Voo-vray) (white) (France)
Made from Chenin Blanc grapes, it is a long-lived white.

White Zinfandel-(Whyt Zin-fan-dell) (pink) (U.S.)
An American original, originally made by mistake.

Zinfandel-(Zin-fan-dell) (red) (U.S.)
Best drunk young. It is full bodied and peppery.

Wine and Food
Matching of wine and food is an individual's choice. For a rule of
thumb, try to match food with wine of similar flavor or try matching
food with wine of a contrasting flavor.

If a dish has a brown sauce or a red wine sauce, red wine is
suggested.

If a dish has a white sauce or a cream sauce, white wine is
suggested.

Dear Reader,

I am pleased to bring to you the following special features: Robert M. Parker, Jr.'s *Vintage Guide,* and his selection of *The World's Greatest Wine Values*. Robert M. Parker, Jr. is a world-renowned and respected wine critic. Categorized by region and vintage, this guide will be of great assistance to you as you make your wine purchase or serving decision, as will the list of *The World's Greatest Wine Values*.

Stephen Kittredge Cunningham

Stephen Kittredge Cunningham
Author, THE BARTENDER'S BLACK BOOK

The Wine Advocate's Vintage Guide
1970-2000® (Current as of 3/1/02)
By Robert M. Parker, Jr.

"Robert Parker is easily the single most influential person in the world of wine."

-Paul Levy, The Observer

"By Dint of Talent and a Formidable Capacity for Thoroughness, Robert M. Parker, Jr. has become one of the most respected American wine authorities."

- The New York Times

"The world's most experienced and trustworthy palate."

- London Times

"When Robert Parker spits, people listen....Parker has revolutionized American wine criticism to the genteel and snobbish world, Parker brought the forthright tastes of a middle class American ... the stringent standards of a fanatic, the high moral purpose of a reformer."

- Newsweek

"The most powerful and influential critic in any field."

- 60 Minutes II

THE WINE ADVOCATE'S VINTAGE GUIDE

	REGION	2000	1999	1998	1997	1996
Bordeaux	St. Julien/Pauillac St. Estephe	94T	89E	85T	87E	94T
	Margaux	93T	90E	86T	86E	88T
	Graves	93T	89E	89T	87E	86E
	Pomerol	94T	89E	96T	88R	85E
	St. Emilion	94T	89E	96T	87R	87T
	Barsac/Sauternes	88E	88E	87E	89E	87E
Burgundy	Côte de Nuits (Red)	?	88E	83C	90R	92T
	Côte de Beaune (Red)	?	91E	82C	89R	92T
	White	?	90E	86R	89R	92T
Rhône	North-Côte Rôtie, Hermitage	87E	95T	90T	90E	86R
	South-Châteauneuf du Pape	94E	90E	98E	82R	82R
	Beaujolais	91R	89R	84R	87R	82C
	Alsace	88R	87R	90R	87R	87R
	Loire Valley (Sweet White)	85R	84R	84R	88R	91R
	Champagne	?	?	86C	86R	91E
Italy	Piedmont	94E	90T	96E	94E	95T
	Tuscany	92E	94E	86C	95E	78R
	Germany	?	88R	85R	88R	93R
	Vintage Port	?	N.V.	N.V.	89T	N.V.
Spain	Rioja	?	86E	82C	86R	85R
	Ribera del Duero	?	91E	88T	86R	92R
Aust	South Austraila	88C	88E	95E	88R	90E
California-N. Coast	Cabernet Sauvignon	87E	88T	85R	94C	90T
	Chardonnay	88R	89R	89R	92C	87C
	Zinfandel	87R	90E	86C	85E	89E
	Pinot Noir	88R	90E	89R	90E	88R
Ore	Pinot Noir	?	92E	89T	87C	76C
Wash	Cabernet Sauvignon	?	90T	90T	88T	88T

Robert M. Parker, Jr's. The Wine Advocate, P.O. Box 311, Monkton, Md. 21111 © Copyright 2002

ABOUT VINTAGE CHARTS

This vintage chart should be regarded as a very general overall rating slanted in favor of what the finest producers were capable of producing in a particular viticultural region. Such charts are filled with exceptions to the rule ... astonishingly good wines from skillful or lucky vintners in years rated mediocre, and thin, diluted, characterless wines from incompetent or greedy producers in great years.

1995	1994	1993	1992	1991	1990
93T	87T	85C	79C	75R	98T
88E	86T	85C	75C	74R	90E
89E	88E	86C	75C	74R	90R
92T	89T	87C	82R	58C	95R
88E	86T	84C	75C	59C	98R
85E	78E	70C	68C	70C	96T
90T	72C	76C	69C	86T	92R
88T	73C	68C	82R	72E	90R
91E	77C	72C	90R	70C	87R
90T	88C	58C	78R	92R	92T
92T	86C	85C	78C	65C	95R
87C	85C	80C	77C	88C	86C
89R	90R	87R	85R	75R	93R
88R	87R	86R	80R	75R	90R
87R	N.V.	88E	N.V.	N.V.	96E
87C	77C	86E	74C	76C	96R
88T	85C	86C	72C	85C	90R
87R	90R	87R	90R	85E	92E
N.V.	92T	N.V.	95E	90E	N.V.
90R	90R	87R	85R	76R	87R
90R	90R	87R	82R	74R	89R
87R	90R	87R	87R	89R	88R
94T	95E	93T	93E	94T	94E
92C	88C	90C	92C	85C	90C
87R	92R	90R	90R	91R	91R
88R	92R	88R	88R	86R	86R
76C	92R	89R	88R	87C	90C
86R	90R	87R	89R	85C	87R

KEY (General Vintage Chart)   *Explanations of*

90-100 = The Finest   C=Caution, too old or irregular in quality
80-89 = Above Average   E=Early maturing and accessible
      to Excellent   T=Still tannic or youthful
70-79 = Average   R=Ready to drink
60-69 = Below Average   NV=Non-vintage
Below 60 = Appalling   ?=No impression yet formed

THE WINE ADVOCATE'S VINTAGE GUIDE

	REGION	1989	1988	1987	1986	1985
Bordeaux	St. Julien/Pauillac St. Estephe	90E	87R	82R	94T	90R
	Margaux	86E	85R	76R	90T	86R
	Graves	89R	89R	84R	89E	90R
	Pomerol	93R	89R	85C	87T	88R
	St. Emilion	88R	88R	74C	88E	87R
	Barsac/Sauternes	90R	98T	70R	94T	85R
Burgundy	Côte de Nuits (Red)	87R	79C	75C	65C	87R
	Côte de Beaune (Red)	88R	86C	79C	72C	87R
	White	92T	82R	79R	90R	89R
Rhône	North-Côte Rôtie, Hermitage	92T	92R	86R	84C	90R
	South-Châteauneuf du Pape	94T	88R	60C	78C	88R
	Beaujolais	92C	86C	85C	84C	87C
	Alsace	93R	86R	83C	82C	88R
	Loire Valley (Sweet White)	92R	88R	82R	87R	88R
	Champagne	90R	88E	N.V.	89R	95R
Italy	Piedmont	96T	90R	85C	78R	90R
	Tuscany	72C	89R	73C	84C	93R
	Germany	90E	89R	82R	80R	85R
	Vintage Port	N.V.	N.V.	N.V.	N.V.	95R
Spain	Rioja	90R	87R	82C	82R	82C
	Ribera del Duero	88C	87C	88C	77C	85C
Aust	South Australia	88C	85C	87C	90R	86C
California-N. Coast	Cabernet Sauvignon	84E	75E	90E	90R	90T
	Chardonnay	76C	89C	75C	90C	84C
	Zinfandel	83C	82C	90C	87C	88C
	Pinot Noir	85C	87C	86C	84C	86C
Ore	Pinot Noir	86C	88C	72C	85C	87C
Wash	Cabernet Sauvignon	92R	88R	90R	78R	86R

Robert M. Parker, Jr's. The Wine Advocate, P.O. Box 311, Monkton, Md. 21111 © Copyright 2002

For subscription information to
The Wine Advocate
Call 410.329.6477 • Fax 410.357.4504
or Write to
Robert M. Parker, Jr's. ***The Wine Advocate***
P.O. Box 311, Monkton, MD 21111

1983	1982	1981	1980	1979	1978
86R	98R	85R	78R	85R	87R
95R	86R	82R	79C	87R	87R
89R	88R	84R	78C	88R	88R
90R	96R	86R	79C	86R	84R
89R	94R	82R	72R	84R	84R
88T	75R	85R	85R	75R	75R
75C	75C	50C	84C	77C	88C
78C	80C	74C	78C	77C	86R
85C	88C	86C	75C	88C	88C
89C	85C	75C	83C	87C	98R
87C	70C	88C	77C	88C	97R
86C	75C	83C	60C	80C	84C
93R	82C	86C	80C	84C	80C
84C	84C	82C	72C	83C	85C
84C	90R	84C	N.V.	88C	N.V.
75C	92R	80R	70C	86R	95T
80C	86C	82C	70C	75C	85C
90R	80R	82R	65R	84R	72C
92R	86R	N.V.	84R	N.V.	83C
74C	92C	92C	75C	79C	84C
85C	87C	84C	85C	-	-
76R	83C	85C	88C	-	-
76C	86R	85R	87R	80R	92R
85C	85C	86C	88C	83C	86C
78C	80C	82C	82C	83C	86C
85C	84C	83C	85C	80C	84C
90C	84C	86C	86C	-	-
92R	78C	-	-	-	-

KEY (General Vintage Chart)	Explanations of
90-100 = The Finest	C=Caution, too old or irregular in quality
80-89 = Above Average	E=Early maturing and accessible
to Excellent	T=Still tannic or youthful
70-79 = Average	R=Ready to drink
60-69 = Below Average	NV=Non-vintage
Below 60 = Appalling	?=No impression yet formed

THE WINE ADVOCATE'S VINTAGE GUIDE
1970-2000 (Current as of 3/1/2002)

REGION		1975	1970			
Bordeaux	St. Julien/Pauillac St. Estephe	89T	87R			
	Margaux	78E	85R			
	Graves	89T	87R			
	Pomerol	94R	90R			
	St. Emilion	85R	85R			
	Barsac/Sauternes	90T	84R			
Burgundy	Côte de Nuits (Red)	50C	82C			
	Côte de Beaune (Red)	50C	82C			
	White	65C	83C			
Rhône	North-Côte Rôtie, Hermitage	73C	90C			
	South-Châteauneuf du Pape	60C	88C			
	Beaujolais	-	-			
	Alsace	82C	80C			
	Loire Valley (Sweet White)	-	-			
	Champagne	90C	85C			
Italy	Piedmont	65C	84R			
	Tuscany	84C	84C			
	Germany	85R	80C			
	Vintage Port	82R	90R			
Spain	Rioja	84C	90C			
	Ribera del Duero	-	-			
Aust	South Australia	-	-			
California-N. Coast	Cabernet Sauvignon	85R	92R			
	Chardonnay	86C	83C			
	Zinfandel	80C	89C			
	Pinot Noir	-	-			
Ore	Pinot Noir	-	-			
Wash	Cabernet Sauvignon	-	-			

Robert M. Parker, Jr's. The Wine Advocate, P.O. Box 311, Monkton, Md. 21111 © Copyright 2002

KEY (General Vintage Chart)

90-100 = The Finest	
80-89 = Above Average to Excellent	
70-79 = Average	
60-69 = Below Average	
Below 60 = Appalling	

Explanations of

C=Caution, too old or irregular in quality
E=Early maturing and accessible
T=Still tannic or youthful
R=Ready to drink
NV=Non-vintage
?=No impression yet formed

The World's Greatest Wine Values
by Robert M. Parker, Jr.
(This list is organized by wine producing region)

BORDEAUX

St.-Estèphe: Meyney, Les-Ormes-de-Pez, Phélan-Ségur, Tronquoy-Lalande Pibran

St.-Julien: Clos du Marquis, Gloria, Hortevie

Margaux and the Southern Medoc: d'Angluder, La Gurgue, Labégorcé-Zédé

Graves: Bahans Haut-Brion, La Louvière, Picque-Caillou

Moulis and Listrac: Fourcas-Loubaney, Gressier Grand Poujeaux, Maucaillou, Poujeaux

Médoc and Haut-Médoc: Beaumont, Le Boscq, Lanessan, Latour St.-Bonnet, Moulin Rouge, Potensac, Sociando-Mallet, La Tour de By, Tour Haut-Caussan, Tour du Haut-Moulin, Vieux-Robin

Pomerol: Bonalgue, L'Enclos

St.-Emilion: Pipean

Fronsac and Canon-Fronsac: Canon de Brem, Dalem, La Dauphine, Fontenil, La Grave, Haut-Carles, Mazeris, Moulin-Haut-Laroque, Moulin-Pey-Labrie, du Pavillon, Pez-Labrie, Rouet Les Trois-Croix, La Vieille-Cure

Lalande-de-Pomerol: Bel-Air, Bertineau-St.-Vincent, de Chambrum, du Chapelain, La Fleur-Bouard, Grand-Ormeau, Jean de Gué Cuvée Prestige, Haut-Chaigneau, Les Hauts-Conseillants, La Sergue

Côtes de Bourg: Fougas-Maldoror, Guerry, Haut-Maco, Mercier, Roc des Cambes, Tayac-Cuvée Prestige

Côtes de Blaye: Bel-Air La Royère, Bertinerie, Clos Lascombes, Garreau, Gigault Cuvée Viva, Grands Marechaux, Pérenne, Peyraud, Roland La Garde, La Rose-Bellevue, La Tonnelle

Bordeaux Premières Côtes and Supérieurs: Carsin, Carsin Black Label, Clos Chaumont, Domaine de Courteillac, Le Doyenné, De La Garde, Jonqueyrès Marjosse Parenchère Cuvée Raphaël, Le Pin Beausoleil, Plaisance, Prieuré-Ste.-Anne, Recougne, Reignac Cuvée, Speciale Reynon

Côtes de Castillon: d'Aigulhe, Brisson, Cap de Faugè res, Dubois-Grimon, Le Pin de Belcier, Pitray, Sainte-Colombre, Veyry, Vieux-Champ-de-Mars

Barsac/Sauternes: Bastor-Lamontagne, Doisy-Dubroca, Haut-Claverie, de Malle

Entre-Deux-Mers (dry white wines): Bonnet, Bonnet-Cuvée Réserve, Tertre-Launay, Turcaud

Generic Bordeaux: Bonnet, La Cour d'Argent, Thébot, Thieuley

Miscellaneaous: Branda (Puisseguin-St.-Emilion), La Griffe de Cap d'Or (St.-George St.-Emilion,), Marsau (Côtes de Francs), La Mauriane (Puisseguin-St.-Emilion), La Prade (Côtes de Francs)

RED BURGUNDY

Saint-Romain Appellation (Côte de Beaune): Bernard Fevre St.-Romaine), Alain Gras (St.-Romaine), Taupenot Père et Fils (St.-Romain, René Thévenin (Monthélie St.-Romain)

Saint-Aubin Appellation (Côte de Beaune): Jean-Claude Bachelet (St.-Aubin Derrière la Tour), Raoul Clerget (St.-Aubin Les Frionnes), Marc Colin (St.-Aubin), Larry-Pillot (St.-Aubin), Langoureau-Gilles Bouton (St.-Aubin en Remilly), Henri Prudhon (St.-Aubin Les Frionnes, St.-Aubin Sentiers

The World's Greatest Wine Values

by Robert M. Parker, Jr.

(This list is organized by wine producing region)

RED BURGUNDY *continued*

de Clou), Domaine Roux Père et Fils (St.-Aubin), Gérard Thomas (St.-Subin Les Frionnes)

Rully (Côte Chalonnaise): Michel Briday (Rully), Domaine de la Folie (Rully Clos de Bellecroix), Jacqueson (Rully Les Chaponnieres, Rully Les Cloix), Domaine de la Rénard (Rully Premier Cru), Antonin Rodet (Rully), Château de Rully (Rully). Domaine de Rully St.-Micheal (Rully Les Champs Cloux, Rully Clos de Pelleret)

Mercurey (Côte Chalonnaise): Château de Chamirey (Mercurey), Chartron et Trébuchet (Mercurey Clos des Hayes), Faiveley (Mercurey Clos des Myglands, Mercurey Clos du Roi, Mercurey La Croix Jacquelet, Mercurey LA Framboisière, Mercurey Les Mauvarennes), Michel Julliot (Mercurey Clos des Barraults, Mercurey Clos Tonnerre), Domaine de Meix Foulot (Mercurey Clos du Château de Montaigu, Mercurey Les Veleys), Domaine de a Monette (Mercurey), Domaine de Suremain (Mercurey Clos L'Eveque, Mercurey Clos Voyen)

Givry Appellation (Côte Chalonnaise): Jean Chofflet (Givry), Domiane Joblot (Givry Clos du Bois Chevaux, Givry Clos du Cellier aux Moines, Givry Clos de la Servoisine), Louis Latour (Givry), Thiery Lespinasse (Givry en Choué), Gerard Mouton (Givry), Domaine Veuve Steinmaier (Givry Clos de la Baraude), Domaine Thenard (Givry Cellier aux Moines, Givry Clos St.-Pierrem, Givry Les Bois Chevaux)

Beaujolais: Domaine Bacheard - Georges Duboeuf (Fleurie), René Berrod (Moulin à Vent), Rene Berrod-Les Roches du Vivier (Fleurie), Guy Braillion (Chenas), Domaine des Brureaux (Chenas), Manoir du Carra-Sambardier (Beaujolais-Villages), Domaine des Champs Grilles-J. G. Revillon (St.-Amour), Domaine Chauver-Georges Duboeuf (Moulin a Vent), Michel Chiguard Les Moriers (Fleurie), Clos de la Roilette-F. Coudert (Fleurie), Domaine de la Combe-Remont - Georges Duboeuf (Chenas), Château des Deduits - Georges Duboeuf (Fleurie), Jean Descombes - Georges Duboeuf (Morgon), Domaine Diochon (Moulin à Vent), Domaine des Grandes Vignes - J. C. Nesme (Brouilly), Domaine du Granit - A. Bertolla (Moulin à Vent), Domaine des Héritiers-Tagent - Georges Duboeuf (Moulin à Vent), Jacky Janoder (Moulin à Vent), Domaine de la Madone - J. Bererd (Beaujolais), Château Moulin à Vent - Jean-Pierre Bloud (Moulin à Vent), Domiane des Terres Dorées - J. P. Brun (Beaujolais-Villages), Domaine de la Tour du Bief - Georges Duboeuf (Moulin a Vent), Jacques Trichard (Morgon)

WHITE BURGUNDY

Jean-Claude Bachelet (St-Aubin Les Champlots), Michel Briday (Rully-Grésigny), Château de Chamirey (Mercurey), Chatron et Trébuchet (Rully Chaume, St.-Aubin, St.-Aubin La Chatenière), Raoul Clerget (St.-Aubin Le Charmois), Marc Colin (St.-Aubin La Chatenière), Joseph Drouhin (Mâcon La Forêt, Rully), Faiveley Bourgogne, Mercurey Clos Rochette), Domaine de la Folie (Rully Clos de Bellecroix, Fully Clos St.-Jacques), Jean Germain (St.-Romaine Clos Sous Le Château), Alain Gras (St.-Romaine), Jacqueson (Rully-Grésigny), Louis Jadot (Bourgogne Blanc), Robert Jayer-Gilles (Bourgogne Hautes Côtes de Beaune, Bourgogne Hautes Cotes de Nuits), Michel Julliot (Mercurey), Louis Latour (Mâcon Lugny, Montagny, St.-Veran), Lequin-Roussot (Santenay Premier Cru), Moillard (Montagny Premier Cru), Bernard Morey (St.-Aubin), Jean-Marc Morey (St.-Aubin Le Charmois), Michel Niellon (Chassagne-Montrachet), Prieur-Brunet (Sanrenay-Clos Rousseau), Henri Prudhon (St.-Aubin), Francois et Jean-Marie Raveneau (Chablis), Antonin Rodet (Bourgogre Blanc, Montagny), Château de Rully (Rully), Domaine de Rully St.-Michel (Rully Les Cloux, Rully Rabourcé), Château de la Saule (Montagny), Erienne Sauzer (Puligny-Montrachet), Gerard Thomas (St.-Aubin Murgers des Dents de Chien), Jean Vachet (Montagny les Coeres), Aubert de Villaine (Bourgogne Aligoté, Bourgogne Le Clous)

The World's Greatest Wine Values
by Robert M. Parker, Jr.
(This list is organized by wine producing region)

LOIRE VALLEY
- terrific dry, crisp, virgin whites (no oak) -

Muscadet: Michel Bahuand, Domaine de la Borne, Andre-Michel Brégeon, Château de Chasseloir, Chèreau-Carré, Joseph Drouard, Domaine de l'Ecu, Domaine du Fief Guérin, Marquis de Goulaine, Domaine Les Hautel Noëlles, Château de la Mercredière, Louis Métaireau, Domaine Les Mortaine, Domaine des Mortiers-Gobin, Château La Noë, Domaine La Quilla, Sauvion Cardinal Richard, Domaine le Rossignol, Sauvion Château de Cléray, Domaine des Sensonnieres, Domain de la Vrillonnière

Sancerre: Paul Cotat, Château du Nozet-Ladoucette, Edmond Vatan

Savennieres: Domaine des Baumard (Clos du Papillon, Trie Spéciale), Clos de la Coulée de Sérrant (N. Joly), Domaine du Closel (Clos du Papillon)

Vouvray: Domain Bourillon-Dorléans, Philippe Foreau Clos Naudin, Gaston Huet

LANGUEDOC-ROUSSILLON
- gutsy red wines, improving whites -

Domaine l'Aiguelière-Montpoyroux (Coteaux du Languedoc), Gilbert Alquier-Cuvée Les Bastides (Faugères), Domaine d'Aupillac (Vin de Pays), Château La Baroone (Corbières), Château Bastide-Durand (Corbières), Domaine Bois Monsieur (Coteaux du Languedoc), Château de Calage (Coteaux du Languedoc), Château de Campuget Cuvée Prestige (Costières de Nimes), Domaine Capion (Vin de Pays), Domaine Capion Merlot (Vin de Pays), Château de Casenove (Côtes du Roussillon), Les Chemins de Bassac Pierre Elie (Vin de Pays), Domaine La Colombetre (Vin de Pays), Daniel Domergue (Minervois), Château Donjon Cuvée Prestige (Minervois), Château des Estanilles (Faugeres), Château des Estanilles Cuvée Syrah (Faugères), La Grange des Péres (Vin de Pays-Herault), Château Héléne Cuvée Héléne de Troie (Vin de Pays), Domaine de l'Hortus (Coteaux du Languedoc), Château des Lanes (Corbières), Domaine Maris (Minervois), Mas Amiel (Maury), Château des Estanilles (Faugeres), Château des Estanilles Cuvée Syrah, Mas de Daumas Gassac (L'Hérault), Mas Jullien Les Cailloutis (Coteaux du Languedoc), Mas Jullien Les Dedierre (Corteaux du Languedoc), Château d'Oupia Cuvée des Barons (Minervois), Château Les Palais (Corbieres), Château Les Palais Cuvée Randolin (Corbières), Château de Paraza Cuvée Speciale (Minervois), Dr. Parté Mas Blanc (Banyuls), Domaine Peyre Rose Clos des Sistes (Coteaux du Languedoc), Domaine Peyre Rose Clos Syrah (Coteaux du Languedoc), Château Routas Agrippa (Coteaux Varois), Château Routa Infernet (Coteaux Varois), Château Routas Truffière (Coteaux Varois), Prieuré de St.-Jean de Babian (Vin de Pays), Catherine de Saint-Juery (Coteaux du Languedoc), Château La Sauvagéonne (Coteaux du Languedoc), Château Le Thou (Vin de Pays d'Oc), Domaine La Tour Boisée Cuvée Marie-Claude (Minervois)

CALIFORNIA

Alderbrook (Sauvignon Blanc, Chardonnay), Amador Foothill Winery (White Zinfandel), Arrowood Domaine du Grant Archer (Chardonnay, Cabernet Sauvignon), Bel Arbors - Fetzer (Zinfandel, Sauvignon Blanc, Merlot), Belvedere (Chardonnay Cuvées), Beringer (Knights Valley Chardonnay, Sauvignon Blanc, Meritage white, Gamay Beaujolais), Bonny Doon (Clos de Gilroy, Ca'Del Solo cuvées, Pacific Rim Riesling), Carmenet (Colombard), Cartlidge & Browne (Chardonnay, Merlot, Zinfandel), Cline (Côtes d'Oakley), Duxoup (Gamay, Charbono), Edmunds St.-John (New World and Port o'Call reds, Pinot Grigio and El Nino whites), Estancia (Chardonnay cuvées, Meritage red), Fetzer (Sundial Chardonnay), Guenoc (Petite Sirah, Zinfandel), Hess Collection (Hess Select Chardonnay, Cabernet Sauvignon), Husch Vineyard (Chenin Blanc, Gewüztraminer, La Ribera Red), Kendall-Jackson (Vintner's Reserve Chardonnay, Fumé Blanc, Vistner's Reserve

The World's Greatest Wine Values
by Robert M. Parker, Jr.
(This list is organized by wine producing region)

CALIFORNIA *continued*

Zinfandel), Kenwood (Sauvignon Blanc), Konocti (Fumé Blanc), Laurel Glen (Counterpoint and Terra Rosa proprietary red wines), Liberty School--Caymus (Cabernat Sauvignon, Sauvignon Blanc, Chardonnay), J. Lohr (Gamay, Cypress Chardonnay), Marietta Cellar (Old Vine Red, Zinfandel, Cabernet Sauvignon), Mirassou (white burgundy--Pinot Blanc), Monterey Vineyard (Classic cuvées of Merlot, Cabernet Sauvignon, Chardonnay, Sauvignon Blanc, and Zinfandel, generic Classic White and Classic Red), Moro Bay Vineyards (Chardonnay), Mountain View Winery (Sauvignon Blanc, Chardonnay Pinot Noir, Zinfandel), Murphy-Goode (Fume Blanc), Napa Ridge (Chardonnay, Cabernet Sauvignon, Sauvignon Blanc), Parducci (Sauvignon Blanc), Robert Pecota (gamay), J. Pedroncelli (Sauvignon Blanc, Zinfandel, Cabernet Sauvignon), Joseph Phelps (Vins du Mistral cuvées), R. H. Phillips (Night Harvest cuvée of Chardonnay and Sauvignon Blanc), Château Souverain (Chardonnay, Merlot, Cabernet Sauvignon, Sauvignon Blanc), Ivan Tamas (Trebbiano, Fumé Blanc, and Chardonnay), Thentadue (Old Patch Red, Zinfandel, Cariguane, Sangiovese, Petite Sirah, Merlot, Salute Proprietary Red Win, N. V. Alexander Valley red), Westwood (Barbera)

WASHINGTON STATE

Arbor Crest (Merlot), Columbia Creat (Chardonnay, Sauvignon Blanc/Semillon, Merlot), L'Ecole No. 41 (Semillon), Hogue (Chardonnay, Merlot, Chenin Blanc, Dry Riesling, Fumé Blanc)

SPAIN

Abadia Retuerta (Prumicia, Rivola), Argicola de Borja (Vina Borgia, Vina Borsao), Agricola Falset Marca (Etim), Albet I. Noya (Cava Brut Reserve), Joan d'Anguera (La Planella), Bodegas Aragoneas (Monte Corba), Capafons (Masia Esplanes), Capcanes (Mas Donis Barrica), Casa Castillo (Monastrell), Casa de la Ermita (Tinto), Castano (Hecula, Solana), Bodegas Martin Codax (Burgans Albarino), Dehesa Gago, Dominico de Eguren (Codice, Protocolo Tinto), El Cep (Marques de Gelida), Erate (Crianza, Gewurztraminer), Farina (Colegista Tinto), Bodegas Godeval (Vina Godeval), Garmona (Gessami), Granja Filliboa (Albarino), Finca Luzon (Merlot), Castillo de Maluenda (Vina Alarba), Bodegas Nekeas (Vega Sindoa cuvées), Palacio de Menade (Rueda), Pazo de Senorans (Albarino), Pergolas (Crianza Old Vines), Real Sitio de Ventosilla (Prado Rey), Castell de Remes (Gotim Bru), Herencia Remondo (Rioja, Tempranillo), Telmo Rodrigueez (Basa Rueda, Dehesa Gago), Sierra Cantabria (Rioja, Rioja Crianza), Bodegas Solar de Urbezo (Vina Urbezo), Tresantos, Valminor (Albarino), Bodegas Vina Alarba (Old Vines Grenache, Vina Alarba), Vina Mein (Vina Mein), Bodegas Y Vinedos Solabal (Rioja Crianza), Vinicola del Priorat (Onix)

ITALY

Giovanni Abrigo (Dolcetto Diano d'Alba Sori Crava), Alario (Dolcetto d'Alba Costa Fiore), Allegrini (Vaipolicello), Almondo (Arneis cuvées), Altesino (Rosso di Altesino), Ambra (Barco Reale, Carmignano San Cristina), Anselmi (San Vincenzo), Apollonio (Copertino), Badabing (Bianco, Russo), Badia a Colibuono (Chianti Cetamura), Boschis (Dolcetto cuvees), Ca del Vispo (Chainti Colli Senesi Rovai), Castello di Cacchiano (Rosso Toscano), Le Calcinaio (Vernaccia Vigna Al Sassi), De Calvane (Chianti Classico Riserva Il Trecione), La Carraia (Sangiovese), I Casciani (Chanti di Montespertoli), Catalci Madonna (Montepulciano d'Abruzzo), Cavalchina (Bianco di Custoza), Censio (Chanti Erte), Clerico Dolcetto Laughe Visari), Coffele (Chardonnay, Soave), Colli Amerini (Carbio), Colognole (Chianti Rufina), Coppo (Barbera d'Asti l'Avvocata), Corrina (Bianco Vergine di Baldichiana, Sangioves), Elisabetta (Aulo Rosso, Le Marze Bianco), Falesco (Poggio dei Gelsi Est! Est! Est!, Vitiano), Fontaleoni (Chianti, Rosso di San Gimignano), Nino Franco (Prosecco di Valdobbiadene Rustico), Gini (Soave Classico), Laila (Rosso Piceno), Lamborghini (Truscone), Lanari (Fibbio), Lucignano

The World's Greatest Wine Values
by Robert M. Parker, Jr.
(This list is organized by wine producing region)

ITALY *continued*

(Chianti Classico Colli Fiorentini), Maculan (Pinot et Toi), Di Majo Norante (Biblos, Ramitello,Sangiovese San Giorgio), A'Mano (Primitivo), Manzone Dolcetto d'Alba), Marcarini (Dolcetto d'Alba Fontanazza), Monte Antico (Monte Antico), La Montecchia (Cadetto), Cantina Monrubio (Rosso), Tenute Montepulischio (Verdicchio di Matelica), Giacomo Mori (Chianti), I. Mori (Chianti, Chianti Colli Fiorentini), Nalles and Magre-Miclara (Chardonnay Lucia, Pinot Bianco Lucia, Pinot Grigo Lucia), Parusso (Dolcetto d'Alba), Elio Perrone (Biagaro, Moscato Clarte), Petrolo (Terre di Galatrona), Piazzano (Chianti Classico Reserva Rio Camarata, Chianti Rio Camarata), Pieropan (Soave Classico), Pira (Dolcetto d'Alba Vigna Fornaci), Poderi Alasia (Arneis Roero, Sauvignon, Camillona), Poggio Turana (IGT), Pojer and Sandri (Chardonnay, Muller Thurgan, Nosiola, Traminer), Maso Poli (Chardonnay, Pinot Grigio), Promessa (Negroamaro, Rosso Salente), Pruntto (Barbera d'Asti Hulot, Dolcetto d'Alba), Tenuta Le Querce (Aglianico), Rebuil (Prosecco Valbobbiadene), Revello (Barbera d'Alba, Dolcetto d'Alba), Rocca di Fabbri (Sangiovese Satiro), Ronchi di Menzano (Chardonnay, Pinot Grigio, Tocai Friuliaco), Castel di Salve (Rosso del Salentino Priante, Rosso del Salentino Santi Mediei), San Biagio (Chianti Colli Senesi), San Fabiano (Chianti Putto), Feudi di San Gregorio (Falanghina), Fattoria San Lorenzo (Montepuliano), Sandrone (Dolcetto d'Alba), Santa Cristina (Rosso), Saracco (Moscato d'Asti), Scavino (Rosso, Rosso Corale), Fattoria Le Sorgenti (Chianti Colli Fiorentini), Sportoletti Assisi Rosso), Tamellini (Scave Superiore), Taurino (Notarpanaro, Salice Salentino), Tavignano (Rosso Piceno, Verdicchio dei Castelli di Jesi Misco), Tiefenbrunner (Pinot Bianco, Pinor Grigio), Cantina Tollo (Montepulciano d'Abruzzo Collect Secco, Sangiovese Villa Diana), Gianolio Tomaso (Arneis, Barbera d'Alba, Dolcetto d'Alba, Nebbiolo d'Alba), Tormaresca (Bianco, Rosso), Giuseppe Traverse (Moscaro d'Asti Vigna Canova), Villa del Borgo (Chardonnay, Merlot, Pinot, Grigio, Refosco), Villa Giada (Barbera d'Asti cuvées), Villa Matilde (Falerno del Massico), Villamaga (Rosso Paceno), Zardetto (Prosecco Brut), Zemmer (Chardonnay, Pinot, Grigo, Sauvignon), Zenato (Valpolicella Classico)

SICILY and SARDINIA

Argiolas (Costere, Perdera Selegas Vermentino), Colosi (Rosso), Morgante (Nero d'Avola), Planeta (Rosso la Segreta), Santa Anastasia (Passomaggio), Cantina Santadi (Vermentino Cala Silente), Tasca d'Almeria (Regaleali Bianco, Regaleali Rosso, Regaleali Rose)

AUSTRALIA

Berry Estates (Semillon), Brown Brothers (Cabernet Sauvignon, Chardonnay King Valley, Muscat Lexia), Jacobs Creek (various cuvées), Peter Lehmann (Cabernet Sauvignon, Shiraz), Lindermans (Chardonnay Bin 65), Michelton (Semmillon/Chardonnay), Montrose (Cabernet Sauvignon, Chardonnay, Shiraz), Orlando (Cabernet Sauvignon Jacob's Creek, Chardonnay Jacob's Creek), Oxford Landing (Cabernet Sauvignon, Chardonnay), Rosemount (various cuvées), Rothbury Estate (Chardonnay Broken Back Vineyard, Shiraz), Seppelt (various cuvées), Tyrells (Long Flat Red), Wolf Blass (Cabernet Sauvignon, Yellow Label, Shiraz President's Selection), Wyndham Estates (Cabernet Sauvignon Bin 444, Chardonnay Bin 222), Yalamba Clocktower Port

SOUTH AMERICA

Argentina: Bodega Weiner (Cabernet Sauvignon), Erchart (Cabernet Sauvignon)

Chile: Casa Lapostelle (Sauvignon Blanc), Cousino Macul (Cabernet/Merlot Finis Terrae, Cabernet Sauvignon Antiguas Reserva)

GLOSSARY

Absinthe: A green 150-proof hallucinogenic liqueur. Banned in the U.S.

Akvavit or Aquavit: A Scandinavian liqueur made with rye and caraway. Means "water of life".

Ale: A fermented beverage containing malt and hops similar but heavier than beer.

Alize: A bottled mixture of fruit juice and Cognac 32-proof. French. Means "gentle trade wind".

Amaretto: Originally from Italy, made from apricot pits and herbs. With an almond and vanilla taste.

Amer Picon: A French cordial with a bitter orange flavor.

Anisette: A very sweet liqueur made from anise seed. Tastes like black licorice.

Aperitif: An alcoholic drink to stimulate the appetite before a meal. Originally referring to wine, but may mean a liquor or liqueur.

Armagnac: Brandy from Gascony, France. A smaller growing area than the well-known Cognac region.

Babycham: A sparkling alcoholic pear flavored drink. Pear cider.

Barley Wine: A dark, rather strong ale.

Beer: An alcoholic beverage brewed from malt and flavored by hops.

Benedictine: A liqueur produced by monks, with a secret formula.

Bitters: A bitter tasting alcoholic liquid made from herbs and roots.

Black Raspberry Liqueur: Chambord is by far the most popular Black Raspberry Liqueur.

Blanc: French for white wine.

Blended Whiskey: A whiskey made by blending 2 or more straight whiskeys. Some Scotch as well as Canadian.

Body: The weight or consistency of a wine.

Bourbon: Solely American made. Aged 4 years or more. Named after Bourbon County, Kentucky.

Brandy: An alcoholic liquor distilled from wine or from fermented fruit.

Brut: Very dry Champagne.

Campari: A bitter Italian apertif.

Canadian Whiskey: Made under strict government regulations. With a lighter taste and color than other whiskeys. Primarily distilled from rye and grains.

Cava: Sparkling wine from Spain. Champagne like.

Chambord: A French black raspberry liqueur.

Chartreuse: An herb liqueur. Developed by Carthusian monks in 1605. Comes in yellow and green.

Coffee Liqueur: The most popular brands are Kahlua from Mexico and Tia Maria from Jamaica.

Cognac: Basically cognac is brandy from the Cognac region of France.

Cointreau: An up-scale, French orange liqueur, in the Curacao family.

Cordial: A straight liqueur drink to stimulate or enhance a warm or friendly situation.

Corked: Refers to a wine ruined by a faulty cork. Air entered the bottle.

Cream of Coconut: A coconut base or syrup used for many exotic drinks, the most popular being the Piña Colada.

Creme De Cacao: A liqueur which comes in either dark or white (clear) form. Made from cacao and vanilla beans.

Creme De Cassis: A liqueur made from European Black Currants (berries).

Creme De Menthe: A liqueur which comes in either green or white (clear). Made from peppermint.

Creme De Nouyax: A brilliant red liqueur made from almonds.

Curacao: A liqueur made from orange peels. Produced in the Dutch West Indies.

Dash: Approximately 1/4 teaspoon.

Drambuie: A liqueur made from Scotch whiskey and honey.

Dry: Pertaining to wine, without sweetness in flavor. Low in residual sugar.

Dry Vermouth: A white wine flavored with herbs and spices.

Dubonnet: An aromatic wine from France. Usually kept refrigerated.

Dumb: A wine opened before maturation.

Falernum: A spicy sweetener from Barbados, with almond and ginger undertones.

Finish: The last taste left by drink in mouth.

Fino: Pale Sherry. Most often from Portugal and Spain.

Flabby: A watery tasting wine.

Forbidden Fruit: A liqueur made with brandy and shaddock (grapefruit).

Framboise: Means raspberry. May refer to either beer or liqueur.

Frangelico: A hazelnut liqueur.

Galliano: An Italian liqueur named after Major Giuseppe Galliano. Sweet and spicy.

Garnish: A garnish is no more than a decoration, sometimes functional, either eaten or squeezed into drink.

Gin: A liquor made by distilling rye or other grains with juniper berries.

Goldschlager: High proof cinnamon Schnapps with floating flecks of gold leaf.

Grain Alcohol: Made from sugar or other starches. Pure alcohol diluted with water usually to 190 proof.

Grand Marnier: A highly prized cognac-based triple orange liqueur.

Grappa: Unaged Italian brandy. Made from the by-products of wine making.

Grenadine: A sweet, red syrup made from pomegranates. Essential for children's drinks as well as adult drinks.

Hazelnut Liqueur: There are many different brands. Frangelico is considered the best.

Irish Cream: A liqueur made from Irish whiskey and cream.

Irish Mist: A liqueur made with Irish whiskey as a base, and heather honey as well.

Irish Whiskey: A blend containing barley whiskeys and grain whiskeys.

Jaegermeister: Considered a form of bitters. It is made of 56 herbs, roots, and fruits.

Kahlua: A coffee liqueur, one of Mexico's most popular exports.

Kirsch: A clear liqueur distilled from black cherries.

Kummel: A liqueur made from caraway and anise.

Lager: A bottom fermented beer.

Legs: (tears) The trails left running down the inside of a wine glass after swirling the wine.

Length: The time the flavor of a wine stays on the palate.

Licor 43: A Spanish brandy-based liqueur with 43 ingredients, with a prominent vanilla flavor.

Lillet: A French apertif wine. It comes in red and white.

Liqueur: A syrupy alcoholic beverage often with a Brandy base.

Liquor: An alcoholic beverage made by distillation.

Madeira: A blended and fortified Portuguese wine.

Magnum: 1.5 liters, two standard bottles of wine.

Maraschino: A Yugoslavian liqueur made from cherries.

Marsala: A full bodied fortified red wine from Sicily.

Mead: Arguably the first alcoholic beverage. Made from honey, herbs and water.

Metaxa: A sweetened Greek brandy.

Midori: A melon-flavored liqueur from the Japanese house of Suntory.

Mist: Is a term meaning "on the rocks" (preferably with shaved crushed ice). Coming from the fact that certain clear liqueurs cloud or mist when poured onto ice.

Muddle: Meaning to mix together or mash.

Neat: Is another way to say straight, no ice, not mixed.

Nose: The scent of any given beverage.

Orange Liqueur: The most common are Triple Sec and Curacao. The best are Grand Marnier and Cointreau.

Orgeat: An almond flavored sweetener.

Ouzo: An anise flavored Greek liqueur.

Passion Fruit Liqueur: A Hawaiian liqueur flavored with peach and mangos.

Peppermint Schnapps: A rather light mint-based liqueur.

Pernod: A French absinthe-type liqueur.

Pilsner: A light bodied beer.

Pisang Ambon: A green colored, banana and herb-flavored liqueur.

Pony: Means 1 ounce. Also refers to a certain glass.

Port: A rich, sweet fortified wine. Originally from Portugal.

Pousse-Café: Refers to either layered drinks, or an alcoholic drink taken with coffee.

Proof: A term to tell alcohol content. 80-proof liquor would be 40% alcohol, meaning 40% of the contents of the bottle would be pure alcohol. Bottled wine at 12% alcohol by volume would be 24 proof.

Robe: The color or look of a given wine.

Rosso: Italian for Red Wine.

Rouge: French for Red Wine.

Rum: A liquor made from fermented molasses or sugarcane. Aged 2-10 years.

Rye: A whiskey made from at least 51 percent rye.

Sabra: An orange-chocolate liqueur from Israel.

Saké: Made from re-fermented rice. It is actually a type of beer.

Sambuca: An Italian liqueur with an anise-like flavor.

Sappy: A young wine that shows great promise for aging.

Schnapps: A common name for a wide range of liqueurs usually light-bodied and flavored. It has many other meanings globally.

Scotch: A liquor from Scotland. They can be either single malts or blends.

Shot: A pour between 1 and 2 ounces.

Sloe Gin: A very sweet liqueur made from sloe berries and steeped in gin.

Soda Water: Carbonated water, sometimes coming in flavors.

Sour Mix: They come in powder and liquid form. Essential at bars. It can be made fresh. Blend 12 oz lemon juice, 18 oz water, 1/3 cup sugar and an egg white.

Southern Comfort: A liqueur made from bourbon and peach liqueur.

Splash: Approximately 1/2 teaspoon.

Stout: A very dark and strong ale.

Strega: A spicy and sweet Italian liqueur made from over 70 herbs and spices.

Sugar Syrup: Basically liquefied sugar. Simply mix sugar to water 2 to 1.

Swedish Punch: A Scandinavian liqueur made from rum, tea and lemon.

Sweet Vermouth: A red wine flavored with herbs and spices.

Tears: (legs) The trails left running down the inside of a glass after swirling the wine.

Tequila: An alcoholic beverage distilled from the Central American Century plant or the Agave plant.

Tia Maria: A coffee liqueur from Jamaica.

Tinto: Portuguese for Red Wine.

Tonic Water: A carbonated quinine-flavored beverage.

Top: Means to add ingredient to top of drink, approximately 1 teaspoon, if alcoholic. Approximately 2 tablespoons if referring to whipped cream. Approximately 1 oz if referring to non-alcoholic ingredient.

Triple Sec: A light-bodied, orange-flavored liqueur.

Tuaca: An Italian brandy-based liqueur, flavored with citrus, nuts, vanilla and milk.

Vandermint: A Dutch chocolate-mint liqueur.

Vermouth: A wine flavored with herbs and spices. Comes in sweet and dry, and is primarily used as an ingredient in cocktails.

Vin: French for wine.

Vino: Italian and Spanish for wine.

Vintage: The year of the grapes' harvest.

Vodka: A liquor originally distilled from wheat. Now made from rye, corn or potatoes.

Wein: German for wine.

Whiskey or Whisky *(European)*: A liquor distilled from grains such as corn, rye or barley.

Wine: A fermented juice of any various kinds of grapes or other fruit.

Yukon Jack: Liqueur made from Canadian whiskey.

INDEX OF DRINKS LISTED
BY INGREDIENT

Use this index to find all of the drinks listed in this book by the ingredients they contain. The ingredients and the drinks are listed in alphabetical order.

DRINKS LISTED IN ALPHABETICAL ORDER

● AMARETTO

Abby Road
Abby Road Coffee
ABC
Alabama Slammer
Alien Orgasm
Almond Enjoy
Almond Kiss
Almond Mocha Coffee
Amaretto Sour
Amarist
Amber Martini
Ambush Coffee
Amore-Ade
August Moon
B-54
B-57
Bahama Mama
Bali Hai
Banana Frost
Beach Hut Madness
Bend Me Over
Biscuit Neck
Black Magic
Black Tie
Bocci Ball
Boss
Boston Iced Tea
Boston Massacre
Brain Eraser
Brandy Almond Mocha
Broken Down Golf Cart
Brown Squirrel
Bubble Gum
Bungee Jumper
Burnt Almond
Butternut Coffee
Café Amore
Café Magic
Café Venitzio
Café Zurich
Capital Punishment
Casino Coffee
Cherry Life-Savor
Chocolate Covered Cherry
Chocolate Squirrel
Christian's Coffee
Climax
Coca Lady
Cocoetto
Cool Aid
Crazy Broad
Cuddler
Cupid's Potion
Day at the Beach
DC-10
Depth Chamber
Dingo
Dizzy Buddha
Dr. P.
Dr. P. From Hell
Dreamsicle
Earthquake
East Side
Electric Cool Aid
F Me Hard
F.E.D.X.
Fern Gully
Ferrari
57 Chevy
57 T-Bird
Filby
Firery Kiss
Flaming Lamborghini
Foxy Lady
French Connection
French Connection Coffee
Full Moon
Gandy Dancer
Gilligan's Isle
Godchild
Godfather
Godmother
Golden Bull
Golden Torpedo
Grand Alliance

Grand Am
Gumdrop
Gummy Bear
Hammerhead
Hard On
Hardcore
Hasta La Vista Baby
Hawaiian
Hawaiian Punched
Heart Throb
Hello Nurse
Homecoming
Hooter
Hurricane
Hussie
Irish Headlock
Italian Coffee
Italian Delight
Italian Iced Coffee
Italian Sunrise
International Incident
Jackalope
Jaeger Monster
Jamaican Mule
Killer Cool Aid
King's Cup
Komaniwanalaya
Lake Street Lemonade
Latin Lover
Laser Beam
Lethal Injection
Liquid Pants Remover
Lobotomy
Long Sloe Comfortable
    Fuzzy Screw Against
    The Wall With A Kiss
Long Sloe Comfortable
    Fuzzy Screw Against
    The Wall with Satin
    Pillows The Hard Way
Lounge Lizard
Moon Chaser
Marlon Brando
Midway Rat
Milano Coffee
Mongolian Mother
Monkey Wrench
Moonbeam
Mooseberry
Mountain Red Punch
Muff Diver
Multipie Orgasm
Mutual Orgasm
Nasty Girl
Naughty Hula Pie
Nutcracker
Nuts and Cream
Nutty Colada
Old Groaner
Old Groaner's Wife
Orgasm
Outrigger
Palm Beacher
Panda Bear
Panty Burner
Paranoia
Peckerhead
Persuader
Pimlico Special
Pineapple Bomb
Pineapple Bomber
Pink Almond
Pink Paradise
Pontiac
Pop-sicle
Prison Bitch
Pterodactyl
Purple Alaskan
Purple Matador
Rasbaretta
Red Death
Red Ruby
Rigor Mortis
Ritz Fizz
Roasted Toasted Almond
Roman Candle
Roman Holiday

Roman Iced Tea
Roman Riot
Roxanne
Royal Canadian
Royal Sheet Coffee
Russian Quaalude
S. O. M. F.
St. Petersburg Sundae
School Bus
Screaming O.
Seventh Avenue
Seventh Heaven
Sex At My House
Sex In The Woods
Shaved Bush
Sicilian Coffee
Sicilian Kiss
Silver Cloud
Skinny Dipping
Sour Apple
Southern Beach
Spanish Fly
Sperm Whale At The Barn
Spilt Milk
Stiletto
Sweet Tart
T-Bird
Tangerine
Tarantula
Tawney Russian
Tennessee Mud
Terminator
Test-Tube Babe
Toasted Almond
Toasted Marshmallow
Top Gun
Tree Climber
Troika
Trophy Room Coffee
Tropical Moon
Turtle Dove
Ugly Ducking
Universal
Vanity Fair
Verona
Watermelon
Wedding Cake
Wench
White Swan
Wiki Waki Woo
Xanadu
Yokohama Mama
Zonker

● ANISETTE

Angel Face
Apple Margarita
Apple Pie
Apres Ski
Bartman
Candy Apple
Café Zurich
Corpse Reviver
Cranapple Cooler
Deauville
Depth Bomb
Diki Diki
Dream Cocktail
Earthquake
Good And Plent-e
Grand Apple
Green Apple
Gumdrop
Happy Jack
Hole In One
Honeymoon
Hot Apple Pie
Hot Apple Toddy
Ichbien
Indian Summer
Jack Rose
Jack-In-The-Box
Jelly Bean
Johnnie
Joll-e Rancher
Ladies

• BEER (continued)
School Bus
Scumbucket
Shante' Gaf
Sizzler
Skip And Go Naked
Snakebite
Strip and Go Naked
Tiger Balls
Train Wreck
Velvet Gaf
Yorsh
Vulcan Mind Probe
Yard Of Flannel

• BENEDICTINE
Aunt Jemima
B & B
C & B
Energizer
Frisco Sour
Froupe
Golden Caddie With
    Double Bumpers
Golden Dream
    (With Double Bumpers)
Gypsy
Highland Coffee
Honeymoon
Honolulu
Hoot Man
Kentucky Colonel
Marmalade
Monk's Coffee
Monte Carlo
Mule's Hind Leg
Oh, Henry
Pleasure Dome
Preakness
Queen Elizabeth Wine
Quiet Nun
Rainbow
Savoy Hotel
Twin Hills
Widow's Dream
Widow's Kiss

• BLACKBERRY BRANDY
Atomic Bodyslam
Black Barracuda
Black Dog
Black Eye
Black Martini
Black Prince
Black Sheep
Blackjack
Bongo
Cadiz
Canadian Blackberry Fizz
Channel
Chi-Chi
Cough Drop
Cramp Reliever
Cure-Ali
Dark Eyes
Elvira
Good And Plent-e
Houndstooth
Jelly Bean
Life-Saver
Miami Vice
Mule Skinner
Naked Lady
Pain In The Ass
Pixie Stick
Poop Deck
Purple Jesus
Rattlesnake
Roman Holiday
Rum Runner
S. O. M. F.

Scorpion
Tequila Sunset
Tidal Wave
Toxic Jellybean
Tropical Storm
Warsaw

• BLACK RASPBERRY LIQUEUR
Abby Road
Abby Road Coffee
Belmont
Black Forest
Black Martini
Black Rose
Black Sheep
Blackberry Swizzle
Bon Bon
Broken Heart
Brut And Bogs
Busted Rubber
Café Marseilles
Candy Ass
Cham Cran Cham
Chocolate Mess
Coca
Cosmopolitan (South Beach)
Cranium Meltdown
Doctor's Elixir
Dry Arroyo
Dusty Road
Dusty Rose
Ecstacy
Elysee Palace
F.E.D.X.
Firecracker
Frankenberry
French Dream
French Martini
French Summer
Frosted Romance
Frutti Nueb
Gloomlifter
Go Girl
Grape Crush
Grape Nehi
Greatful D.
Happy Feller
Hollywood
Hollywood Martini
Hot Raspberry Dream
Hot Tub
Indian Summer Hummer
Jelly Doughnut
Key West
Killer Cool Aid
Killer Whale
Kir Royale
Lady Luck
Left Bank
Little Purple Men
Lobotomy
Macaroon
Mad Max
Madtown Milkshake
Menage a Trois
Midnight Dream
Mocha Berry Frappe
Nervous Breakdown
Nuts And Berries
Oral Sex on the Beach
Panabraitor
Paris Match
Parrot Head
Passionate Screw
Peanut Butter and Jelly
Pez
Phantom
Pink Missile
Purple Alaskan
Purple Dream
Purple Haze
Purple Hooter

Purple Matador
Purple Nipple
Purple Rain
Purple Russian
Raspberry Beret
Raspberry Colada
Raspberry Gimlet
Raspberry Kiss
Raspberry Lime Rickey
Raspberry Margarita
Raspberry Sherbet
Raspberry Smash
Raspberry Sombrero
Raspberry Torte
Restoration
Riviera
Royal Spritzer
S. O. S.
Saint Moritz
Scarlet Letter
Sex at My House
Sex In A Hot Tub
Sex In The Parking Lot
Sex On The Beach
Simply Bonkers
Sour Grapes
Sovereign Coffee
Squid Ink
Sweet Tart
38th Parallel Coffee
Tie Me To The Bedpost
    Baby
Vampire
Wadkins Glen
Wet Crotch
Wet Dream
White Ghost
Y. I.
Zipper Head
Zuma Buma

• BLACK SAMBUCA
Creature From The Black
    Lagoon
Dark Secret
Dragoon
Eclipse
Phantom
Slippery Black Nipple
Squid Ink
Starlight

• BLUE CURACAO
Adios Mother
Agent 99
Air Gunner
Alaskan Iced Tea
Alien Urine Sample
Anti-Freeze
Assassin
Battered Bruised And
    Bleeding
Bazooka Joe
Big Kahuna
Bimini Ice-T
Blue Bayou
Blue Bijou
Blue Canary
Blue Daiquiri
Blue Hawaiian
Blue Kamikaze
Blue Lady
Blue Lemonade
Blue Margarita
Blue Meanie
Blue Shark
Blue Tail Fly
Blue Valium
Champagne Super Nova
Chi-Chi
Code Blue
Deep Sea

DRINKS LISTED IN ALPHABETICAL ORDER

● BRANDY (continued)

Hari Kari
Harvard
Head Wind
Heartbreak
Highland Coffee
Hogback Growler
Hoopla
Hot Toddy
Huetchen
International Stinger
Irish Flag
Irish Headlock
Irish Stinger
Italian Stinger
Jamaican Coffee
Kappa Colada
Kentucky Cooler
Keoke Cappuccino
Keoke Coffee
King Kong Coffee
King's Peg
Kiss The Boys Good-Bye
La Jolla
Lady Be Good
Lallah Rookh
Life Line
Loudspeaker
Luger
Maxim's
Maxim's A Londres
Mediterranean Coffee
Memphis Belle
Minstrel Frappe
Monga Monga
Montana
Morning
Morning Glory
Mountain Red Punch
Naked Lady
Netherland
Odd McIntyre
Olympic
One Seventy
Panama
Paris Match
Peppermint Stinger
Persuader
Phoebe Snow
Picon Fizz
Pierre Collins
Pimlico Special
Pisco Punch
Pisco Sour
Planter's Punch
Pleasure Dome
Poop Deck
Port In A Storm
Port Sangree
Pousse Café
Prairie Oyster
Prince Of Wales
Quaker
Quelle Vie
Restoration
Rhode Island Iced Tea
Ritz Pick-Me-Up
Run, Skip And Go Naked
Russian Roulette
S. O. B.
Sangria
Saratoga
Savoy Hotel
Scorpion
Screamer
Separator
Sherry Twist
Siberian
Sidecar
Sink Or Swim
Sir Walter
Sledgehammer
Sleepy Head
Sloe Brandy
Sloppy Joe's

Snowball
Snowshoe Grog
Spanish Coffee
Spanish Iced Coffee
Special Rough
Stinger
Super Coffee
Tantalus
Third Rail
38th Parallel Coffee
Three Miles
Thumper
Thunder
Tiger's Milk
Tom And Jerry
Tongue Stroke
Toreador
Torpedo
Tumbleweed
Vanderbilt
Vatican Coffee
Velvet Dress
Venetian Coffee
Venetian Frappe
Venetian Sunrise
Via Veneto
Victor
Volcano
Vulcan Mind Probe
Wagon Wheel
Wandering Minstrel
Washington
Waterbury Cocktail
Weep No More
Whip Cocktail
Whisper
White Spaniard
Widow's Kiss
Winter Frost
Yokohama Mama
Zamboanga Hummer
Zoom

● BUTTERSCOTCH SCHNAPPS

Buttafinger
Butter Ball
Butter Shot
Butternut Coffee
Carrot Cake
Gingerbread Man
Jamaican Bobsled
Neutron Bomb
Oatmeal Cookie
Sugar Daddy

● CHAMPAGNE

Ambrosia
April In Paris
Bali Hai
Barracuda
Bellini
Bird Of Paradise
Black Prince
Black Velvet
Bronco Cocktail
Brut And Bogs
Caribbean Champagne
Cham Cran Cham
Champagne Cocktail
Champagne Super Nova
Chicago
Concorde
Death In The Afternoon
Diamond Fizz
Dry Arroyo
Elysee Palace
F.E.D.X.
Flying Madras
French Lift
French 95
French 75
Frozen Bikini

Glenda
Golden Showers
Grand Alliance
Grand Mimosa
Honeydew
Hot Tub
King's Peg
Kir Royale
Lobotomy
London Special
Mad Max
Maxim's
Maxim's A Londres
Me So Horney
Melon Royale
Metropolis Martini
Mimosa
Mind Obliterator
Moscow Mimosa
Nantucket Red
Nelson's Blood
One Seventy
Pan Galactic Gargle Blaster
Peach Mimosa
Pink Slip
Poinsettia
Prince Of Wales
Ritz Fizz
Ritz Pick-Me-Up
Royal Screw
Royal Spritzer
Ruddy Mimosa
Russian Nights
Santiago
Scarlet Letter
Sex In A Hot Tub
Sparks
Thug Passion
Tintoretto
Torque Wrench
Typhoon
Valencia
Velvet Gaf
Volcano

● CHARTREUSE (YELLOW and GREEN)

Dead Rat
Death Mint
Flaming Lamborghini
French Dragon
Golden Dragon
Green Dragon
Green Lizard
Jewel
Jewel of the Nile
Lollipop
Mexican Missile
Pago Pago
Pousse Café
Rainbow
Razorback Hogcaller
Save The Planet
Screamer
Screaming Dead Nazi Digging for Gold
Swampwater
Tipperary
Warday's Cocktail
Whiskey Daisy
Widow's Kiss
Xanthia
Yellow Parrot

● CHERRY BRANDY

Ankle Breaker
Black Cat
Blood And Sand
Busted Cherry
Candy Cane
Casablanca
Cherry Blossom
Cherry Cola

● COFFEE LIQUEUR

(continued)

Café Gates
Café Grande
Café Magic
Café Marseilles
Café Orleans
Café Reggae
California Mother
California Root Beer
Calypso Coffee
Cancun
Cara Sposa
Carrot Cake
Cartel Buster
Celtic Comrade
Cerebral Hemorrhage
Chastity Belt
Chocolate Covered Cherry
Chocolate Kiss
Chocolate Mess
Chocolate Rattlesnake
Christian's Coffee
Climax
Cloudy Night
Cobra
Coca Lady
Cocopuff
Coffee Colada
Coffee Sombrero
Colorado Bulldog
Colorado MF
Colorado Mother
Concord
Cookie Monster
Dallas Alice
Dangerous Liaisons
Dark Side
DC-10
Deep Dark Secret
Deep Throat
Depth Chamber
Dire Straits
Dirty Bird
Dirty G. S.
Dirty Harry
Dirty Monkey
Dirty M. F.
Dirty Mother
Dirty White Mother
Dizzy Buddha
Double Mint BJ
Dragoon
Dry Arroyo
Dublin Coffee
Duck Fart
Embryo
Everglades Special
F-16
Face Eraser
Flaming Hooker
Flaming Lamborghini
French Dream
G. S. Cookie
Gentle Bull
Ghetto Blaster
Gingerbread Man
Good And Plent-e
Ground Zero
Gun Runner Coffee
Hard On
Harbor Lights
Hawaiian Eye
Hot Sex
Hot Young Lady
Hummer
Iguana
Indian Summer
International Incident
Irish Coffee Royale
Irish Maria
Irish Rover
Ixtapa
Jackalope
Jamaica Me Crazy

Jamaican
Jamaican Coffee
Jamaican Dust
Jamaican Kiss
Jamaican Wind
Kahlua Club
Kahlua Coffee
Kahlua Sombrero
Kahlua Sour
Keoke Coffee
King Alphonse
King Cobra
King Kong Coffee
Kingston Coffee
Kioloa
Kowloon
Lebanese Coffee
Leg Spreader
Licorice Whip
Lighthouse
M-16
Mad Cow
Maple Russian
Mexican Cappuccino
Mexican Coffee
Mexican Jumping Bean
Midnight Martini
Midway Rat
Mike Tyson
Millionaire's Coffee
Mind Eraser
Mind Obliterator
Mint Chocolate Chip Ice
  Cream
Minstrel Frappe
Mint Condition
Mississippi Mud
Mocha Berry Frappe
Mocha Mint
Monk Slide
Monte Cristo Coffee
Montego Bay Coffee
Moose Milk
Mudslide
Mudsling
Multiple Orgasm
Neutron Bomb
Nutcracker
Nuts And Berries
Nutty Bitch
Oatmeal Cookie
Orgasm
Panty Burner
Panty Dropper
Playboy Cooler
Port Antonio
Pousse Café
Primal Scream
Pumpkin Pie
Quaalude
Quick F
Rasta Man
Rattle Snake
Rear Buster
Rebel Russian
Rhode Island Iced Tea
Roasted Toasted Almond
Root Beer
Royal Canadian
Royal Sheet Coffee
Russian Quaalude
S. O. M. F.
Screaming O.
Separator
727
747
Sewer Rat
Sex
Sex In The Woods
Sex Machine
Sex On The Beach
Sexy
Shaved Bush
Siberian
Silver Cloud
Skid Mark

Smith And Kerns
Smooth Operator
Snicker At The Bar
Sno Cap
Sombrero
South Of The Border
Southern Bulldog
Spanish Coffee
Spanish Iced Coffee
Spanish Moss
Spooge
Stealth
Steel Helmet
Storm Cloud
Stuffed Toilet
Sugar Daddy
Super Coffee
Swedish BJ
Sweet Cream
T. K. O.
Tam-O-Shanter
Teacher's Pet
Three Kings
Tijuana Bulldog
Toasted Almond
Toblerone
Tootsie
Toreador
Toronto Orgy
Toxic Waste
Trappist Frappe
Trappist Monk
Tumbleweed
Uzi
Velvet Dress
Voo Doo
Wandering Minstrel
Watergate Coffee
Whisper
White Bull
White Jamaican
White Knight
White Roman
White Russian
White Spaniard
Xavier
Y 2 K
Yellow Bird
Yellow Jacket

● COGNAC

ABC
Amber Cloud
B-57
Between The Sheets
C & B
Café Amore
Café Diablo
Café Royale
Café Zurich
Concorde
Copenhagen Pousse Café
Corpse Reviver
Eggnog
Elysee Palace
Fat Cat
Fish House Punch
French Coffee
French Connection
French Connection Coffee
French Dragon
French Iced Coffee
French 75
G & C
Godchild
Grand Apple
Jizz
Keoke Cappuccino
Keoke Coffee
King Kong Coffee
King's Peg
Lallah Rookh
Paris Match
Petrifier

CREME DE MENTHE (continued)

Pink Whispers
Point
Port And Starboard
Santa Shot
Silver Bullet
Silver Spider
Sneaky Pete
Snowball
Spanish Moss
Stinger
Tarnished Bullet
Tequila Stinger
Traffic Light
Turkey Shoot
Velvet Glove
Virgin
Vodka Grasshopper
Vodka Stinger
White Way
Wandering Minstrel
White Mink
White Minnesota
White Spider
Winter Frost

CURACAO

American Sour
Bosom Caresser
Chicago
Diamond Head
East India
Fair And Warmer
Fare-Thee-Well
Hammerhead
Honeymoon
Ichbien
Il Magnifico
Jade
Johnnie
Kiss Me Quick
London Sour
Maiden's Blush
Man O'War
Marmalade
McClelland
Mexican Blackjack
Millionaire
Morning
Morning Glory
Newbury
Nightingale
Olympic
Orange Julius
Parisian Blonde
Park Avenue
Pegu Club
Pineapple Passion
Platinum Blonde
Presidente
Prince Of Wales
Ramos Fizz
Rhett Butler
Sangria
Sherry Twist
Sir Walter
Southern Bride
Suffering Bastard
Tango
Temptation
Tiger's Tail
Velvet Hammer
Vulcan Mind Probe
Whip Cocktail
Whirlaway
Zamboanga Hummer
Zombie

DRAMBUIE

Bent Nail
Black Tie
Celtic Comrade
Crankin' Wanker
Depth Charge
Dundee
Golden Nail
Heather Coffee
Hot Nail
Hot Scotch
Inverted Nail
Jolly Roger
L. S. D.
Point
Prince Edward
Russian Roulette
Rusty Nail
Rusty Nail Coffee
Scottish Coffee
Seventh Avenue
Whiskey Zipper
White Knight

DUBONNET

Dubonnet Cocktail
Dubonnet Manhattan
Mary Garden
Napoleon
Nightmare
Oom Paul
Opera
Phoebe Snow
Princess Mary's Pride
Sanctuary
Silken Veil
Soul Kiss
Temptation
Trois Rivieres
Vancouver
Wedding Belle
Weep No More
Zaza

GALLIANO

Alabama Slammer
Amber Cloud
Barracuda
Bossa Nova
Cactus Banger
Café Venitzio
California Root Beer
Colorado MF
Colorado Mother
Comfortable Fuzzy Screw
    Against The Wall
Creamsicle
Deceiver
Dire Straits
Dirty M. F.
Dr. Funk
Dreamsicle
Fat Cat
Festering Slobovian
Flaming Lamborghini
Hummer
Flying Kangaroo
Freddy Fudpucker
G & C
Golden Caddie
Golden Caddie With Double
    Bumpers
Golden Cappuccino
Golden Day
Golden Dream
Golden Dream
    (With Double Bumpers)
Golden Russian
Golden Screw
Golden Torpedo
Harbor Lights
Harvey Wallbanger
Hillary Wallbanger
International Stinger
Italian Coffee
Italian Iced Coffee

Italian Screw
Italian Stallion
Italian Stinger
Jenny Wallbanger
José Wallbanger
Jump Up And Kiss Me
King's Cup
Leg Spreader
Leisure Suit
Licorice Stick
Long Comfortable Screw
    Against The Wall
Long Sloe Comfortable
    Fuzzy Screw Against
    The Wall With A Kiss
Long Sloe Comfortable
    Fuzzy Screw Against
    The Wall With Satin
    Pillows The Hard Way
Mediterranean Coffee
Oceanview Special
Port Pelican
Pousse Café
Red Zipper
Rocky Mountain Rootbeer
Roman Riot
Root Beer
Russian Roulette
Scotti Was Beamed Up
Sloe Comfortable Fuzzy
    Screw Against The Wall
Sloe Comfortable Mexican
    Screw Against The Wall
Sloe Comfortable Screw
    Against The Wall
Steel Helmet
Three Kings
Toasted Marshmallow
Toxic Waste
Trade Wind
Traffic Light
Tropical Storm
Venetian Coffee
Venetian Frappe
Wally Wallbanger
West Indies Yellowbird
White Mink
Xanadu
Yellow Bird

GIN

Acapulco
Adios Mother
Alaskan Iced Tea
Albatross
Alexander
Alexander's Sister
Angel Face
Appendectomy
Around The World
Asian Martini
Atomic Bodyslam
B-52 with Bombay Doors
Babbie's Special
Bali Hai
Barbary Coast
Bay City Bomber
Belmont
Big Kahuna
Bimini Ice-T
Black And Blue Martini
Black Martini
Blackberry Swizzle
Blue Canary
Blue Lady
Blue Meanie
Boston Iced Tea
Bottom Line
Brave Cow
Cable Car
California Iced Tea
California Lemonade
Chain Lightning
Champagne Super Nova

DRINKS LISTED IN ALPHABETICAL ORDER

● GRAIN ALCOHOL
Assisted Suicide
Big Titty Orgy
Chambered Round
Cherry Bomb
Cherry Cola From Hell
Crippler
Eat The Cherry
Hairy Mary
Hardcore
Leg Spreader
Mad Cow
Pink Panty Pulldown
Polish Butterfly
Primal Scream
Screaming Dead Nazi
  Digging for Gold
Suicidal Tendencies
Tiger Balls

● HAZELNUT LIQUEUR
Amber Martini
Aspen Coffee
Beam Me Up Scotti
Biscuit Neck
Boston Massacre
Butternut Coffee
Café Marseilles
Café Theatre
Chastity Belt
Chocolate Squirrel
Cream Dream
Creamsicle
El Salvador
F-16
F. U.
Friar Tuck
Irish Monk
Irish Monk Coffee
Mad Monk
Madtown Milkshake
Menage a Trois
Millionaire's Coffee
Mississippi Mud
Monk Juice
Monk Slide
Ninja
Nut and Honey
Nutcracker
Nuts And Berries
Nuts And Cream
Nutty Bitch
Nutty Chinaman
Nutty Irish Cooler
Nutty Irishman
Nutty Irishman Coffee
Nutty Jamaican
Nutty Russian
Panty Burner
Peanut Butter And Jelly
Quaalude
Rocky Road
Russian Quaalude
S. O. M. F.
Seduction
747
Simply Exquisite
Smooth Operator
Snicker
Snicker At The Bar
Toblerone
Trappist Frappe
Trappist Monk
Tumbleweed
Vatican Coffee
White Ghost

● HOT CHOCOLATE
Adult Hot Chocolate
Almond Kiss
Black Magic

Brandy Almond Mocha
Chocolate Kiss
Coconapps
Cocoetto
Cocopuff
Dutch Treat
Hot Peppermint Patty
Mad Monk
Midnight Snowstorm
Mound Bar
Mudsling
Peppermint Kiss
Ski Lift
Snuggler
Wooden Shoe

● ICE CREAM
B-52
Banana Colada
Banana Cow
Banana Cream Pie
Banana Frost
Banana Popsicle
Banana Split
Banshee
Bit Of Honey
Black Cow
Black Forest
Black Russian
Blizzard
Boston Massacre
Brandy Alexander
Brandy Hummer
Brown Squirrel
Burnt Almond
Cancun
Chi-Chi
Chocolate Banana Freeze
Chocolate Covered Cherry
Chocolate Mess
Coffee Colada
Cookies And Cream
Creamsicle
Dirty Monkey
Dusty Road
Fat Cat
Flying Grasshopper
Flying Kangaroo
French Iced Coffee
Frosted Romance
Fudgesicle
Funky Monkey
G. S. Cookie
Golden Caddie
Golden Caddie With Double
  Bumpers
Good and Pient-e
Grasshopper
H. Bar
Harvey Wallbanger
Hummer
Jamaican Milk Shake
Kappa Colada
Key Largo
Las Brisas
Love Potion #9
Madtown Milkshake
Meister-Bation
Melon Colada
Mocha Berry Frappe
Monkey Special
Moose Milk
Mudslide
Night Train
Nut and Honey
Nutcracker
Nutty Colada
OR-E-OH Cookie
Orange Julius
Orange Margarita
Orange Whip
Orsini
Panda Bear
Parfait

Peach Alexander
Peach Colada
Peach Velvet
Peanut Butter and Jelly
Pearl Harbor
Piña Colada
Rasbaretta
Raspberry Colada
Roasted Toasted Almond
Roman Cappuccino
Root Beer Float
Russian Quaalude
St. Petersburg Sundae
Snicker At The Bar
Strawberry Blonde
Strawberry Colada
Strawberry Shortcake
Tidal Wave
Tidbit
Toasted Almond
Toblerone
Tropical Breeze
Tropical Moon
Tumbleweed
Velvet Hammer
Virgin Piña Colada
Whisper
White Cargo
White Russian
Winter Frost
Xylophone

● IRISH CREAM
A-Bomb
ABC
After Eight
After Five
After Five Coffee
Angel Wing
Apple Pie
Aspen Coffee
B-12
B-50
B-51
B-52
B-52 Coffee
B-52 On A Mission
B-52 With A Mexican
  Tailgunner
B-52 With Bombay Doors
B-54
Bailey's And Coffee
Bailey's Comet
Bailey's Fizz
Banana Cream Pie
Bazooka Joe
BBC
Beach Hut Madness
Beam Me Up Scotti
Beautiful Thing
Belfast Bomber
Berlin Wall
Biscuit Neck
Black Forest
Black Magic
Blizzard
Bloody Brain
B.J.
Bon Bon
Boston Massacre
Brain
Brain Tumor
Brain Wave
Bush Diver
Bushwacker
Busted Rubber
Buttafinger
Butter Ball
Butter Shot
C-Drop
Café Magic
Café Theatre
Camshaft
Cancun

DRINKS LISTED IN ALPHABETICAL ORDER

● **JAEGERMEISTER**

(continued)
Skid Mark
Stumbling F.
Surfer Taking A Trip
Three Wise Men
Toxic Jellybean
Vegas B J
Yellow Jacket

● **MELON LIQUEUR**

Albatross
Alien Orgasm
Alien Secretion
Alien Urine Sample
Anti-Freeze
Artificial Intelligence
Atomic Waste
Bart Simpson
Battered Bruised And
  Bleeding
Bleacher Creature
Broken Down Golf Cart
Bubble Gum
Cheap Shades
Clouds Over Scotland
Cool Aid
Crocodile Cooler
Dizzy Buddha
E. T.
Electric Cool Aid
Electric Watermelon
F Me Hard
Fairchild
Frutti Nueb
Gangrene
Ghostbuster
Green Apple
Green Demon
Green Goddess
Green Kamikaze
Green Meany
Green Mountain Melon
Green Russian
Green Sneakers
Gumby
Gummy Bear
Happy Summer
Hard Candy
Hawaiian Punched
Head Room
Hole in One
Honeydew
Irish Tea
Itchy Bitchy Smelly Nelly
Jamaican Ten Speed
Juicy Fruit
June Bug
Kuwaiti Cooler
Kyoto
Laser Beam
Leaf
Life-Savor
Lifesaver
Little Green Men
Loch Ness Monster
Los Angeles Iced Tea
Maxim's
Melon Ball
Melon Breeze
Melon Colada
Melon Grind
Melon Royale
Melon Sombrero
Melon Sour
Mexican Flag
Miami Melon
Neon
Nesi
Ninja
Ninja Turtle
Nuclear Meltdown
Oral Sex On The Beach
Pan Galactic Gargle Blaster

Pearl Harbor
Pixie Stick
Puccini
Quick F
Radioactive Iced Tea
Rain Man
Rainbow
Rainforest
Sand In Your Butt
Save The Planet
Scooby Snack
Sex On The Beach
Sex On The Pool Table
Shady Lady
Slimeball
Sour Apple
Spats
Three Mile Island
Three Story House On Fire
Tie Me To The Bedpost
Tie Me To The Bedpost
  Baby
Torque Wrench
Traffic Light
Tropical Hooter
Tropical Lifesaver
Universal
Vulcan Mind Probe
W. W. II
Wall Street Lizard
Watermelon
Y. I.
Yokohama Mama

● **MENTHOLATED
   SCHNAPPS**

Anti-Freeze
Cough Drop
Doctor's Elixir
Dr. J.
Fuel-Injection
Guillotine
No Tell Motel

● **MILK OR CREAM**

Aggravation
Alexander
Alexander The Great
Alexander's Sister
Almond Joy
Amigo
Angel Kiss
Angel Wing
Angel's Tit
Atomic Waste
Babbie's Special
Banana Sombrero
Banana Split
Banshee
Beetle Juice
Belmont
Bikini
Black Cow
Black Rose
BlackJack
Blow Job
Blue Tail Fly
Blood Clot
Bob Marley
Boston Massacre
Bourbon Satin
Brandy Alexander
Brandy Hummer
Brandy Milk Punch
Brown Cow
Brown Squirrel
Bubble Gum
Bull's Milk
Bulldog
Bumble Bee
Bungee Jumper
Burnt Almond
Bushwacker

Busted Cherry
Butt Munch
Buttafinger
Cadiz
California Cool Aid
California Mother
Candy Cane
Canyon Quake
Capri
Cara Sposa
Caribbean Screw
Charro
Chastity Belt
Chiquita
Chocolate Colada
Chocolate Squirrel
Climax
Coca Lady
Coconut Cream Frappe
Coffee Sombrero
Colorado Bulldog
Colorado MF
Colorado Mother
Cowboy
Cream Dream
Creamsicle
Cricket
Deep Dark Secret
Dickie Toecheese
Dire Straits
Dirty Banana
Dirty Bird
Dirty G. S.
Dirty M. F.
Dirty Mother
Dirty White Mother
Dreamsicle
East Side
Eggnog
Embryo
Everglades Special
Festival
Fifth Avenue
Flaming Lamborghini
Flying Grasshopper
Fourth of July
Foxy Lady
Frostbite
Fuzzy Navel With Lint
G. S. Cookie
G-String
Gentle Bull
Godchild
Golden Caddie
Golden Caddie With
  Double Bumpers
Golden Dream
Golden Dream
  (With Double Bumpers)
Golden Torpedo
Grasshopper
Green Russian
Hard On
Head
Hello Nurse
Henry Morgan's Grog
High Jamaican Wind
Hot Milk Punch
Hot Raspberry Dream
Huntress Cocktail
Ice Ball
Ichbien
Il Magnifico
Irish Angel
Irish Cow
Italian Delight
Jamaican Kiss
Jenny Wallbanger
Jizz
Jungle Jim
Kahlua Sombrero
King Alphonse
King's Cup
Kioloa
Kiss
Kremlin Cocktail

DRINKS LISTED IN ALPHABETICAL ORDER

● ORANGE LIQUEUR
(continued)
Passionate Point
Pernod Flip
Platinum Blonde
Prince Igor
Queen Elizabeth
Quaalude
Red Lion
Ritz Pick-Me-Up
Riviera
Royale Gin Fizz
S. O. B.
Sanctuary
Sand Flea
Screaming Orgasm
727
Sex
Sex At The Beach
Sex Machine
Sexy
Shogun
Shot In The Dark
Simply Exquisite
Smooth Driver
Spanish Coffee
Spanish Dynamite
Star Wars
Stealth
Suffragette City
Sun Stroke
Sweet Tart
T-Bird
Tahitian Itch
Tampa Bay Smoothie
Tangerine
Terminal Iced Tea
Top Hat
Toronto Orgy
Trade Wind
Ulanda
Unpublished Hemingway
Visitor
Vodka Grand Marnier
Watergate Coffee
West Indian Frappe
Xanadu
Xavier
Zipper

● PEACH SCHNAPPS
Alien Orgasm
Alien Urine Sample
Antiquan Kiss
Atomic Waste
Bermuda Triangle
Bitch Fight
Brain
Bumble Bee
Cerebral Hemorrhage
Cheap Shades
Comfortable Fuzzy Screw
   Against The Wall
Cool Aid
Corkscrew
Crazy Red Head
Cuban Peach
Dirty Silk Panties
F Me Hard
Fish House Punch
Forbidden Jungle
French Martini
Frozen Bikini
Fru Fru
Fruitbar
Fuzzy Astronaut
Fuzzy Bastard
Fuzzy Fruit
Fuzzy Guppie
Fuzzy Kamikaze
Fuzzy Monkey
Fuzzy Navel
Fuzzy Navel with Lint

Georgia Peach
Ghostbuster
Glass Tower
Glenda
Golden Daze
Hairy Navel
Halley's Comfort
Hand Job
Harmony
Hasta La Vista, Baby
Heatwave
Hollywood
Irish Spring
Joll-e Rancher
Juicy Fruit
June Bug
Killer Cool Aid
Leprechaun
Long Sloe Comfortable
   Fuzzy Screw Against the
   Wall with a Kiss
Long Sloe Comfortable
   Fuzzy Screw Against
   The Wall with Satin
   Pillows The Hard Way
Meltdown
Miami Ice
Mo Fo
Mongolian Mother
Moody Blue
MoonPie
Nasty Girl
Northern Lights
Open Grave
P. M. S.
Passionate Point
Peach Alexander
Peach Blaster
Peach Breeze
Peach Bulldog
Peach Cobbler
Peach Daiquiri
Peach Fuzz
Peach Mimosa
Peaches And Cream
Plaid
Purple Helmeted Warrior
Red Devil
Red Dwarf
Red Panties
Red Silk Panties
Roxanne
Ruddy Mimosa
Sewer Rat
Sex At The Beach
Sex In a Hot Tub
Sex On The Beach
Sex On The Beach In Winter
Silk Panties
Silk Shorts
69er
Ski Lift
Skinny Dipping
Sloe Comfortable Fuzzy
   Screw Against The Wall
Smelly Cat
Southern Beach
Tear Drop
Tight Snatch
Tokyo Express
Tokyo Rose
Top Gun
Tree Smacker
Trip To The Beach
Uncle Sam
Under The Covers
Very Joll-e Rancher
Week On The Beach
Weekend At The Beach
Woo Woo
Yellow Submarine

● PEPPERMINT
SCHNAPPS
Adult Hot Chocolate
After Five
After Five Coffee
Apres Ski
Bavarian Coffee
Beautiful Thing
Beetle Juice
Candy Cane
Chocolate Kiss
Coconapps
Coney Island
Cookie Monster
Cure-All
D. O. A.
Dead Nazi
Death Mint
Death Wish
Depth Charge
Dirty G. S.
Festering Slobovian
Hummer
Fire And Ice
Firestorm
Flaming Blue J.
Four Horsemen
Frostbite
G. S. Cookie
German Leg Spreader
Ground Zero
Hand Release
Hard Candy
Hard Nipple
Hot Pants
Hot Peppermint Patty
Hot Young Lady
Ice Boat
Iceberg
Iron Cross
Jack Frost
Lighthouse
Liquid Coca
Liquid Crack
Liquid Valium
Mad Monk
Mint Chocolate Chip Ice
   Cream
Mint Condition
Mother Love
Naked G S
911
Nutty Bitch
Oil Slick
Peppermint Kiss
Peppermint Patty
Peppermint Stinger
Pitbull On Crack
Purple Jesus
Rattlesnake
Rumplestiltskin
Santa Shot
Screaming Dead Nazi
   Digging for Gold
Screaming Nazi
Skid Mark
Slippery Nipple
Snakebite
Snowball
Snowblower
Snowshoe Grog
Snuggler
Stumbling F.
Three Wise Men
Thunder and Lightning
Tic Tac
24 Karat Nightmare
Urinalysis
Whippet

● RUM (DARK)

(continued)

Spleef
Stonewall
Stupid Cube
Suffering Bastard
Tai Tia
Tiger's Milk
Tiki Bowl
Tokyo Express
Tom And Jerry
Top Gun
Trophy Room Coffee
Tropical Moon
Tropical Storm
Turtle Dove
Voo Doo
Wind Jammer
Wombat
Zombie

● RUM (LIGHT)

Adios Mother
Alaskan Iced Tea
American Graffiti
Antiquan Kiss
Apple Cooler
Artificial Intelligence
B. M. P.
Bacardi Cocktail
Bahama Mama
Bambini Aruba
Banana Colada
Banana Daiquiri
Banana Split
Banana Strawberry Daiquiri
Barbary Coast
Barracuda
Bartman
Bat Bite
Bee's Knees
Between The Sheets
Bimini Ice-T
Black Jamaican
Black Martini
Black Rose
Blast
Bleacher Creature
Bloody Marisela
Blue Bijou
Blue Hawaiian
Bog Fog
Bongo
Bos'n Mate
Boston Iced Tea
Box Car
Brass Monkey
Buckaroo
Bulldog
California Cool Aid
California Iced Tea
Calypso Coffee
Caribbean Champagne
Caribbean Screw With
    A Sunburn
Casablanca
Catfish
Cherry Blossom
Chi-Chi
Chocolate Colada
Coca Lady
Coco Loco
Coconut Cream Frappe
Code Blue
Coffee Colada
Coral Sea
Corkscrew
Cranapple Cooler
Creamsicle
Cricket
Cruise Control
Cuba Libra
Cuban Peach

Daiquiri
Deep Dark Secret
Devil's Tail
Dirty Ashtray
Dr. Funk
Dr. P.
East Side
El Salvador
Electric Watermelon
Everglade's Special
Eye-Opener
Fair and Warmer
Fern Gully
57 Chevy
57 T-Bird
Flamingo
Flim Flam
Florida
Florida Iced Tea
Florida Sunrise
Flying Kangaroo
Fog Cutter
.44 Magnum
Funky Monkey
Gangrene
Gaugin
Gentle Ben
Gilligan
Gilligan's Isle
Glass Tower
Go-Go Juice
Golden Gate
Goombay Smash
Gradeal Special
Grand Occasion
Greatful D.
Guana Grabber
Hammerhead
Hard Hat
Hawaiian Garden's Sling
Hawaiian Nights
Headhunter
Honey Bee
Honolulu
Hop Toad
Hound Dog
Hurricane
Irish Tea
Jamaican Coffee
Jamaican Mule
Jolly Roger
Judge, Jr.
Jump Up And Kiss Me
Key Lime Pie
Key Lime Shooter
Killer Cool Aid
King Cobra
Lallah Rookh
Leaf
'Lectric Lemonade
Liberty Cocktail
Limbo
Little Devil
Little Princess
Long Beach Iced Tea
Long Island Iced Tea
Long Island Lemonade
Los Angeles Iced Tea
Love Potion
Mai Tai
Malibu Monsoon
Mary Pickford
Melon Colada
Melon Grind
Mexicano
Miami Ice
Miami Vice
Midway Rat
Milano Coffee
Mint Julep
Mississippi Mud
Mojito
Mojo
Mongolian Mother
Monkey Special
Monkey Wrench

Naked Lady
Navy Grog
Night Train
Nuclear Meltdown
Nutty Colada
Outrigger
Pain In The Ass
Palmetto
Pan Galactic Gargle Blaster
Pancho Villa
Peach Cobbler
Peach Colada
Peach Daiquiri
Pedro Collins
Pensacola
Piña Colada
Pineapple Bomb
Pineapple Daiquiri
Pineapple Passion
Pink Gator
Pink Lemonade
Pink Panther
Planter's Punch
Platinum Blonde
Porch Climber
Port Pelican
Presidente
Pterodactyl
Puerto Rican Screw
Purple Armadillo
Purple Rain
Purple Thunder
Quaker
Quarter Deck
Quickie
Ranch Valencia Rum Punch
Raspberry Colada
Raspberry Daiquiri
Raspberry Lime Rickey
Red Tide
Release Valve
Riviera
Rockaway Beach
Roman Iced Tea
Rum and Coke
Rum Madras
Rum Punch
Rum Runner
Run, Skip and Go Naked
San Juan Sunset
San Sebastian
Sand Blaster
Sand Flea
Santiago
Scorpion
September Morn
Sevilla
Sex In A Bubblegum Factory
Shark Attack
Shaved Bush
Silver Spider
Sir Walter
Skull Cracker
Sloppy Joe
Smurf P.
Snowblower
South Of France
Spats
Spilt Milk
Spy's Demise
Stiletto
Stock Market Zoo
Strawberry Colada
Strawberry Daiquiri
Stump Buster
Stupid Cube
Summer Breeze
Summer Share
Summer Solstice Sunrise
Sundowner
Susie Taylor
Swamp Water
Sweet Release
Tahitian Apple
Tahitian Itch
Terminal Iced Tea

● RUM (151-PROOF)

● RUM (SPICED)

● SAMBUCA

● SCOTCH

● SLOE GIN

● SLOE GIN (continued)

Kiss The Boys Goodbye
Lemonade (Modern)
Long Sloe Comfortable
  Fuzzy Screw Against
  The Wall With A Kiss
Long Sloe Comfortable
  Fuzzy Screw Against
  The Wall with Satin
  Pillows The Hard Way
Love
McClelland
Mexican Flag
Mich
Modern
Moll
Monogolian Mother
Moulin Rouge
New York Slammer
Panty Dropper
Pink Floyd
Purple Margarita
Red Death
Red Devil
Ruby Fizz
San Francisco
Savoy Tango
Singapore Sling
Sloe Ball
Sloe Boat To China
Sloe Brandy
Sloe Comfortable Fuzzy
  Screw Against The Wall
Sloe Comfortable Mexican
  Screw Against The Wall
Sloe Comfortable Screw
Sloe Comfortable Screw
  Against The Wall
Sloe Dog
Sloe Gin Fizz
Sloe Poke
Sloe Screw
Sloe Tequila
Spats
Spring Action
Spy's Demise
Sweet Release
Tie Me To The Bedpost
  Baby
Traffic Light
Troika
Union Jack
Velvet Glove
Watermelon

● SOUTHERN COMFORT

Alabama Slammer
American Graffiti
Apple Polisher
Avalanche
Banging The Captain 3
  Ways On The Comforter
Bazooka
Bible Belt
Blood Clot
Bootlegger
Bubble Gum
Bucking Bronco
Coca
Comfortable Fuzzy Screw
  Against The Wall
Comfortable Screw
Cool Aid
Crankin' Wanker
Crazy Broad
Dingo
Dizzy Buddha
Double-D
Earthquake
Electric Cool Aid
57 Chevy
57 T-Bird

Flaming Blue J.
Gasoline
Golden Bull
Gorilla Fart
Green Meany
Gummy Bear
Halley's Comfort
Hammerhead
Harbor Lights
Hawaiian
Hawaiian Punched
Jelly Bean
Jezebel
Laser Beam
Lion Tamer
Liquid Pants Remover
Long Comfortable Screw
  Against the Wall
Long Sloe Comfortable
  Fuzzy Screw Against
  The Wall With A Kiss
Long Sloe Comfortable
  Fuzzy Screw Against
  The Wall with Satin
  Pillows The Hard Way
Memphis Belle
Missouri Mule
Mongolian Mother
Open Grave
Oxbend
Paint Ball
Panabraitor
Peckerhead
Pineapple Bomber
Pixie Stick
Pop-Sicle
Pterodactyl
Purple Alaskan
Purple Helmeted Warrior
Quaalude
Rattlesnake
Rebel Russian
Red Death
Red Devil
Rhett Buttler
S. O. B.
Sand In Your Butt
Saturn's Ring
Scarlet O'Hara
Sex At The Beach
Sicilian Coffee
Sicilian Kiss
Sloe Comfortable Fuzzy
  Screw Against The Wall
Sloe Comfortable Mexican
  Screw Against The Wall
Sloe Comfortable Screw
Sloe Comfortable Screw
  Against The Wall
Southern Beach
Southern Belle
Southern Bulldog
Southern Comfort
  Manhattan
Stevie Ray Vaughan
Southern Comfort Old
  Fashioned
Spring Action
Star Wars
Sunny Day Dream
Test-Tube Babe
Tidal Wave
Tie Me To The Bedpost
  Baby
Tool
Top Gun
Urinalysis
Vibrator
Vulcan
Wagon Wheel
Watermelon
White Trash

● STRAWBERRY LIQUEUR

Banana Split
Banana Strawberry Daiquiri
Big Titty Orgy
Bikini Line
Bloody Brain
Brain
Brain Tumor
Flaming Noriega
Kiwi
Metropolis Martini
Monga Monga
Red Russian
Snowberry
Strawberry Blonde
Strawberry Daiquiri
Strawberry Shortcake
Watermelon
Wombat

● TEQUILA

Acapulco Gold
Adios Mother
Alice In Wonderland
Amigo
Apple Margarita
Arizona Lemonade
B-52 With A Mexican
  Tailgunner
Baja Margarita
Bay City Bomber
Big Daddy
Bimini Ice-T
Black Rose
Bleacher Creature
Bloody Maria
Blue Margarita
Blue Meanie
Blue Shark
Body Shot
Boomer
Bootlegger
Border Crossing
Brahma Bull
Brass
Brave Bull
Bucking Bronco
Buffalo Piss
Buffalo Sweat
Burning Bush
Burnout Bitch
Cactus Banger
California Iced Tea
Cartel Buster
Chambered Round
Charro
Chiles Fritos
Chupacabra
Code Blue
Colorado Mother
Dallas Alice
Darth Vader
Deceiver
Desert Sunrise
Dirty Ashtray
Dirty Bird
Dirty Mother
Don Juan
El Cid
El Diablo
Electric Lemonade
Elmer Fudpucker
Fire And Ice
Firecracker
Florida Iced Tea
Four Horsemen
Freddy Fudpucker
Frostbite
Fubar
Fuzzy Mother
Gang Banger
Gasoline

DRINKS LISTED IN ALPHABETICAL ORDER

● TRIPLE SEC
(continued)
Mexican Blackjack
Millionaire
Mimosa
Mississippi Mud
Mongolian Mother
Monmarte
Morning
Mount Vesuvius
Muscle Beach
Netherland
Nuclear Meltdown
Odd McIntre
Olympic
Orange Julius
Orange Krush
Orange Margarita
Oriental
Orgasm
Orsini
Pacific Pacifier
Paint Ball
Pan Galactic Gargle Blaster
Panabraitor
Panama Red
Parisian Blonde
Pernod Flip
Petrifier
Pink Caddie
Platinum Blonde
Polly's Special
Pop-Sicle
Prison Bitch
Pterodactyl
Purple Rain
Quickie
Quiet Nun
Radioactive Iced Tea
Ramos Fizz
Rattler
Rebel Yell
Red Death
Red Devil
Roman Iced Tea
Run, Skip And Go Naked
S. O. B.
S. O. M. F.
Samari
San Sebastian
Sangria
Santiago
Scotch Bird
Sherry Twist
Sidecar
Silver Spider
Singapore Sling
Sloppy Joe
Sloppy Joe's
Southern Belle
Southern Bride
Southern Maiden
Spanish Dynamite
Spring Fling
Stevie Ray Vaughan
Strawberry Margarita
Suffering Bastard
Sunburst
Sundowner
Sunspot
Sweet Patootie
Tango
Temptation
Texas Tea
Three Mile Island
Tiger's Tail
Tijuana Titty Tickler
Top Gun
Trois Rivieres
Tropical Storm
TTT
Ulanda
Upside Down Margarita
Velvet Dress
Velvet Hammer

Venetian Coffee
Venetian Frappe
Volga Boatman
Vulcan Mind Probe
W. W. II
Waikiki Beachcomber
Wet Crotch
Whip Cocktail
White Baby
White Cadillac
White Heat
White Lady
White Lily
White Mink
White Water
White Witch
Wiki Waki Woo
Wild Thing
Will Rogers
Wind City
Wind Surf
Xango
XYZ
Zamboanga Hummer
Zaza
Zipper
Zombie
Zonker

● TUACA
Café Italia
Hot Apple Pie
Il Magnifico
Lemon Frappe
Puccini
Stuffed Toilet
Thumper
Tiger's Milk
Tijuana Titty Tickler
Tuaca Cocktail

● VANDERMINT
Black Cow
Dutch Coffee
Dutch Pirate
Trophy Room Coffee
Wooden Shoe

● VODKA
A-Bomb
Adios Mother
Agent O.
Air Gunner
Alabama Slammer
Alaskan Iced Tea
Amber Martini
Anna's Banana
Anti-Freeze
Apple Pie
Asian Martini
Atomic Bodyslam
Atomic Waste
B-50
Bailey's Comet
Balalaika
Bambini Aruba
Banana Cream Pie
Banana Popsicle
Banana Split
Bart Simpson
Bay Breeze
Bay City Bomber
Beam Me Up Scottie
Beer Buster
Bend Me Over
Berlin Wall
Big Daddy
Big Titty Orgy
Bikini
Bikini Line
Billie Holiday

Bimini Ice-T
Black And Blue Martini
Black Cat
Black Cow
Black Eye
Black Forest
Black Magic
Black Russian
Bleacher Creature
Blizzard
Bloody Brew
Bloody Bull
Bloody Caesar
Bloody Mary
Blow Job
Blue Bayou
Blue Hawaiian
Blue Kamikaze
Blue Meanie
Blue Shark
Bocci Ball
Boston Iced Tea
Brain Eraser
Brain Wave
Brass Monkey
Broken Down Golf Cart
Broken Heart
Brown Derby
Bubble Gum
Bull Shot
Bulldog
Bullfrog
Burnout Bitch
Burnt Almond
Buttafinger
Butter Shot
California Breeze
California Cooler
California Driver
California Iced Tea
California Lemonade
Cape Codder
Celtic Comrade
Chambered Round
Champagne Super Nova
Cheap Shades
Cheap Sunglasses
Cherry Bomb
Cherry Pie
Chi-Chi
Chicken Shot
China Beach
Chocolate Banana Freeze
Chocolate Covered Cherry
Chocolate Martini
Chocolate Thunder
Clam Digger
Climax
Cloudy Night
Coca
Coca Lady
Coco Loco
Code Blue
Colorado Bulldog
Colorado MF
Colorado Mother
Comfortable Fuzzy Screw
    Against the Wall
Comfortable Screw
Cookies and Cream
Cool Aid
Cool Breeze
Copperhead
Cosmopolitan
Cranapple Cooler
Cranes Beach Punch
Crankin' Wanker
Crazy Broad
Creamsicle
Crocodile Cooler
Dark Eyes
Dark Side
Darth Vader
Deep Throat
Devil's Tail
Dickie Toecheese

DRINKS LISTED IN ALPHABETICAL ORDER

● **VODKA** *(continued)*
Raspberry Soda
Raspberry Torte
Rear Entry
Red Apple
Red Death
Red Devil
Red Eye
Red Panties
Red Russian
Red Silk Panties
Red Zipper
Release Valve
Rhode Island Iced Tea
Rigor Mortis
River Berry
Roasted Toasted Almond
Rocky Mountain Rootbeer
Rosy Dawn
Roman Iced Tea
Root Beer
Root Beer Float
Roxanne
Ruby Red
Russian
Russian Banana
Russian Bear
Russian Coffee
Russian Nights
Russian Pussy
Russian Quaalude
Russian Rose
Russian Roulette
Russian Sunrise
S. O. S.
St. Petersburg Sundae
Saketini
Salty Dog
Save The Planet
Scorpion
Screaming Banshee
Screaming O.
Screaming Yellow Monkey
Screwdriver
Screw-Up
Sea Breeze
727
Sewer Rat
Sex At The Beach
Sex In A Hot Tub
Sex In The Parking Lot
Sex In The Woods
Sex Machine
Sex On The Beach
Sex On The Beach In Winter
Sex On The Pool Table
Siberian
Silk Panties
Silk Shorts
Silken Veil
Silver Cloud
Silver Spider
Silverado
Sinner
Sizzler
Skinny Dipping
Skip And Go Naked
Skylab Fallout
Slim Jim
SlimeBall
Sloe Ball
Sloe Comfortable Fuzzy
 Screw Against The Wall
Sloe Comfortable Mexican
 Screw Against The Wall
Sloe Comfortable Screw
Sloe Comfortable Screw
 Against The Wall
Sloe Dog
Sloe Screw
Smooth Driver
Sno Cap
Snowberry
Sour Ball
Sour Grapes
Soviet Cocktail

Spring Fling
Spring Thaw
Spy's Demise
Star Wars
Starlight
Steel Helmet
Strawberry Shortcake
Strip And Go Naked
Stump Buster
Summer Share
Summer Solstice Sunrise
Sun Stroke
Sunburst
Swedish B J
Sweet Release
Sweet Tart
Swedish Bear
T-Bird
Tampa Bay Smoothie
Tangerine
Tawny Russian
Terminal Iced Tea
Texas Mary
Texas Tea
Three Mile Island
Thug Heaven
Tidal Wave
Tie Me To The Bedpost
 Baby
Tiny Bowl
To Hell You Ride
Top Banana
Top Gun
Toronto Orgy
Tovarich
Toxic Shock
Traffic Light
Transfusion
Trip To the Beach
Troika
Tropical Storm
Tuaca Cocktail
Twister
Under The Covers
Universal
Vampire
Very Joll-e Rancher
Visitor
Vodka Collins
Vodka Cooler
Vodka Gibson
Vodka Gimlet
Vodka Grand Marnier
Vodka Grasshopper
Vodka Martini
Vodka Saketini
Vodka Sling
Vodka Soda
Vodka Sonic
Vodka Sour
Vodka Stinger
Vodka Tonic
Volga Boatman
Volga Cooler
Vulcan
Vulcan Blood
Vulcan Mind Probe
W. W. II
Wadkins Glen
Wall Street Lizard
Wally Wallbanger
Waltzing Matilda
Wandering Minstrel
Warsaw
Watermelon
Well Red Rhino
Wet Dream
Whale's Tail
White Death
White Elephant
White Mink
White Russian
White Spider
Wiki Waki Woo
Wild Thing
Windex

Woo Woo
Y. I.
Yellow Bird
Yellow Fever
Yellow Russian
Yellow Snow
Yo Mama
Yorsh
Zhivago Standard
Zipper Head
Zonker

● **VODKA** (CITRUS)
Blue Lemonade
Cosmopolitan (South
Beach)
Crocodile Cooler
Lemon Drop
Neon
Pink Lemonade
Ragnar
Salty Dogitron
Samurai
Shogun
Smelly Cat
Tie Me To The Bedpost
Toxic Shock
Tropical Lifesaver
Zuma Buma

● **VODKA** (PEPPERED)
Afterburner
Cajun Martini
Creole Martini
Fahrenheit 5
Firebird
Holy Hail Rosemary
Hot Dog
Louisiana Shooter
Oyster Shooter
Pepper Martini
Sparks

● **WHISKEY**
Alabama Slammer
Algonquin
Belfast Bomber
Bend Me Over
Bent Nail
Big Daddy
Black Hawk
Blinker
Blue Valium
Boilermaker
Bop The Princess
Cablegram
California Lemonade
Canada Cocktail
Canadian Blackberry Fizz
Canadian Cider
Depth Charge
De Rigueur
Dog Sled
Dry Manhattan
Dubonnet Manhattan
Duck Fart
Eden Roc Fizz
Empire State Slammer
Firecracker
Fox River
Frisco Sour
Gaelic Coffee
Gloomlifter
Hawaiian
Heartbreak
Henry Morgan's Grog
Highball
Horse's Neck
Hot Apple Toddy
Hot Toddy
Hunter's Cocktail

For Notes & Phone Numbers